Homesickness

Homesickness

An American History

Susan J. Matt

OXFORD
UNIVERSITY PRESS

OXFORD
UNIVERSITY PRESS

Oxford University Press, Inc., publishes works that further
Oxford University's objective of excellence
in research, scholarship, and education.

Oxford   New York
Auckland   Cape Town   Dar es Salaam   Hong Kong   Karachi
Kuala Lumpur   Madrid   Melbourne   Mexico City   Nairobi
New Delhi   Shanghai   Taipei   Toronto

With offices in
Argentina   Austria   Brazil   Chile   Czech Republic   France   Greece
Guatemala   Hungary   Italy   Japan   Poland   Portugal   Singapore
South Korea   Switzerland   Thailand   Turkey   Ukraine   Vietnam

Published by Oxford University Press, Inc.
198 Madison Avenue, New York, NY 10016

www.oup.com

Oxford is a registered trademark of Oxford University Press

Library of Congress Cataloging-in-Publication Data
Matt, Susan J. (Susan Jipson), 1967–
Homesickness : an American history / Susan J. Matt.
    p.   cm.
Includes bibliographical references and index.
ISBN 978-0-19-537185-7
1. Nostalgia—History.
2. Homesickness—History. I. Title.
BF575.N6M295   2011
155.9′2—dc22   2011004603

1 3 5 7 9 8 6 4 2

Printed in the United States of America
on acid-free paper

In memory of Joseph Matt
and in honor of
Barbara J. Matt,
Elizabeth Matt Turner,
and
Luke O. Fernandez

CONTENTS

ACKNOWLEDGMENTS

I have incurred many debts while writing this book.

First, Susan Ferber, executive editor of American and world history at Oxford University Press, was extraordinarily patient and supportive while waiting for me to finish this book. Always helpful and encouraging, she brought to the manuscript great historical knowledge and keen insight about how to improve it. It is much stronger because of her. Thanks to Joel-lyn Ausanka, senior production editor at Oxford, for shepherding the project through production, and Judith Hoover for her careful copyediting.

I started this project long after graduate school, but I might never have become interested in homesickness and nostalgia were it not for my graduate school advisors. Thanks to Michael Kammen, a good friend and mentor, who read an early draft of the project and offered both encouragement and citations. It was more than twenty years ago, in his seminar on social memory and the transformation of tradition, that I first became aware that nostalgia had a history. His work—and his work ethic—have been inspiring models. Joan Jacobs Brumberg introduced me to historical studies of disease and psychology, and this work shows her influence as well. Over the years she has been a source of good advice on a range of topics. In fascinating lectures on the bourgeois personality, Isaac Kramnick started me thinking about the traits most suited to capitalist endeavor. Stuart Blumin's work and perspectives on class and capitalism influenced me as well.

Peter N. Stearns of George Mason University has offered me opportunities to delve more deeply into the history of the emotions. He has been a thoughtful reader and a supportive mentor from afar. I have benefited from his great knowledge and groundbreaking work on the emotions.

Ed Linenthal, the editor of the *Journal of American History*, helped me hone my argument and clarify my ideas for an exploratory essay on homesickness that appeared in the journal. Thanks to him for strengthening my work and to the *Journal of American History* for allowing portions of that essay to appear here.

Monroe Friedman, a guest editor of the *Journal of American Culture*, asked me to write an essay on consumerism and emotions. That piece helped me outline ideas about immigration, food, and homesickness. Portions of that essay also appear in this work.

James Grossman, James Gregory, and James Horn answered queries I sent them and pointed me to good sources. Members of CASHOU— Cultural and Social Historians of Utah—including Dan McInerney, Lawrence Culver, Colleen McDanell, Phil Barlow, Jennifer Ritterhouse, Stephen Francis, Brady Brower, and John Sillito, offered comments on portions of the manuscript. Thanks as well to Bill Allison for providing me with good insights and sources on the connections between military history and homesickness and for inviting me to present my work at Georgia Southern University. Readers for the *Journal of American History*, the *Journal of American Culture*, and Oxford University Press provided useful feedback.

When I was at an early stage of writing and researching this project, John Mack Faragher offered encouragement and the crucial advice that I look at the resources of the Beinecke Library at Yale University. A month-long fellowship from the Beinecke in 2007 offered me the opportunity to explore their rich holdings, which George Miles, curator of the Western Americana Collection, helped me navigate.

Thanks to the archivists at the Bancroft Library at the University of California, Berkeley, the Manuscripts Division of the Princeton University Library, the Immigration History Research Center at the University of Minnesota, the Ebling Library for the Health Sciences at the University of Wisconsin, the Society of California Pioneers, the Avery Institute and the College of Charleston Library, the South Carolina Historical Society, the University of Miami, and the University of Rochester. I am also grateful to these institutions for giving me permission to quote from their sources.

Thanks to Abel Eduardo Castillo Valtierra and the many people he introduced me to in Tepic and Villa Hidalgo, Mexico. Their willingness to talk about their experiences as immigrants in the United States was invaluable. I learned so much from them. Thanks as well to the many people in Ogden and Salt Lake City, Utah, who shared their stories with me.

This book is about home, and there are many people at my home institution, Weber State University, who deserve acknowledgment. Joan Hubbard, university librarian at WSU, made this project possible. She is unstinting in her generosity and heads a remarkable staff at Stewart Library. Jamie Johnson Weeks, associate curator of Digital and Archival Collections, gave me friendship, humor, lots of Cokes, and a carrel. John Sillito, former director of University Archives and Special Collections, and history bibliographer par excellence, provided me with great resources and good conversation. Kathy Payne, head of Reference and Information Services, helped me track down obscure sources, sent citations whenever she came across them, and found useful databases. Sandi Andrews, circulation services manager, was so helpful and always cheery, even when I had overdue books. Misty Allen, coordinator of interlibrary loan, worked with me to gain access to distant resources. Debbie Stephenson, the interlibrary loan specialist for the library, brought the world's resources to Ogden. She worked tirelessly and did extra research to find rare books and articles. I owe her special thanks. Bob King of Multimedia Services helped me obtain images for the illustrations.

Two graduates of Weber State University worked for me as research assistants. Michelle Braeden, a gifted student and now a talented teacher, worked on this project for nearly two years. I am grateful for Michelle's conscientious industry as well as her warm friendship. Irasema Rivera traveled with me to Mexico to interview returned immigrants. Back in Ogden she found more people for us to interview, and she translated and transcribed the interviews. She was insightful, competent, and very good company.

Thanks to Weber State University and its administration for supporting this project. A year-long sabbatical in 2007 provided time for writing and research. The College of Social and Behavioral Sciences Endowed Professorship and the University's Presidential Distinguished Professorship provided me with much appreciated funds for travel, supplies, and research assistants. Funding from the Hemingway Foundation supported research in Nayarit, Mexico.

Provosts Michael Vaughan and Kathleen Lukken have encouraged faculty research, and I thank them for their support and leadership. Dean Richard Sadler has been a good colleague and friend since I arrived. I am grateful to have wonderful colleagues, who are also dear friends, in the History Department. Thanks to Gene Sessions, Kathryn MacKay, M. Brady Brower, Sara Dant, Richard O. Ulibarri, Greg Lewis, Branden Little, Bob Becker, Henry Ibarguen, Lee Sather, Stan Layton, John Sillito, LaRae Larkin, Stephen Francis, Vikki Vickers, and Angela Swaner.

Special thanks to Kathryn MacKay for her good company and conversation and her wonderful lending library, and to Brady Brower for his thoughtful comments on a chapter of the manuscript and on the project as a whole. The incomparable Angela Swaner, secretary for the History Department, kept everything running smoothly. She transcribed interviews and notes and also proofread the entire manuscript. She is the most efficient person I know and makes coming to work a pleasure.

Vikki Vickers kept her eyes open for citations and gave me advice about colonial historiography. Even more she has been a great and caring friend, funny and smart. Stephen Francis has offered me sound advice and understanding, great wit, and general jollity. I am grateful for his friendship—and his familiarity with the *Chicago Manual of Style*. He deserves special acknowledgment for helping me with my bibliography, a very generous gift of time and energy.

Dear friends outside the department also deserve thanks. Lauren Fowler of the Psychology Department and Marjukka Ollilainen of the Sociology Department are treasured friends who have exposed me to other disciplinary approaches and shared many lunches.

Thanks are due as well to Christine Y. Todd, my rival and best friend since high school. A gifted conversationalist, lyricist, and doctor extraordinaire, she is like a sister to me. She sent me medical studies of homesickness, widening my perspective on that topic and so many others.

My in-laws, James and Renate Fernandez, asked interesting questions about homesickness, exposed me to anthropological works on the topic of home, and made me feel at home with them. Lisa Fernandez, Richard Remnick, and Will and Talia were wonderful hosts during my month in New Haven. Andrew Fernandez has become a brother.

I began to write this book in earnest in January 2007, when my year-long sabbatical began. In August of that year, my wonderful, funny father, Joseph Matt, died quite suddenly. While he was alive, he gave me love and a sense that all was well in the world. When he died, I felt his absence profoundly. As I wrote about homesickness, I realized how integral he was to my sense of home.

Thankfully there are others who give me a sense of home. My mother, Barbara J. Matt, an editor and writer, taught me to write and to be curious about the world. She has heard endless discussions of this topic and offered ideas, encouragement, and love. Thanks to my sister, Betsy Matt Turner, and her family—Jonathan, Alex, and Josh—who bring great fun to family happenings. Finally, thanks to my wonderful husband, Luke O. Fernandez. He has read and edited countless iterations of this manuscript, conducted and translated interviews, helped me untangle difficult theories, and brought me new perspectives. Since we met in Ithaca, New York, in 1990, we have lived in six states and traveled many places, but no matter where we are, when I am with him, I am at home.

Homesickness

Introduction

In 1887, forty-two-year-old Rev. Father J. M. McHale left Ireland to take up a position in a Brooklyn parish. Shortly after arriving in New York, he became afflicted with nostalgia and began to waste away. Newspaper accounts reported that McHale proclaimed, "'I cannot eat; my heart is breaking.' In his troubled sleep he talked of Ireland and his friends there. He often murmured: 'I am homesick. My dear country, I will never set a foot on your green shores again. Oh, my mother, how I long to see you.'" He eventually lost consciousness and died.[1] His death was attributed to homesickness, or nostalgia, as it was then called. Such a diagnosis was not unusual in nineteenth-century America, nor was the newspaper coverage of McHale's death. Papers sometimes reprinted the pathos-filled letters of migrants separated from their loved ones and sometimes carried news of their sorrowful deaths.

Before the twentieth century, homesickness was a widely acknowledged and discussed condition. Throughout the eighteenth and nineteenth centuries, Americans moved frequently, but they were not fully accustomed to leaving home and did not find the process easy or natural. There was a trauma associated with migration, a trauma they did not shy away from expressing. Americans took homesickness seriously—as did their doctors, many of whom maintained that the only cure was to return sufferers to their homes before the condition turned fatal.

More than a century after Rev. McHale's death, the *New York Times* carried news of another homesick migrant to New York. In 2004, the writer Katherine Lanpher moved from Minnesota to Manhattan. She found the move painful: "My first week ended with a sharp bout of homesickness." To cheer herself up she decided to get a manicure. She told the Korean woman who was doing her hands, "I'm pretty homesick," but encountered little sympathy. The manicurist, herself far from home, looked at Lanpher with impatience: "Her eyes narrowed, she sucked in some breath and then she barked out an uppercase admonition: 'DON'T BE BIG BABY.'"[2] This is the modern attitude toward homesickness, an attitude predicated on the belief that movement is natural and unproblematic and a central and uncontested part of American identity. Today those who suffer from homesickness are considered immature and maladjusted. To feel pain at migration and to discuss it openly is, as one psychologist noted, "taboo."[3]

While this perspective on homesickness is now widespread, it developed slowly. Americans have not always been able to leave home with ease. This book explores how they learned to do so. It begins with European colonization and continues up through the twenty-first century, tracing changes both in emotional prescriptions and lived experience. It examines how homesickness was transformed from a dire and potentially fatal malady to an inconsequential emotion rarely mentioned, and from an adult condition to a childhood one. The book explores how love of home, once seen as the mark of a refined and sensitive nature, eventually came to signify backwardness, prissiness, and a lack of ambition. It seeks as well to illuminate how Americans dealt with these changing norms, and how, in doing so, they gradually learned the habits of modern individualism.

During the colonial era, a significant number of those who came to America hoped to return home. Those who could go back did so, at a surprisingly high rate; for instance, as many as one in six Puritans eventually left New England and returned home to old England.[4] Many more colonists would have liked to do the same, but could not, for a majority came to America in some state of unfreedom. Whether slaves, servants, or wives, they had to submit themselves to the patriarchal and communal order that guided social life and subordinate their desires to the will of the larger society. They grappled with their longings. Some regarded their circumstances as God's will and resigned themselves to sadness. Others took action to resolve their homesickness, but often to no avail since an ocean separated them from their homes.

By the mid-eighteenth century, a new set of ideas began to alter both the colonial social order and individual outlooks. Enlightenment philosophy celebrated the freely moving individual who maximized happiness and who could be at home anywhere in the world. Colonists who could act on this cosmopolitan philosophy—generally white, generally male—began to develop new expectations about their lives. They became less willing to submit to communal imperatives that dictated their location, and they manifested a new spirit of autonomy as they searched for contentment. For some this independence led to novel opportunities and points unknown;

for others it carried them home. Faced with unprecedented liberty, many individuals came to realize that even freely made decisions—to leave home or to stay—carried hefty emotional costs.

This became more apparent to nineteenth-century Americans who lived through the market revolution and the emergence of a full-fledged capitalist economy. Influenced by the ideal of the self-made man, American men and women abandoned the familiar in search of new profits and possibilities. Yet they did so with some hesitation. Although later remembered as a period of great restlessness and individualism, antebellum America also was characterized by a great deal of homesickness. Explorers, pioneers, gold miners, and mill girls all moved forward, but often did so with some reluctance and looked back with regret. To them their destiny was not manifest, whether they should go or stay not a settled question. They discussed publicly their reservations about moving and worried about the implications of their restlessness, since love of home and mother was a mark of good and refined character.

While attentive to their own pain at parting, white Americans were often unmoved by the emotional plight of Native Americans, who were forced to vacate ancestral lands. Natives' attachment to home was seen as an atavistic trait, standing in the way of progress. Similarly, the homesickness that slaves experienced as they were bought and sold generally went unacknowledged by whites, who presumed that "primitive" blacks lacked their level of emotional sensitivity and capacity.

The phenomenon of homesickness, so widespread during the antebellum period, received systematic attention during the Civil War. During that time, European conceptions of the condition as a disease became popular, and the diagnostic category of nostalgia gained acceptance. The term *nostalgia* was used to describe the acutely homesick, who many doctors believed might die if their condition went untreated. In fact, during the war, Union doctors diagnosed more than five thousand soldiers as suffering from nostalgia, seventy-four of whom succumbed to the condition. Given such alarming statistics, some army bands were prohibited from playing "Home, Sweet Home" for fear the song might provoke the deadly illness in soldiers.

After the war, the idea that homesickness might be fatal continued to circulate among laypeople and physicians alike. Native-born Americans flocked from farms to cities, and European and Asian immigrants streamed into the United States, and these migrations inspired prolific commentary on homesickness and nostalgia. As the nation's racial and ethnic diversity increased, many observers claimed they saw patterns among homesick populations and suggested that nostalgia was a condition to which particular groups were especially susceptible. For instance, psychologists and social commentators influenced by Darwinian theory hypothesized that the groups least able to conquer their homesickness were the least culturally advanced. Those who succumbed to it were unfit for life in modern American society, for they lacked the prized characteristic of adaptability. As the charity worker Morris Fishberg observed in 1906, "Nostalgia . . . is the first and most effective aid to the natural selection of desirable immigrants."[5] According to this view, those unable to adapt to a new environment and stricken with nostalgia were doomed to fail in life and business, perhaps even to perish. Observers maintained that a variety of different ethnic groups as well as African Americans, Native Americans, and women of all races were unsuited to movement and independence because of their alleged vulnerability to homesickness. Homesickness gradually became a marker of dependence and inadequacy.

If there was a new condemnation of homesickness, there were also new ways to assuage it, for during the late nineteenth century and early twentieth, revolutions in transportation made migration easier. Transcontinental railroads spanned the country, and fast steamships linked nations. Leaving and returning home became much easier for migrants and immigrants, rich and poor alike. Yet the rapid industrialization of the late nineteenth century that produced these new technologies also led to radical transformations in daily life. Migrants who returned after years away discovered that home was no longer what they had imagined it to be. Their homes had changed and so had they. As a result, many Americans began to yearn not just for a lost home—the longing of the homesick—but for a lost time as well. As they journeyed between old homes and new, many began to wonder if they had any home whatsoever. A sense of homelessness began to emerge that would become endemic to modern life.

In the twentieth century, the imperative to move became greater, the need to accept dislocations more pressing. From expanding corporations, government agencies, and the military, Americans heard they should subordinate themselves to the large institutions of modern society and move cheerfully when asked. Child-rearing experts suggested that parents prepare their offspring for these inevitable partings by sending them away from home so that they might master their homesickness early in life. Psychologists, corporate leaders, and government officials hoped that ultimately individuals would learn to transfer their loyalties from mother, home, and hometown, to their employers and the government, and would be transformed from mama's boys into organization men. Impatience with those reluctant to leave home grew over the course of the twentieth century, and the perception that homesickness was a sign of immaturity solidified. Americans learned a code of behavior and emotion management that taught them to repress all signs of homesickness in public life in order to appear modern and mature.

Only in the late twentieth century and early twenty-first, as faith in organizational culture declined, did Americans begin to publicly question the relocations that the modern workplace demanded of them. Yet even today, those who resist moving on are reluctant to discuss their misgivings in terms of homesickness or the love of home, for this would mark them as lacking ambition and drive. Instead they express their emotions in other ways. As the historian Peter Stearns has noted, in the twentieth century individuals faced increasing pressure to restrain their emotions in public yet found greater opportunities in leisure time and private life for emotional release.[6] As they type on their Facebook pages or email accounts, watch Bollywood films on satellite television, or visit the taqueria to eat foods redolent of the flavors of home, Americans move through a culture of memory and connection and try to re-create what they have left behind. Although it has been repressed in speech and overt action, homesickness makes its appearance in daily rituals, in ways that often go unnoticed precisely because they are so commonplace.

The history of homesickness recovers the story of how Americans learned to manage their feelings, but beyond that, it reveals how Americans learned habits of individualism that supported capitalist activity. Central to modern individualism is the ability to separate oneself from home and family, to wander in pursuit of happiness, to leave communities (if only to rejoin others), to be fluid and unfettered.[7] That ability has been portrayed by some observers as a trademark American behavior; however, the ability to be mobile is not innate. This book explores the long education Americans went through in order to be able to act like rugged individualists and to make movement appear unproblematic. In so doing it offers a new history of mobility and individualism, a history that shows the ambivalence, hesitation, and reluctance so often experienced by those who moved on. As their society came to enshrine movement as necessary for an expanding, capitalist order, Americans learned to live with these mixed feelings and to subordinate the desire to stay behind to the goal of getting ahead.

Being a rugged, mobile individualist involves mastering an emotional code, knowing how and when to express some emotions and repress others. It means acting optimistically, cheerfully, and with little regret, while embracing change and novelty. The demands for such traits first emerged in the late eighteenth century but did not become dominant until the twentieth. Individuals and families were watch-guards of emotional expression and helped to inculcate such habits and behaviors in each other, but so too did influential success advisors, child-rearing experts, and modern psychologists, who helped shape emotional norms and worked to create models of personality well suited to the needs of the capitalist economy. During the twentieth and twenty-first centuries, they have celebrated those individuals who can separate and move on and have portrayed as pathological and maladjusted those who cannot. Scholars commenting on contemporary attitudes toward homesickness suggest that in modern America, since "homesickness is seen as something childish, it is socially sanction[ed] even among children."[8]

Because it has become a taboo emotion, homesickness is not a category that Americans use to assess their society or their past. The emotion is absent from nationalist narratives, in which historical actors are largely portrayed as happy movers. Alexis de Tocqueville offered perhaps the most famous sketch of American mobility when he wrote, "An American will build a house in which to pass his old age and sell it before the roof is on; he will plant a garden and rent it just as the trees are coming into bearing; he will clear a field and leave others to reap the harvest; . . . settle in one place and soon go off elsewhere with his changing desires."[9] Later commentators such as Frederick Jackson Turner elaborated on this vision, portraying unceasing movement as essential to American identity.[10] Modern historians have continued to use this interpretative mode, describing Americans as "uprooted," "restless," and a "nation on the move."[11] The emphasis on effortless mobility and the silence on the topic of homesickness have been self-perpetuating. Because homesickness is absent from modern accounts of the past, it is seen as an illegitimate emotion in the present. For instance, the mythology of individualistic pioneers has been used to motivate successive generations to move on bravely and without hesitation, despite the fact that the pioneers themselves were homesick and hesitant, and that many hoped to—and sometimes did—return home.

In telling their stories, the history of homesickness restores emotional complexity to U.S. history and undercuts the idea that American society and culture is strictly a product of individualism. Again, Tocqueville was an early exponent of this view, suggesting that everything from newspapers to civic associations to familial relations bore the imprint of individualism. Turner elaborated on this idea, describing the "dominant individualism" of American culture and character.[12] Understanding the mix of feelings that Americans experienced as they moved allows for a different interpretation, for American culture was created by people in search of connection and community, trying to restore and re-create what they had left behind. Their yearnings left an indelible mark on the physical and social landscape of America. For example, the paths of homesick migrants can be traced through the repetition of place-names across the American landscape. English town names were transplanted to New England; subsequent generations settling in the Midwest and West carried these names with them and tried to reestablish a sense of place by affixing old names to new locales.[13] In gardens around their newly built homes, settlers planted seeds and cuttings they had carefully transported over land and sea in order to establish a semblance of the landscapes they had left behind. That lilacs bloom in southern California yards is testimony to the homesickness of eastern migrants trying to make foreign terrain familiar.[14] National patterns of culture and communication also reflect longings for connection. For decades, American men and women sang songs and read novels that mourned the necessity of leaving home and celebrated the prospect of return. Whether sitting around campfires on the Overland Trail or at pianos in comfortable parlors, Americans sang with passion melodies like "Home, Sweet Home," "Old Folks at Home," and "My Old Kentucky Home." To maintain connections with the old folks at home, Americans became a letter-writing nation in the nineteenth century, and a telephoning, emailing, and texting population in the twentieth and twenty-first.[15] These patterns illustrate that other values besides individualism left a deep and enduring mark on American social and cultural life.[16]

The history of homesickness also challenges the myth of America's magnetic allure. Rather than the United States exerting an irresistible pull on immigrants, home, wherever it was, was frequently the true magnet. Early colonization efforts were carried out by individuals who often intended to go back home, who regarded America as settlers at Jamestown did, "not as a place of Habitacon but onley of a short so[j]ourning." They were interested not in long-term settlement but in "present profit."[17] That motivation has been shared by generations of immigrants. Although millions end up staying, they often set out with the belief that they will soon return to England, Italy, China, Poland, or Mexico. For many, the American dream has always been to come to America, get rich, and return home.

What the history of homesickness, and the history of the emotions more generally, brings to the American narrative is a record of intention, motivation, and feeling. To focus only on external behaviors misses much of what went on in the past. Understanding how individuals felt about their migrations and how they responded to social rules that guided their behavior and their feelings allows for a more nuanced appraisal, both of how society shapes personality and how emotions shape history.[18] While generations of scholars long assumed that emotions were "tangential" to the fruitful study of the past, historians of the emotions argue that they are central to historical narratives, for their shifting meanings reveal much about the social attitudes and outlooks that were prevalent in earlier eras.[19] This is clear in the case of homesickness, for the fact that it was a problem emotion for much of the nation's history suggests that at one time many people were unaccustomed to long-distance migrations. Indeed, before the seventeenth century, the word *nostalgia* did not exist, and before the eighteenth century the English word *homesickness* did not either. The invention of these terms reflected a new concern about the emotions that were becoming apparent in early modern society; their recent disappearance from adult conversation is a sign that, at least to some degree, modern Americans have become accustomed to moving on.

Jean Starobinski, the first historian to critically study homesickness and nostalgia, maintained that while individuals longed for home throughout history, the invention of new names for the longing changed the meaning and experience of the emotion, transforming private feelings into a socially recognized problem and a disease.[20] This book builds on that observation, beginning its examination in the colonial period, when the words *nostalgia* and *homesickness* first were coined. It employs the words in accordance with their historical usage. It also takes seriously the fact that homesickness meant different things to different people at different times. Some who used the word longed for family, some for houses, others for towns or landscapes, for all of these were constituents of the idea of home. By including all of these meanings, this book allows the historical actors themselves to define their feelings.

Although the book focuses on homesickness, it does not deny that other emotions played a role in patterns of mobility, nor does it deny that some individuals felt no homesickness whatsoever. Nevertheless, the emotion has been far more common than previously acknowledged. Chapter 1 explores the feelings of colonists far from home and examines how a hierarchical social order shaped opportunities for emotional expression. It also charts the ways that Enlightenment philosophy and revolutionary social movements began to alter these patterns. Chapter 2 examines the antebellum period, the era of the highest rate of interstate mobility in U.S. history. Americans coming of age in the early nineteenth century—explorers, farmers, mill girls, and miners—had to learn how to move on. Despite the distances they traveled, many continued to hold out hope that they might return to and reunite with those they had left behind.

Civil War soldiers, raised in the midst of this culture, experienced homesickness and nostalgia with great frequency and expressed it quite publicly. They found that civilians and military officials alike took their condition seriously and gave it unprecedented attention. Chapter 3 examines soldiers' experiences of the emotion and the larger society's evolving views of the condition. The trauma of the war, as well as changes brought on by industrialization and urbanization in the years that followed, made many wonder if they could ever really return to the homes—or the pasts—they had left behind. Late nineteenth- and early twentieth-century culture was marked by widespread longings for homes lost in time as well as in space, the subject of chapter 4. Chapter 5 examines how the 20 million immigrants who flooded into the country during these years regarded their old and new homes, and how homesickness shaped their social lives. Able to avail themselves of rapid transportation, they traveled back and forth between their native lands and their adopted one, and often wondered where their true home was. Their sense of placelessness was part of an emerging modern sensibility.

That sensibility was increasingly necessary during the twentieth century. An organizational society began to take shape that required mobility of workers, soldiers, and citizens. Psychologists and child-rearing experts urged families to push their children out the door to prepare them for life in the mobile world. Chapter 6 examines the expansion of this organizational culture during the first half of the twentieth century and explores how the homesick fared within it. Chapter 7 looks at its postwar growth and eventual decline and considers modern responses to mobility. The conclusion looks at commercial culture and technology and how they have both affected and been affected by the longing for home.

Although the book ends there, the emotion continues. Over the years, many observers have predicted that rapid transportation, high-speed communication networks, and the global consumer economy, which provides a smorgasbord of the world's goods, would eventually eradicate homesickness, making it an artifact of earlier times. That has not proven to be the case, however. While internal migrants and immigrants can find many of the tastes of home on grocery store shelves, and while they can travel and phone home with unprecedented ease, their homesickness has yet to be conquered. It may have disappeared from adult conversation, but homesickness lurks inside the heads of many Americans on the move.

CHAPTER 1

✧

Emotions in Early America

In reports he sent back to the West India Company, Johan Printz, the governor of New Sweden (now Delaware), repeatedly asked that he be allowed to return home to Sweden. In 1644, he wrote, "It is . . . my humble prayer and request that when this term of three years is over I may be relieved and allowed to return again to . . . my Most Gracious Queen and my Fatherland, especially since I am no longer young and since the greatest part of my days have been hard and toilsome." In 1647, he asked again: "I for a great while (namely twenty-eight years) have been in the service of my dear native country. . . . My humble request . . . is, that I be relieved, if possible, and sent home by the next ship to my beloved native land."[1] Although Printz was a man of power and prominence, he could not control where he went or when he could return home. It was only in 1653 that his wish was granted and he was able to return to Sweden.

Three hundred miles to the north, Peter Bulkeley, a Puritan minister who emigrated to America in 1635 and founded Concord, Massachusetts, still looked homeward after more than a decade. In a sermon he exclaimed, "*O England*, my deare native Countrey (whose womb bare me, whose breasts nourished me, and in whose arms I should desire to dye)."[2] Despite his longing for home, Bulkeley remained in Massachusetts for the rest of his life, believing that this was God's will and desire for him.

Almost a century later, in 1733, the *Boston Gazette* carried news of the disturbing actions of a woman who had similar longings for her native land and even fewer options: "A Negro woman at Salem determined to go into her own Country, as she call'd it, took a Bottle of Rum & two Biskets and carried them into the Burying Place there where she dug a hole & cover'd 'em, and then took a Knife and cut her Belly so much that her Guts came out, her Wound was sew'd up but she dy'd a day or two afterwards."[3] The woman acted on the belief, common among slaves imported from West Africa, that after death, individuals were reincarnated in Africa and would be free. Without liberty or income, her best hope for returning home lay in death.

Despite differences in race, religion, gender, and power, Printz, Bulkeley, and the anonymous slave woman all experienced the same powerful emotion, which today is termed homesickness. The ways that they coped differed dramatically from one another and from modern ways of coping with the yearning for home.

During the seventeenth and eighteenth centuries, many colonists felt constrained and unable to act on their longings, since a startling number could not control if they left home or if they might return to it. Between 1607 and 1789, roughly half of the 600,000 Europeans and all 300,000 of the Africans who landed on American shores were not free, arriving either as servants or slaves.[4] They frequently had little control over their destinations or their destinies. Even those with greater power and independence still faced limits on their migrations. European nations imposed a variety of restrictions on their citizens' movements, for they regarded their populations as part of their national wealth. In some countries, citizens were blocked from leaving their native lands without government permission and frequently faced questioning if not outright prohibition when they desired to return.[5] Some migrants also felt controlled by divine edict and feared their migrations might offend God. Their lack of autonomy influenced how they thought about the places they left and the journeys they made.

Those European colonists who longed for home, however, probably had different expectations about pain and suffering than do modern Americans, for they came from societies that assumed that unhappiness, discontent, and pain were to be expected and were to be dealt with patiently and passively.[6] This melancholy but accepting disposition was well suited to life in a society where individuals frequently had little control over their fates.[7]

Then too, Europeans and American colonists often thought of their emotions as unruly passions that needed to be subordinated to community will or religious injunction. Many Protestants believed that sadness and pain were signs of an unholy life, evidence that an individual lacked God's grace.[8] Too much interest in the state of one's emotions, whether happy or sad, was sinful as well. Some Puritan divines believed that the more individuals focused on their own desires and feelings, the further they were from God.[9] Such attitudes informed how colonial Americans understood their longings for home and how they responded to them; many felt they had little choice but to tolerate and accept the pain they experienced.

These attitudes began to change in the mid- to late eighteenth century, as new ideas of personal autonomy and volition began to spread and as a social order built on deference and hierarchy gradually crumbled. Alongside revolutionary views of the place, power, and role of the individual came new expectations about personal happiness. This gave select groups within the American colonial population more control over their migrations and conferred legitimacy on their efforts to find personal happiness. Yet such attitudes did not always eliminate homesickness, for the new spirit of individualism that emerged in the mid-eighteenth century could as easily propel people away from their homes as toward them. Many Americans during the Revolutionary era came to see homesickness as the price of independence.

EMOTIONS AMONG EARLY COLONISTS

European colonists began to stream into the Americas after Columbus's voyages, as nations across Europe competed to lay claim to the abundant land and resources of the Western Hemisphere. In search of opportunity and prosperity, many made the voyage willingly, but did so with the hope of eventually returning to their native lands.[10] As many as 10 to 20 percent of all Spanish immigrants returned home after years, and in some cases, decades in the Americas. Those who remained in the colonies generally kept their eyes and thoughts on their native land, sending back remittances to support their kin. Some French colonists likewise saw their time in America merely as a way to gain wealth that would ultimately enable them to enjoy a better life back in France.[11] British colonists nursed similar hopes, and these sometimes undermined their early efforts at colonizing. In 1585, English settlers made the first of two ill-fated attempts to establish the colony of Roanoke. They lasted only a year and then, according to reports, grew homesick, and imposing on the goodwill of Sir Francis Drake, managed to return to England. An attempt in 1607 to colonize along the Kennebec River in Maine lasted for just a year. A seventeenth-century report explained, "They[,] after a winter stay dreaming to themselves of new hopes at home[,] returned backe with the first occasion."[12]

Even the colonies that became permanent settlements initially attracted colonists who envisioned their time in America as temporary. In Jamestown, Virginia, the first successful English colony, Capt. John Smith reported that members of his company attempted to commandeer a ship and sail back to England. These efforts were put down and the men punished, since returning so early would doom the colonizing enterprise.[13]

Those who stayed on in Virginia, often against their will, suffered greatly from a combination of afflictions. Conflicts with local Native Americans led many to fear for and ultimately lose their lives. Brackish water and malaria were natural hazards of the locale; colonists also lacked sufficient food.[14] While violence, starvation, disease, and poor protection from the elements contributed to a high mortality rate, so too did mental turmoil. One early colonist, George Thorpe, who arrived in 1620, believed that his comrades' ill health indicated more than just physical pain. He noted, "I . . . am pswaded that more doe die here of the disease of theire minde then of theire body."[15] The more apathetic and depressed colonists became, the less able they were to provide for themselves.[16]

Even colonists who did not withdraw fully from life displayed their depression and their pain at being so far from home. Those who lived in Virginia during its first few decades often turned to alcohol to drown their sorrows. Edmund Morgan suggested that Virginians consumed substantial amounts of liquor "to solace them for losing the comforts of a settled life." Because they had come to make a quick profit and planned to go back to England, they invested little time or effort in making the colony habitable or pleasant. As a result, the settlement was hastily and poorly constructed, full of "ramshackle hovels."[17] The colonist Edward Hill wrote to his brother that the poor conditions in Virginia made him want to return to England; as soon as he earned sufficient profit, he would do so. "And to speake the truth I stay to get what I haue lost and then god willing I will leaue the Countrey: for this is the worst yeare here that . . . [ever] I saw like to bee." Phoebus Caner described his desperate desire to go back to England: "I beseech god to give me life & health that I may this yeare end this troublesome voyage. I am quite out of hart to live in this land god send me well out of it."[18]

In the early years of Virginia's history, colonists expressed such laments repeatedly, and the colony's leaders looked for a way to allay settlers' homesickness. Some concluded that a chief source of discontent that prompted colonists to return to England was the dearth of women. Without wives men could not establish households or a sense of home. To rectify that problem, Sir Edwyn Sandys, leader of the Virginia Company, recommended in 1619 that the colony import women. Sandys wanted women who were "young and uncorrupt to makes wifes to the Inhabitñnte." The motive was "to make the men there more settled & lesse moueable who by defect thereof . . . stay there but to gett something and then to returne to England, wch will breed a dissolucon, and so an ouerthrow of the Plantacon."[19] If women came, perhaps the men could be induced to put down permanent roots in Virginia. John Smith's history of the colony reports that as a result, ninety "young women to make wives" were imported to America.[20] They agreed to marry colonists once they disembarked in Virginia, and their future husbands agreed to pay the cost of their journey, which was about 120 pounds of tobacco.[21]

Women were not sufficient to diminish the men's desire for England, and in fact, they themselves often longed for home. William Rowlsley wrote to his brother from Jamestown, "My wife doth nothing but talke of going home."[22] Some men and women made good on such dreams of return. Affluent settlers in Virginia could afford to make migrations back and forth across the Atlantic, some returning to England for supplies, others to visit family and friends, and still others to settle back in their native homes for good. In a letter written in 1614 telling of his marriage to Pocahontas, John Rolfe noted that he still had "hope but one day to see [his] Country," and eventually did return to it, bringing with him his bride, who died there, far from her own home.[23] The Virginia Assembly was troubled by the significant number of departures for England, but nevertheless decided in 1626 that rather than prohibit returns they would monitor them: "It *is thought fitt at this quarter Court*, that there shall be noe generall restraint of people frō goeing for *England*, but yᵗ such as desire their passes shall repaire to the Court held weekely at *James Cittye*."[24]

Virginia colonists with the lowest social status generally had most cause to long for home and the least ability to act on their longings. During the seventeenth century, ninety thousand indentured servants were brought into the colony (75 percent of the total European population there), and few were pleased with their new circumstances.[25] Some objected to the harsh living conditions, others to the grueling work, and many to their distance from home. Richard Frethorne, a servant, wrote his parents in 1623, "This is to let you understand that I yoʳ child am in a most heavie Case by reason of the nature of the Country, [which] is such that it Causeth much sickness, as the scurvie and the bloody flix and diverse other diseases, wch maketh the bodie very poore, and Weake and when wee are sicke there is nothing to Comfort vs." So wretched and hard were the conditions, so hungry were the colonists, and so fearful were they of Indian attack that Frethorne heard "people crie out day, and night, Oh that they were in England without their lymbes—and would not care to loose anie lymbe to bee in England againe, yea, though they beg from doore to doore." He told his parents, "If you love me you will redeeme me suddenlie, for wch I doe Intreate and begg." A few weeks later, he made another plea, telling them that could they see his condition they would be moved: "Oh, that you did see may daylie and hourelie sighs, grones, and teares, and [the] thumpes that I afford mine owne brest. . . . I thought no head had beene able to hold so much water as hath and doth dailie flow from mine eyes." Despite his wrenching pleas, he remained in Virginia; by 1624, he was listed among the colony's dead.[26]

Another indentured servant, James Revel, described servants' predicaments in a poem. After being transported to America as punishment for a crime and forced to do labor, he fell sick and despaired both of his condition and his slim chances of returning home:

> Oft on my knees the Lord I did implore,
> To let me see my native land once more,
> For through his grace my life I would amend,
> And be a comfort to my dearest friend.

His prayers were eventually answered, and he returned to England and his parents.[27]

Colonists forced to remain in Virginia during the early decades of settlement had to reconcile themselves to the fact that they were in a new and unfamiliar world, where English village order, traditions, and populations were largely absent. There were very few towns for most of the seventeenth century; instead settlers established widely scattered plantations on which they built small and rather sparsely furnished houses.[28] Such living arrangements left individuals separated from one another, exacerbating feelings of loneliness, alienation, and homesickness.

Over time, however, they gradually transformed this bleak world so that it came to resemble the one they had left behind. Although it took several decades, the architecture and physical landscape that the colonists built and named gradually embodied their longings for England.[29] Their new towns and counties were named after those they left behind: Norfolk, Southampton, New Kent.[30] Through this landscape moved many who continued to wish that they were back home in the real Norfolk, Southampton, or Kent.

The Pilgrims, who established Plymouth Colony in 1620, and the Puritans, who settled the Massachusetts Bay Colony in 1629, felt at least as constrained in their movements and choices as those who settled in Virginia, perhaps more so, because they believed that they were bound by divine edict. In their view, the Church of England had not distanced itself sufficiently from Catholic doctrine and practice. They risked incurring the wrath of God if they stayed in corrupt England and believed the Lord wanted them to remove themselves to a purer place.

Most of the 21,500 settlers who arrived in New England between 1620 and 1641 believed that while leaving England might result in pain and sorrow, God's will could not be denied. William Bradford, who became governor of the Plymouth Colony in 1621, explained that the move was emotionally wrenching for some. First they had left England for Holland, and this had been very difficult, for, "being thus constrained to leave their native soil and country, their lands and livings, and all their friends and familiar acquaintance, it was much; and thought marvelous by many. . . . It was by many thought an adventure most desperate; a case intolerable and a misery worse than death." If that move was hard, the Pilgrims' next migration, to America, was even more daunting, for they remembered "their former troubles and hardships in their removal into Holand, and how hard a thing it was for them to live in that strange place, though it was a neighbour countrie." Consequently, when they bid adieu to friends and family and embarked for America, "truly dolfull was the sight of that sade and mournfull parting; to see what sighs and sobbs and praires did sound amongst them, what tears did gush from every eye." Yet they set forth, believing they were following God's will.[31]

Despite their belief that God had brought them to New England, many still yearned for their native land, particularly once they saw the rough conditions of their new one. Bradford reported that in 1623, the ship *Anne* arrived at the Plymouth Colony. The ship's "passengers, when they saw their low and poore condition a shore, were much danted and dismayed, and according to their diverse humores were diversely affected; some wished them selves in England againe; others fell a weeping, fancying their own miserie in what they saw now in others; other some pitying the distress they saw their friends had been long in, and still were under; in a word, all were full of sadness."[32] Settlers coming to the Massachusetts Bay Colony reacted similarly to their new home. The combination of harsh living conditions, inadequate food, and great distance from England made colonists miserable, and they showed both physical and emotional symptoms. Governor John Winthrop claimed that while many of the new settlers suffered from scurvy, it became fatal only to those longing for home: "It hath always been observed here, that such as fell into discontent, and lingered after their former conditions in England, fell into the scurvy and died."[33] Edward Johnson, in his *Wonder-Working Providence of Sion's Savior*, reported of the settlers, "That which added to their present distracted thought, the Ditch betweene England and their now place of abode was so wide, that they could not leap over with a lope-staffe." Of the early years in Massachusetts Johnson noted that "the beginning of this worke seemed very dolorous."[34]

What offset the pain for many was the conviction that God wanted them to go to America. The Puritan Roger Clap explained that he was grateful to God for giving him "contentedness": "I do not remember that ever I did wish in my Heart that I had not come into this Country, or with my self back again to my Father's House: Yea I was so far from that, that I wished and advised some of my dear Brethren to come hither also." Clap believed it was the Puritans' religious fervor that made them content in their new home: "Our Hearts were taken off from *Old England* and set upon *Heaven*. The Discourse . . . was not, How Shall we go to England? (tho' some few did not only so discourse, but also went back again) but, How Shall we go to heaven?"[35] Like Clap, many Puritans took comfort in the belief that their real home was wherever God was, and as He had withdrawn his grace from England, so they should withdraw themselves from it too.

Calvinists also tried to console themselves by remembering the teaching that all places were equally distant from God, and that earth was but a temporary resting stop on the pilgrimage to heaven. Consequently, they should not be overly attached to particular places. Some Puritans saw their ability to withstand separation as proof of their piety; others reminded themselves that mortal life and earthly homes were but temporary and that their true home and eternal life were in heaven.

Yet such ideas went only so far in soothing the homesick; and despite their piety, many colonists in Massachusetts ultimately returned to England. Their willingness to pay a return fare indicates the depth of their desire. The cost of passage across the Atlantic has been estimated at £5.[36] Not only did boat fare cost dearly, but colonists who came to New England had already sold land and outfitted their families for the journey to America. For a household of six to move to America might cost between £50 and £80—this at a time when small farmers earned between £20 and £60 per year.[37] Yet despite the considerable investment they had made to come to America, a significant number were willing to spend more to return home. Perhaps as many as one out of six migrants to New England eventually sailed back to England during the seventeenth century, some after the installation of a Puritan government following the English Civil War.[38]

Those homesick colonists who returned often earned the animus and contempt of those who remained in New England. Return migrants were accused of being weak in their faith. John Winthrop, for instance, cast a harsh judgment on "one Austin (a man of good estate) [who] came with his family in the year 1638 to Quinipiack, and not finding the country as he expected, he grew discontented, saying that he could not subsist here, and thereupon made off his estate, and with his family and £1000 in his purse, he returned for England in a ship bound for Spain." When that ship was captured by the Turks, and Austin and his family were sold into slavery, Winthrop saw it as divine retribution sent to punish those who undermined the colonizing enterprise. True and devout Christians would stay in New England rather than return home and ignore divine ordinance.[39]

Like Virginians, homesick Puritans who remained in the colonies tried to make the new and unfamiliar landscape of Massachusetts more comforting and homelike. A significant portion of Massachusetts towns founded in the seventeenth century were named after English towns: Haverhill, Ipswich, Cambridge, Groton, Dedham, Springfield, Marlborough, Lancaster, Andover, Gloucester. Their streets were lined with Cape Cod, saltbox, and gabled box houses, styles reminiscent of homes left behind but not forgotten.[40]

While Massachusetts, Virginia, and all the other colonies differed from each other in culture, religion, and settlement patterns, there were commonalities. They all were populated by individuals who looked backward rather than forward, who nurtured a connection to the land and cultures they had left behind, and who often tried to replicate at least some part of those cultures. As they established homes and towns, they were guided by practical concerns, but they were also motivated by a desire for the familiar, for objects, rituals, and architecture that could bring order and comfort in a new land.[41]

To hold on to an identity, to preserve a continuity of self, some went home, some imagined themselves there, and some tried to create their old world in the new. Their children and their children's children, to varying degrees, clung to a sense of their Englishness. David Cressy maintains that it took until the third generation for colonists in New England to feel at home there, to no longer believe that their true home was in England.[42] A new sense of nativity grew slowly.

Alongside these English colonists, who only gradually came to think of themselves as Americans, were colonists from other nations who looked back to their own homelands. Between 1700 and 1775, more than 110,000 Germans emigrated to America, a significant portion of whom settled in the mid-Atlantic colonies.[43] Between the late seventeenth century and the early nineteenth, more than 400,000 Irish immigrants came to North America. The majority were Protestants, arriving with a mix of motives—some religious, others financial. Many came with very high expectations of what they would find in the colonies; many were disappointed. A common lament among newcomers to America, even those coming to colonies that had been established for some years, was the lack of town culture, familiar faces, cultivated landscapes, and communal life.[44] An Irish poem from the mid-eighteenth century described a new immigrant's experiences in America:

> I once took a notion that I would leave my people and depart for the
> New Island, and so I did. . . .
> Once there I walked twenty miles and never met a Christian—
> No, nor even a horse or a cow or a sheep grazing on the meadow.
> There was nothing but dense woods and deep glens resounding
>   with the roar of wild beasts. . . .

Continuing on his journey, the narrator came upon a house occupied by Irish people from his own region, and determined to return home. Although the verse was fiction, it represented a widely acknowledged reality.[45]

In some colonies, immigrants who found such conditions dispiriting could find help returning home, particularly if they hailed from the British

Empire. Private charitable organizations such as the Scots Charity Box, founded in 1657 in Boston, and the Friendly Sons of St. Patrick, founded in New York in 1784, offered funds for immigrants to "enable them to return to their native land."[46] Immigrants from countries outside of the British Empire who wanted to return home often found that their native lands forbade it. In Germany, immigrants' lands were confiscated when they left the country, so there was little to return to. Basel, Switzerland, allowed its citizens to migrate only so "that they might see how foolishly they had acted." Upon departing they lost all of their land and their inheritance and were barred from ever returning.[47] The idea was to discourage potential emigrants and make them hesitant to sever home ties.

As a result, for many colonists there was no way to remedy the yearning for home. Hierarchical communities shaped their emotional lives, teaching them to obediently subordinate themselves and their desires to the larger social order. Individual needs and feelings were accorded little importance in colonial society, and many expected sadness and submission as their lot in life.

THE EMOTIONAL EXPERIENCE OF BONDAGE

While the principle of order and the expectation that life was a vale of tears influenced how European colonists viewed their separations from home, it offered little comfort to African slaves. Slaves expressed a mix of emotions, including anger at the injustice of their situation, despair at their lack of control, and fear about the future, but a recurring theme in the writings of and about those sold away from their families and their native lands was the desire to return home.

The first slaves brought from Africa to America were twenty individuals delivered to Virginia in 1619, but their numbers soon increased. During the colonial period, around 300,000 slaves were imported to the colonies, with the pace of importation accelerating over time.[48] A far larger number started the journey than arrived; some estimate that 15 percent died during the sea passage, and on some ships mortality rates were far higher.[49] En route to America, slaves were stripped naked and faced dreadful and life-threatening conditions on the overpacked ships that transported them across the Atlantic. They also suffered psychological trauma. Separated from their communities and families, many succumbed to a condition called the "fixed melancholy," a state of such despondency that they could not eat and soon died.[50]

Other slaves, overcome with despair, threw themselves overboard. Thomas Phillips, captain of the slave ship *Hannibal*, wrote of his captives' behavior on a voyage in the 1690s: "The negroes are so wilful and loth to leave their own country, that they have often leap'd out of the canoes, boat and ship, into the sea, and kept under water till they were drowned, to avoid being taken up and saved by our boats, which pursued them; they having a more dreadful apprehension of Barbadoes than we can have of hell, but home is home, etc. We had about 12 negroes did wilfully drown themselves, and others starv'd themselves to death; for 'tis their belief that when they die they return home to their own country and friends again."[51] Many slaves en route to the Americas took less drastic measures, but still felt and expressed their deep pain at being forcibly removed from their homes. One ship's doctor reported, "They sing, but not for their amusement. The captain ordered them to sing, and they sang songs of sorrow. Their sickness, fear of being beaten, their hunger, and the memory of their country, &c, are the usual subjects."[52]

Those who survived the arduous journey did not easily relinquish memories of home, and many attempted to return to Africa. Colonial newspapers carried ads for slaves who had tried to make their way back to their own countries. Five slaves tried to float down the Ogeechee River in a canoe, hoping the river would lead them back to Africa, and a group of Angolans enslaved in South Carolina struck an eastward course, hoping they could find their way home.[53] In the *Virginia Gazette*, George Robertson offered "twenty pounds reward" for the return of his slaves, twenty-year-old Step, who "has his Country Marks on his Temples," and twelve-year-old Lucy. "Neither of them can speak good English, as they have not been long in the Country. They went off with several others, being persuaded that they could find the Way back to their own Country."[54] By 1768, Will, a thirty-year-old slave, had already made three unsuccessful attempts to "get to his country." When he made a fourth attempt, his master, Jordan Anderson, warned all vessels against letting him board and aiding his escape.[55] Although slaves' efforts to return to Africa were futile, they attest to the depth of desire to return home and the limitations slaves faced when trying to act on those desires.

Africans were forced into slave labor throughout the Atlantic world. Many were sent to the West Indies before being imported to British North America. Some started families in these locations, and when moved from them they tried to return. Very quickly, enslaved people began to define home not only as a particular place in Africa from where they or their parents had been taken, but as the spot where their immediate family lived. This could be Antigua or Jamaica or Bermuda or any number of locales in the Atlantic world. A Virginia slave owner, Robert Donald, described Brazil, who had run away from him, as a "Negro man" and "a Spaniard" and a "very good seaman," and noted, "I imagine his intention is to get to his own country, therefore I forewarn all masters of vessels, and others, from

RUN away from the fubfcriber in *Chefterfield*, about the end of *Auguft* laft, a middle fized Negro man named WILL, about 30 years old, of a yellowifh complexion, very much marked on his face, arms, and breaft, his country fafhion, fpeaks very broken, and can hardly tell his mafter's name; had on when he went away a new ofnabrugs fhirt, *Virginia* linen fhort troufers, old cotton jacket, and felt hat, with part of the brim burnt off. He has made three attempts, as he faid, to get to his country, but was apprehended. All mafters of veffels are hereby fore-warned from carrying the faid flave out of the colony. Whoever apprehends him, and brings him to me, fhall have 20 s. reward, befides what the law allows.   JORDAN ANDERSON.

Ad for an escaped slave, Will, who had made three previous escapes in an effort to return to his native land. *Virginia Gazette*, October 27, 1768, supplement.
Source: Library of Virginia, Courtesy of the Colonial Williamsburg Foundation.

carrying him off." Similarly, seventeen-year-old Jack, born in Antigua, was suspected of trying to run either to his former plantation in Norfolk or trying "for a passage to the West Indies."[56] In 1766, the *Georgia Gazette* carried an advertisement for a runaway described as a "mulatto boy named Billy," who had been born in Jamaica. He had run away from his Georgia master and was "supposed to be skulking about some vessels in order to get there [Jamaica] again."[57] Sue, "Bermuda born" and described as "of a middle size inclinable to be fat," was believed to have run from South Carolina to a vessel bound for her birthplace.[58]

Some slaves who were born in Africa eventually developed roots in America and were loath to leave their new connections. Rather than trying to return to another continent, they often tried to maintain connections in an adjoining county. For instance, Aberdeen, an enslaved blacksmith born in Africa, missed his family in Virginia when he was sold away from them. His master, William Black, reported, "He ran away from the Falls Plantation, in Chesterfield. . . . He is an African, but came in the Country young, and speaks very good English. . . . He had a wife at the Plantation of John Parke Curtis, Esquire, in King & Queen, where I formerly lived, and it is probable he may be in that Neighbourhood, as he would sometimes stay a Month there when I gave him liberty to go and see his wife, or he may be lurking about my plantation in Prince George."[59] Aberdeen was no anomaly. Philip Morgan tells of a "'Mandingo' slave, [who] after spending most of his youth in South Carolina, was shipped off and sold in Jamaica; he was captured in Charlestown a year later." Such patterns demonstrate "the early identification of African-born slaves with particular New World neighbourhoods."[60]

Slaves born in America also felt homesick for the places where their kin lived and from which they had been taken.[61] Colonial newspapers were full of notices for slaves who had run back to their former plantations. Sufferer, "a Virginia born negro fellow" with a "country made shirt and breeches, a short brown cloth coat turned up with white, with pewter buttons," ran away in June 1778, and his master, John Armistead, believed he was heading to Elizabeth City County, where he was born and raised.[62] Theodorick Bland suspected that his slave Harry, clad in "a dark brown Cloth Livery Coat turned up with Green, Waistcoat of the same, striped velvet breeches," had left in such finery to be with "his Mother, an old Negro Woman formerly the Property of the late Parson Green." Fanny, about "45 years of age, rather of a short size, but lusty," was suspected of "lurking in the neighborhood of Petersburg, having many children there."[63] While slaves of both sexes were more likely to run off to visit relatives and friends than to run to freedom, this pattern was especially pronounced among women.[64]

Both slaves born in Africa and their children born in America looked for consolation in their spiritual practices and displayed religious sensibilities shaped by the longing for a lost home. Before the religious revivals of the Great Awakening, when many converted to Christianity, slaves frequently mixed the signs and symptoms of homesickness with traditional West African religious practices, believing that after death they would return to Africa and be free.[65] Masters were aware that their slaves harbored such hopes. Rev. Ebenezer Dovtrion bought Phillis, a slave newly arrived from Guinea. According to Dovtrion's family, Phillis "endured bondage, civilization, and Connecticut only in the prospect of returning at death to freedom, barbarism, and Guinea. This idea she hugged to her poor, homesick old heart with a sort of ferocious faith. Ever in her dreams gleamed before her the golden sands of Benguela, ever beckoned its palms."[66]

Some did not wait for their natural death but hoped to speed their return to Africa by committing suicide. A chronicler of New England recorded the story of "haughty Congo Pomp," who "escaped to a swamp near Truro on Cape Cod—a swamp now called by his name—and placing at the foot of a tree a jug of water and loaf of bread to sustain him on his last long journey, hanged himself from the low-hanging limbs, and thus obtained freedom."[67] Young Chloe Spear, captured from the coast of Africa in the 1760s, when she was around twelve, and transported to Massachusetts, was separated from all she knew. So desperate did she feel in America that one New England writer said of her, "She sighed, and wished for *death*; supposing that when she died, she would return to her country and friends. This imagination she derived from a superstitious tradition of her ancestors, who she said, supposed that the first infant born in a family after the decease of a member, was the same individual come back again."[68]

Others did not commit or contemplate suicide but instead nursed the hope of return throughout their lives. Jin Cole, who lived in Deerfield, Massachusetts, and who had been taken from Africa in 1715, when she was twelve, "could not forget her early life, its sunny days, her royal blood, and her cruel wrongs. And she fully expected at death, or before, to be transported back to Guinea; and all her long life she was gathering, as treasures to take back to her motherland, all kinds of odds and ends, colored rags, bits of finery, peculiar shaped stones, shells, buttons, beads, *anything* she could string."[69] Phillis, the slave of Reverend Dovtrion, had similar habits and beliefs; she too was from Guinea and longed to return. During her life in Connecticut she hoarded goods in a chest for her own final journey back to Africa. Descendents of her master recalled, "When she died, it was found to contain pies, cakes, nuts, raisins, shawls, aprons, and handkerchiefs—some of which had been stored there fifty years. My mother remembers, as a child following this old servant about, questioning Phillis, Phillis, where do you expect to go when you die? . . . 'Why, go Guinea, whar udder folks go—fool you!'"[70]

For slaves in colonial America, a permanent home often proved elusive. For some, home was in Africa, impossibly far away, across a distance that could be covered only by supernatural means. For others, home was where mother and father and spouse were, and slaves were often forced to leave these places and people as they passed from the hands of one owner to the next.

The emotional problems that slaves faced when they were forced to leave their homes were no doubt more acute than those of other colonists. Nevertheless, they shared with whites some similar circumstances. All were living in a hierarchical, patriarchal society that dictated the movements of its members, in some cases denying freedom of mobility altogether. Slaves' migrations were dictated by their masters, servants by theirs, sons by their fathers, wives by their husbands, religious colonists by God. While many felt pain at such movements, few had recourse to relieve it.

THE ENLIGHTENMENT, NOSTALGIA, AND HOMESICKNESS

While generations of colonists, white and black, felt a longing for the land they or their ancestors had left, and some quite intensely, their understanding of their emotions was characterized by a sense of restraint. Those without resources had no choice but to live with the pain of separation. Those with greater means still felt the press of communal and religious obligations that limited their opportunities to return home. All lived in a culture where pain and suffering were seen as natural and inevitable components of the human condition, and these beliefs shaped the ways they expressed and acted on their yearnings.

During the Enlightenment, however, as scientists and philosophers began to study the workings of human nature, the view that God caused suffering to promote character gradually lost power and persuasiveness, and the desire to eliminate suffering and increase happiness gained currency.[71] As philosophers developed new views about feelings, they also began to study them more closely in an effort to understand their causes and their meanings.

In 1688, a Swiss scholar, Johannes Hofer, accorded formal medical status to the longing for home, a condition he claimed had not previously been "observed properly or explained carefully." He described the plight of a man from Berne, Switzerland, who had gone to Basel in order to study. While there he suffered "sadness for a considerable time," and then became afflicted with "a burning fever." His symptoms worsened with each passing day, and it appeared that he would soon die. His doctors concluded that to save him he must "be returned to his native land." Although he was "half dead" by this time, he was placed on a bed and transported the sixty miles back to Berne. As soon as the trip was under way, the patient was suddenly able "to draw breath more freely ... to show a better tranquility of mind." As the party came closer and closer to Berne, "all the symptoms abated to such a great extent they really relaxed altogether, and he was restored to his whole sane self before he entered Berne."[72]

While the Germans already had the word *heimweh*, and the French the phrase *la Maladie du Pays* to describe the painful longing for home, Hofer claimed that there was no word in medicine to describe the feelings and symptoms of the condition. He therefore created a new word, *nostalgia*, from two existing Greek words, *nostos*, meaning "return home," and *algia*, the word for "pain." He also offered a medical explanation for what caused this newly identified condition. He claimed it was caused by what he termed the "living spirits" that flowed throughout the body. In the nostalgic individual, the mind was focused on the powerful idea of home, and because the living spirits were "occupied much for a long time around the arousing of one idea in the mind, it scarcely could be otherwise than that these same ones [were] either wearied or exhausted," and could not attend to other bodily needs, functions, or ideas.[73]

Hofer's discussion inspired other doctors and scholars to address the problem. A flurry of studies in the early eighteenth century focused mostly on Swiss examples of nostalgia, and for a time doctors believed the condition to be unique to Switzerland. Eventually, cases were identified across Europe and later in the Americas. In detailing these cases, the writers tried to understand why some people succumbed to the emotion while others did not. Often they pointed to national traits and habits, claiming that the Swiss were most tied to home, but that other nations, such as France, also inspired longing in their citizens.[74] Many believed the English were unlikely to contract the illness because they were accustomed to commerce and colonization, and therefore to relocation. One British physician suggested that nostalgia was a species of "pathetic insanity" and a condition to which his countrymen were utterly invulnerable. He claimed that because the English were worldly, they would not suffer from nostalgia, as it was the "offspring of an unpolished state of society."[75]

Evidence from the eighteenth century, however, shows that many British people were not immune to the "pathetic insanity" of nostalgia. Doctors used the diagnostic category of nostalgia to describe the condition of Welsh soldiers in the 1780s. It was also during the eighteenth century that an English word for the condition, *homesickness*, was coined, becoming part of the language in the 1750s.[76] *Homesickness* crossed the Atlantic before the American Revolution and became a part of common parlance in the colonies. The medical diagnosis, and the term *nostalgia*, while evident in the colonies by the late eighteenth century, took somewhat longer to become part of popular speech.

The interest in naming and categorizing emotions was symptomatic of Enlightenment culture. Philosophers came to see feelings as a potential source of goodness and virtue and, in the words of one historian, "a basic attribute of humanity."[77] In particular, members of the Scottish Enlightenment focused on the power of emotions and praised the "social affections" or "benevolent affections" that bound humans to each other.[78] In addition to these affections for family, there were even more exalted emotions that people should strive to experience. Philosophers believed that individuals, particularly men, should cultivate "a universal love of the human."[79] One should not be too tied to family or farm, but instead should be at ease in the whole world and consider it home. The broader one's connections, the wider one's circle of attachments, the more enlightened one was. As an eighteenth-century English poet, Aaron Hill, wrote,

> Base are these *local* limits to mens hearts,
> That canton out *humanity*, in parts.
> *Truth* has no *districts*, to divide her toil;
> And *virtue* is at *home*, in ev'ry soil.[80]

This cosmopolitan vision challenged older notions of locally based communal life that had governed both European and colonial society in earlier centuries. Rather than seeing individuals as defined by their communities and divine will, followers of the Enlightenment came to see them as having the potential to be self-directed and autonomous, pursuing happiness, possessing rights and abilities that went beyond those conferred by their families, their churches, or their towns. They would be citizens of the world.

In such a vision, nostalgia was a problem, for it kept people rooted and provincial. The English physician Thomas Arnold condemned it, calling it an "unreasonable fondness for the place of our birth." He noted that the emotion was not visible in "the populous, wealthy, commercial city, where a free intercourse with the rest of mankind, and especially the daily resort and frequent society of foreigners, render the views and connexions more extensive, familiarize distant nations with each other, rub off the partiality of private and confined attachments." Admittedly, the cultivation of a cosmopolitan outlook might "diminish the warmth" of private connections, but it had the potential to "vastly increase the extent of affection."[81] Not all were convinced, and a debate of sorts raged in Europe between strict adherents to cosmopolitanism and those who were willing to accord value to more provincial ties.[82]

Yet the idea of cosmopolitan, unfettered, happy individuals, open to the offerings of the world, was powerful and liberating. It suggested that individuals should work to increase their fortunes and improve their futures rather than let community will dictate their place in society. If opportunities for wealth, distinction, and greatness beckoned men away from home, they must follow. By pathologizing any tenacious attachment to the local, this philosophy, blossoming in the eighteenth century, began the process of naturalizing wandering and placelessness as essential and celebrated human behaviors and traits, and marginalizing the homesick as unpolished provincials.

Alongside this new evaluation of emotions came related changes in political culture and social order. During the eighteenth century, traditional authority began to break down across the colonies, and individual passions and interests were given a new centrality in social and political life. In earlier decades, private interests had been subordinated to communal ones, but that was changing as individual desires were afforded more significance.[83] Obedience as a social and political value was increasingly undermined over the course of the eighteenth century.[84] Colonists moved more frequently than before and created a wealth of new settlements, often at greater distances from their families and churches. They also began to distance themselves from the rigid hierarchical order that had dominated colonial life.[85]

One sign of individuals' emerging sense of autonomy, rejection of hierarchy, and quest for happiness was the way unfree people began to regard their obligations and the way they asserted greater control over their whereabouts. Rather than accept subservient roles in society, they struck out on their own. White servants and apprentices, for instance, began to flout their masters' will, leave their servitude, and return home, at least temporarily. In a world where authority was being questioned, many claimed the right to act on the promptings of their own feelings. Colonial newspapers testified to this, carrying countless ads for runaway servants and apprentices that detailed both the disobedience and the homesickness of the colonial labor force. In the *Virginia Gazette* in 1767, Samuel Lemberd advertised a reward of three pounds for his runaway apprentice, Absalom Spicer, who worked as a ship's carpenter and was suspected of running to Caroline County, where his parents lived.[86] Thomas Roberts advertised for John Bailey, another apprentice who had run away, suspecting him of "lurking about Hampton, as he was born there."[87]

Those who were free to contract their labor and move where they wanted to also gave new attention to their homesickness, for with their freedom came the responsibility of deciding where they should go and what they should leave behind. They could pursue happiness, but it was not always clear if that pursuit led away from or back to home. The experiences of Philip Vickers Fithian, a New Jersey native employed as a tutor on a Virginia plantation, offer a window onto the new emotional conundrums faced by free men who felt in control of their own migrations but somewhat overwhelmed by their competing choices. Fithian was an eager individualist, willing to travel from New Jersey to the wealthy Carter plantation in Virginia in order to secure a well-paying job and put his Princeton education to work. Once there, however, he complained repeatedly in his journal about his separation from friends and family and used the new word *homesickness* to describe his feelings. He wrote in 1773, "Rode to Church. . . . Dined at home—Mr Lee dined with us. . . . Feel very home-sick—Saw two Brothers quarrel—Doleful sight."[88]

Fithian was not sure what he should do or what significance he should attribute to his emotions. On the one hand, he longed for his New Jersey home and confided to his journal that he had taken a break from his reading to "look over Potowmack through Maryland towards Home." On the other hand, he tried to be cosmopolitan in his outlook, reminding himself, "How insignificant . . . is it for me and how foolish to be uneasy, & solicitous whether I live in *Cohansie*, In *Princeton*, or in *Virginia*."[89] After a trip home to New Jersey he reflected on the many advantages in his situation in Virginia: "Yet I love Cohansie! And in spite of my resolution, when I am convinced that my situation is more advantageous here, yet I wish to be there—How exceedingly capricious is fancy! When I am Home I then seem willing to remove, for other places seem to be full as desirable."[90] He ultimately concluded that he must return home. "Strong, & sweet are the bands which tye us to our place of nativity; If it is but a beggarly Cottage, we seem not satisfied with the most elegant entertainment if we are totally separated from it." Fithian's confusion over where his freedom should take him was never resolved. He did return to New Jersey, but he died away from home, while serving in the army in 1776.[91]

Another young man in New Jersey felt equally mixed emotions as he tried to find the place that would make him happiest. In 1768, Hugh Simm, a native of Paisley, Scotland, went to Princeton, New Jersey, with John Witherspoon. Witherspoon became president of the College of New Jersey; Simm was given the post of college librarian. He tried to embrace the cosmopolitan individualism of the era, but during his first year in New Jersey, he had mixed emotions, writing to his brother, "I hope yet to have the comfort of seeing you. . . . I am not Sorry for my coming here but I do not incline to spend all my life in it tho I find nothing so dissagreeable as my being at so great a distance from you—Send me an account of evry thing that is particular in the place the death person new building accidences and occurrences with whatever is remarkable every thing any thing." Four years later he was still in the colonies, although he had resettled in New York. He longed to return to Scotland but also saw advantages to prolonging his stay, for doing so might enable him to eventually buy a house in Paisley. He wrote, "I can say little about returning to Scotland at present tho nothing could be more desirable that is Still more doubtfull all I can say is that perhaps next year I may send you as much money as will purchase a house near you and return Some time After my self."[92]

Simm and Fithian believed that they should be comfortable at large in the world, citizens of the universe, but they were not always so at ease. They displayed a greater sense that they could control their own movements than had earlier generations, but they were not yet sure where they should go, how far they should wander. To be a cosmopolitan individual took work and training and did not come naturally.

REVOLUTIONARY SENTIMENTS

Enlightenment philosophies of rights, happiness, and freedom undergirded the revolutionary movement, yet as many a military leader of the Revolution was to discover, this new spirit had the potential not just to inspire revolutionary action, but to lead away from it. While a number of historians have focused attention on the way that emotional sensibilities motivated colonists to join the revolutionary cause, little has been said of how this increased emphasis on individual happiness could also undermine the cause.[93] The tension between individual happiness and political imperatives was clearly evidenced in the problem of homesick soldiers, who often joined the war effort out of deeply held civic allegiances, but eventually abandoned it because of the press of their own individual emotional and material needs.

In the early months of the conflict with Britain, Americans, animated by political enthusiasms, eagerly joined the revolutionary armies. For a time it was believed that this patriotic spirit would be sufficient to motivate common citizens to fight for liberty, but as the war effort dragged on, their ardor for the cause dimmed, and many left the army for home. As a result, the citizen army had to be replaced with a professional one, well trained in obedience and duty and less likely to desert.[94]

The problem was that citizen soldiers, free to follow their own desires, found that those desires often led away from the army and toward home. Daniel Barber, born in 1756 in Simsbury, Connecticut, joined the cause in 1775, after Bunker Hill. He wrote of both the initial excitement and the unexpected pain that leaving home to fight occasioned.

> [Before setting off] each soldier had the opportunity of mingling for a few moments with his dearest friends and companions. The tender feelings of love—of friendship—of affection—again burst forth. While the fond father and tender-hearted mother are bidding adieu to their sons, the husband, the wife, the children—brothers, sisters, and best friends—are exchanging, as for the last time, the tokens of their love, and the best affections of the heart.... The drums beat to arms. Soldiers, take your places, is the word; the line of march is formed; we add one more wishful, lingering look, while many a silent tear bespeaks the real feeling of the heart. The word is given. We begin our march with silence, downcast looks, and pensive feelings and reflections. We were now leaving our homes, our friends, and all our pleasant places behind, and which our eyes might never again behold.

Adding to the poignancy of the departure was its strangeness: "Most of us had not, at that time, I believe, been twenty miles from home."[95] Josiah Atkins, who joined the army and ventured from his native Connecticut to Virginia, also felt unsettled by his unprecedented distance from home. When he reached Baltimore he observed, "O Lord my God, how lamentable my circumstances! Once I liv'd in peace at home, rejoicing in the divine favor & smiles; but now I'm on the field of war, surrounded with circumstances of affliction & heart felt disappointment! ... Once I enjoy'd the pleasant company of many friends; but now I am among *strangers* in a *strange land*."[96]

Many soldiers could not grow accustomed to life away from home and returned as soon as their terms of service expired, deaf to pleas to reenlist. In 1775, Gen. Charles Lee described this problem when he wrote of troops from Connecticut who garnered great attention when they decided to leave the army and return to their families: "Some of the Connecticutians who were homesick could not be prevailed on to tarry." Their fellow soldiers shamed them for succumbing to their emotions: "In passing through the lines of other regiments, they were so horribly hissed, groaned at, and pelted that I believe they wished their aunts, grandmothers, and even sweethearts, to whom the day before they were so much attached at the devil's own palace."[97] Again and again, officers were frustrated by soldiers' unwillingness to reenlist. Gen. Philip Schuyler wrote to Governor Jonathan Trumbull in 1776, "I was in hopes that experience would have taught us not to depend on the patriotism of our common men—they left both armies last year at very critical moments. . . . As soon as the first cold is felt, we are seized with the home-sickness, and it increases with the severity of the weather."[98]

It was not just cold weather that triggered homesickness. Another part of the problem was that soldiers' sense of home was still quite geographically bounded. Home was not yet the new nation; it was the local neighborhood or, at best, the colony. The historian Charles Royster notes, "In June 1775, eighteen men from Captain Winthrop Rowe's New Hampshire company deserted outside Boston, saying 'that they didn't intend when they enlisted to join the Army, but to be station'd at Hampton' on the New Hampshire coast."[99] George Washington commented on the problem, noting that local militia men "just dragged from the tender Scenes of domestick life" were emotionally unequal to the task before them. Then too "the sudden change in their manner of living, (particularly in the lodging) brings on sickness in many; impatience in all, and such an unconquerable desire of returning to their respective homes that it not only produces shameful, and scandalous Desertions among themselves, but infuses the like spirit in others."[100] Desertion rates were extremely high; on average, 20 to 25 percent of soldiers deserted each year, although the numbers declined over the course of the war, as Washington came to rely on professional rather than volunteer armies.[101]

Some conjectured that while common soldiers might succumb to homesickness, officers, animated by a sense of gentlemanly honor and duty and seeking glory and distinction in the service of their country, would be better able to master their yearnings for home. Yet they could not always escape the feeling of homesickness themselves. Even George Washington wrote to his wife of the conflict he felt between home and duty. After being appointed to lead the Continental Army, he wrote, "You may believe me, my dear Patsy, when I assure you, in the most solemn manner that, so far from seeking this appointment, I have used every endeavor in my power to avoid it. . . . I should enjoy more real happiness in one month with you at home, than I have the most distant prospect of finding abroad."[102] Yet he soldiered on. Those officers who did not uphold their commitments to the nation as he did earned his scorn. When, for instance, Col. William Malcolm asked for a furlough in 1778, Washington fired back, "I have received your Letter of the 4th Instt. When you reflect how lately you joined the Army. What indulgencies you have had, and how long you were at and in the Neighbour-hood of your Home, after your appointment, you cannot be surprised, that I disapproved your application for a Furlough and with some degree of dis-pleasure."[103] Elsewhere Washington made it clear that acting on homesick-ness was dishonorable, ignoble behavior, writing dismissively of those "disgracefully desiring to go home."[104]

Given such attitudes, officers struggled to master homesickness, risking dishonor and humiliation if they did not. Gen. Richard Montgomery criti-cized New England troops for their homesickness, yet before the Battle of Quebec, Montgomery decided he himself would soon resign from the army. He wrote his wife, "I wish it were well over, with all my heart, and sigh for home like a New-Englander."[105] Many officers struggled with their feel-ings. Samuel Kennedy, an army surgeon stationed on Long Island, wrote to his wife in 1776, "My separation from you and my dear little one becomes daily more Intolerable, so that sometimes I feel almost ready to resign." A few days later he wrote again: "My dearest self. . . . I apprehend myself de-clining in flesh, which must undoubtedly arise from local separation from you. How time and a greater distance may operate I know not, but at pre-sent I feel as much as my constitution will bear."[106] Another surgeon, Albig-ence Waldo of the First Connecticut Infantry Regiment stationed at Valley Forge, worried about others reading the soft sentiments in his journal: "If I should happen to lose this little Journal, any fool may laugh that finds it. . . . Am sure there is much Sincerity, especially when I mention my family, whom I cannot help saying and am not asham'd to say that I Love. But I begin to grow Sober, I shall be home sick again.—Muses attend!—File off to the right grim melancholly."[107] The expression of too much affection for home might compromise the carefully constructed demeanor of the hon-orable gentleman.

In their efforts to promote honor and civic virtue in their troops, Amer-ican military commanders had little patience for the homesick. In Europe, army commanders often dealt sympathetically with homesick men, calling them nostalgics, admitting them to military hospitals, and in some cases securing them furloughs, because they considered nostalgia to be a debili-tating mental condition with real physical consequences.[108] To commanders of the Continental Army, however, the emotion signified a failure of will, character, and civic commitment. Soldiers should endure the temporary discomforts of separation from their families for the sake of the new nation. After the war, Benjamin Rush summed up this view, suggesting that the republican citizen must "be taught to love his family, but let him be taught at the same time that he must forsake and even forget them when the wel-fare of his country requires it."[109]

Rush admitted that men could not always achieve such an ideal. In his account of the Revolution's effects on the human body, published in 1789, he offered one of the earliest medical discussions of nostalgia in America, explaining how it had affected colonial soldiers: "Nostalgia . . . was a frequent disease in the American army, more especially among the soldiers of the New England states." He claimed it had been particularly acute in 1776, but when men perceived a true threat they were able to master their feelings and suppress the desire for home. "The patience, firmness, and magnanimity with which the officers and soldiers of the American army endured the complicated evils of hunger, cold, and nakedness, can only be ascribed to an insensibility of body," which was the result of "an uncommon tone of mind excited by the love of liberty and their country." According to Rush, in the end, civic commitment conquered nostalgia.[110] Such idealism may have pervaded accounts, particularly retrospective ones, of the Revolution but did little to allay the actual homesickness so many soldiers felt.

Rush was an astute observer and recognized that there was a variety of new emotional and medical conditions that arose as a result of the Revolution. He suggested, for instance, that loyalists who opposed the Revolution and were forced to leave the colony suffered something akin to the pain of nostalgia: "In some of them, the terror and distress of the revolution brought on a true melancholia." That melancholy sprang from, among other causes, their loss of power, a change in diet and habits, and the "neglect, insults, and oppression, to which the loyalists were exposed." Rush termed their suffering "*revolutiana*," noting, "In some cases, this disease was rendered fatal by exile and confinement."[111] Loyalists themselves gave different names to their suffering, but they would have agreed with Rush that their condition, and particularly their exile, caused them anguish. Like soldiers who deserted, they were seen by Americans who supported the cause of independence as lacking a vital commitment to the communal will and the civic good. When forced to leave the colonies, the majority traveled in Canada, with smaller numbers settling in England and the West Indies. Once installed in their new homes, however, they missed America, even if they were at odds with its political rulers.

The loyalist Joseph Stansbury, forced to leave Philadelphia after the war's end, wrote to his wife,

> Believe me, love, this vagrant life,
> O'er Nova Scotia's wilds to roam,
> While far from children, friends, or wife,
> Or place that I can call a home,
> Delights not me;—another way
> My treasures, pleasures, wishes lay.[112]

Thomas Hutchinson, the former governor of Massachusetts, lamented, "I would rather die in a little country farmhouse in New England than in the best nobleman's seat in Old England."[113] Samuel Curwen, a loyalist living in England, shared that sentiment and spoke of his time there as "an unhappy banishment from [his] family, friends and country." Curwen was excited when a club of New Englanders was to be formed in London and spent much of his time while in that city at the New England Coffee House, often reading New England papers and conversing with other exiles from the region. Little wonder, then, that he returned to Massachusetts after the war.[114]

The Revolution brought forth many conflicting notions of home. Homesick soldiers sometimes had a profoundly local sense of home, and when taken away from their farms and villages and forced to act for the larger polity, found themselves "strangers in a strange land." Loyalists too considered the colonies home, but tied to that conception of home was a set of political allegiances and a long nurtured connection with England, which, when severed, left them homeless. Compared to their fathers, grandfathers, and great-grandfathers, both revolutionaries and loyalists asserted far more independence in deciding who they would or would not support. They listened to the promptings of their own feelings and followed where they led. They had to weigh allegiances and balance competing senses of home as they tried to set their course. The emerging ideology of individualism posed these conundrums for them; their children would confront an even wider and often more confusing array of choices in the decades that followed.

CHAPTER 2

◈

Painful Lessons in Individualism

I n popular mythology, the icons of nineteenth-century life are people who were on the move: pioneers in wagon trains, gold miners heading west, mill girls and young clerks swarming into American towns. Observers of American life long have celebrated the willingness of antebellum citizens to leave their families, dwelling on their individualism and depicting a time when motion was prized for its own sake. Alexis de Tocqueville offered such an interpretation, describing men who migrated from the East and "rush[ed] so boldly onwards in pursuit of wealth," despite the fact that they "were already in the enjoyment of a competency in their own part of the country."[1] Another visitor, Domingo Sarmiento, offered a portrait of what such mobility looked like on a grand scale: "If God were suddenly to call the world to judgment He would surprise two-thirds of the American population on the road like ants."[2] By the late nineteenth century, when historians looked back to the era, many agreed with Frederick Jackson Turner that "movement has been its dominant fact."[3] These observers perceived Americans' migrations as easy, unproblematic, and inevitable. Yet while they captured the mobility of the era, they missed the fact that Americans often moved on hesitantly, sometimes regretfully, and frequently with the intention of eventually returning home.

Despite the mixed feelings of those on the move, move they did. From 1800 to 1850, a higher percentage of people, almost half of the population, crossed state lines to change residences than in any comparable later period.[4] As a new political order based on individual rights and the pursuit of happiness developed in the wake of the Revolution, the old bonds of fealty and obedience, which had linked individuals and kept them in place during the colonial period, weakened, at least among white citizens.

The early nineteenth century was also witness to a market revolution that encouraged ambition and competition. Capitalist activity, what Wordsworth decried as mere "getting and spending," became more valued, and Americans increasingly celebrated and strived for financial success. No longer was it sufficient to have a comfortable competency on which to survive; instead many hoped to acquire small fortunes.[5] In such a context, freedom of movement, both social and geographic, became a right, and for some even a necessity.[6]

Yet this capitalist activity and desire for more was often based on hopes for family improvement rather than mere individual enrichment. Nineteenth-century Americans endlessly extolled domestic life as the chief source of happiness and virtue, celebrating the warmth of mother love, the charms of cozy cottages, the tranquility of rooted family life. While on the surface, restless mobility ran counter to such a vision, in actuality, restlessness often reflected migrants' hopes of improving domestic life. Some planned to venture to the West or to growing towns, make a fortune, and return home; others thought they might build a home with their families on new land. In either case, the dream of family unity undergirded much of the mobility of the age. Migrants' letters bore witness to this, for they were full of hopes and plans for reunion and return. In the event that this proved impossible, they comforted themselves with the vision that they would rejoin their kin in heaven, for increasingly during the nineteenth century, Americans imagined heaven as a family home in which the scattered would be brought together once more.[7] Often it was only the conviction that they eventually would be reunited with their families, either on earth or in heaven, that allowed prospectors, farmers, missionaries, and soldiers to leave home in the first place. These mobile individuals were hardly full-fledged individualists.

Consequently, as they moved, many Americans worried about the miles that separated them from loved ones. Some thought leaving home and family in search of better prospects was unnatural; when they did leave they did so with grave misgivings. Commentators fretted that migration carried a heavy price for society and for individuals. Some worried that those who left home defied God. Foreign immigrants had to overcome this anxiety as they made their way to America. Native-born citizens also harbored concerns about the restlessness they saw about them, believing that it undermined civilization.[8] Whether they were concerned about moral or social backsliding, the extraordinary mobility of the nineteenth century left many unsettled, in every sense of the word.

One sign of this anxiety was the attention that newspapers paid to the problem of homesickness, often publishing dramatic accounts of the sad fates of melancholy migrants. Some were caught up in overseas migrations: the *Federal Mirror* told the tale of a homesick Portuguese boy, apprenticed to the captain of the ship *Britania*, who had thrown himself overboard in the futile hope of reaching a nearby ship bound for Lisbon; the *Alexandria Gazette* reprinted a letter from a homesick New England sailor anchored on the River Tigress, near Canton; the Charleston, South Carolina, *City Gazette and Commercial Daily Advertiser* discussed the plight of a homesick naval officer in Valparaiso, Chile; the *Boston Weekly Messenger* described Chinese workers afflicted by the emotion after traveling to work on tea plantations in Brazil.[9]

Papers often focused on suicides that homesickness prompted. For instance, a number of newspapers carried news of the slave ship *Le Rodeur*. In 1819, on a voyage from Africa to Guadeloupe, many of the slaves onboard began to suffer from disease. The ship's surgeon advised that they be brought above deck in order to get fresh air. However, that solution was abandoned after "many of those Negroes, affected with Nostalgia (that is a passionate desire to revisit their native land), threw themselves into the sea, locked in each other's arms."[10] San Francisco papers covered the suicides of homesick German immigrants in California.[11] The *New York Herald* carried news of the death of a schoolgirl, Sophia Defoe, living in Towanda, New York, far from her parents in Michigan: "Her suicide is attributed to grief at being separated from her relatives. Just before she went out to commit the crime she complained of being homesick."[12] A few weeks later, in January 1857, the *Herald* reported on "another homesick suicide." This time the victim was an English immigrant, Sarah Bentley, who committed "the rash act" because of her "deep despondency . . . owing to her separation from friends and home scenes across the water, to which she ha[d] pined to return."[13]

Such suicides were one response to the hard realities of distance, for during the antebellum era, even short distances were great. To travel from New York to Boston in 1800 took seventy-four hours by stagecoach. Travel time improved somewhat after the introduction of the steamship; by 1816, the journey from Philadelphia to New York City took thirteen hours by boat and stage.[14] Longer distances were still daunting, for roads were rough and poorly maintained, but in the late 1820s, railroads began to chug across the countryside, and by 1850, 7,500 miles of track had been laid across the eastern United States.[15] Still, train service extended no farther west than Omaha until 1869, when the transcontinental railroad was completed. To make it to the western edge of the continent therefore required expensive and lengthy overland or sea journeys.[16]

Given such conditions, leaving home was often quite painful. Although only a small number of Americans committed suicide because of grief at their distance from kin, many more expressed great homesickness in letters, journals, songs, and stories. They bore witness to the real difficulties of migration and the emotionally trying process of embracing individualism.

Americans did not hide their homesickness, for they lived in a culture that valued displays of family love, grief, and what the historian Peter Stearns has called "tearful sadness." These emotions needed to be channeled appropriately, but they did not need to be repressed. They were constituent parts of homesickness, and consequently that emotion had some legitimacy. Yet Americans also were embracing an ethic of cheerfulness, which suggested that men and women should show a sunny disposition in the face of life's challenges.[17] During the early nineteenth century, Americans were trying to balance these emotional demands. They were not always proud of their homesickness, but they did not deny the emotion and often expressed it quite openly.

TRAILS OF TEARS

One group eager to discuss the costs of their migrations was Native Americans. Forced off ancestral lands, they appealed to fellow Americans on the basis of rights and treaties, but also on the basis of feeling.

Their forced migrations in the nineteenth century were the culmination of many generations of coerced leave-takings. Algonquin moved on as colonists streamed into the Northeast; Iroquois gave way as later generations pressed west into New York. Cherokee, Creek, Pottawattamie, Shawnee, Ottawa, Miami, and Chippewa were forced off their native lands, and European Americans swarmed into them.[18] While this had been the case since the seventeenth century, the pace of displacement quickened after the Revolution.

During the first half of the nineteenth century, perhaps as many as 100,000 Native Americans were pushed west of the Mississippi.[19] During Andrew Jackson's presidency alone, forty-six thousand Native Americans were forced to leave their homes.[20] The most publicly debated removals were those of the Five Civilized Tribes—the Choctaw, Chickasaw, Creek, Seminole, and Cherokee—many of whom had adopted white ways. In 1830, the Indian Removal Act authorized the government to offer land west of the Mississippi to those tribes in the way of white settlement. Despite financial inducements (which were minimal), most tribe members wished to stay in their homes. However, a series of treaties, which a majority of Indians did not assent to, forced them off their lands.[21] The first to go west were the Choctaw, and many in the tribe shared the feelings of their chief, George Harkins, who proclaimed, "Friends, my attachment to my native land is strong—that cord is now broken; and we must go forth as wanderers in a strange land! . . . Here is the land of our progenitors, and here are their bones; they left them as a sacred deposit, and we have been compelled to venerate its trust; it is dear to us yet we cannot stay."[22]

Even before the treaties that forced them to leave were written, the Chickasaw felt similar dismay at the prospect of removal. Levi Colbert, a representative of the tribe, told government officials pressuring them to vacate their Tennessee lands, "We never had a thought of exchanging our land for any other, as we think that we would not find a country that would suit us as well as this we now occupy, it being the land of our forefathers." The tribe feared that moving from their land might "be similar to transplanting an old tree, which would wither and die away." Such fears went unheeded. In 1836, the government forcibly removed Creek Indians; in the next two years, some four thousand Chickasaw had no choice but to head west.[23]

The Cherokees' struggle to remain on their own lands received the most attention. The tribal leader John Ross described their plight: "We have been made to drink of the bitter cup of humiliation . . . our country and the graves of our Fathers torn from us . . . through a period of 200 years, rolled back, nation upon nation [until] we find ourselves fugitives, vagrants, and strangers in our own country."[24] The tribe's cause excited sympathy in many quarters. In 1835, John Howard Payne was arrested while visiting Cherokee lands. Payne was a national celebrity, for in 1823, while living in Paris, he had written the lyrics to "Home, Sweet Home," which soon became the most popular song in America.[25] When the controversy over the Cherokee broke out, Payne went to investigate conditions among the tribe and was affected by their plight. As the composer of the national anthem to homesickness, he was perhaps particularly sensitive to the domestic emotions. Then too, he saw in the Cherokee a style of living that closely resembled white ways, and this excited his sympathy. In a letter published in newspapers across the South, Payne adopted a Cherokee's perspective, writing, "The eyes of avarice are gloating on our lands, and cannot see our wives, nor our children, nor the heart strings which bind us to our sacred home; and its coarse voice can utter nor sound but that to us most withering one— 'Remove!'"[26] Despite such protests, the Cherokee were forced to vacate their homes, pack up their belongings, and embark on a trek of more than a thousand miles to Oklahoma. A missionary who witnessed the exodus wrote, "It is mournful to see how reluctantly these people go away, even the stoutest hearts melt into tears when they turn their faces towards the setting sun—& I am sure that this land will be bedewed with a Nation's tears—if not with their blood."[27]

President Jackson, a chief architect of Indian removal, was unmoved by such accounts and suggested that the tribes should master their emotions. He admitted, "It will be painful to leave the graves of their fathers," but then asked, "What do they more than our ancestors did or than our children are now doing?" Learning to swallow the pain of moving on was a particular talent of whites, he claimed. "To better their condition in an unknown land our forefathers left all that was dear in earthly objects. Our children by thousands yearly leave the land of their birth to seek new homes in distant regions." Jackson believed that migration had become so normal that leave-takings were happy occasions for whites. "Does Humanity weep at these painful separations from everything, animate and inanimate, with which the young heart has become entwined? Far from it. It is rather a source of joy that our country affords scope where our young population may range. . . . These remove hundreds and almost thousands of miles at their own expense, purchase the lands they occupy, and support themselves at their new homes from the moment of their arrival." Jackson maintained that the migrations Native Americans were forced to make were no different from those whites undertook voluntarily, and suggested that a white man would jump at the chance to have the government buy new land for him and "pay the expense of his removal." It was impossible for him to believe that "the wandering savage has a stronger attachment to his home than the settled, civilized Christian."[28] However, Jackson underestimated the pain that Native Americans experienced and overestimated the ease with which whites moved from place to place.

THE MARKET REVOLUTION

Into the lands the Native Americans had been forced to leave streamed white settlers. Hoping to cash in on the booming cotton market, they moved into the "Old Southwest," an area that contained Alabama, Tennessee, Mississippi, Louisiana, Arkansas Territory, and later Texas. There farmers found incredibly fertile land that could produce twice and sometimes three times the amount of cotton that land in the Southeast yielded.[29] This thriving economic sector attracted individuals eager to rise in the world, a goal shared by an increasing number of men in antebellum America. Once interested in earning a comfortable living, they became increasingly interested in amassing a fortune.[30]

Pulling up stakes and relocating to the Southwest was a family enterprise, yet men were generally the ones who made the decision to do so. Overall, southern women were hesitant to leave their homes and suggested in letters and diaries that their husbands were motivated by greed and materialism. Women had been raised to regard family relationships as sacred connections, divine in their origin, and therefore precious and worth conserving; men seemed less worried about moving on. This difference was apparent in their letters home. After following her husband from North Carolina to Mississippi, a woman wrote her mother, "It seems so unnatural for me to be living so far from you that I can never visit you or have the pleasure of your company at my house."[31] In contrast, many young men felt less troubled by the distance. When Allen Brown and his wife migrated from North Carolina to Tennessee in 1841, he reported that he was "well pleased" with his new home. In her letters home, however, his wife confided that she pined for North Carolina and that her thoughts often returned to her "native hill."[32]

Yet even for men, migration was sometimes harder than expected. John Owens, born in 1789 in North Carolina, moved first to Virginia and then, in 1818, to Alabama. With him on his journey over very rough terrain were his wife, two children, his mother-in-law, and three or four slaves. In the journal he kept, his entries were frequently tinged with despair: "Started early bad roads Old mair fell down carriage run back very much alarmd Mother & Ann . . . much distress[d] & low spirited almost wish I was dead or that fate had bloted the day in which I was born out of the calendar & left a perfect Blank." On other days, he compared his low spirits with those of his wife; she seemed to be holding up better than he. In early December, he wrote, "Felt Bad wife more fortitude than my self." Owens's feelings improved when he finally reached Alabama and settled for good in Tuscaloosa.[33] Unlike Owens, some settlers found that neither their situations nor their moods improved once they were settled, and they returned home after trying their luck and failing in their new homes.[34]

Families who stayed on in the Southwest settled into a pattern of life that differed from the one they had left behind. Most had started lives in extended rather than nuclear families , and they were not able to re-create these arrangements in their new homes. Families were much smaller in the frontier towns and farms and had fewer connections with each other. This made the pain of being away from home more acute, particularly for southern women who had left sprawling webs of brothers, sisters, cousins, and parents.[35]

SLAVES' MIGRATIONS

When southerners moved, they took with them what they considered to be their most valuable assets: their slaves. As a result, slaves faced a great deal of unwelcome mobility. In one study, researchers found that over the course of twenty-eight and a half years, men and women in bondage moved an average of 5.4 times.[36] Yet white masters downplayed the emotional suffering such moves caused their slaves. Whites often viewed African Americans as more expressive of what were presumed to be cruder emotions, but denied they possessed true emotional sensitivity and doubted that they loved their homes and families enough to experience much pain at separation from them. The escaped slave Harriet Jacobs said of her mistress, "It had never occurred to Mrs. Flint that slaves could have any feelings."[37] It was not just southerners who nursed this belief. John Ball, born in Vermont in 1794, wrote of the slaves he saw in Darien, Georgia, "Saw much that satisfied me that the African and Caucasian are constitutionally unlike, and cannot by an education be made, even to fully understand each other, any more than the ox and the horse. The negro docile or he could not be enslaved, cheerful under all circumstances, never committing suicide."[38]

Slaves' true feelings were often hidden from sight because masters mandated that their slaves be cheerful and sunny and show no sadness, anger, or resistance. If they were homesick, they could not express the emotion in front of their masters without repercussions. The former slave Elizabeth Keckley recalled that her master, Colonel Burwell, did not like "to see one of his slaves wear a sorrowful face, and those who offended in this particular way were always punished. Alas! the sunny face of the slave is not always an indication of sunshine in the heart." Henry Watson, an escaped slave, recalled, "The slaveholder watches every movement of the slave, and if he is downcast or sad,—in fact, if they are in any mood but laughing or singing, and manifesting symptoms of perfect content at heart, they are said to have the devil in them . . . and they are often whipped or sold."[39]

Some whites grudgingly admitted that despite the fact that they had to mask feelings, slaves had emotions similar to their own. John Knight, a Mississippi merchant who had purchased slaves in New Orleans, realized that these men and women still longed for their homes in Maryland, but he thought that most of them would eventually get over the yearning: "I consider all my N. Orleans negroes will be well acclimated after two years. . . . It is much more difficult to acclimate *old* negroes than young ones; and after their removal from their old homes to new ones, they seldom, if ever, become reconciled to the change."[40] Realizing that moves could cause pain, some owners were more active in trying to assuage it. John Cotton of Leon County, Florida, wrote a friend asking that he help reunite a young slave girl with her parents. He asked his friend to purchase the girl, noting of her parents, "I know they are human and have feelings as well as white persons and it is my earnest desire to gratify them."[41] In 1804, Henry Tucker came to a similar conclusion. He took his young slave Bob away from his family in Williamsburg and brought him to Winchester, Virginia. When Tucker discovered that Bob missed his mother, he was taken aback. He had been awakened "by a most piteous lamentation": "I found it was Bob. . . . 'I was dreaming about my mammy Sir'!!! cried he in a melancholy & still distressed tone. 'Gracious God!' thought I, 'how ought not I to feel who regarded this child as insensible when compared to those of our complexion.'

In truth our thoughts have been starting the same way. How finely woven, how delicately sensible must be those bonds of natural affection which equally adorn the civilized and the savage. The American and the African— nay the man and the Brute!"[42]

Slaves and masters had the same emotional bonds to home, but when forced to move, slaves, unlike their masters, had neither the hope of a brighter future nor the comfort of kin to offset their homesickness. This difference was clear when William Helm decided to leave Virginia for brighter prospects in western New York. He took with him his slaves, among them Austin Steward, who noted, "[We] thought Capt. Helm's prospects pretty fair, and yet we shuddered when we realized our condition as slaves." Helm's slaves "looked upon this removal as the greatest hardship they had ever met; the severest trial they had ever endured; and the separation from our old home and fellow slaves, from our relatives and the old State of Virginia, was to us a contemplation of sorrowful interest."[43]

Some slaves had to move because their masters were setting off for new locales, but often masters stayed put and auctioned off their slaves. Even those sold short distances away from their homes found the experience painful. James Mars, born in Connecticut in 1790, was sold when he was eight years old. As he moved from one master's house to another, his thoughts turned gloomy. Almost seventy years later, the memory of that day was still vivid: "I thought of my parents; should I, oh! should I never see them again? As I was taught to obey my superiors, I set out; it was a little over a mile. The way was long. I went alone. Tears ran down my cheeks. I then felt for the first time that I was alone in the world, no home, no friends, and none to care for me. Tears ran, but it did no good; I must go, and on I went."[44]

The pain was no less for adults. Slaves who told their stories in abolitionist appeals recalled the trauma of being sold. Charles Ball, born in 1781, was sold away from his family in Maryland and transported to South Carolina when he was in his early twenties. Of this separation he wrote, "I was far from the place of my nativity, in a land of strangers, with no one to care for me beyond the care that a master bestows upon his ox; with all my future life one long, waste, barren desert, of cheerless, hopeless, lifeless slavery." Ball eventually escaped slavery and returned to his family, but in 1830, he was kidnapped and sold to a master in Georgia; upon regaining his freedom and returning home in 1832, he found his free-born wife and children had been enslaved as well.[45]

In other cases, free blacks were enslaved and taken away from their families. Solomon Northup, a free man carried into slavery in 1841, contemplated his bleak situation: "Thoughts of my family, of my wife and children,

Watercolor by Lewis Miller, showing a coffle of Virginia slaves who had been sold to Tennessee. Traders often forced slaves to sing as they marched, and Miller recorded the lyrics of one song: "Arise! Arise! And weep no more[.] Dry your tears, we shall part no more. Come rose we go to Tennessee, that happy shore. To old Virginia never-never-return."

Sources: Courtesy of the Abby Aldrich Rockefeller Folk Art Museum, Colonial Williamsburg Foundation, Williamsburg, Va. Gift of Dr. and Mrs. Richard M. Kain in memory of George Hay Kain.

continually occupied my mind. When sleep overpowered me, I dreamed of them—dreamed I was again in Saratoga—that I could see their faces, and hear their voices calling me. Awakening from the pleasant phantasms of sleep to the bitter realities around me, I could but groan and weep." Northup eventually regained his freedom and rejoined his family in 1853. Less fortunate were slaves he met in the South. Clem, sold away from his home in Washington, D.C., "was wholly overcome. To him the idea of going south was terrible in the extreme. He was leaving the friends and associations of his youth—every thing that was dear and precious to his heart—in all probability never to return." Northup came to know slaves in Louisiana: "Often they recalled the memories of other days, and sighed to retrace their steps to the old home in Carolina."[46]

Despite the hardship and brutality of life in bondage, slaves often considered the plantations they had grown up on to be home and despaired at leaving them. Although there were numerous factors, from slave patrols to the threat of harsh punishment, limiting the number of slaves who ran away, love of family kept many from fleeing permanently. The fugitive Harriet Jacobs described the "desolate feeling" she experienced upon finding herself "alone among strangers" in New York. Although happy to be away from her oppressive and predatory master, she missed those she had left behind, particularly her grandmother, whom she never saw again.[47] Like Jacobs, many ran north to freedom, but perhaps an even larger number ran toward family, even if it meant remaining in the slaveholding South. One slaveholder estimated that half of the runaways were men, women, and children trying to rejoin kin.[48] These efforts often proved futile. A former slave from South Carolina recalled, "People wus always dyin' frum a broken heart."[49]

Often the only consolation that slaves had was the hope that they would be reunited in heaven, for many believed that there they could bind back together the families broken up by slavery. Abream Scriven, an educated slave sold away from his family, wrote to his wife at their separation, "If we Shall not meet in this world I hope to meet in heaven. . . . My pen cannot Express the griffe I feel to be parted from you all."[50] Others sang songs that promised, "My soul and your soul / will meet in de day / When I lay dis body down."[51]

While many hoped for such reunions in the future, in the short term they had to prepare themselves and their families for the realities of separation. Black parents tried to teach their children how to leave home and family under the very worst of circumstances. The slave auction was perhaps the most obvious and extreme example of the way that human affections and emotions came to be shaped by market forces in antebellum America. The historian Stephen Deyle writes, "Most parents tried to soften the blow of separation for their children as best they could. Thomas Jones recalled that his parents were aware of the 'inevitable suffering in store for their beloved children,' and they 'talked about our coming misery, and they lifted up their voices and wept aloud, as they spoke of our being torn from them and sold off to the dreaded slave trader.'" Deyle notes that some parents "emphasized the need to be stoic when faced with suffering and to never complain. Others were like the Virginia mother who advised her daughter before the girl's departure to 'Be good an' trus' in de Lawd.'" Despite such advice, children could not help but find their sale away from home profoundly painful. If they expressed their fear and sorrow publicly during the auction, they ran the risk of facing ridicule; if they bore up stoically, they might earn the onlookers' respect, for what that was worth.[52] Enslaved children needed to learn the lesson of repression early, for it would be required of them all their lives. They needed to be the masters of their own emotions even if they could not be the masters of their selves.

THE MARKET REVOLUTION IN THE NORTH

White children's initiation into the pain of separation was somewhat easier. Many affluent families believed their offspring would eventually leave them, not because they were forced to, as were slaves, but because they should make the most of economic opportunities. To prepare them for a mobile future, middle-class parents frequently sent their children away to school. By 1850, there were six thousand academies across the country, where students either boarded or took lodgings in houses nearby. Although each school had its own educational philosophy, one goal that unified many was the desire to provide a place where students could make a transition from home in a safe and protected environment and learn virtues and habits of industry that would equip them for later life.[53]

Parents sent both daughters and sons to schools. Designed to fit a girl for domestic life, going to school removed her from her own domestic circle, and in so doing often caused pain. How to master that pain was another lesson that boarding schools taught. In 1797, Eliza Southgate's parents sent her to a school in Medford, Massachusetts, some distance from the family home in Scarborough, Maine. The fourteen-year-old wrote her "Honored Parents," telling them that the transition to school had been a hard one: "When first I came here . . . I burst into tears and instead of trying to calm my feelings I tried to feel worse." Showing that she was learning the lessons of emotional control that society, and her parents, demanded, she wrote, "I begin to feel happier and will soon gather up all my Philosophy and think of the duty that now attends me, to think that here I may drink freely of the fountain of knowledge, but I will not dwell any longer on this subject."[54] Fifteen-year-old Mary Ann Bacon, a student at Sarah Pierce's Litchfield, Connecticut, school, confided to her diary in 1802, "[I have been] reflecting with many disagreeable feelings upon have [sic] parted from my kind Parents and Acquaintances to live with strangers." These feelings returned during her early days in Litchfield, although Mary worked to conquer them.[55] By the 1820s, Pierce's school mandated that students who displayed homesickness would lose thirty "credit marks," while those who manifested a contented spirit would be rewarded.[56] Pierce wanted her students to master their emotions and learn to rationally accept the pain that came from leaving the protective circle of the family. Self-mastery was necessary for self-improvement.[57]

Other young women faced similar battles. Emily Dickinson struggled mightily with her homesickness as she braved a year at Mount Holyoke

Academy, some ten miles from her family's house in Amherst, Massachusetts. She wrote her brother Austin, "I have been quite lonely since I came back, but cheered by the thought that I am not to return another year I take comfort & still hope on. . . . Home was always dear to me & dearer still the friends around it, but never did it seem so dear as now." Of her efforts to cope with her unruly feelings she wrote:

> When tempted to feel sad, I think of the blazing fire, & the cheerful meal & the chair empty now I am gone. I can hear the cheerful voices & the merry laugh & a desolate feeling comes home to my heart, to think I am alone. But my good angel only waits to see the tears coming & then whispers, only this year!! Only 22. weeks more & home again you will be to stay. To you, all busy and excited, I suppose the time flies faster, but to me slowly, very slowly so that I can see his chariot wheels when they roll along & himself is often visible.[58]

Unexpectedly, in March 1848, Dickinson's family, worried about her health, retrieved her from Mount Holyoke. Despite her earlier homesickness, she was reluctant to leave school and resented the lack of control she had over her life.[59] Yet this experience too was an important part of female education. For girls, the family claim trumped individual desire. Parents or schoolmistresses might dictate their whereabouts during girlhood; thereafter, husbands would. Consequently, young women had to learn to control their homesickness and deny their own desires in order to advance family interests.

At male boarding schools, young boys also learned to sever family ties in preparation for adulthood and successful careers, but the goal was independence, not subordination. In 1843, young Sidney Roby's family sent him away to an academy in Brockport, New York, 135 miles from his home in Sconondoa. From there, he wrote a stream of letters, begging his family to let him return home. In 1844, he wrote, "Dear Aunty I arrived here safe last evening, but was very tired and homesick. . . . I went up to school today. . . . Almost as soon as I got there I began to be homesick and could not hardly keep from crying." Sidney's homesickness set in on the trip to Brockport: "I would almost cry right out I would think of you and the folks at Syracuse all down there in the parlor. Then I would think of being at home . . . talking with Grand Father and Mother, and then be over to the store talking with Uncle Sidney, and then I would think of my situation. . . . Oh Aunty . . . the tears come down so fast that I can hardly write. Oh Aunty you cant think how I feel."[60] Sidney, as well his grandparents, aunt, and uncle who had raised him, all found consolation in the hope that the painful separation would yield future rewards. Sidney wrote, "If it was not for one thing Grand Father I think I could not stay here that is that I am now fitting myself to be something and to come home in time and be Uncle Sidney's clerk and be whare I can see you every day and near the place whare I was brought up I shall improve my self as much as I can while I am here." A year later, when Sidney still complained of homesickness, his grandfather reminded him, "You must . . . not suffer your feelings to impede your progress in your studies—remember that a good education will be invaluable to you when you become a man."[61] Homesickness, Roby and his family believed, was one of the costs of rising in the world, part of the process of learning to delay gratification. Hopes for the future might offset homesickness in the present. Children at boarding schools were not only learning music and drawing, mathematics, and literature, but they were also learning how to be apart from family and home, abilities increasingly in demand in the industrializing and urbanizing economy of nineteenth-century America.

Going to boarding school was one way to learn how to leave home, but not the only way; people of lesser means often found that economic need propelled them away from home with very little notice or preparation. In search of greater opportunities, many migrants left farms for factories that were springing up in towns and cities across the Northeast.

Young women moved to mill towns to take advantage of the unprecedented opportunity for paid industrial work. One woman described her desire to set off for a factory job in Nashua, New Hampshire, as a symptom of her "mill fever."[62] The mill worker Harriet Robinson wrote that across the countryside, stories circulated about the good pay at the mills, "stories that reached the ears of mechanics' and farmers' sons, and gave new life to lonely and dependent women in distant towns and farmhouses. Into this Yankee El Dorado these needy people began to pour by the various modes of travel known to those slow old days." Robinson noted that the mills gave single women "a place in the universe; they were no longer obliged to finish out their faded lives mere burdens to male relatives. . . . For the first time in this country woman's labor had a money value."[63]

Some who came to the mill towns reflected cheerfully on the economic and social opportunities that factory work presented them. Sally Rice, born in 1821, explained to her parents in Dover, Vermont, why she wanted to remain at work in the mills at Union Village, New York: "I have but one life to live and I want to enjoy my self as well as I can while I live. If I go home I can not have the privelage of going to meting nor eny thing else."[64] Others, however, found the transition from home to mill too abrupt. Harriet Robinson recalled of the mill girls she knew, "They had all left their pleasant country homes to try their fortunes in a great manufacturing town, and they were homesick even before they landed at the doors of their boardinghouses. Years after . . . whenever anyone said anything about being homesick, there rose before me the picture of a young girl with a sorrowful face and a big tear in each eye, clambering down the steps at the rear of a great covered wagon, holding fast to a cloth-covered bandbox."[65]

Mill girls who longed for home emphasized that the move to an industrial location was jarring and expressed the desire to live closer to nature. The urban landscapes to which they had migrated were far different from the rural ones they had left behind, and their new identities as factory workers were foreign to their sense of self. In essays and poems, they frequently expressed longings for their bucolic farming villages. Lucy Larcom, a worker in Lowell, Massachusetts, waxed poetic about her hometown of Beverly, Massachusetts: "There is something in the place where we were born that holds us always by the heartstrings." She missed Beverly's "beautiful scenery and ancestral associations . . . its miles of sea-border, almost every sunny cove and rocky headland of which was a part of some near relative's home-stead." In this case, the desire to go home was a desire not only to visit kin and return to familiar places but to retreat from the industrial order.[66]

Leaving home for the factory also meant becoming an unfettered individual in a capitalist economy, a feat many found harder than they had imagined. Susan Brown, of Epson, New Hampshire, wrote of her life at the Middlesex mill in Lowell, Massachusetts, "Seven months . . . since I saw home! Alone & among strangers! Oh, when shall I return?"[67] Mary Ann Smith, a native of New Hampshire who had moved to Lowell, wrote her brother, who had himself struck out in search of greater opportunity, "Do you get *home sick* any? I do. If mother was here I should 'like' right well. . . . Dont see any prospect of mother's coming."[68]

Older women found the transition equally hard. Jemima Sanborn, born in 1798, was forced by financial difficulties to leave her Bristol, New Hampshire, farm. She moved to Nashua in 1843, where she set up housekeeping with her daughters, who were working in mills. Unlike her husband, who traveled back and forth between farm and town, she could not easily move or choose her location, and this exacerbated her homesickness. She confided to relatives, "It don't seeme much like home. It would seeme more like home if any of my folks lived here you know I never was weaned from fathers house before. . . . I suppose I must try and bare with it. . . . I am as lonesome as you can think here among all strangers."[69] Jemimah Sanborn, Lucy Larcom, Susan Brown, and the thousands of other women working in factories were being "weaned" from home. Some ultimately found their departures liberating, but many found them unsettling.

Young men, who more often expected to make such transitions, still struggled with them. As a boy, John Albee, of Bellingham, Massachusetts, was apprenticed to his uncle, who lived one town away. Sent there to learn the trade of boot making, Albee was profoundly unhappy: "I found myself cut off from all the objects and persons I had ever known, thrown into a strange world, my own lost as completely as if I had gone to another. . . . A deadly homesickness at once seized upon me, of which I could not be cured. . . . A kind of depression and melancholy took the place of my natural gaiety. I can readily believe . . . that one might die of homesickness." His uncle returned him to his mother, and his attempt to leave home was temporarily delayed.[70] Archelaus Putnam, who had spent some homesick days at boarding school, also found it difficult to leave home in the pursuit of a career. In 1809, he left New Mills, Massachusetts, where he had been working for his brother, to try his luck at his own business, an apothecary shop in Lynn, some six miles away. He spoke of his departure as if he were traveling hundreds of miles, lamenting, "[I am leaving my] birthplace & abode . . . where reside my brothers, sisters, & near & familiar connexions. . . . [I am being] transplanted into an untried soil where it is doubtful if I shall take root & live, much more grow & flourish." He did not last long in this foreign soil; within eight months he was back home, once again working for his brother.[71] Another New England boy, Francis Bennett, age seventeen, moved from Gloucester to Boston to work in a store in 1854. When he left he had to struggle not to cry. Even six months later he mourned the fact that to seek his fortune he had to leave his "beloved home and mother and little sister."[72]

Those who grappled with such feelings as they tried to make their future in new towns and cities often looked for ways to strengthen their ties to home. Many formed fraternal organizations, celebrating their shared place of origin. The Sons of Maine organized in Boston; the Sons of New York congregated in Wisconsin and in Keokuk, Iowa.[73] Virginians eager to reestablish home ties formed the Old Dominion Society in New York City in 1860.[74] Although not terribly far form home, New Hampshire migrants to Boston established the Sons of New Hampshire and for a time held annual Festivals of the Sons of New Hampshire.[75] They also settled near each other in the same Boston neighborhood, hoping for the comfort of familiar faces in an alien environment.[76]

Much has been written of the vaunted American optimism that led so many young men to become entrepreneurs in the nineteenth century, but that emotion was often challenged by other feelings: hesitation, anxiety, sadness, a desire to stay put. While the economic growth of the market revolution offered tantalizing profits and opportunities, Americans living through this time of transformation also recognized that financial gains might result in emotional and familial losses.

PIONEERS

The same tendency that motivated farm boys and girls to go to mill towns motivated others to look for new land. During the first half of the nineteenth century, hundreds of thousands of settlers moved into Ohio, Indiana, Illinois,

Wisconsin, and Iowa; once there many moved repeatedly within the region, and even farther west.[77] Such movement not only indicated a restless spirit, but also often reflected frustrated hopes and unrealized dreams.[78] When settlers did not find success, moving on preserved the hope that fortune might still await them in the future.

While their eyes were fixed on distant prizes, their minds were often on the homes they had left behind. In 1817, a Maine newspaper, the *Hallowell Gazette,* reprinted a letter from Zacheus Parker, formerly of Waterville, who had "supported his family here in easy and comfortable circumstances, till he was attacked by the *prevailing fever* for Western Emigration." Of his new residence in Marietta, Ohio, he wrote, "I find this to be a poor, muddy hole. . . . My advice to all my friends is not to come to this Country. I intend to leave it as soon as the spring opens. . . . And there is not one in a hundred but what is discontented, but they can't get back having spent all their property here. . . . This Country has been the ruin of a great many poor people."[79] The crude cabins, the difficulties of starting a new farm or business and making it pay, led many to regret having left their settled lives in the East. A tongue-in-cheek guide written by a migrant from Maine to Illinois claimed that all that could be gained on the frontier was "a broken down wagon!—a broken winded horse!—A broken hearted wife—a Broken legged dog!" The author suggested, "Who have a *good home* and don't *realize* it, / 'A trip to the *West*' will teach you to *prize* it."[80]

"I am going to Illinois." This guide warned that those who traveled to the frontier would soon long for their eastern homes. Walter Wilkey, *Western Emigration: Narrative of a Tour to, & one year's residence in "Edensburgh" Illinois* . . . (New York: Sackett & Sargent, 1839), frontispiece.

Sources: Image courtesy of the Yale Collection of Western Americana, Beinecke Rare Book and Manuscript Library.

In 1843, Elias Lothrop wrote that he was learning to prize his old home. Lothrop moved from Durham, Maine, to Chicago to open a store. He wrote back to his wife with a mixed assessment of the move: "My dear wife ... whether to tell you that I am doing well or not I can hardly know which to say as yet but—I think that at all events that I shall never regret coming here. . . . I have many lonesome hours but that is to be expected." As the letter continued, Lothrop made it clear that he was pulled by two very different sets of desires, and that on some days he did indeed regret his move: "Sometimes I think that I will give up all my ambitious ideas of trying to make money and content myself at home on my farm and enjoy what little I have among my friends as I begin to ... think that happiness is as often found in a comparritively humble place as among the great and rich." Yet he could not fully abandon his goals and told his wife that perhaps they should settle permanently in Illinois: "You must expect if we emigrate here that you will be homesick enough for a while—I confess that I have been so though not without reason."[81] His homesickness must have been substantial, for he returned to Maine in 1845 and stayed there for four years. Then, once more beset by the desire for success and distinction and lured by the possibility of gold, he again set off, this time for California.

Another New England native who also traveled to Illinois, Samuel Francis, wrote of his regrets as he found himself far from his wife, children, and Vermont home. His calculating instincts took him in one direction, his affections in another. In January 1846, Francis meditated on his distance from home: "I feel in rather low spirits, far from home & all those that I hold most dear, my Wife and little ones. O! that I could see them, it would be great pleasure to me if I could only receive an epistle from them it would be some comfort and I hope soon to receive one." He hoped as well "soon to meet with them and enjoy their society again."[82] After his lonely sojourn in the Midwest, Francis returned to Vermont in 1846, gathered up his family, and brought them to Illinois with him. There the family stayed until 1852, when they relocated to Oregon. What his wife thought of such relocations goes unrecorded.

Yet other women who faced similar patterns of removal did record their thoughts about leaving for the Midwest. Many believed they had little choice but to accompany their husbands, though they often did so unwillingly and with trepidation. Domestic ideology suggested that married women should accede to their husbands' decisions and go wherever they went, but many found it hard to do so when faced with the reality of leaving their extended families, perhaps forever. The ideals of feminine behavior did not always sit easily together, as women were supposed to be defined by home but also willing to leave it.

Throughout the Midwest, resigned and melancholy women who had left behind friends and family were legion. In 1837, the *New Hampshire Sentinel* reprinted excerpts of a letter from a woman newly settled in Illinois. Many nights she imagined herself back in her Connecticut home: "But alas! in the morning it is all a dream, and I find myself in our little log cabin, which is about 16 by 16 feet—only one room." Not only did she miss her family, but she pined for the refinements of eastern living, complaining, "Our children have not been to school a day since they have been in the country. . . . I have not attended public worship since I left the State of New-York. . . . I must confess that I am somewhat homesick."[83] Thirty-three-year-old Elizabeth Fickes, a native of Ohio, shared those sentiments. She moved with her husband and children to Iowa in 1856. In her diary, she recorded her feelings as the family moved to and settled in their new home. Her sense of dislocation began when they departed from Ohio: "April 17, 1856 Left home (for Steubenville was sweet home) this morning on steamboat Convoy. . . . This has been a wet cold and disagreeable day according well with my feelings. Goodbye to Steubenville and many dear dear friends, perhaps in this world forever." Eleven days later her feelings about the undertaking had not changed much: "Sunday April 28, 1856 I have spent some time in writing home this afternoon but Oh! how it seems to carry me back to dear ones there." Settled into the new house by early June, Fickes continued to struggle with her homesickness: "June 8, 1856 Cold and rainy this morning, the first Sunday in our new home. I feel very lonely today." When it came, correspondence from her family cheered her considerably: "June 19, 1856 Received letters from home. They were sent to Washington and forwarded here. It seems as if we are very near home when I read their letters." But the letters were only temporary salves for her pain. "July 20, 1856 A pleasant Sabbath day this day. We feel more lonely than any other day in the week." Six months later her feelings had not much changed. "January 1, 1857 New Years Day. How much I think of our old home and dear friends far away for whom this is a day of pleasant meetings."[84]

While married women who felt homesickness could do little about it because of their subordinate position within the family, single women found a greater sphere of action and liberty. Lucy Larcom, who was unmarried and had already tried and abandoned mill work, moved to Illinois with her sister's family in 1846. She began to feel sad "when good-bys had to be said," and she "wish[ed] it was not to be." She promised that she would return to Massachusetts but worried that might prove impossible: "The West was very far off then,—a full week's journey. It would be hard getting back. Those I loved might die; I might die myself." Once the party arrived in Illinois they found the place lacking: "Ours was at first the roughest kind of pioneering experience; such as persons brought up in our well-to-do New

England could not be in the least prepared for." Larcom returned to Massachusetts in 1852, confiding, "I could not stay at the West. It was never really home to me there, and my sojourn of six or seven years on the prairies only deepened my love and longing for the dear old State of Massachusetts. I came back in the summer of 1852."[85] Unmarried, she could control her own migrations.

For men and women who could not return home, some solace could be found in the widespread belief in heavenly reunions. Clarissa Ward wrote to her sister, Mary Angell, in 1825, lamenting the fact that her sister "live[d] so far of[f]." Given that she could not overcome the reality of distance, she wrote, "I hope and trust that if we never meate Again in this world we shall all meate in heave[n] where parting is no more. Where I trust we shall meate our dear Sister that has gone but A little before us."[86] Ward's sentiments were typical of antebellum Americans on the move. They were able to endure distance and separation only because they believed they would not be permanently apart.

Homesickness among pioneers did not easily or quickly abate. Women and men moved to the newly available land in the Midwest, but their ties to the East were not severed, just stretched; their memories were not erased, but instead etched deeper as a result of frequent recollection.

While those moving from Ohio to Iowa found relocation painful and looked back to their eastern homes with affection and longing, others on the midwestern prairies had emigrated from Europe and traveled much greater distances. For instance, by 1860, 140,000 new English immigrants had settled in Ohio, Michigan, Indiana, Illinois, and Wisconsin.[87] A majority of the more than 2 million German immigrants who came to the United States between 1820 and 1870 also settled in the Midwest.[88]

A plethora of guides encouraged such emigration to America, touting the advantages of life there and suggesting that the pain of relocation was ultimately worth the price. *The Emigrant's True Guide*, written for English immigrants to America, warned readers to carefully consider the decision to emigrate, for such migrations would cause "many discomforts and sore trials." For those who made the decision to go, the guide advised, "The emigrant's *home-sickness* will wear off by degrees. . . . It is among the keenest of trials to bid farewell, perhaps for ever, to the friends and home of one's childhood, and to see no more the old familiar scenes." Immigrants must remember, however, that the "toil, and trouble, and trial" they might experience was necessary for success. To shore up the flagging feelings of heartsick readers, the book included tales of immigrants who had succeeded in America.[89] Other guides suggested that to steel themselves against homesickness migrants abandon the idea of returning home and plan on a permanent separation from their native lands. *Errors of Emigrants* recommended, "If a man comes to Illinois, he must come with a singleness of purpose, with an intention and desire of finding some occupation by which he can support his family in happy mediocrity of circumstances." The best way to make the transition to a new life abroad was with one's family; they would afford him comfort and company and allow him to transplant his idea of home.[90] Yet the guides admitted that migrants' families might be reluctant to leave home. One guide noted that the only barrier to male settlers finding success in the United States was a "home sick Wife," while another contended, "Women, and especially English women transplant very badly."[91]

These guides anticipated some of the emotional problems faced by European immigrants to America, but wrote of them as small inconveniences, easily overcome through careful planning. Immigrants themselves, however, found the distance between their old home and their new depressing. Rebecca Burlend and her family, natives of Yorkshire, left England for Pike County, Illinois, in 1831. Like many of the women who would be her neighbors on the prairies, she felt compelled to leave because of her husband's plans and economic necessity. Before her voyage to America, she had never been more than forty miles from her village, Barwick-in-Elmet. She began her account of her travels with the comment, "Whatever may have been our success in America, I can attribute but little of it to myself; as I gave up the idea of ending my days in my own country with the utmost reluctance, and should never have become an emigrant, if obedience to my husband's wishes had left me any alternative." After a year on the Illinois frontier she was suffering from low spirits: "The first Sunday in November was the anniversary of our landing in America. . . . It was further distinguished as being the day on which the yearly feast is held at the little village where we had lived in England. This circumstance . . . had a tendency to bring to our recollection in a most vivid manner, bygone associations and endearments, the value of which we only discovered when they were lost." Burlend remarked that she and her husband now understood more fully the lines of a poem by Cowper:

> When I think of my own native land,
> In a moment I seem to be there;
> But alas! recollection at hand
> Soon hurries me back to despair.

Although she carried such feelings with her for decades, Burlend spent her remaining years in Illinois, with the exception of a brief trip back to England in 1846 to satisfy a longing "which [she] had never ceased to indulge, of visiting once more the shores of Old England."[92]

Other foreign immigrants shared her sentiments, and after arriving in America, nursed dreams of returning home. In 1856, twenty-four-year-old Jan George Zahn wrote regretfully of his decision to come to America. Having arrived in Muscatine, Iowa, he realized that it did not live up to the stories he had heard:

> The situation here is not always as it is described to us in the Netherlands. These people admitted that they were better off in Holland. . . . P.S. Do answer soon. Please. I am waiting eagerly. Believe me, I have not yet had a happy moment here in America. If it must always be like this for me I will certainly return. My trunks all arrived in good condition. Heaven only knows how I am to get over this. Oh, it would be worth anything if I could just talk to one or all of you sometime. My advice to everyone is, "Be satisfied to remain in Holland."[93]

In 1844, Jon N. Bjørndalen wrote that he felt he had made a mistake in leaving Norway for America: "Time is heavy on our hands, and we are not happy in our emigration. If the Almighty grants us good health and we can make enough money, our greatest wish is to go back to old Norway. When you have neither health nor any pleasures here in America, it is better to live in your native country even if you own nothing. America will always be unhealthful, and no Norseman is ever going to be happy here."[94]

Lonesome immigrants looked for ways to return home, at least for a visit and perhaps for good. The steamship excited hope in many. Carl Blümner, born in 1805, emigrated from Brandenburg, Germany, in 1832. After a decade in America, during which he lived first in Missouri and then in Santa Fe, he still missed his family. He wrote his sister, "My hand pauses involuntarily as I am writing the date above! 1841! I ask myself 'Is it possible that 10 years have already slipped by since I said my last farewell to my beloved sister?!' . . . But, my sister, whether my life is short or long, I will see you again! The dark ruler of our fates will not refuse to grant this wish, when he sees how heartfelt and sincere it is!" He held out hope that he might be able to see her soon, given recent advances in transportation: "We sometimes receive newspapers . . . and then with what emotion I read that this or that steamship has gone from England to Neu York in the unbelievably short time of 12–14 days. In my mind, I see myself transported to Neu York! I go on *bord* the mighty ship! Fly across the enormous ocean in 8–10 days! Land in Liverpool! In 2 or 3 says I'm in Hamburg! From there—But halt! I am traveling too fast! You laugh at me, dear Hannchen! You laugh at my somewhat overly 'swift fantasy'!!" It was a fantasy, for he never made it back.[95]

Other immigrants, however, were able to make good on their dream of returning home. Indeed in some years, particularly during hard economic times, as many as twenty thousand immigrants returned to England—this at a time when the annual migration from England to the United States totaled sixty thousand.[96] Likewise, in a study of German immigrants from 1853 to 1892, remigration numbers fluctuated from a low of 4.7 percent in 1859 to a high of 49.4 percent in 1875.[97]

Those who stayed on resigned themselves to the painful trade they were making: exchanging the love and comfort of family and homeland for greater opportunity. Henrietta Jessen reconciled herself to the reality that she would not return to Norway, writing to her sisters from Milwaukee in 1850, "Fate has indeed separated me from my native land and all that was dear to me there. . . . Cannot deny that homesickness gnaws at me hard. When I think, however, that there will be a better livelihood for us here than in poor Norway, I reconcile myself to it."[98]

Learning to accept separation in the hope of future profit was not easy, and some worried that it was not even right. Many foreign immigrants were guilt-stricken at having left their families behind, a preoccupation that cut across ethnic lines. Gro Svendsen, who left her family in Hallingdal, Norway, in 1862 to follow her husband to Iowa, wrote, "I do hope my dear parents are not heavy-hearted because of my leaving them. . . . My conscience tortures me for the grief and pain that I have brought upon them."[99]

Another source of guilt that often exacerbated homesickness came from religious teachings. Many Christians believed that leaving one's native land and family was sinful and represented a rebellion against God's will. Clergy were among the most outspoken critics of emigration. Irish priests throughout the nineteenth century often preached against leaving Ireland.[100] Protestant ministers offered harsh warnings to their flocks as well. In 1837, Bishop Jacob Neumann of the Archdiocese of Bergen, Norway, preached against migration in *A Word of Admonition to the Peasants in the Diocese of Bergen Who Desire to Emigrate*, a copy of which the Norwegian immigrant Sjur J. Haaeim found in Illinois. He read it aloud to other Norwegians there, many of whom broke down in tears after hearing their migrations condemned. "Then I told them frankly that if God the Almighty would help me save up enough capital to pay my way back to Norway, I should be happier than I could say; and many of those who had arrived there with me said the same thing."[101] A Swedish minister tried to elicit a similar response from would-be migrants, telling his parishioners that they should not leave home casually: "Without a call from God or being in peril of one's soul no one ought to desert his native country, and . . . those who carelessly or thoughtlessly can exchange all these advantages for something uncertain are ungrateful and act foolishly."[102]

These sermons represented a response to the new individualism, which severed ties between fathers and sons, citizens and their native land. They were a call to return to a more stable social world. Such sermons drew mixed reactions from immigrants. Some came to regret their migrations and saw themselves as alienated from what they cared most about. Others defended the choice they had made to come to America, believing that the decision to stay or go was their own to make. The idea that mobility was legitimate opened up the world, and its opportunities, to ambitious individuals. It would become a central belief in capitalist ideology, built upon the idea of open markets and free individuals. But as many would discover, it was often more emotionally wrenching to act on than they expected.

THE WESTERN FRONTIER

While there were many who journeyed from foreign countries to the United States, there were also many Americans who traveled into what they considered foreign lands: the Rocky Mountain West, the American Southwest, California, and the Oregon Territory. The earliest pioneers in these regions—trappers, explorers, and missionaries—have often been portrayed as the stalwart vanguard of manifest destiny. Under a façade of optimism and adventurousness, however, often lurked regret and a deep longing for home and family.

During his journeys through the Southwest, Zebulon Pike occasionally alluded to the undercurrents of homesickness that he and his party felt during their explorations. On an expedition in 1806, he wrote of the dark mood that prevailed on Christmas Day: "The hardships and privations we underwent, were on this day brought more fully to our mind." Among those deprivations were lack of warm clothing, bad weather, and cold, as well as being "800 miles from the frontiers of [the] country." At the end of an expedition in 1807, he expressed relief at being back home: "Language cannot express the gaiety of my heart, when I once more beheld the standard of my country waved aloft!—'All hail' cried I, 'the ever sacred name of country in which is embraced that of kindred, friends, and every other tie which is dear to the soul of man.'"[103]

To be sure, some explorers showed little if any homesickness. John Charles Frémont, who led a series of expeditions to the West, expressed few misgivings about his distance from home. Those in his party, however, were less sanguine about it. Frémont's cartographer, Charles Preuss, longed to leave the prairie and return east. During the expedition of 1842, while making maps for the "Great Pathfinder," as Frémont was called, Preuss was mentally following trails back home. Early on in the expedition, he wrote, "To the deuce with such a life; I wish I were in Washington with my old girl." That thought would plague him. His journals were peppered with entries like this one, from August 1842: "Oh, I wish I were home again!"[104] His mind turned eastward, but his maps guided others west.[105]

Those who felt that God was calling them west were no more immune to homesickness than those guided by a spirit of adventure. Narcissa Whitman, the first woman of European origin to travel across the Rocky Mountains, repeatedly voiced her commitment to missionary work in Oregon Territory, where she hoped to convert Native Americans to Christianity. In her journal and letters, however, signs of homesickness surfaced.[106] She admitted that she found great comfort in the thoughts and things of home. On her journey, she wrote that knowing that her family and friends were praying for her gave her solace: "O, how comforting is this thought to the heart of the missionary. We love to think and talk of home." On days when she felt particularly anxious about her new undertaking, she tried to distract herself "and [be] carried out of [her]self in conversation about home and friends." She also took comfort in items she had transported from the East. When her luggage became too much of a burden, and she had to discard a trunk, she lamented, "I regret leaving anything that came from home, especially that trunk, but it is best."[107] Another missionary, Mary Richardson Walker, also struggled to match her emotions with her sense of having a divine calling. She often wanted to cry as she traveled from Maine to Oregon in 1838, pregnant with her first child. Once installed in Oregon Country, at Waiilatpu, her melancholy did not abate. In September 1838, she wrote, "After crying a little picked up and found myself somewhat tired. Oh! dear how I would like to be at home about this time, and see brothers, hear from all the good folks! I wish I could have a letter from some of them."[108]

Other vanguards of the western movement felt similarly. The soldiers who fought in the Mexican-American War and ultimately added more than half a million square miles of territory to the Union found the process of expansion arduous and often longed to return home. James K. Holland, a volunteer in the Texas militia, recorded in his journal, "I have been thinking of home . . . and feel disposed to wish [myself] there enjoying the luxuries that offered in the way of fruits—melons—camp meeting—clean clothes—good Razor—corn bread—and pretty women—[rather] than here knee deep in dust in the boiling sun—beef and crackers to eat and nasty water to drink."[109] An Ohio volunteer shared similar feelings in a letter written in 1846: "Here we are in a barren island, with nothing to be seen but sand—sand—sand. There is not a bush large enough for a fly to light upon as far as the eye can see. . . . Every morning and evening we bathe in the Gulf, and I believe it is the only thing that keeps us alive, yet this hasn't prevented some of our boys from getting homesick."[110] Another soldier from Ohio felt despair at the interminable marches and abominable food, including weevil-filled biscuits, and concluded, "Musquitoes abound, the 'boys' are getting homesick, and trying to get discharged. . . . Some of the 'boys' who used to sing 'Rio Grande, I would I were upon your banks,' now reverse the case, and wish they were three thousand miles away from it."[111]

If they could not be back at home, soldiers at least wanted news of home. Benjamin Franklin Scribner, a volunteer from Indiana, wrote his sister of his joy at receiving a letter from her, as well as his frustration when mail did not come: "How lonely and melancholy it makes me feel to see others around reading epistles from their friends, while I am apparently forgotten and uncared for." On one frustrating day, he walked sixteen miles to see if any letters from home had been delivered, but found nothing waiting for him.[112] While soldiers did not receive as many letters as they desired, they wrote great numbers of them back to the folks at home. An observer in Baltimore noted in 1848, "One of the largest mails ever received from the army, was opened at our post office yesterday. It consisted of more than a thousand letters, principally from the Maryland troops; most of them are quite home-sick, and are looking with great anxiety for a termination of hostilities."[113]

In the meantime, soldiers looked for ways to assuage their yearnings for home. In Mexico City, some merchants found that a good income could be made catering to the homesick. A number of restaurants, including the United States Hotel, the Anglo-Saxon House, the Soldier's Home, and the Washington Hotel, advertised "American style" menus and offered comfort food to soldiers longing for a taste of the familiar.[114]

During the war, army physicians paid new attention to homesickness, particularly when it had grave effects on sufferers. Many of the doctors who served in the U.S. military's medical corps were conversant with European discourses on homesickness and nostalgia, likely from reprinted accounts of nostalgic soldiers in the Napoleonic Wars.[115] As a result, the Mexican-American War was the first time the U.S. Army employed the diagnosis of nostalgia on a broad scale. One army surgeon addressed the condition in his article "The Medical Topography of Texas and the Diseases of the Army of Invasion," noting, "I saw a few cases of pure nostalgia, and I believe there were many such, during the first six months of service, amongst the young men of the army."[116] The *Boston Medical and Surgical Journal* carried a long article on nostalgia and homesickness by Dr. W. G. Proctor, who served as hospital steward to the Louisville (Kentucky) Legion during the war. Proctor explained that external factors influenced the mental and physical dispositions of soldiers. Men were most susceptible to nostalgia when they were idle: "The disease was always most rife when we had been encamped for a considerable length of time in one position, and when the soldiers were permitted to remain in idleness: this disease was manifesting itself to a fearful extent in a company of young country-men who had been idle for several weeks encamped in one position and permitted to remain idle." Once the men resumed marching, however, they recovered.[117]

It is perhaps surprising to find homesickness among soldiers, missionaries, and explorers—those who seemed most daring in their migrations, who seemed to act on the belief in manifest destiny, and who have become symbolic of the westering movement. And yet the West was explored and mapped by individuals with mixed feelings about their migration. Despite these pioneers' inner conflicts, which most did not share with the broader public, the well-publicized accounts of their expeditions to the frontier promoted the idea of western settlement. The mere fact that they had made the trip made it seem both practically and emotionally possible for others to follow. Their journeys were mythologized, and the mythology had little room for homesickness. Future generations would hear only of the bravery, not the misgivings, of such wanderers.

CALIFORNIA

If these vanguards of manifest destiny had mixed feelings about leaving the East to settle in the Far West, so too did the men and women who followed them and streamed into the region during the late 1840s and 1850s, attracted by the discovery of gold in California in 1848. Many would-be prospectors deliberated about setting off for the gold fields. Some wondered if they were flouting God's will by so obviously pursuing wealth. Moralists, ministers, and wives added to these doubts, warning men seeking gold that they were choosing lucre over love, money over home, and by extension, mammon over morality.[118]

The gold seekers themselves were not completely comfortable with the capitalist credo of wealth accumulation, a credo that seemed to contradict many of the tenets of Christian morality and domesticity. Some justified their decision to go to California by describing their expeditions as means by which they might ultimately improve their families' position and prospects; gold would enrich home life, not threaten it. This was not mere rhetoric, for most who set out clearly expected to return home. A life in California was not what they were after; they went with thoughts of an improved existence back in Connecticut, Ohio, or Vermont. One miner, Prentice Mulford, explained the plans most men had in mind when they migrated: "Five years was the longest period any one expected to stay. Five years at most was to be given to rifling California of her treasures ... and the rich adventurers would spend the remainder of their days in wealth, peace, and prosperity at their Eastern homes."[119]

Stephen Crary of Plainfield, Connecticut, had just such plans. He went twice to the California gold fields, the second time informing his wife of his plans in a letter he sent only after he had departed: "Dear Rowena . . . as soon as I can make a 'stake' I will come right home to you and we will have a *good little home,* for us, and *our* children the first thing we will do. Then I am going to get a nice 'pianoforte' for *you,* and as for the '*ponies*' for Blanche and Grace,—why you may have the choice of *animals,* and may pick out such ones as you would like for them to ride."[120] Although the search for money took him from home, Crary believed it also enabled him to provide his family with refinement and gentility. He saw his migrations as supporting rather than undermining domestic life. Elbridge Gerry Hall of Connecticut wrote his wife from Granada as he made his way by sea to California: "But dearest when I think of home and my dear dear wife and the kind friends I have left behind I feel a little sad for I cannot really enjoy life without the One I so fondly love—but I am acting for the future, and I hope my labour will meet with success."[121]

Once they made the momentous decision to go, prospectors faced a choice of routes. To go by sea meant traveling from the East Coast to Central America and then either across the Isthmus of Panama or around Cape Horn. The majority went overland, across the Plains, an arduous journey that took three months but was far cheaper than ocean travel.[122] Whether they traveled by land or sea, many had second thoughts along the way.

In June 1849, Enos Christman, a native of Westchester County, Pennsylvania, chose the sea route. He wrote his fiancée, Ellen Apple, from the ship, admitting, "Hot tears from the fountain within have flown freely and I now feel some relief." In his visibly tear-smudged journal he elaborated:

> My feelings and emotions on leaving my friends and my native land can better be imagined than described. I left all that is near and dear and turned my face toward a strange land, expecting to be absent two or three years hoping in that time to realize a fortune; and then return and be greeted by kind friends; and this hope is my greatest consolation and comfort. . . . Often memory carries me back . . . and were I of a desponding temperament I should wish myself back again; but hope whispers all is well and so I proceed . . . with bright anticipations of joy and happiness in the future.[123]

Like many other miners, Christman used hopes for the future to ameliorate pain in the present, believing homesickness to be the price of advancement.

Those hopes could not always conquer homesickness, however, and en route to California some men capitulated to the emotion and joined the ranks of the "Go Backers," those who turned around on the trail.[124] Each year between 1849 and 1852, hundreds, and in some years, thousands, of migrants on the Overland Trail turned around, despite the fact that they were disparaged as lacking manly courage, perseverance, and virtue.[125] Others were sorely tempted to do so but resisted because they did not wish to mar their reputations. William Peacock of Chemung, Illinois, was one who wrestled with his feelings as he traveled overland to California in 1850. He had gotten only as far as St. Louis when he wrote, "I have the horrors every day since I never knew what real homesickness was Before. There has not been a day or an hour since I left Belvidere But what I have longed to BE again with my wife and children happy as we once was. I feel and now in my heart that you have been praying for me dayly." He vacillated about continuing on: "I would have staid at Dixon [Illinois] But for my pride of feeling as i don't like to undertake anything and give it up."[126] Masculine pride, a desire to appear brave and to complete what they had started led many others to suppress their sadness and head on. In April 1849, early on in his expedition from Mt. Pleasant, Iowa, to California, P. C. Tiffany wrote that he was "in rather low spirits": "[I am] reflecting on the step that I have taken; the probability of my not seeing my family for a long time, the hardships that I must encounter on the way." Yet he assured his wife, "Not for one moment have I harboured the idea of turning back. I would not 'back out' as the saying is for the sum of two hundred dollars, offered as an inducement."[127]

The depressed spirits that miners experienced as they went west sprang from trepidations about the future and a sense of loss. Traveling through the unorganized territories made them feel that they were in an alien place, removed from their nation. The Fourth of July figured in many accounts as a particularly sad day, for it evoked memories and yearnings for the familiar. Traveling to California in July 1849, Kimball Webster of Pelham, New Hampshire, wrote, "The Fourth of July will remind an American of his home wherever he may be or however far he may be separated from it. Early in the morning we fired several rounds, and made as much noise as possible in honor of the day of Independence."[128] P. C. Tiffany recorded how his company celebrated while camped along the Bear River: "It being the anniversary of our National Independence we took rather longer nooning than usual today." The party ate cake that Tiffany's wife had packed for the day. Another in the group, Mr. Grantham, shared a song he had written:

> Tho' far from our homes,
> Still we hail thee with joy;
> There's naught on this earth
> Shall thy memory destroy.
> . . . . . .
> Our friends we have left,
> To be gone for a time

And have wandered far off
In a mountainous clime;
We are searching for Gold,
And we love it, 'tis clear
But our glorious country
Is ever most dear.

The song suggested that although the men might appear to be abandoning home and nation for gold, in reality they remained loyal patriots. Summing up the day's events, Tiffany wrote, "In this manner we remembered this glorious day with some feelings of patriotism although in a country inhabited only with wild & rude Savages, & a great distance from our friends our homes, & everything that is dear to us."[129]

These men not only missed their sense of connection to the polity; they also pined for organized religion, for refinement, for women. On Sundays, both on the trail and once in California, they felt more disconnected from their families and old lives than on other days. Some kept the Sabbath, but many did not. In either case, they were aware that how they were observing it differed greatly from how their kin were. Gurdon Backus wrote in 1849, "My thoughts today have been more than usual turned towards *home* & the *sanctuary* of God. I have longed to again hear the voice of the living 'minister of Christ.'"[130] In a letter to his wife in 1850, William Peacock confided that he sorely missed religious observances because they offered a counterweight to the all-consuming materialism he saw about him: "How I would like to Be with you at your Evening Devotion till I should get my heart warmed and my hopes of heaven strengthened for I almost dispair at times. there is nothing thought of or sought for here But gold and it is a Poor Consolation when the heart is not at ease."[131]

Once settled in California, the men missed a familiar style of home life, the tone of which was set by women. Joel Brown, a miner, noted that his longings for domesticity were not at all unusual among other California miners: "I expect that you will think . . . that I am crying to see my wife. Well suppose I am and what then? I am not the only one that is crying to see the wife and baby."[132]

The relatively few white women who lived in California found themselves sought out by lonely men in search of home life left behind. Margaret Kroh Blake Alverson, a minister's daughter, recalled how miners flocked to her family's home in Stockton. Shortly after their arrival in 1851, the family invited several men to dinner to celebrate Thanksgiving: "[We] gave a homelike welcome to these men who for months had not eaten a home dinner or enjoyed the society of women. As the darkness came on, we lit up the room with candles. . . . Some of the gentlemen looked sad, some dignified, others joked and others related stories of home."[133]

It was not just the comfort of home-cooked food that time and again drew men to the Kroh house, but the comfort of family and domestic culture. The Reverend Kroh and his friends purchased a piano for Margaret's sister, Mary, and when she began to play the listeners were transfixed.

> [Father] had occasion to answer a call at the front door and before closing he accidentally looked out, and to his surprise the sidewalks and porch were filled with old and young men. Along the side of the house stood scores of men in the street as far as the eye could see and some were sobbing. On entering the room he said, "We have an immense congregation outside. Get out your familiar tunes—'Home, sweet home.' Etc." He then drew aside the curtains and raised the windows, "Now, my children and friends, give these homesick sons and fathers a few songs more."

The men came back on other nights to listen from the porch.[134] Indeed, whenever "Home, Sweet Home" was played in California, listeners seemed spellbound by memories. William Taylor, a Methodist minister, described the scene in a California saloon when musicians played the song: "Homeless wanderers, by hundreds, would stand entranced, seeming to live for a time in the embrace of loved ones, surrounded by all the sweet associations of the past."[135] At a mining camp, Enos Christman heard two Mexican women play the song on guitars: "Suddenly a sob was heard, followed by another, and yet another, and tears flowed freely down the cheeks of the gold diggers. Pieces of gold were generously tossed into the tambourine held out to receive them."[136]

If the men in the Far West missed the comforts, melodies, and refinements of home life, the very small number of white women in California missed them even more, since part of their identity was lodged in the domestic environments they created. Of course some women welcomed the adventure and the liberation from the more rigid and confining gender roles of the East.[137] Others, while intrigued by the new society they saw springing up around them, missed the old society, the old homes, and the things they had left behind. Mary Alverson's mother reluctantly sacrificed the comforts of familiar possessions for the journey to California. The family had moved a great deal and so they did not balk at the thought of this journey: "After inquiry and instructions from the steamship company, we found to our dismay that no furniture could go, as there was no way of getting it over the Isthmus. All our long-cherished household furniture must remain behind." Alverson's mother felt great "anguish of mind to see the familiar things of her girlhood scattered here and there and her claim to them forever gone. She had heretofore been able to go willingly to different places because the familiar things made it homelike when settled in new surroundings, but this time all must be left behind. California was too far— she was going out to the great unknown world, far from civilization."[138]

Many women shared these feelings. Mary Ballou, who made the voyage by sea in 1851, felt homesick as she traveled through Panama, which she found disconcertingly foreign and wild: "Arrived at Chagres Dec 22 stopt at a ranch had coffee Boiled rice and Stewed Beans for supper. The Beans cooked in a pot hung to a tree in the Bushes.... No floor but the ground for my bed, a valiece for my pillow a hard bed indeed." The crude conditions she faced and the contrast to what she had left behind made her despondent: "I wept Biterly there were twenty five in our company all Laid on the ground. The monkies were howling, the Nighthawks were singing, the Natives were watching." She continued to make her way across Panama: "Stopt at a ranch, laid myself down a the ground a weeping. I thought if I had had wings how swiftly I would fly to my Home."

Once settled in Negrobar, California, Ballou's feelings did not improve. The kitchen of her new house was full of mud and water: "I felt badly to think that I was de[s]tined to be in such a place. I wept for a while and then I commenced singing and made up a song as I went along." While the song temporarily alleviated her blues, they came back with great frequency as she contemplated the differences between her old life and her new. Although she found profitable work in California, she did not believe that it was worth the attendant hardships: "I am taking care of Babies and nursing at the rate of fifty dollars a week, but I would not advise any Lady to come out here and suffer the toil and fatigue that I have suffered for the sake of a little gold, neither do I advise any one to come. Clark Simmons wife says if she was safe in the States she would not care if she had not one cent. she came in here last night and said, Oh dear I am so homesick that I must die and then again my other associate came in with tears in her eyes and said that she had cried all day.... My own heart was two sad to cheer them much."[139]

Part of their sadness sprang from their living conditions. How they lived, cooked, cleaned, and interacted with strangers was dramatically different from what they were accustomed to. In mining camps, they lived in tent cities, where disorder and violence were common; in San Francisco, Stockton, or Sacramento, they found chaotic, dirty streets, hastily erected buildings, and lots of mud. Food supplies increased over the years but still made for a diet markedly different from East Coast menus.[140] Ballou wrote, "Sometimes I am cooking rabbits and Birds that are called quails here, and I cook squirrels. Occasionly I run in and have a chat with Jane ... and Mrs. Durphy and I often have a hearty cry, no one but my maker knows my feelings and then I run into my little cellar which is about four feet square, as I have no other place to run that is cool."[141]

Ballou wrote of these details to her son, and in that she was quite typical. The historian J. S. Holliday observed that through letters home "the entire nation was emotionally involved in the rush to California."[142] A national letter-writing culture sprang up in America in the 1840s and 1850s as postage rates fell, and scattered Americans, eager to stay connected with their families and friends, became prolific correspondents.[143] While those in the East waited for word from California, Californians waited equally breathlessly for the post. When it came, its arrival in San Francisco was announced by the raising of a black ball on Telegraph Hill.[144] Miners quickly gathered in the hope of receiving letters from home. Enos Christman wrote of the queues he saw outside the post office in 1850: "I strolled up towards the post office, and there witnessed a novel and interesting sight. A vast crowd had assembled and placed themselves in a line long before the office had been opened: and when the window opened every man awaited his turn with the greatest impatience. The line was long enough to keep the last ones waiting until after dinner and so I walked away concluding that I stood no chance there." He returned later in the day, but still had to wait an hour to pick up a letter from his brother.[145] William Taylor, the Methodist minister, told of men so impatient for their mail that they would pay five dollars to others who had reserved places at the head of the line. He believed that the "long lines of anxious faces, formed several hours before the opening of the office, furnished evidence of the social longings of their hearts. It was interesting to mark the countenances and conduct of men as they turned away from the delivery windows at the horrible announcement, 'Nothing for you, sir,' or as they grasped and broke open the letters which brought them news from home." Taylor heard a distraught man declare, "I have not received a letter from my family for two years. . . . I have come down here, three hundred miles, and have spent one hundred fifty dollars to try to get one letter from home, and I can't get it. I'll just quit writing! It's no use!"[146]

Prospectors relied on the mail to reassure them that their families had not forgotten them. Simon Brown of Pittsfield, Massachusetts, implored his parents to write. He denied he was homesick, but wondered, "if all the home ones have forgotten me? So far as hearing from them is concerned I might well think they have, as I have not received a letter or paper since I left you, nearly a year ago. . . . Would it be requesting too much to ask both of you to write me occasionally, even if you say but a few words? It will seem so good to get a letter now and then directly from home. . . . Letters in this far-off land are pearls of great price."[147]

Almost as coveted as letters were hometown newspapers. Tocqueville commented on the multitude of newspapers to be found in America and suggested that their purpose was to foster solidarity among men who otherwise would have "no firm and lasting ties" to one another. He saw them as a means of uniting strangers for useful, civic purposes.[148] Many Americans, however, saw papers not as a way of connecting with strangers, but as a means of sustaining "lasting ties" with their home communities. Richard

THE POST-OFFICE, CORNER OF PIKE AND CLAY STREETS.

Miners waiting for mail in California. William Taylor, *California Life Illustrated* (New York: Carlton & Porter, 1861), 202.

Henry Dana felt the Boston newspapers he was able to read in California linked him to his friends and family. He was overjoyed to find copies of the *Boston Transcript*, noting, "There is nothing in a strange land like a newspaper from home."[149] A prospector observed, "The sight of a late newspaper is rare among us and when one arrives . . . it is read and reread, with all its advertisements even, and then it passes from hand to hand till little is left to entitle it to the distinction of being a newspaper."[150]

Miners pleaded with their families to send them letters and papers, but sometimes they wanted more than mere words. They often asked their kin to enclose daguerreotypes in their letters, seeing them as a balm for their homesickness. Invented in France in 1839, the technology of daguerreotyping quickly spread to the United States, where it became enormously popular among displaced populations. In California, a surprisingly large number of studios carried on a lively trade in portraits, destined to be sent to points east. In turn, those in the West waited eagerly for images from family left behind.[151] Abby Mansur was one new Californian who eagerly watched the mails, hoping for letters and pictures from home. She had traveled to the gold fields with her husband, but she missed her family and begged her sister to send her family portraits. She wrote her in 1852, "i am so homesick i do not know what to do but i am afraid i never shall reach my native shore again if i could have your miniature and Eds and mothers and Phebes i should feel a great deal better do make mother have hers taken without fail and phebe to I trust you will have regard enough for my feelings to not fail to put them up to it and do not neglect yours and Eds." In December 1852, she once again reminded her sister of her urgent desire for portraits of them:

> i hope you will remember those miniatures I will willingly wait for the lord knows I do not know but I will go out of my skin when I receive them may god spare my life to enjoy that scene when you wrote me you was keeping house and living so comfortable it seems as though my heart leaped home with you and life was estinct you cannot think my feelings Hannah for I tell you I often think can it be possible that I shall ever put my foot on my native shore once more o god forbid I must not think of it carry me away.... my feelings is better imagined than described

In a postscript she added, "The thought of those miniatures stops my breath for a minute when I look forward to the time of getting them I hope my hopes will not be blasted."

Her hopes, however, were not immediately fulfilled. In 1854, she was still reminding Hannah of her desire for the portraits, with some disgruntlement. She felt that her sister did not recognize how lonely she was, far from home and desperately in need of tokens of her family: "I think Hannah you do not serve me right.... Just imagine to yourself Hannah if you was where I am and then perhaps you can sympathize with me." Finally, two years after her initial request, Abby received the portraits. The effect on her was dramatic. She wrote her family on December 9, 1854, "Dear Mother and Sister and Brother I seat myself to answer your letter and also to thank you for your kindness in sending those miniatures, Hannah I cannot describe to you with pen and ink how thankful I was to receive them I liked to have cried myself to death over them Horace cried our partner cried also."[152] Abby was lucky to see her family's portraits, for she never again saw them in person; she died in California eight months after the images arrived.

Letters, portraits, and papers offered some relief, but those at the far edge of the continent found other ways to cope with their yearnings for distant homes. William Taylor reported that some miners made surrogate families out of local wildlife: "A pet coon made a pretty good companion for some, others preferred a caged wild cat, or California lion. One man ... had a large family which accompanied him wherever he went. His family consisted of a bay horse, two dogs, two sheep, and two goats. . . . They seemed to be a very harmonious family indeed. Now these animals seemed to be very mean substitutes for families 'at home,' but, poor fellows, what better could they do?"[153]

Prospectors, separated from their own families, also took pleasure in watching the reunions of other miners and their kin. Taylor reported, "The fact is, men by hundreds assembled through social sympathy to witness the happy greeting of men and their wives who had not seen each other for years, accompanied by dancing and shouting for joy, embracing, kissing, laughing and crying, all to the great amusement of the excited throng."[154] In 1852, William Murray, who joined the crowds to watch the steamships dock, wrote to his wife of his wistful feelings as he watched reunions taking place:

> I have been down to see the Steamers come in. I have wished that I might see yours, anxious faces among the crowd who cast their wishful eyes on shore to look for some dear friend whom they expect to meet, here after a being separated for a time, and meeting again in this country where real friendship is more dearly prized than in any other Country. . . . I most wonder at myself that I don't get so homesick as to break over every other consideration and take the first boat and all the speed that, steam and wind, could carry me.[155]

Desperate for such reunions, many swallowed their pride and returned to their native states and families, often with little to show for their months or years in California. William Murray explained men's decisions, writing his wife, "A great many stay but a short time, get discouraged and start for home. It is a great expedition for a man . . . and if they dont happen to have good luck rather discouraging."[156] Sometimes miners took up collections to fund return journeys. William Peacock wrote in 1851, "There are a great many here going home as soon as they get enough to Carry them there and I have seen Several Round among the miners with a Subscription to get to go Home."[157] Often they left in great numbers, as Daniel W. Coit explained to his wife: "More people seem to be returning to—than coming from—the Atlantic states. Some 250 persons went on the small steamer *Antelope* and some 300 now go on the *Tennessee*."[158] Although more migrants went to California than left it, each year during the 1850s, around twenty-five thousand men went home to the East.[159]

Others wanted to head east but had to stay on. William Peacock wrote his family that, having spent nine months away from home, he would like to return to them and to his life in Chemung, Illinois, but both lack of money and fear of dishonor prevented him from doing so. Writing from Ophir,

California, in early 1851, he confessed, "I would Come home if I was not Ashamed to as i feel you & my friends would have just Cause to Reproach me with folly in Coming here against your advice. I hope you will forgive me & receive me kindly if I come home For which i fear will be the Case, I shall stay and try it this summer and if I can do nothing I will be Satisfied to Return & spend my Days in Peace and Poverty with my family. I sometimes get the Blues when I think of home wife & children."[160] In 1852, Peacock returned to Illinois, disappointed that he had not made more in the gold fields but happy to be home.

Others, fueled by dreams of great success, moved from one mine to the next, hoping to find something better to take home to their families, and never made it home.[161] Elias Lothrop gives a face and a name to this pattern. Lothrop, who had left Maine for a brief sojourn in Chicago during the 1840s, set out once again in search of fortune in 1849. This time he headed to California. There he missed his wife and longed to go back. He wrote in the fall of 1850, "I have an intense desire to see my own little family but do not feel at present as though I was willing to return home with so little means of contributing to their future comfort. . . . If I go home now it must be with far less than any one ought to have who has had to undergo what I have here." Lothrop noted that many miners wanted to return to their homes: "The tide of people which has been so long flowing into this country is now on a rapid ebb owing to the bitter disappointment of the people who came here with the expectation of getting a fortune for the bare trouble of picking it up—this reaction will serve one good purpose—that of keeping the rest of the *fools* at home—Still for all this I can make money much faster here than I should ever dream of doing at home."[162] Fueled by these hopes, he stayed on, but never saw his home again, dying of cholera in 1852.

Those who wanted to return but kept prolonging their stays in California sometimes found their characters changed by their absence from home. Enos Christman, who himself returned to Pennsylvania, saw the emotional toll that extended absence could take. He wrote his fiancée, "Long absence from friends . . . deadens or at least blunts the warmer instincts of our nature, and while we form no new friendships here we gradually lose those at home. We are strangers where ever we go and we imagine we would even be strangers at home. There some of our friends have died, others moved away, and their places are filled by strangers—we think we are forgotten, or at most, seldom thought of, and so lose all desire to return; one place seems as good for us as another."[163] That one place was as good as another, that home was impermanent, was a foundational belief in the capitalist ideology being constructed during the nineteenth century, but it was not yet a comfortable idea.

Levi Kenaga, a native of New York, believed the hard conditions of mining drove men mad: "There is a greade meny young men in this country that never will see thair home again for they give up all hopes and get discouraged and regluss [reckless] and they is a grade meny crasy. The Stockton asilum is fill for if a person gets to mining ones they thinks they cant do nothing els they is a grade meny that way but that is all foolishness."[164] Kenaga's belief that the disappointments of mining and the distance from home brought on insanity was widely shared. In the mid- to late nineteenth century, California was reputed to have a higher insanity rate than other places. Doctors of the era found one explanation in a report published in 1873 describing "the general character of a people who have left their homes to colonize a distant country. . . . Discontented, restless, enterprising and ambitious, they combine the elements of character prone to mental aberration." Another cause of instability was "absence from home and the want of domestic and family ties, to give response and relief to body and soul. . . . The want of fixedness—the idea that this is but a temporary home, creating the sensation of being adrift in the world. . . . Nostalgia—longing for the old home, the father land, the scenes of childhood and the objects of early attachment." All of these, the doctors reasoned, caused the high rate of insanity in the state.[165]

Many of the personality traits found in asylum populations—restless discontent, ambition and enterprise, the ability to sever bonds with home—were also constituent traits of rugged individualists. While these behaviors were pathologized when seen in their extreme state, they were considered benign and even desirable attributes in other contexts. The problems California's itinerant residents faced as they searched for opportunity were shared by others in the rising capitalist order. Compared to the colonial era, when community sanctions often prevented individuals from following their desires for fortune or family or freedom, many in the nineteenth century saw greater possibilities for movement. Yet they were not completely unfettered individualists, for they felt deeply attached to home and kin.

Many also searched for new selves in these faraway locales, optimistically believing that something better awaited them—better luck, better jobs, better land. When the gold did not pan out, when the plans did not come to fruition, disappointment replaced optimism and led them to stay where they were rather than carry themselves and their shame back home. They stayed away not because they did not want to see their kin but because they were embarrassed by their lack of success. Homesickness, then, was not just the cost of success; it also was the price of failure.

Although traces of homesickness can be found everywhere in writings from the antebellum era, they were increasingly erased from popular memory by the new ethic of cheerfulness overtaking American society. Over the course of the nineteenth century, people felt increasing pressure to express publicly only happy feelings.[166] Cheerfulness would not vanquish homesickness until the twentieth century, but by the end of the nineteenth century, when Americans looked back on their pioneering experiences, they often left out the emotional difficulties that they faced, and focused instead on the fact that they had triumphed over adversity. As a result, when Americans came to characterize the restless mobility of the age, they saw optimistic movement rather than decisions tinged with regret and nostalgia. Much emotional nuance was lost in the retelling. The complex reality of movement became obscured, and later generations were left with the mythology of the pioneers who set forth bravely to embrace the future. That myth would encourage later generations to do the same and leave them unprepared for the emotional challenges they would face.

CHAPTER 3

◇

A House Divided

In June 1862, Col. Alexander Hays of the 63rd Pennsylvania Volunteers wrote his wife from the Fair Oaks battlefield, "Last night as the whippor-will sang on the outskirts of camp, I thought of you all, and felt homesick, but I dare not entertain even that disease, for the thought is followed with serious consequences."[1] Another officer, higher up in the ranks, shared similar worries about his emotions. In August 1864, Gen. Benjamin Butler wrote again and again to his wife of his yearnings for home: "My dearest little Wife . . . you do not know how homesick you make me feel." Although he admitted to the melancholy feelings, he worried about indulging the emotion and warned his wife to avoid provoking it in her letters. Two days later he warned her, "Don't write me to come home any more. You make me so homesick. I shall have *nostalgia* like a Swiss soldier." A day later he implored, "My own dear Wife: You must not write me any more about coming home. You have made me so homesick now I am almost unfit for duty."[2]

In their worries about homesickness these two officers were typical of Civil War soldiers. They lived in a culture that celebrated home life, but the war required them to transform that love of home into martial spirit. It was a not an easy task. Soldiers had grown up steeped in a domestic sentimentalism that regarded the love of home, family, and, in particular, mother as ennobling. Ideally, this love prompted men to be honorable sons, husbands, fathers, and citizens. During the Civil War, however, they found that their love of home could be a double-edged sword: it could motivate them to fight but might also lead to homesickness, which could render them unfit for battle.[3]

How to love home and simultaneously leave it was a question that nagged at thousands, if not millions, of men between 1861 and 1865. Over the course of the war, more than 850,000 soldiers served the Confederacy and more than 2.1 million fought for the Union. They wrote millions of letters, and in them homesickness was a recurring and central topic.[4]

Homesickness often grew in the gaps between the ideals of warfare and the realities. In the early days of the war, after the Confederate victory at Fort Sumter, passions ran high and men on both sides rushed to enlist. Initially, the U.S. government asked men to volunteer for ninety days, but soon thereafter asked for a three-year commitment; the Confederacy asked for a one-year commitment.[5] Both northern and southern men responded enthusiastically, motivated by faith in their cause and a desire to display manly courage.[6] When the war dragged on, when there were long lulls of inactivity between battles, when the hardships of camp life became acute, many soldiers who had eagerly volunteered for service became despondent. Some were disappointed and bored; others wished themselves home again, comparing their circumstances with the comforts of family life; still others expressed great fears and presentiments that they might never again see loved ones. Those who were conscripted, by the Confederacy starting in 1862, or the Union in 1863, had even more reason for homesickness, since their desire to stay at home was not offset by an eagerness to serve. Conscripts were more likely to desert both armies, for they had left home unwillingly.[7] While their motivations for leaving home to fight differed from those of the volunteers, their desire to return to it did not.

Civil War soldiers' homesickness, evident in their letters home, reflected a mix of longings: a desire to return to the known, the comfortable, the safe, and the familiar, and a desire to be farther away from danger and death. While Americans felt homesick in peacetime as they migrated across the country, the homesickness that soldiers felt was intensified by the possibility that they might die violent deaths far from home. Their letters also indicate that many worried their homesickness might be a sign of weakness, make them unfit for duty, or even kill them.

The fear that homesickness might kill soldiers was a sign that American doctors and a growing number of laypeople were becoming familiar with the European discourses on homesickness and nostalgia and were applying them to American circumstances. These imported theories about the ravages of nostalgia had special currency in America, for many citizens attributed great emotional and moral power to family life and could easily believe that those removed from its good influences might suffer greatly.[8] Consequently, both the Union and the Confederate armies paid close attention to the domestic yearnings visible among their troops. They listed nostalgia in their medical manuals and tallied the number of men whom it felled. The U.S. government revealed that between 1861 and 1866, 5,213 white Union soldiers and 324 black soldiers suffered homesickness acutely enough to

"The Soldier's Dream of Home," a Currier & Ives lithograph produced during the Civil War, was one sign of the great attention that soldiers' homesickness received.
Source: Courtesy of Library of Congress.

come to a doctor's attention; fifty-eight white and sixteen black soldiers died of the disease.[9] No frivolous condition, homesickness became a subject of national attention and concern during the Civil War.

LEAVING HOME

Men who willingly enlisted in the war effort experienced homesickness as they tried to balance the competing demands of a love of home and a desire for honor. Such demands left many soldiers confused. Take William B. Greene, a seventeen-year-old from New Hampshire, who in 1861 enlisted in a special regiment of skilled marksmen, Berdan's Sharpshooters. In doing so, he defied his mother's wishes, yet he was intent on his plan. To join the regiment he had to prove he could shoot "ten consecutive shots in a ten inch bulls eye at 200 yards."[10] Once inducted, he found soldiering to be less glorious, more frustrating, and more frightening than he had imagined. Early on, he and his fellow soldiers were dismayed to discover that the guns they were provided with were unreliable. That William was frustrated, and that his family missed him, is evident in the fact that shortly after leaving

home in 1861 his mother asked various authorities about getting him discharged from the unit, but to no avail. His complaints were doubtless
many—the letter detailing his woes does not survive—but among them
was a feeling of profound homesickness. His mother reported to her friends
and relatives that William was homesick, and his cousin, Clara E. Downing,
wrote him in January 1862, telling him that he must conquer such feelings:
"Everybody must be homesick sometime and it would be very strange
indeed if you were not when you are so far away from home and friends."
After expressing her sympathy for his situation, she urged him to practice
techniques of self-mastery: "You will soon overcome such feelings, you will
think you are working in a glorious cause that you are there with thousands
of others to defend your noble country's rights and to crush out rebellion.
Now that you have entered the army look not back but forward. Let your
motto ever be upward and onward forever until my country is free and liberty and peace is restored to these United States."[11]

Clara Downing's response to William was typical of many women's
views during the war. Although they loved their husbands, sons, fathers,
brothers, and cousins, and rejoiced that they in turn loved them, these
women also wanted their menfolk to act nobly. Like William Greene's
mother, many were reluctant to see their kin leave home, but they generally
believed that once they did, the men should comport themselves honorably, without fear or misgivings. They certainly should not bring dishonor
on themselves or the household by coming home without permission.[12]

William's mother, Susan Greene, desperately wanted her son to return
but feared he might desert the army.[13] She confided her misgivings to her
extended family. As a result, William continued to receive a stream of letters
from various female relatives who warned him against capitulating to his
homesickness and spoke of the dishonor he would incur should he desert.
His cousin, for instance, wrote him:

> I see by last nights Journal that "desertion" is openly talked of in your camp. . . . Willie for
> the love of God & your friends, let it never be said that Willie Greene brought disgrace
> upon himself by deserting his regiment or that he died the deserter's death. It makes
> me shudder at the thought of such an awful death and the disgrace in consequence
> thereof. . . . I do not think you would do such a mean thing. I think you have too much
> pride and honor, too much regard for your mother's feelings, too much love for your
> country & friends. I think you would turn in horror from such an ignominious death as
> the "deserter" must *surely die.*[14]

William became, at least temporarily, ashamed of his homesickness and
denied that he was experiencing the emotion. He wrote his mother that she
should stop broadcasting his feelings to others. She had told many in their

community of his homesickness; those people in turn had written to other soldiers in his regiment, and suddenly his condition had become public both in his hometown and in his regiment, filled as it was with his neighbors and schoolmates. He chided his mother for sharing his confidences with others. "Warren received a letter from his wife last night. He said that she stopped with you the other night and that you were worried about my being sick and homesick. What do you mean by my being sick? I am not sick nor have I been since I came. . . . He told me what Wealthy's said about my being homesick. If you told her what I wrote in my first letter I shant like it for I don't feel so now. I am contented now better than Warren or Augustus, but you need not go tell their folks of it."[15]

Although he denied being homesick in this letter, he continued to long for home, and his mother continued to miss him. He wrote her in early February that he might be able to return home if his brother were to write a letter saying that she was sick.[16] Later he abandoned this plan and attempted to make himself appear ill, with the hope that he might thereby earn a discharge. He wrote to her in the summer of 1862, "I suppose I could go into the hospital and play pretty sick and get discharged." Two years later he was still trying to return home, writing, "I expected to be transferred home then, but I find I was not sick enough for that & so I have come to the conclusion to be very sick. I think I shall either come home by transfer or by furlough. I trust I shall get home some way."[17] Despite his homesickness and his efforts to return home—he did in fact take an extended leave but was never convicted of desertion—William stayed in the army until 1865. But his letters offer clear evidence of an individual struggling to adjust to the demands of duty, the distance from home, the danger of war, and the difference between his expectations of battle and the reality.

Across the country, both northern and southern soldiers faced similar experiences. They had been brought up in a culture that allowed, and in fact encouraged, men to display tender emotions about home life.[18] Once at war, however, they found that if those feelings were not kept in appropriate bounds, if they competed too much with the imperatives to fight, they were unwelcome.[19] Like William, soldiers were fighting a multifront war with their feelings. They needed to make certain that the men around them did not think they were soft, they had to manage their reputations back home, and they had to maintain a sense of self and a connection to loved ones under trying circumstances.

In such a climate, soldiers saw their homesickness as a problem because it drew into question the level of their commitment to the cause. When word leaked out that a soldier was homesick his comrades sometimes judged him harshly. Sixteen-year-old Chauncey Herbert Cooke of the 25th Regiment, Wisconsin Volunteer Infantry, wrote his parents from his sick bed. He and ten other soldiers had come down with measles. Lying in bed, with little to occupy him, Chauncey thought of home. But he worried as he did so: "God knows I never felt before what it meant to have a good home and a kind father and dear mother. . . . Don't think I am homesick, mother, you know I can say all these things and still not be homesick. When a fellow is sick and all broke up he can't help saying soft things." Apparently the "soft things" he said about home made him an object of derision. "Some of the fellows here are awful rough in their talk. They wasn't very sick and they are joking me and a young fellow in Co. E. because we are talking so much about our home and our mothers. I don't deny that I long to see my dear mother, and when the tears come into his eyes I know the poor boy that lays next to me is thinking of home too."[20] Like the men who taunted Cooke, an Illinois soldier, Charles Wright Wills, looked down on those who were too soft, too homesick. He confided to his diary, "Our boys are singing, 'Home Again' as they lie around me in our tent. I thank goodness that none of them get homesick like some do that I know. . . . I do despise these whiners."[21]

It was not just other soldiers who criticized the homesick; the men also judged themselves harshly. Calvin Shedd, a soldier in the New Hampshire Volunteers, 7th Regiment, tried to downplay his emotions, writing, "I am going to be just as little homesick as possible do my duty & let come what will I have a good reputation as a Soldier in this Regt."[22] William G. Vardell, a quartermaster in the 23rd South Carolina Infantry Regiment, wrote to his wife, Jennie, of his own struggles. He did not want to forget the comforts and delights of home life, but he did not want his longings for home to interfere with his performance of his duties: "Dearest Jennie . . . some argue that you become accustomed to being away from [home] & they feel the separation less, the longer the time of separation, not so with me—I feel it more than ever, but must learn to feel it properly & without interfering with discharge of my duties. . . . My *duty* is here & to feel & act accordingly."[23]

Soldiers, especially volunteers, felt trapped. They genuinely missed home, and they knew that love of home was an acceptable feeling; however, they worried about what it indicated about them as soldiers. Consequently, they often ended their letters with a denial that they were homesick. The Gould family of central New York sent six of seven sons to the Union Army. They all longed to return to their farm in Delaware County but were hesitant about admitting to their homesickness. For instance, William Gould wrote his sister in 1862, "Some times I long to be at home to see things there, but will not for one moment suffer my self to get home sick, as this would do no good & would be injourest [injurious] to me. . . . Nothing but the hope of returning home does keep us so contented as we are." His brother Richard wrote of his welter of emotions. He hoped the war would end so he could "come home and live a farmers life." But he added, "You must not think I am homesick, for I am not."[24]

Benjamin Kenaga of New York wrote his wife, Fanny, of his emotions and his attempts to grapple with them: "I get lonesome to think of home of the dear ones I have left home. . . . Dear Fanny my thoughts are to home very much but I must stick . . . her through."[25] Kenaga came to regret that letter and followed up with another one in which he asserted his mastery of his emotions: "I have heard that [it] was said at home that I was home sick and that I cried half the time. Since I am here I have god for my witness that I never shead a tear while I was a way from home put them fears out of your mind and be calm for you make me feel bad by discouraging me."[26]

In addition to worrying that their local reputations might be harmed by homesickness, some worried that their actual military performance might be affected. After the Union's defeat at Bull Run in 1861, a reporter for the *New York Herald* observed, "It is thought by many who have studied the matter, that the sending forward of the three months men, whose time of enlistment was nearly out, was a fatal error. They were already homesick, and the near approach of the time for their return had dampened their ardor, and rendered them less anxious to court danger."[27] Other reporters suggested that the defeat at Bull Run had shamed homesick Union soldiers and made them recommit themselves to the cause. A *New York Times* reporter noted, "I heard a Massachusetts man who was in the fight, and whose time was out, say that he was homesick enough until last night, but that now he would not go home until this war was ended, and that nine out of twelve of his regiment would reenlist for the war without going home."[28] No matter how much these soldiers wanted to return home, to do so after a stinging and surprising defeat would only bring dishonor upon them. So they remained, but their battle with homesickness was not over.

THOUGHTS OF HOME

Homesickness was worrisome; it could lay low men's spirits and defeat armies, but it was also unpredictable, striking at different times and for different reasons. Some found that homesickness attacked them when they ceased to believe in the cause for which they were fighting. Morale was already low in the Union Army in 1862, but it sank lower after Abraham Lincoln issued first a preliminary proclamation in September of 1862, declaring that slaves in the Confederate states would be freed, and then signed the final Emancipation Proclamation in January 1863. Many northern soldiers who did not support abolition felt less inspired by the Union cause than they had before the proclamations.[29] To their mind, the fundamental nature and purpose of the war had suddenly changed with the stroke of Lincoln's pen. General McClellan himself declared the Proclamation "infamous." He wrote to his wife, "[I] could not make up my mind to fight for such an accursed doctrine as that of a servile insurrection."[30] McClellan eventually overcame his misgivings, but many of his men did not. For instance, James Fortiner, Company D., 2nd Illinois Cavalry, wrote to his sweetheart, Emma, "If i could i would get out of this Niger War it has com to a Abolition war and i am tired of fighting to free Nigers The armys are not fighting fore that same thing that they was when we first started." The war had changed and become less compelling. And home had become more so. "Emma do you ever think of days past promises maid and . . . the pleasant hours gone by do you ever look back and wish fore those time to bee again I do and if God spares me I will endeavor to fulfill my part of vows that I have maid to you."[31] A Union captain from New York noted that he heard soldiers declaring that the conflict had "turned into a 'nigger war' and all are anxious to return to their homes for it was to preserve the Union that they volunteered."[32]

After the Emancipation Proclamation, African Americans were allowed to serve in the U.S. Army, a change in policy that led to protests and flagging commitment to the cause among whites. Many white soldiers felt their own sense of manly courage would be diminished if black soldiers could now participate in the same civic rituals of soldiering.[33] Sympathetic to the cause of the black soldier, Calvin Shedd of the New Hampshire Volunteers responded to rumors that blacks were being treated better than white soldiers. Shedd chalked such stories up to "Homesick Traitorous Dough-Faces that have just political knowledge enough to D—n the Niggers & abolitionists & hurrah for Sham Democracy." These malcontents complained about the war because they wanted to go home. "They have no manhood left or love of Country & hate to own they are homesick so vent their Billingsgate on the Government & the Nigger-War as they are pleased to call it. When they enlisted they were in favor of 'crushing the rebellion' at any cost & all hazzards; but their present position shows how much stamina they have got, & their sincerity at the beginning."[34] The perceived change in the purpose of the war may have been a convenient excuse for some discontented soldiers to express, and perhaps act on, their homesickness. They had joined the war effort out of a sense of duty, with the goal of preserving the Union. If that was no longer the purpose of the fight, then perhaps they were freed from their original obligations and could return home—or so they hoped.

Many other, more mundane occasions caused homesickness, too. Sending and receiving mail was one of these occasions. The letter-writing habits that Americans had developed in the 1840s and 1850s shaped troops' emotional experiences during wartime. One Union doctor noted, "Ours is emphatically a letter-writing army. At all times, and amid the most varied scenes the American soldier is in correspondence with home. . . . The constant correspondence with home serves to keep vividly before the imagination the homes scenes and home ties."[35] This certainly was the case for William Atwell of the 27th Ohio Infantry Regiment, who wrote in his diary in March 1862, "I write a letter home today.—This is a pretty picture here I am sitting before a guard fire writing at midnight—with my knee for a desk all around the fire are sleeping guards. I being the only one awake it is not the time to wright—but the time for thought!—and I guess I will lay this aside and think of my dear old *home* and my many friends there."[36] Although Atwell was the only one writing that night, he generally would have had more company. Mary Livermore, a nurse for the Union Army, noted, "If you went into any camp at any time, you would see dozens and sometimes hundreds of soldiers writing letters. Some would be stretched at full length on the ground, with a book or a knapsack for a table—some sitting upright against the trunks of trees, with the paper resting on their drawn-up knees—others would stand and write."[37]

The volume of letters that soldiers sent was staggering. Livermore estimated that each day, forty-five thousand letters were sent to Union soldiers on the Atlantic coast, and soldiers sent an equivalent number daily, "making an aggregate of ninety thousand daily letters that passed through the post-office at Washington." An additional ninety thousand or so passed through the Louisville, Kentucky, post office, another distribution point for the Union army, leading Livermore to conclude that on average 180,000 letters were sent each day.[38]

These letters were crucial for maintaining morale. Indeed Daniel Holt, a surgeon with the 121st New York Volunteers, wrote to his wife, thanking her for a "soul inspiring letter" she had sent him: "I am firmly of the opinion that were more of such letters written to desponding soldiers, we should have less desertion and harder fighting. . . . It is only those who are the recipients of complaining, fault-finding letters—letters worthy of no virtuous Christian mind . . . and *those who receive no letters*, who are found in the rear when a battle is raging."[39]

Letters from home might temporarily assuage homesickness, but they also might intensify longings. Capt. Geo. W. Dawson of the Confederate army wrote of his reaction to a letter from his wife in 1861: "Oh how I wish last night (after reading Your letter twice) to be with you and our sweet Children. I can hardly sleep my thoughts were of My Happy Home and Dear kind sweet wife and our sweet ones." Dawson was killed in battle the following year.[40] Another Confederate soldier, Tally Simpson, of the 3rd South Carolina Volunteers, wrote to his sister that for every soldier "there is a moment of his life which is transcendently sweet, rendered still sweeter the more seldom it appears, and that is the moment he is made the recipient of a precious letter from home. . . . A letter from home renders him oblivious of all his trials and sends him dreaming such dreams as thought of home can alone suggest."[41] Dreams of home might bring comfort, but they might also renew longings.

While receiving letters could provoke the yearning for home, not receiving them could as well.[42] Sgt. John Collins, an African American soldier in the 54th Massachusetts Infantry, wrote in 1865 from South Carolina of the sadness he felt when "looking around and seeing [his] fellow soldiers-in-arms standing in groups, and some looking with a wishful eye and palpitating heart for the mail, to see what our people north are doing, and to see if any news comes from the loved ones at home." Of course, not all soldiers received letters. Collins wrote, "You can just imagine how they feel, when finding no news from home, from mothers, sisters, wives, nor friends, they exclaim, 'Well, I'm forgotten.'"[43] Soldiers, white and black, frequently complained to their families that they did not receive enough mail and blamed their kin for being lazy and neglectful. While this was no doubt the reason some soldiers failed to receive letters, far more often the problem lay with the armies' mail service.

The war not only affected the pace of mail delivery, it also affected the supply of paper and ink, necessities for the corresponding soldiers. As a result, many used improvised materials. Marion Hill Fitzpatrick wrote to his wife, "I am writing with ink of my own make which is simply polk berries squeezed out. I want you to put a little coppera in your next letter for me to put in it. They say it will turn it black and make it more indelible."[44] Other soldiers asked their families to send stationery, envelopes, and stamps, all of which were scarce.[45]

The mail carried not just letters, but also packages. Tally Simpson of South Carolina wrote to his sister in 1861, "I have been wanting something good to eat till I am nearly dead. I crave peach pie, honey and good buttermilk & cc. Is there no way of sending us a box of some kind?"[46] To sate such yearnings, many families did send packages to their soldiers. William Watson, a surgeon in the 105th Regiment of the Pennsylvania Volunteers, was expecting a box of treats for Christmas. He wrote his sister Ella in December 1862, "I informed Pa in my letter how to direct my box. I only hope I will receive it—as I am heartily sick of Army rations."[47] Families sent every conceivable foodstuff as well as other little reminders of domestic life. One soldier reported that the mail was filled with "apples, eggs, and doughnuts . . . pickle and jam bottles . . . flannel shirts and quires of writing paper . . . packages of tea . . . ink bottles."[48] These humble items were portable bits of home and connected soldiers to remembered kitchens, parlors, and routines of daily life.

Sometimes soldiers, particularly wounded men in hospitals, received packages sent to them by strangers. Despite the anonymity of the transaction, such parcels could easily provoke homesickness. These parcels often originated in the voluntary organizations that northern and southern women had established with the goal of provisioning hospitals and the sick and wounded within them. In the North, an estimated ten thousand to twelve thousand soldiers' aid societies sent $15 million worth of supplies to support Union troops.[49] They sent boxes of socks, handkerchiefs, combs, dried berries, shirts, towels, and the like. Almost always, the women who made these goods enclosed notes to the unknown soldiers who would receive their handiwork and treats. Even though their letters were directed to strangers, the writers assumed the role of mothers and wives and spoke of family love. For instance, one box sent through Chicago and intended for a wounded soldier contained a note that read, "My Dear Friend,—You are not *my* husband nor son; but you are the husband or son of some woman who undoubtedly loves you as I love mine. I have made these garments for you with a heart that aches for your sufferings, and with a longing to come to you to assist in taking care of you. . . . God loves and pities you, pining and lonely in a far-off hospital." Another woman sent a dressing gown, its pockets filled with hickory nuts and gingersnaps, designed for an anonymous soldier in a hospital. A note was pinned to it: "My Dear Fellow,—Just take your ease in this dressing gown. Don't mope and have the blues, if you *are* sick. Moping never cured anybody yet. Eat your nuts and cakes, if you are well enough."[50] The authors of such missives assumed that sick men longed for domestic life, and they felt little compunction about trying to reproduce it for them.

The mail also carried hometown magazines and newspapers that families had forwarded on to their sons.[51] Probably more Union troops received such publications than Confederates, both because there was more printed material in the North and because the literacy rate was higher there. Because newspapers had a more local flavor than national magazines, they were all the more appreciated. A soldier from the town of Urbana, Ohio, told his parents, "The most satisfaction I have is in reading the news from home. . . . I would like to have the Urbana paper sent me once in awhile I would sooner read it than any paper I can get hold of."[52]

While letters, boxes of food, and newspapers provided the most immediate links to home, there were other reminders that played on soldiers' emotions. Sentimental music, so much a part of domestic civilian life, played a significant role in the lives of soldiers on duty. Sometimes, army bands could relieve the blues by playing rousing music designed to lift the spirits of the soldiers. One soldier reported in his diary, "Time hangs heavily and were it not for the bands I should be almost homesick."[53] Many bands resorted to old favorites; "Home, Sweet Home" was reportedly the most popular song among soldiers on both sides during the Civil War. For Union soldiers, the next most popular songs were "Auld Lang Syne," "Annie Laurie," "Old Hundred," and "I'm a Pilgrim." To this list, southern soldiers added such nostalgic favorites as "Dixie Land," "My Old Kentucky Home," and "Swanee River."[54]

As these song titles make clear, both northern and southern soldiers had grown up in a sentimental culture, and there were moments when young men on opposite sides of the battlefield could draw on the same tunes and lyrics and find a common means of expressing their feelings. Bell Irvin Wiley noted, "The spirit of friendliness that sprinkled Yankee-Rebel relations had no more eloquent expression than the musical fetes in which the two armies occasionally participated." He described a Union band at Fredericksburg that played an assortment of popular northern tunes. "'Now give us some of ours,' shouted Confederates across the river. Without hesitation the band swung into the tunes of 'Dixie,' 'My Maryland,' and the 'Bonnie Blue Flag.' This brought forth a lusty and prolonged cheer from the Southerners. Finally the music swelled into the tender strains of 'Home, Sweet Home,' and the countryside reverberated with the cheers of thousands of men on both sides of the stream."[55]

The war also inspired new sentimental songs, and a great many of them juxtaposed soldiers' memories of home with their daily realities. For instance, "Tenting Tonight" pulled at heartstrings as it explained,

> We're tenting tonight on the old camp ground,
> Give us a song to cheer
> Our weary hearts, a song of home
> and friends we love so dear.

"Just before the Battle, Mother" suggested that thoughts of home made soldiers strong. Troops were homesick, but home impelled them to fight and mother was the motivation for martial valor.

> Just before the battle, Mother,
> I am thinking most of you,
> While upon the field we're watching,
> With the enemy in view.
> Comrades brave are 'round me lying,
> Filled with thought of home and God.

Despite the fact that soldiers' heads were full of visions of home, the song affirmed that good men would fight on in the name of honor and duty:

> Oh, I long to see you, Mother,
> And the loving ones at home,
> But I'll never leave our banner,
> Till in honor I can come.[56]

Yet even during the war, some questioned whether the songs of home were a good tonic for homesickness. While sentimental music could raise spirits, it could also depress them. Union bands sometimes were forbidden to play "Home, Sweet Home" or other songs that might render soldiers melancholic. Such a rule was not frivolous. Numa Barned, a Union soldier forced to listen to new "homesick recruits" playing "Home, Sweet Home," confided, "I don't like to hear it for it makes me feel queer."[57] Another soldier wrote of the emotional effects of camp songs, "If I ever get Back I can give you some songs that will make your eye water."[58] The Confederate soldier William G. Vardell, admitted the songs affected him. In early June 1863, he wrote his wife, "Last night a band came up near our quarters & played beautifully for an hour or more, I enjoyed it but partially, for it made me feel sad; whilst listening I thought of you & home. . . . Then they played Home, sweet home." Bands must have played the air often, for he wrote again to his wife some three weeks later, reporting that all was "quiet save the chirp of the katydid, & band playing 'Let me kiss him for his Mother' I think of a little circle at home around the Piano: dearest Mamma seated & our two boys singing, & then away would memory run. . . . The band is playing 'Home sweet home' so plaintive, how that song appeals to every heart, for the humblest know some home."[59]

While letters and music brought bits of home life to soldiers far from home, other prompts to homesickness came from the disjuncture between their old lives and their new. Many worried about how the war was changing them, and as the conflict stretched on, the normal routines of home life seemed ever more distant.[60] Being away from home and church on the Sabbath made men homesick. Henry Greenwood of the 15th Regiment of the Massachusetts Volunteer Infantry, Company C, wrote on a Sunday in 1861, "Some are reading their testaments; some, books or papers, and others are writing. My thoughts wander back to home, and it seems as if I could see the people in the streets, wending their way to the various places of worship, and could hear the prayers which go up from the pulpits in our little town for our welfare and safety."[61] W. C. Porter struggled with the gap between his religious and his military duties; being a soldier meant leaving part of his old churchgoing identity behind. He wrote in his diary in the summer of 1861, "Captain says we have to drill. Don't like to on the Sabbath, but he says 'No Sundays in time of war.'"[62]

Holidays, particularly Christmas and Thanksgiving, were also occasions that sparked memories of family and home life. Soldiers knew that everyone else in the family was together, heightening their feelings of absence. Samuel Fiske, a Connecticut soldier who wrote letters about army life to the Springfield paper under the pseudonym Dunn Browne, reported how the soldiers felt on Thanksgiving: "Our thoughts reverted to the far off home scenes; our wishes, desires, affections, prayers were hovering over the New England fire-sides left behind."[63] Sgt. Thomas W. Smith, of the 6th Pennsylvania Cavalry, wrote his brother from the hospital of the fine feast that was prepared for him. Women at the hospital had given them "a big Dinner on Thanksgiving Day": "We had Turkeys, Geese, Ducks, and Chickens, with Mashed Potatoes, Cold Sloughs, Apple Saus, Cranberry Saus, all kinds of Jelleys and Preserves, Oyster Soup, and Oyster Pie, Cranberry Pie, Minse Pie, Peach Pie, Apple Pie, and Pumpkin Custard." Ultimately, however, the food did not make up for the missing warmth of kin: "But Bennie do you know that a Crust of Bread and a Glass of Water at Home, would have been much better relished by me, than all the big Dinner that we had here."[64]

Union surgeon Charles Brackett thought back to his family in Indiana on Christmas Eve in 1862 and wrote of how the holiday intensified his longings for home: "I have been thinking how this Christmas Eve would be, if I could be with my loved ones at home instead of being here . . . with the enemy harassing our Pickets." He compared the traditional home-cooked meal he usually ate on Christmas with the "Coffee, Sugar, Salt Pork, & Bread" that he was eating alone that year. He imagined himself decorating the Christmas tree and preparing presents for the family. The contrast with his current conditions made him "love his neat wife, & home comforts more than ever."[65] On the same night, Christmas Eve, 1862, John Apperson, a Confederate hospital steward, let his thoughts wander homeward. He wrote in his diary, "This is Christmas Eve. . . . How it will be spent by the good folks at home is not for any of us to say. . . . How I do wish to be at home!"[66]

While holiday meals could excite the imaginations of homesick soldiers, so too could everyday meals. Many men longed for familiar tastes and dishes, and even on those occasions when they found the local cuisine satisfying, it nevertheless could not measure up to the remembered meals of home. F. O. Danielson wrote to his parents back in New Sweden, Iowa, that terrible army food made him homesick. "P.S.," he wrote, "Tell Mama that I wish I were home and could sit down at her table, for I am utterly tired of hardtack and bully beef. I hope to come home soon. Don't forget to write."[67] Other soldiers shared similar dreams of family meals. Richard Gould wrote his sister Hannah in 1864, "I am rather slim now, I tell you. . . . I dream of home most every night and of being at your house & of going in the buttery & down in the cellar and eating pie & cake. If I should come there and act so, I would not blame you if you took the broom stick and drove me out of the house, but if I had the chance I

Thomas Nast's portrayal of a homesick soldier on Christmas Eve, 1863.
Source: Courtesy of the Library of Congress.

would willingly run the risk of that." When Hannah sent him food, Richard wrote, "Was very glad to get them. They tasted like home."[68]

Food that "tasted like home" was welcomed by soldiers who subsisted on pork, beans, flour, potatoes, and very strong coffee. The other dietary staple was hardtack, which the men suggested was best consumed at night so that diners would not have to see the weevils that infested the crackers.[69] Good food was one of many creature comforts soldiers missed. They had little protection from rain or snow and lived in muddy, waste-filled encampments. There were few opportunities for bathing or cleaning up, and many opportunities to become sweaty, dirty, and exposed to lice, rashes, and disease. Troops often lacked such essentials as blankets and shoes.[70] Their lives in war stood in marked contrast to their lives at home, and the misery of their condition often added to their yearnings.

PATHS BACK HOME

At times the misery of camp life and the imagined happiness of home life proved too much for soldiers, and they deserted. Estimates vary, but some suggest that on the Confederate side more than 100,000 soldiers deserted, and more than 250,000 soldiers left the Union army.[71] High desertion rates were often linked to homesickness, although there were a number of other compelling reasons to leave: the slow pace at which they were paid, concern for their families' well-being, and fear for their lives. Some deserters would run off, visit home, and then return; others, once home, remained there. Soldiers frequently deserted when the army was moving close to their homes because the temptation was so strong; some jumped off troop trains when they passed through their hometowns. Desertions may have been evidence not of disloyalty, but of a desire for greater rights within army life, such as the right to visit family occasionally.[72] Confederate soldiers tried to exert control over where they served, often hoping to stay in the vicinity of their homes. Faced with the possibility of transfer to distant locales, many deserted.[73] They were fighting for home, but for a very local sense of it.

Union soldiers deserted as well. William Greene, the sharpshooter from New Hampshire, took a leave but then returned to service. Gen. Benjamin Butler appealed to Lincoln for clemency for another soldier who had temporarily abandoned his duty as a result of homesickness. Butler wrote Lincoln in 1864, detailing the sorry case of Lt. Daniel Russell of the 10th New Hampshire Volunteers. Russell had initially enlisted for a three-month term of service, during which time he had "served faithfully and well." He subsequently joined the 19th Massachusetts Volunteers, with which he served for ten months. Thereafter, he decided "to desert and go to his home, having, as he alleges and he seems truthful, home-sickness to such a degree as to amount to the disease *nostalgia*." Russell stayed home for a few months, but then "he came to a sense of his situation, and enlisted in the 10th New Hampshire. Served bravely and faithfully with them, was in the battle of Fredericksburg, and was promoted for good conduct to be *second lieutenant*, which office he now holds. He has been in actual service of the United States thirty-three and a half (33½) months out of thirty-six." The missing two and a half months were the problem, however. Despite his return, Russell was arrested for desertion. Butler was sympathetic to the young man because of "his youth, and the strong effect of home-sickness upon youth," as well as his good conduct. He had released Russell from arrest but needed Lincoln to officially pardon the young man so that he might escape further prosecution.[74]

Not all commanding officers were as sympathetic as Butler, and men who deserted knew they ran the risk of being prosecuted, and in some cases executed. Those who wanted to leave the army without earning the dishonorable label of deserter or facing legal or mortal peril therefore often chose to fake an illness in order to return home. Medical authorities were on the lookout for such hoaxes and devised ways to distinguish between real disease and feigned conditions. In 1864, Second Assistant Surgeon

William Fuller noted that these "malingerers" had many motivations. Some simply did not like service; others found it tiring and difficult and resented the discipline. Still others were "troubled with nostalgia, and desire to procure a discharge from service, so as to be with their friends at home once more." Those soldiers most likely to malinger were "married men . . . who have families at home, and whose malingering is generally brought about from nostalgia caused by this strong attachment to home, and by the reception of letters that are not calculated to raise the spirits of any man. . . . They generally feign diseases of the lungs, heart, genital organs, diarrhea, and epilepsy."[75]

Some soldiers either could not pull off the deception that they or a relative were ill or they did not want to act dishonorably, and so they remained in service, but their thoughts were often troubled. They agonized not only about when they would next see their families, but if they ever would. The threat and fear of death pervaded many a soldier's letter. These men frequently sought comfort in the belief that families would be reunited in heaven, which they envisioned as their true and ultimate home. Some scholars maintain that it was this faith in heavenly reunion that made it possible for both armies to mobilize—and lose—such large numbers of men. Without the promise of heavenly family gatherings, few would have been willing to make such sacrifices.[76]

The belief in heavenly reunions offered at least some relief to the homesick and scared soldier. The Gould brothers, who wrote so frequently to their sister Hannah, displayed their conviction that a heavenly reunion was possible. Wesley Gould, for instance, wrote to Hannah of their brother Charles's death in 1862: "I have often thought how happy we would be if we should all meet at home after the war was over. But alas we can never meet with him again on earth, but let us try and meet him in heaven. What a joyfull meeting that will be when we shall meet to part no more." A year later, his brother Richard wrote to Hannah, "You must not think I am homesick for I am not, but I long to see the day when we shall hear peace proclaimed throughout our land and when friends shall meet friends." In the event that he did not live that long, Richard took comfort in the idea that if he lived honorably they would "meet in heaven where there is no wars." A few months later, another Gould brother, William, wrote his sister, "If we meet no more on earth we, I hope, may make an unbroken family in heaven. O when that eloustrious day shall come."[77]

Soldiers on both sides of the lines shared the Goulds' faith. William R. Barry, a native of South Carolina, wrote, "Dear Sally I do not want you to fret about me remember that the same kind providence watches over us when we are separated that does when we are together and if it is his will we will meet again, and live happy together in this world if it is not I hope that we may meet in heaven where there is no parting no wars to trouble. . . . if we never meet in this world god grant that we may all meet in heaven where parting is no more."[78] Dr. Charles Brackett of Rochester, Indiana, wrote to his daughter in 1861, "If death (the common lot of us all) takes any of us before that time my trust is that we may all meet in the Spirit land were partings, & sorrows ar no more, & all is love, peace, & joy." Brackett later wrote to his family of a young dying soldier he had treated who also shared this conception of heaven: "His last words were 'I am going home now.'"[79]

As he lay dying, Confederate J. R. Montgomery wrote his father a letter that showed how he thought about his impending death, far from his family. Injured at the battle of Spotsylvania, he told his father, "[My] right shoulder is horribly mangled & I know death is inevitable." He knew his father would want to know his last thoughts and words, and so he wrote, "I know death is near, that I will die far from home and friends of my early youth," but he comforted himself that he had good comrades around him. "My grave will be marked . . . so that you may visit it if you desire to do so." After death, he hoped he might rejoin his family, first by being reburied near them, then by being reunited with them in heaven. "I would like to rest in the grave yard with my dear mother and brothers but it's a matter of minor importance. Let us all try to reunite in heaven. . . . May we meet in heaven. Your dying son, J. R. Montgomery."[80] The hope of reunion and return that allowed many men to go into battle and meet the enemy was the only consolation Montgomery had as death approached. He died four days later.

DEBATES

Montgomery longed for family as he lay dying; according to medical wisdom of the time, some soldiers lay dying because they longed for family. If a soldier had an unremarkable case of homesickness, few worried. However, if it grew acute doctors might classify it as nostalgia and regard the afflicted with greater concern. Alfred Lewis Castleman, a surgeon serving in the 5th Regiment of Wisconsin Volunteers, wrote in his diary in October 1861 of the first death in his regiment: "The poor fellow died of Nostalgia (home-sickness), raving to the last breath about wife and children. . . . Deaths from this cause are very frequent in the army."[81]

Not all soldiers knew the word *nostalgia*, but they knew that homesickness could take on an intense form, lead to deep depression and debilitation, and have accompanying physical distress. Most did not think they had the condition, although they knew of its dangers. Gen. Joseph Shields of the Union army wrote in 1862, "If not allowed to go home and see their families . . . [soldiers] droop and die. . . . I have watched this."[82] Common soldiers too worried about their emotions. Richard Gould wrote his sister in 1864, "This being homesick and worrying kills more soldiers then bullets dose."[83] A soldier in the 15th Iowa Infantry, Cyrus Boyd, wrote in 1863, "More men *die* of homesickness than all other diseases—and when a man gives up and lies down he is a *goner*. Keep the mind occupied with something new and keep *going all the time* except when asleep."[84] Others provided more concrete examples of the ravages of homesickness. Benjamin Kenaga described the condition of one of his friends who had languished as he thought of home: "Now Riser he was sic and homesick at that and he would have died if he would have State free he fell away to almost to a skeleton then they saw him fit to sent him home."[85]

Prisoners of war were particularly susceptible to homesickness. Languishing in unsanitary prisons with little to occupy their minds, many perished. Often their deaths were attributed to nostalgia. Union soldier Charles Mattocks of Maine wrote his mother from a military prison in Charleston, South Carolina, in 1864. He told her he was better off than men at the infamous Andersonville Prison in Georgia: "During two months 8000 and more of our soldiers [at Andersonville] died of scurvy, and nostalgia, which is merely the medical term for homesickness. The whole number confined there was about 24000. So one out of three died in two months. At this rate all would have died in 6 months."[86] A soldier recalling his days at Andersonville described the dramatic effects of nostalgia on inmates. He told of a fellow prisoner, a man from Pennsylvania who came from a loving family, "When he first came in he was thoroughly dazed by the greatness of his misfortune." He sat still for hours, gazing off into space, and could not be diverted from his ruminations. He spent most of his time paging through letters from his family and gazing at "a melaineotype of a plain-faced woman—his wife—and her children." He grew more and more dejected as time passed. He stopped eating after a time and soon became "delirious with hunger and homesickness." Hallucinating, he imagined himself back at home with his family and reenacted dinnertime rituals. His fellow inmate recalled, "Making a motion, as if presenting a dish, he would say: 'Janie, have another biscuit, do!' Or, 'Eddie, son, won't you have another piece of this steak?' Or, 'Maggie, have some more potatoes,' and so on through a whole family of six or more. It was a relief to us when he died about a month after he came in."[87]

An observer summed up the effects of nostalgia on prison populations: "[It] fastens upon the breast of its prey, and sucks, vampyre-like, the breath of his nostrils. Many a heroic spirit after braving death at the cannon's mouth . . . has at length succumbed unresistingly to this vampyre, Nostalgia, and found release in the end only through the gloomy portal of dissolution."[88] This understanding of nostalgia as a physical illness that could suck the life out of a soldier had been slowly emerging in America during the antebellum period. It became far more widespread during the Civil War as doctors and laypeople north and south came to see acute homesickness not just as an emotional condition, but as a physiological one as well.

The U.S. Army began collecting statistics on the number of soldiers afflicted with various maladies, including nostalgia. During the first year of the war the Union counted 572 cases of nostalgia among white troops, and the numbers rose in subsequent years. The highest tally came in the year ending in June 1863, after the draft had begun. That year, more than two thousand white men were listed as suffering from nostalgia; twelve succumbed to it. The year with the most fatalities was 1865, when twenty-four men died of the disease. Black soldiers serving in the Union army were also diagnosed with the condition, with an estimated 324 cases and sixteen deaths.[89] The Confederate army likewise tracked the disease, listing it as an official diagnostic category in its medical regulations.[90]

In addition to documenting cases of nostalgia, physicians during the Civil War wrote more extensively on the subject than ever before. Army doctors filled the pages of government reports and medical journals with discussions of the condition.[91] Additionally, a number of books dedicated to war medicine came out in the middle of the conflict and took up the subject. Volumes such as Joseph Woodward's *Outlines of the Chief Camp Diseases of the United States Armies*, Roberts Bartholow's *A Manual of Instructions for Enlisting and Discharging Soldiers With Special Reference to the Medical Examination of Recruits, and the Detection of Disqualifying and Feigned Diseases*, and John Ordronaux's *Manual of Instructions for Military Surgeons* all listed the symptoms of and described cures for nostalgia.[92]

Medical authorities agreed that nostalgia was a serious condition; what they could not agree on was precisely how to regard and treat it.[93] Some viewed nostalgics with great compassion. Assistant Surgeon Dewitt Peters sympathized with sufferers, noting that the disease could transform healthy young men into hollow shells of their former selves: "The fresh and youthful American volunteer leaves his home flushed with patriotism, and animated by new associations. . . . Stimulated by bright anticipations of the future, he may for a time resist the inroads of disease; but in a few months the novelty of long marches, guard duty, exposure, and innumerable hardships, has vanished, his mind begins to despond, and the youth is now a fair victim for fever or some other terrible scourge that is to wreck his constitution and blight his hopes." Peters suggested that camps be well run, food tasty, and life structured in order to ward off nostalgia.[94]

Other doctors assigned more blame to the sufferers themselves and described nostalgia as a failure of character. Dr. John Taylor of the 3rd Missouri Cavalry believed that those who suffered from it were frequently indolent hypochondriacs.[95] Theodore Calhoun suggested that nostalgics needed to be "render[ed] ... more manly." If necessary, commanders might subject homesick soldiers to "ridicule" in order to shame them out of their condition.[96] To Calhoun, nostalgia, though a common condition, undermined the ideal of the masculine warrior essential to the successful prosecution of the war.

While some observers painted nostalgia as the result of a general failure of will, others pointed to its presumed connection to other vices. John Taylor was the harshest on the topic. He treated his homesick men by pointing out the relationship between nostalgia and various moral pitfalls. He told sufferers that their "disease was a moral turpitude; that soldiers of courage, patriotism and sense should be superior to the influences that brought about their condition, and that to speak of home as inseparably connected with their recovery, and all that constituted happiness, was petty and degenerating." He told all the nurses who worked for him to regard nostalgics in this way, "and every opportunity was taken to inflame the feelings of their patients by impressing them with the idea that their disease was looked upon with contempt—that gonorrhœa and syphilis were not more detestable."[97]

The association of nostalgia with venereal disease was not accidental. Some doctors, such as Roberts Bartholow, believed that a strong libido and the tendency to masturbate predisposed soldiers to homesickness. He wrote, "In our army married men of middle life are more liable to it [nostalgia], particularly those given to solitary vice or the victims of spematorrhoea."[98] Soldiers who lived in a dream world, prone to fantasies, either about home, or sex, or both, became disconnected from their actual surroundings and wished for different circumstances. Other vices believed to be associated with nostalgia were drinking, gambling, and tobacco use.[99]

Some doctors believed that those who suffered possessed weak characters; others pointed to environmental factors. Many physicians claimed that rural young men were more likely to be dangerously homesick than urban soldiers. Country boys, with less exposure to crowds and stronger ties to home, felt the pain of leaving more than their cosmopolitan counterparts. One physician wrote, "The most liable to disease were those from the country, who had never been away from home, or left the quiet comforts of domestic life in the country. ... Those not accustomed to a perambulating life ... are more liable to disease, and the inference can scarcely be avoided, that this is due to the depressing effects of nostalgia upon the system."[100] Another concluded, "Men raised in towns and cities ... bore best the vicissitudes of the camp. They are more cosmopolitan in habit, thought, and feeling, and they were much less subject to home-sickness."[101]

Experts also claimed that homesickness had a regional dimension. Doctors frequently contended that men from New England were more attached to home than other soldiers. Perhaps this view sprang from the fact that many had migrated from New England to points west; those who had remained, therefore, seemed more attached and more homebound than men hailing from more recently settled regions. The *Medical and Surgical Reporter* suggested that troops from Vermont were in poorer health overall than other troops.[102] DeWitt Peters noted that the majority of men treated for nostalgia in a New Orleans hospital during the war were "from the Eastern states, whose love of home and kindred is a characteristic trait."[103]

Some maintained that African American soldiers were prone to the illness. Thomas Wentworth Higginson, who commanded the African American regiment of the 1st South Carolina Volunteers, noted that his men had started out "home-bound" but had gradually become less so over the course of the war.[104] Others thought a love of home was an innate trait of African Americans, and that it was and would always be harder for blacks to leave home. A *New York Times* reporter, commenting on former slaves who had run behind Union lines, wrote in 1863, "Perhaps the most marked trait in the negro character is his love of home and of the localities to which he is accustomed. They all pine for their homes." U.S. government records show a higher rate of nostalgia among black soldiers than white, but this may reflect white doctors' biases rather than a higher incidence of the condition.[105]

Still others pointed to the age of the soldier as determinative, although few could agree as to which age group was most vulnerable to the condition. Some suggested that youth might make one susceptible to homesickness, for the war might be the first occasion for leaving home. On the other hand, middle-aged married men, long used to the comforts of domestic life, also seemed to suffer greatly.[106]

If the precise causes of nostalgia were open to debate, so too were its cures. In many cases there was a division between those doctors serving in "general hospitals," away from the battlefield, and military doctors serving in field hospitals, in the midst of the conflagration. Those in the general hospitals were still connected to domestic life and civilian society; consequently they affirmed its values and considered homesickness to be almost noble. Those in the field, separated from civilian life, adopted a harsher set of policies, perhaps because they were daily exposed to brutal conditions and medical emergencies far more dire than nostalgia.[107]

John Taylor, a physician who served in the field and who had likened nostalgia to gonorrhea and syphilis, contended that there should be little sympathy and no mollycoddling for the homesick. He reported that in the first year of his regiment's operations, twenty-three soldiers had been profoundly homesick, five of whom suffered "some mental alienation." Some also suffered from maladies that ranged from palpitations to indigestion, which Taylor counted as signs of hypochondria. Most manifested a "stubborn indolence" and a lack of interest in the world. They claimed their symptoms would abate only if they were sent home. At first, Taylor and his staff tried a sympathetic approach, endeavoring to amuse the patients and offering them pleasant words, but this did not alter their condition, so Taylor concluded that sympathy was a worthless approach. He rejected a variety of other treatments as well. For instance, he believed that furloughs were counterproductive, for they spread the desire to return home throughout a regiment. Instead, he mandated vigorous physical exercise to distract the men, and treated homesickness as though it were a moral vice. The combined effects of this new regimen were at first "excited resentment—Passions were aroused, a new life was instilled and the patients rapidly recovered. Within two years not a single case of nostalgia has occurred, which may be attributed to the fact that idleness is unknown in the regiment, while the odium attached to the disease has played a part in causing the men to overcome the influences which tend to its production."[108]

Taylor was not alone in advocating a tough response to the condition. Theodore Calhoun maintained that *"battle is to be considered the great curative agent of nostalgia in the field,"* for after surviving the onslaught, men developed bonds with their fellow soldiers. Their thoughts gradually lingered less over memories of home, and more over the challenges they and their comrades faced. Should battle not help the afflicted, other techniques might. While Calhoun believed homesickness caused physical ailments, it was ultimately an "affection of the mind" and a sign of weakness. "Any influence that will tend to render the patient more manly, will exercise a curative power. . . . Ridicule . . . will often be found effective in camp. . . . The patient can often be laughed out of it by his comrades, or reasoned out of it by appeals to his manhood."[109] Taylor and Calhoun wanted to inculcate an ethic of courageous self-control among soldiers, believing they should conquer the sentimentality that made them weak and effeminate and that interfered with war aims.

More influential during the war were those physicians and nurses who took a sympathetic approach to the problem of homesickness. Some soldiers who were suffering acutely from it received much compassion from the medical authorities who tended them, particularly if they were treated away from their units. Doctors sometimes suggested hospitalization. Thomas Wentworth Higginson described a "convalescent camp" in Saint Augustine, Florida, "whither they send homesick officers to cure them by contraries—getting them farther from home." More serious cases might require sending the patient home if a fatal outcome was to be avoided. A medical manual suggested that in the early stages, "a furlough . . . will often suffice to restore the moral vigor of the young soldier. But when it has long resisted treatment, and gone so far as to produce sensible external lesions . . . or structural changes in large organs, a discharge must unquestionably, be granted."[110]

Physicians were not the only caregivers to weigh in on the debate over how to treat the homesick.[111] Nurses did as well, and they almost uniformly suggested a softer and more sympathetic response. During the Civil War, American women from north and south volunteered to treat the wounded. More than three thousand women served as paid nurses for Union troops, organized under the auspices of a variety of agencies and associations. Most notable was the U.S. Sanitary Commission, created in 1861.[112] This organization, as well as a variety of other groups, put women eager to serve the war effort in the role of caregivers. This was a controversial policy, given long-standing fears of women treating and touching the bodies of men unrelated to them. Indeed, up to this point, nursing had been a somewhat disreputable occupation in the United States. To avoid allegations of impropriety, Dorothea Dix, the superintendent of nursing during the war, tried to recruit middle-aged women of plain looks, sensible dress, and respectable background.[113] While outside observers worried about the effects of this unorthodox mingling of the sexes, nurses and patients had fewer qualms, and quickly came to envision the relationship between wounded soldier and nurse as a domestic one.

When nurses encountered homesick men, they offered nurturing care rather than shame or criticism. Louisa May Alcott, who worked briefly in a hospital during the war, reported in a fictionalized account of her experiences that the mere presence of women on a hospital ward could have curative effects: "I had forgotten that the strong man might long for the gentle tendance of a woman's hands, the sympathetic magnetism of a woman's presence." She realized that her patients, some of them mortally wounded, appreciated "those little cares and kindnesses that solace homesick spirits, and make the heavy hours pass easier." She and many other nurses became like mothers and sisters to their charges.[114] Another Civil War nurse, Mary Livermore, visited wounded soldiers who were being cared for in ramshackle hospitals in Cairo, Illinois. She believed the men in those facilities suffered greatly because the buildings were filled with "filth and discomfort, neglect and suffering." They had a "fetid odor of typhoid fever, . . . measles, and healing wounds." Adding to the stench was the scent of "unwashed bodies" and "boiling meat and coffee." Men who were patients in such hospitals welcomed the presence of women, who not only provided nurturing care, but also cleaned up the place. Livermore said of her patients, "They were very young, homesick, and ready to break down into a flood of weeping at the first word of sympathy." The worst off were those who were very ill, "for under the wasting of camp diseases they became mentally as weak as children." She told of one young soldier haunted by memories of home as he lay stricken with "the delirium of brain fever. He fancied himself at home with his mother" and repeatedly called out to her.[115]

Without hesitation, nurses took on the role of mother for these ill and dying soldiers who so clearly longed for their own, and soldiers themselves readily assented to such surrogate relationships, often calling nurses "mother" or "sister."[116] The poet Walt Whitman, who worked in a hospital during the war, suggested that because they sparked memories of home, women were the most appropriate people to care for the wounded: "For nurses, middle-aged women and mothers of families are best," for they were "full of motherly feeling" and brought to their patients "reminiscences of home" and tender caresses.[117] Nurses and their patients did not see these domestic touches as antithetical to the martial effort. They envisioned the wounded as their own sons, fathers, and brothers, and they worked to create a domestic environment for them in the hospitals. If they could not immediately bring the men home, they could at least bring a bit of home to them. These reminders of domesticity would have alarmed the far stricter field doctors, but they proved popular with the soldiers themselves and were consistent with the ways that most Americans thought about the war.

BACK AT HOME?

Throughout the conflict, during marches, at camp, on the battlefield, and in the hospital, men longed for home. This longing may have been a useful psychological tool. Wartime experiences were so sharply different from peacetime existence that for soldiers to feel some continuity with their old, prewar selves, they needed a touchstone, a reference point, a stable source of identity, and they found it in their visions of home. As William Vardell confided to his wife, he did not want the war to make him "feel satisfied away from home, I always hope to love my home & desire to be there above all places, & therefore I never fly the feeling."[118] If he did grow satisfied away from home, he would have become a different man. By clinging to thoughts of home, by imagining it as unchanging, and by continually expressing their longings for it, soldiers could maintain a coherent identity in circumstances unlike any they had known before. They could also maintain a sense of integrity and reaffirm their fundamental values. Asked to fight and kill, soldiers could maintain a sense of their "true" selves by asserting an affection and affiliation for home life, the central symbol of morality in nineteenth-century culture.[119]

Yet despite such psychological tactics, even if their love of home held steady, their sense of self often did not. While they wanted to be reunited with their families, they felt increasingly alienated from all they had left behind. Union and Confederate soldiers had witnessed death and carnage, horror and trauma, and could not adequately convey all they had seen to their families. Nor did they want to. On the one hand, they wanted their nearest and dearest to understand what they had gone through; on the other hand, they did not want their loved ones to be damaged by the traumatic events they themselves had witnessed.[120] Union soldiers probably felt this sense of separation much more than Confederates, for in the South, civilians had been subjected to hardship and grim scenes of carnage.[121]

As a result, to truly return home proved difficult for both northern and southern soldiers at the end of the war. Many found home was not as they recalled it, not quite what they had imagined. It had changed, and they had too.[122] In the years after the war, many concluded that although they had

"Home Again" (1866), a lithograph by Dominique Fabronius of a painting by Trevor McClurg, depicts the widely shared hopes for homecoming after the Civil War. Even if they returned to their houses and families, however, it was not always easy or even possible for soldiers to return to their former lives.
Source: Courtesy of the Library of Congress.

returned home, they had never made it all the way back to what they had left behind. The chasm created by the Civil War was uncrossable. It was not just the distance from the battlefield to the front porch that separated soldiers from home; it was the experience, the knowledge of death, suffering, misery, and reality, that might forever keep them from going back to what they had been and believed before the war.[123]

Throughout the conflict, Americans had taken homesickness and nostalgia quite seriously, believing that the mass exodus of young men from their homes was a traumatic event for the nation and for the men themselves. Few realized, however, just how far the men would go from home, not just physically, but mentally. After the war was over, many men found a cure for the festering homesickness they had felt over the course of the conflict, for they went home to the places they had left. Yet some longed to return to a lost time as well, and found that that was a far more difficult journey to make.

CHAPTER 4

ᴄᴠᴏ

Breaking Home Ties

At the end of the Civil War, it was not just soldiers who felt displaced by their experiences. Civilians too had made journeys, both mental and geographical, between an old world and a new. Some found their new conditions liberating; others found them foreign and difficult to embrace. Many individuals in late nineteenth- and early twentieth-century America found ample cause for homesickness in the midst of a new social order that seemed to celebrate a new kind of self.[1] They also found new encouragement to master their homesickness so that they might better adapt to the modern society emerging around them.

From their abandonment of premodern forms of forced labor to their embrace of urbanization, industrialization, and international expansion, Americans were leaving behind not just their old homes but their old ways. Homesickness was pervasive, and during this period, Americans often used the word *nostalgia*, popularized during the Civil War and still used as a synonym for homesickness, to describe their feelings.[2] Most continued to believe that homesickness and nostalgia were troubling conditions, but they began to offer new assessments about why the feelings occurred and how they should be handled. Many came to see leaving home as necessary for progress, both for individuals and for society as a whole. Not all Americans were perceived as mentally and emotionally equipped to leave home, however, and the ability to conquer homesickness came to be seen as a sign of one's adaptability, fitness, and modernity.

At the same time, Americans began to express not just a longing for a home left behind—the characteristic yearning of the homesick—but a longing for a home lost in time. In the twentieth century, that longing gradually became known as nostalgia, but when nineteenth-century Americans used the word *nostalgia* they still meant homesickness.[3] Yet they often felt this other mood, this yearning for the past. Homesickness sometimes became subsumed under this new longing, as many wondered if the homes they had left behind even existed anymore. Perhaps home had become lost in time as well as space.

AFTERMATH

The Civil War disrupted civilians' lives as well as soldiers.' In the South, whites were uprooted by the armies' advances and retreats. African Americans, who welcomed the end of slavery, often found their world transformed and their sense of home changed. Whites and blacks lived through the same conflict, but found it had very different implications for their lives, their futures, and their sense of place.

In the summer of 1861, Mrs. S. H. Reed confided to a friend that she had been forced to leave her home in Charleston and settle in Orangeburg, South Carolina: "You cant imagine how dreadful it is to have to leave your home not knowing but the next news we hear will be that it is in the possession of our heartless enemy.... [We were] compelled to leave our home and some of our loved ones in danger and the graves of those we loved dearer than life itself. It makes me feel sad. I felt this morning that if I could only get to Charleston and go to my Dear Husband's grave and weep there it would be such a relief to my burdened heart."[4]

Sometimes such dislocations caused clinical cases of homesickness. Looking back on the war years, Dr. W. T. Taylor of Kentucky recalled a difficult case of nostalgia he had observed while the battles raged. He told of the sad case of a sixty-five-year-old supporter of the Union who had been forced to flee his native Tennessee. He moved to Kentucky with his family, his slaves, and enough money to set himself up fairly comfortably. Despite this, Taylor reported, "after the family settled, the old man became despondent, silent, and preoccupied." His family's attempts to cheer him failed, and his wife called on Dr. Taylor for help. Taylor recorded his initial impressions: "He was pining for his home.... If he could see his native mountains over which he roamed when a boy, and out of sight of which he had never been until the armies in their destructive marches, back and forth, laid waste the country, he would be happy. But he knew this could never be. 'He was heart-broken; he knew he would die; did not want to live.'" Taylor concluded that although there was nothing physically wrong with the man, he was afflicted with nostalgia: "I called on him twice a day, and by every means in my power strove to divert his mind from the fatal despondency which held him in its grasp, but without avail. He continued growing weaker day after day—reiterating the assertion that he was 'heart-broken,' that 'nothing else was the matter with him.' Toward the last, hectic symptoms set up, after which he declined more rapidly. He retained his consciousness, however, up to the last, talking about and pining for his home."[5]

Even those who could return home after the war often found that their homes were no longer there. When Mary Boykin Chesnut returned to her devastated house after the war, she wrote to a friend, "There are nights here with the moonlight cold and ghastly & the whippoorwills, & the screech owls alone disturbing the silence when I could tear my hair & cry aloud for all that is past & gone." Another white southerner, Sara A. Pryor of Virginia, wrote, "All the cords binding us to the past were severed, beyond the hope of reunion. We sat silently looking out on a landscape marked here and there by chimneys standing sentinel over blackened heaps, where our neighbors had made happy homes."[6] Assessing the toll of the Civil War on his family home, Charles Jones Jr. wrote in 1882, "The entire region is changed. It is peopled only with phantoms of things that were, and present images are a mockery of the blessed idols here enshrined."[7] Pervasive in white southerners' accounts of life in the aftermath of the Civil War was a sense of loss and longing. As they watched their former slaves leave them, as they witnessed social conventions change and racial relations transformed, whites felt their universe had shifted.[8] After the emancipation of her slaves, another white southerner, Grace Elmore, lamented "this breaking up of old ties, the giving up of those with whom your life has been spent, and making a new and wholly unknown start."[9] These white southerners' sense of displacement was sometimes homesickness and was sometimes that newer emotion, which we today call nostalgia, for they longed for a lost era as much as a lost place.

Newly liberated slaves felt the world had changed as well, although for them this was a joyful rather than a melancholy event. During the war, thousands of slaves left plantations to win their freedom and ran behind Union lines for protection. Initially, many were housed in contraband camps. Although free of their masters, they often missed those they had left behind. In 1863, the *New York Times* described the emotional problems of escaped slaves working on government-run plantations, far from family and friends:

> Scarcely any of the negroes on the plantations hereabouts were raised in this immediate part of the country. . . . Perhaps the most marked trait in the negro character is his love of home and of the localities to which he is accustomed. They all pine for their homes. They long for the old quarters they have lived in; for the old woods they have roamed in, and the old field they have tilled. The surgeons in charge of contraband camps tell me that a great many of them actually die from home-sickness . . . in scientific language, nostalgia. They get thinking of their old homes and if they have left their families or any part of

them behind, they long to see them, and so they become depressed in spirits and yield readily to the first attack of disease, or succumb to the depression alone.

Given how profoundly their lives, circumstances, and locales had changed, the reporter wrote, "it is inevitable that there should be a great deal of discontent and complaint among the negroes. They are in a strange place among strangers. They are unsettled, and know not where they may be the next year."[10] Indeed, while they had gained freedom, their new world was filled with great uncertainty.

Roughly 4 million slaves were emancipated, many of whom faced the problem of deciding where to go and defining where home was. Sometimes the comfort of the familiar and the opportunities of freedom seemed to be at odds with one another. Some went off in search of family from whom they had been separated by sale. For these men and women, home was tied more to people than to place. Others moved away from their masters' plantations. One black minister advised in 1865:

> You ain't, none o' you, gwinter feel rale free till you shakes de dus' ob de Ole Plantashun offen yore feet an' goes ter a new place whey you kin live out o' sight o' de gret house.... You mus' all move move—you mus' move clar away from de ole places what you known, ter de new places what you don't know, whey you kin raise up yore head douten no fear o' Marse Dis ur Marse Tudder. Take yore freedom, my brudders an' my sisters. . . . Go whey you please—do what you please—furgit erbout de white folks—an' now stan' up on yore feet.

Thousands of blacks believed this and left the plantations.[11]

Many left the spots they had occupied when emancipation came, but few struck out toward totally alien destinations. Often freed slaves tried to return to scenes from earlier in their lives. Even when they had good prospects elsewhere, they frequently chose to stay near or return to the vicinity of their old plantation, because they wanted to be in a familiar place, filled with old friends and neighbors. One man decided to "put out for de place where he fust belong," the plantation he had lived on until he was sold. In Mississippi, the freed slave Jane Sutton walked back to her former plantation after emancipation, explaining, "I wanted to see Old Mis' an' my Mammy an' my brothers an' sisters."[12]

African Americans also felt connected to the land itself. A white officer in the Freedmen's Bureau, working in South Carolina, noted that the emancipated slaves he met "were crazy to get back to their native flats of ague and country fever." Former slaves on Edisto Island, when petitioning the federal government to allow them to occupy the land owned by their former masters, wrote, "This is our home. We have made these lands what they are."

One historian observed that when emancipated bondsmen and women sought land to farm for themselves, they "did not want just any land; they wanted land that was familiar to them, plantation land with which they had developed a personal bond."[13] As a result, the majority of freed slaves stayed in the counties or states where they had been living prior to emancipation.[14]

In the years after the war, however, many African Americans had to confront the fact that racism and inequality had not died alongside slavery, and they came to believe that their home was not in their former neighborhoods or states or even in America at all. This realization sent them in search of new homes. Although never large in numbers, some African Americans hoped that a true home could be found in Liberia. The American Colonization Society, founded in 1817, had established that colony as refuge to which freed slaves might return. In the years before the Civil War, the Society had relocated a relatively small number of people; it continued promoting migration after the war and piqued the interest of African Americans who were coming to grips with the limited nature of their freedom. In 1877, a former slave, Henry Adams, informed the Colonization Society that he had a list of more than sixty thousand people from across the South who wanted to leave that "horrible part of the country." Although many hoped to leave for Africa, few could afford to, and the American Colonization Society was itself chronically short of funds. In all, between the Civil War and the start of the twentieth century, only 2,500 African Americans emigrated to Africa. Among them were residents of Charleston, who launched one of the most successful expeditions to Liberia.[15] In 1878, 252 African Americans set sail from Charleston. A white reporter accompanying the immigrants noted that, at least at first, those aboard felt no homesickness, only jubilation, for South Carolina had not been a good home for them. When they were some ninety miles from Charleston and "all traces of land had faded from sight," the reporter "felt some curiosity to see how the sentimental, or love of home, would display itself. Careful observation, however, failed to discover an indication of either of those feelings. When the strip of mist, representing the land of these people's birth and bringing up, which contained all the memories, sweet and bitter, of their past lives, and on which their friends and kind yet remained, was fading from their sight forever, there was no development of any feeling other than a slight interest in the distance from them at which it could be seen!"[16]

Despite their high hopes for their new home, life in Liberia was not as easy as many expected. Newcomers were shocked by the harsh conditions they found there and disappointed by the lack of support that the American Colonization Society offered them as they tried to settle in.[17] A significant number of colonists decided to return, though this represented more of a rejection of African conditions than a fondness for life in the segregated

South. Rufus Clark found he could not make a living in Liberia and promised a correspondent, "If you will aid and assist me to get away from this country I would be willing to bind myself and family to work for you on your place. . . . We will all work for you if you will only put me in a place where I can make corn and cotton and rice. I thought that I could live in this country, but I find that no man can live in this country. Please make arrangements . . . to bring me home again."[18] In 1879, newspapers carried accounts of three other colonists who returned to Milledgeville, Georgia, and reportedly "expressed much satisfaction at being so near home once more."[19]

Throughout the late nineteenth century, blacks continued their search for a welcoming home. Some moved to southern cities; between 1860 and 1870, Mobile, Montgomery, Selma, and Huntsville, Alabama, saw their black populations increase by 57 percent. Between 1880 and 1890, Savannah's and Nashville's black populations increased twofold, and Atlanta's and Memphis's grew even faster.[20] While many longed for the places and family they left behind as they resettled in cities, they were eager to escape the sharecropping system that dominated the agricultural South.

An estimated fifty thousand freed slaves moved west between 1878 and 1881.[21] In the late 1870s, a group of African Americans from Mississippi, Louisiana, Texas, and Tennessee, dubbed the Exodusters, set out for Kansas to escape the oppressions of the Deep South. In 1881, a reporter observed, "Homesickness afflicts them not a little." The Exodusters were "homesick for clean brooks running over clean pebbles . . . and for the round domes of the hill's that they left behind them." Nevertheless, they found it necessary to move from such landscapes in order to "better their condition." Few returned to the South, enjoying the greater freedom of Kansas.[22] Any homesickness they felt was offset by the far greater sense of liberty they had on the plains.

A significant number moved north as their civil liberties in the South dwindled. In the 1870s, an estimated 68,000 moved north; by the 1890s, the human stream had increased to 185,000.[23] Many migrated north because they had no choice; they would have liked to stay near their families but their lives and livelihoods were in danger. Ida B. Wells, forced out of her Memphis home in 1892 because of her antilynching writings, called herself a "homesick exile." Staying in New York City for a time, Wells still thought of Memphis: "A feeling of loneliness and homesickness for the days and the friends that were gone came over me and I felt the tears coming."[24]

Unable to gain equal footing in the southern economy, members of the rising black middle class also found it necessary to leave the South. In 1904, the attorney Julius Mitchell explained, "Things have become so very dull in my native state and the prejudice against us so great that it is almost impossible for the professional Negro to amount to much. . . . I had 43 offers to leave the state and better my condition. Accordingly, I left home on the 18th ult. to visit New England and the West and look at some of the places to which I have been invited to go with a view to accept the best that was offered me."[25] Another migrant to the North was Edward Harleston. Born in Charleston in 1869 and educated at Claflin University, Harleston faced prejudice in South Carolina and eventually left. He expressed his attitude about rising in the world in a poem, where he advised his readers, "Look not backward."

> Look not backward into the past;
> They're drones who linger to complain.
> Move on and manfully meet the task;
> Look forward, success thou wilt obtain.

Harleston settled in New Jersey, where he became the mechanical superintendent and custodian of Heinz Ocean Pier in Atlantic City. He still thought of home, however, titling one of his verses "Home, Sweet, Home" and describing in it his longing for "my own, 'sweet home.'" He filled other poems with his memories of Charleston.[26]

Home for African Americans in the post–Civil War South, then, was sometimes a difficult thing to define. Most felt that home was where they had been born, despite the fact that they had to endure great oppression there. Given that in 1910, 90 percent of the black population still lived in the South, and 75 percent in the rural South, and that most black southerners continued to live in the states in which they had been born, it seems clear that the idea of home, the dream of return to kin and familiar places, exerted a powerful, almost magnetic pull.[27] After Reconstruction ended, however, many found it difficult to make a home in an inhospitable society and kept looking for some other place, be it Kansas, New York, or Liberia, that offered greater freedom and opportunities to rise in the world. African Americans' feelings toward home were ambivalent, to say the least.

Southern whites had a vested interest in where blacks decided to locate, for they could preserve a hierarchical social order and labor market if blacks remained in the South. Accordingly, many discouraged African Americans from migrating, some using force, some withholding wages. Southern states passed laws punishing those who encouraged black migration and black workers themselves if they left before their labor contracts expired.[28]

These political barriers to opportunity were buttressed by rhetoric claiming that African Americans were unsuited to migration because of their unusually strong ties to home, family, and the rural southern way of life.[29] Even a Freedmen's Bureau official organizing Reconstruction efforts in Mississippi noted, "This love for home will be of great service to us in reorganizing this Country under the new order of things."[30] Other observers suggested that blacks would always want to stay in the South because of their great vulnerability to homesickness. In 1890, a *Chicago Herald* article claimed, "There is not a race of men on the face of the earth that has such strong attachments for place and people as the negro race. The pangs of nostalgia have no such stamping ground in the universe as the negro heart." The author admitted that whites were similarly tied to home, yet suggested that their nostalgia was counteracted by their "ambition to acquire wealth," as well as by "energy and intelligence.... The negro, on the other hand, has a stronger love for place and people, without any business ambition or hope and without any energy or intelligence with which to overcome his nostalgia." Consequently, African Americans would never succeed at leaving the South, much less the United States, for if they did they would "all die of homesickness."[31]

Even some African Americans embraced the idea that their population was emotionally tied to the region and to agricultural life, and therefore they should not uproot themselves. Shortly after the war's end, Frederick Douglass warned emancipated slaves in Maryland that they should not flock to Baltimore, for the city held perils and problems. If they did set out for the city, "sad, indeed, will be their fate! They must stick to the country and work."[32] In a speech at Carnegie Hall in 1912, Booker T. Washington claimed that African Americans should not move away from their rural roots: "In the rural districts, the Negro, all things considered, is at his best in body, mind and soul. In the city he is usually at this worst."[33] He also suggested that blacks were poorly suited for the work, living conditions, and competition they would face in the North.[34] They should stay in the South because they would become homesick if they left; they should also remain on farms to avoid the corrupting urban influences that might ruin their characters. True safety and moral purity could be maintained only in rural districts.

The idea that African Americans were rural people, tied to the soil and to their homes, reflected the white view that they were not yet ready for the modern life emerging in American cities. While white men were encouraged to leave home in search of opportunity during the late nineteenth century and early twentieth, blacks were not. The presumption that they would be too homesick was also a presumption that they were premodern. In dwelling upon the alleged homesickness of African Americans, many commentators revealed the prejudice that only whites possessed the ability to cut ties, the propensity to be ambitious and competitive capitalists, and the strength and discipline to avoid moral peril.

This was an ironic twist, for in the antebellum years, southern whites had vociferously denied that African Americans experienced pain or homesickness when they were sold and forced to leave home and family behind. This willful blindness to the feelings of slaves enabled masters to conduct the economic transactions that tore families apart. In the years after the Civil War, however, in an effort to maintain an economic order that depended on a stable labor force, southern whites claimed that blacks experienced a surfeit of homesickness and a deficit of ambition. In reality, it was often whites who wanted to remain lodged in the ways of the past and blacks who wanted to move on, but discussions of emotions were more than idle explorations of social psychology—they were a way of defining and justifying power relations in the racially divided South.

INDIAN WARS

The connection between emotions and power was also illustrated in the relations between whites and Indians in the late nineteenth century. Whites interested in the Indian question (and also interested in Indian territories) recognized that Indians were tied to their land—too tied, they believed. Nevertheless, they hoped Native Americans would master their homesickness and move into the modern world. Supposedly this would benefit the tribes themselves, but even more obviously it would benefit land-hungry white settlers. While southern whites hoped to keep their fields filled with homebound black laborers, those contemplating Indian territories hoped to dissolve Indians' strong connections to the land.

The Indians, however, resisted giving up their land or severing their emotional, social, and economic bonds to it. As a result, by the end of the nineteenth century, Native American tribes and U.S. Army soldiers had fought each other in an estimated 1,065 engagements.[35] Repeatedly pushed from their homelands, Indians had been promised a permanent safe haven beyond the Mississippi in "Indian Territory," a territory that continued to shrink as white settlers moved west. Battles ranged from Texas to Washington, from Minnesota to California throughout the late nineteenth century, resulting in the forced relocation of tribes onto reservations. In 1870, the U.S. census estimated that 383,000 Native Americans lived in the United States, 234,740 of whom "freely roamed" in areas of the American West. The majority could be found in Alaska, Arizona, Nevada, Montana, Oklahoma, and the Dakota Territories. By the end of the century, with the exception of the Alaskan tribes, America's 267,000 Indians lived on reservations, many of them in Oklahoma.[36]

Col. Richard Irving Dodge of the U.S. Army had witnessed the relocations of many of these tribes. In his book, *Our Wild Indians: Thirty Three
Years Personal Experience among the Red Men of the Great West*, published in
1883, he noted that although whites generally considered Native Americans to be nomadic, they actually felt deeply connected to the land on
which they lived: "Their attachment to it is one of the strongest traits of
their character. No people are more truly 'lovers of their country,' no people
suffer more from 'homesickness,' when forced to leave it." He suggested that
nostalgia was killing off large numbers of Indians: "Like most people who
live much in the fresh air, the Indians are a healthy race, but their condition
of health seems to be in a great degree dependent on their remaining in the
country to which they are accustomed." Once tribes were moved onto reservations, their populations declined steeply. Dodge maintained that this
was not the result of an unhealthy environment on the reservation: "Homesickness is the foundation of this ill effect, and . . . the extraordinary and
unnatural diminution in the numbers of certain tribes is due to nostalgia
more than any other cause." Nearly every year a tribe was compelled to
leave its ancestral lands. "Those old enough to appreciate the misfortune,
disheartened, despairing, in no mood to maintain the struggle for existence,
are ready to fall, almost willing victims, to the first malady that assails them.
The young grow up, and learn to love the country of their adoption, only in
time to be themselves removed, and go through with the wretched experience of their fathers."

Dodge made an appeal to his readers and to the government, noting that
by removing Indians, particularly peaceful tribes, from their lands, the
United States was creating unnecessary problems for itself and for the
Indians. Much of the discontent that Indians manifested on reservations
grew out of simple homesickness. When faced with relocation, some
became "despairing and desperate" and more militaristic toward the U.S.
government. Dodge concluded his discussion of nostalgia with a plea: "It is
time that the government began to understand that homesickness with
Indians is a disease, a most dangerous malady, resulting in death to them, in
loss of life and money to us."[37]

Dodge was right: the homesickness of Indians on reservations caused
problems within tribes as well as with the federal government. Many of the
tribes he mentioned had made similar pleas to the government, asking to
remain on their lands. Some tried to resist relocation, but this generally was
a losing battle. Countless examples abound. In 1863, the U.S. government
forced the Navajos to vacate their lands and move on to the Bosque
Redondo reservation, which was situated on poor land and offered residents little wood, few provisions, overcrowded conditions, and widespread
disease. To get to Bosque Redondo, the Navajos traveled three hundred

miles from their traditional territories on foot, in what came to be known as "the Long Walk." General Carleton of the U.S. Army, who oversaw this migration, wrote, "The exodus of this whole people from the land of their fathers is not only an interesting but a touching sight." He believed that the Navajos had "sacrificed to us their beautiful country, their homes, the associations of their lives," but that such a sacrifice was necessary for progress. If Carleton saw the Indians' losses as necessary, the Navajos disagreed. Manuelito, a tribal leader, noted, "My God and my mother live in the West, and I will not leave them. It is a tradition of my people that we must never cross the three rivers—the Grande, the San Juan, the Colorado. Nor could I leave the Chuska Mountains. I was born there. I shall remain. I have nothing to lose but my life. . . . I will not move." Eventually Manuelito surrendered to the U.S. Army, but in 1868, the federal government made a rare reversal and allowed the Navajos to leave Bosque Redondo and return to their own lands. Manuelito wrote of the tribe's reactions, "The day before we were to start we went a little way towards home, because we were so anxious to start. . . . We told the drivers to whip the mules, we were in such a hurry. When we saw the top of the mountain from Albuquerque we wondered if it was our mountain, and we felt like talking to the ground, we loved it so, and some of the old men and women cried with joy when they reached their homes."[38]

Like the Navajos, other tribes displaced from their ancestral lands missed them acutely, but most had to spend their lives away from them. After the brutal Sand Creek Massacre in Colorado in 1864, in which U.S. troops attacked Arapaho and Cheyenne Indians, the tribes were forced to give up their claims to land in Colorado. The Arapaho chief Little Raven said, "It will be a very hard thing to leave the country that God gave us. . . . Our friends are buried there, and we hate to leave these grounds." Yet they had no choice, and with members of the Southern Cheyenne, the Arapaho were forced on to a reservation in Indian Territory.[39] In 1876, the U.S. Congress listed the Poncas as a tribe that should be relocated from their land in Nebraska to Indian Territory. When tribal leaders were taken to Oklahoma to inspect their designated homeland, they did not like what they saw. One told a government official, "It makes my heart feel sad . . . as I do not know this land." The New York Times reported, "The strip of country they had seen along the route traversed was unprepossessing, and the Poncas became homesick, and asked to be taken back to their homes. Eight of the delegation . . . started back to their homes in Dakota afoot."[40] The Nez Percé likewise faced removal and lobbied aggressively to preserve their homeland. In 1877, the government sent military forces to clear the tribe off their lands, with the hopes of settling them on the Lapwai Reservation in Idaho. Chief Joseph and his tribe fled the army, but eventually surrendered. The Nez

Percé were sent to Oklahoma. After many years and much pleading, a portion of the group was able to return to the Nez Percé reservation in Lapwai, which was not home, but was closer to it. Chief Joseph, however, was barred from returning and was sent instead to a reservation in Washington, where he died in 1904. His death was attributed to a broken heart, a diagnosis that became common on Indian reservations.[41]

While earlier generations of whites had viewed Indians as too nomadic, the prevailing view in the late nineteenth century was that they were too tied to particular plots of land and to each other. Loyalty to the tribe, to tribal traditions, and to old homes had no place in a modernizing nation. Over the course of the nineteenth century, as the reservation system expanded, the U.S. government attempted to sever these bonds to the land and make Native Americans modern. To do this, they tried to forcibly assimilate Indian children into American society and teach them about American values at government schools. John Oberly, the superintendent of Indian schools, explained in 1888 that the goal was to teach the Indian to dispense with the communitarian values of the tribe and to embrace instead "the exalting egoism of American civilization, so that he will say 'I' instead of 'We,' and 'This is mine,' instead of 'This is ours.'"[42] The Indian child was to be taught the ethic of rugged individualism, including the ability to separate oneself from the group, leave home, and pursue individual advancement.

To accomplish this, the government built schools. By 1877, there were 150 Indian schools that enrolled more than three thousand students; by 1900, there were 307, educating more than twenty-one thousand.[43] There were three types of schools. Day schools, which were located near Indian settlements, were often considered ineffectual because the students were never far enough away from their parents or tribal influences to learn white ways. Reservation boarding schools were perceived as weak for similar reasons. Educational experts believed that off-reservation boarding schools, situated far away from tribal influences, were the best places to educate Indian youth.[44]

Tribal leaders and Indian agency policy often forced children to go to these schools against their will.[45] Consequently, students at both the reservation schools and the more distant off-reservation schools experienced intense homesickness as they faced involuntary migration and a dramatic rupture between their past life and present circumstances. Irene Stewart, a Navajo born in 1907, was placed at the Fort Defiance Boarding School when she was about six years old: "This sudden change in my life was a shocking experience. . . . I feared everything, especially the people and the strange facilities." In the dormitory, she recalled, "there was always someone crying, mostly because of homesickness." After graduating from Fort Defiance, Stewart attended the Haskell Institute in Kansas. She had trouble

A sketch from the Carlisle Indian School depicting the difficult adjustment many Native American students had to make.
Source: Image courtesy of the Yale Collection of Western Americana, Beinecke Rare Book and Manuscript Library.

settling into the new dormitory: "I sat there without even unpacking my suitcase.... Then the other girl and I broke down and cried.... The loneliness stayed with me for almost two years."[46]

The founder of the Carlisle School in Pennsylvania, Lt. Richard Henry Pratt of the U.S. Army, encountered a great deal of homesickness among his students, although he tried to turn a blind eye to its existence. The first question a *New York Sun* reporter asked Pratt in an interview was, "How do you overcome home-sickness?" Pratt replied, "By occupation, entertainment and attention to the individual. There are very few cases of homesickness, and they are seldom of long duration or of any seriousness." When the first students came to the school, Pratt made efforts to keep them occupied, encouraging them "to dance and sing their Indian songs ... [we] did not prevent it because we had nothing to give them in exchange then.... They brought their tom-toms from the west with them, and I allowed them to have them. In the evenings they would sit around and pound them and sing, and you could have heard them in town.... I said to myself that it was not fair to take these things away until something could be given them in their place." Eventually, the tom-toms were replaced with brass instruments. Yet apparently the amusement Pratt had devised did not keep the students adequately distracted, for as the *Sun* reporter noted, few students actually stayed at Carlisle long enough to graduate from the school. Pratt explained the cause: "Simply because of the pulling back influence of the reservation.

The sentiment, not more Indian, however than white, that exists there for holding them together and is not willing to let any escape."[47]

Children at the Carlisle school surely felt the pull of the reservation. In letters reprinted in the school newspaper, they described their longings for home. In 1880, the paper reprinted the letter of Joseph Vetter, who wistfully contrasted his life at home with his life at school: "I am trying hard to learn my shoemaker trade and I think it is a very nice trade and when I was home I always hunted ducks and squirrels. . . . When I first came here I was very lonesome. . . . We always had nice times down home."[48] In 1882, a letter from Harry Shirley showed his distress at being separated from home and family: "My Dear Father . . . we got at Carlie on Thursday and when we got here I did not like the place but sence I have been here two or three days I have got used to the place and I like it very well but when we got [here] I felt very homesick." Not yet ready to completely shed his past, he told his father, "Be shure and send my bow and some spike arrows."[49]

A significant number of those who were homesick tried to run away from school. Historians have documented that the runaway problem was extensive, but few school administrators wanted to admit the dimensions of the problem.[50] Students too scared to run away sometimes resorted to more desperate measures. In 1898, the *New York Times* reported on events at Carlisle: "Elizabeth Flanders and Fannie Eaglehorn, Indian girls, who tried to burn the girls' building at the Indian school here, to-day pleaded guilty, and were sentenced to one year and six months imprisonment. They said they were homesick, and wanted Capt. Pratt to send them home."[51]

Instead of running away, some conquered their homesickness by telling themselves that eventually they would be able to return home and, armed with the knowledge they had gained at school, help the folks back home. In a letter reprinted in the *School News*, Moses Nonway wrote to his mother:

My Dear Mother:—I thank you very much for the picture . . . of yourself and my little sister. Oh, I was so glad when I saw your faces looking at me out of the picture I kissed it over and over, and then showed it to all my friends, they like it very much. I am very glad that you are all very well as you tell me, but it makes me very sad when I think how poor my people are, this is one very good place, and I will try to learn all that I can while I stop here, for I know that it is for my own good that I should try all I can to learn, that I may be able to teach my people how to do and how to live to be good people.[52]

Roman Nose had similar plans: "When I get through school and work then I will return to my old home in Indian Territory. When I get there I think maybe I will help all my Indian people and teach them about the good way of the white man road and to love God."[53]

A magazine published by the Carlisle Indian School shows the path students should follow. While they might nostalgically recall what they had left behind, they should move away from their tribes and traditions and embrace white ways. "Memories." Cover Illustration, The *Carlisle Arrow and Red Man*, Outing Number (7 June 1918).

Source: Image courtesy of the Yale Collection of Western Americana, Beinecke Rare Book and Manuscript Library.

Carlisle officials advised students returning home to retain the new, modern identities the boarding school had bequeathed them and not revert to old ways: "Remember if you go back home and forget all you had learned, and go back to your old Indian ways, everybody will point their finger at you and say: 'That's the boy that went to school among white people and got his education. But now there he is, in his Indian ways.'"[54] Female students were supposed to return to their families and teach them how to make American homes, modeled after white styles of domesticity. They should resist the temptation to follow the traditions of their parents. In a story published in 1892, supposedly based on the experiences of several children who had returned from the Carlisle school to their families, Stiya, a young girl, was overjoyed to be able to return home after five years. But her return was not what she expected. The sight of her parents was a shock.

> "*My* father? *My* mother?" cried I desperately within. "No,
>   never!" I thought, and I actually turned my back upon them.
> I had forgotten that home Indians had such grimy faces.
> I had forgotten that my mother's hair always looked as
>   though it had never seen a comb.
> I had forgotten that she wore such a short, queer-looking
>   black bag for a dress, fastened over one shoulder only, and
>   such buckskin wrappings for shoes and leggings.
> "My mother?" I cried, this time aloud.

Instead of hugging her mother, she hugged the school matron who had chaperoned the trip from Carlisle, and asked to return to the school, but to no avail. Stiya followed her parents to their house, with its dirt floor and abundant flies. That night she said, "I was so desperately homesick for Carlisle." She encountered great opposition as she tried to change tribal ways and introduce white customs, but she did succeed in changing her own family's manner of living: her parents decided to leave their pueblo; her father found a job shoveling coal and bought a three-room house in a town that had a school and a white teacher. The moral of the tale was this: "If every returned girl could resist the first efforts of her home friends to drag her back into the old Indian ways, and make them feel in a kind but decided way that they were no longer right for her, she would eventually enjoy untold satisfaction and happiness."[55]

Few found this "untold satisfaction and happiness." After staying several years at boarding schools, students could not fit back into their old life. Youths who returned to their families had changed, and their sense of home had been lost in the process. Thomas Wildcat Alford wrote of his return to Oklahoma, "My homecoming was a bitter disappointment to me. Noticing

Few students found going home as emotionally easy as the portrayal of this girl's return from the Carlisle Indian School to the Pine Ridge Agency in 1884.

Source: Image courtesy of the Library of Congress.

at once the change in my dress and manner, in my speech and conduct, my people received me coldly and with suspicion. Almost at once they suspected that I had taken up the white man's religion, along with his habits and manner of conduct. There was no happy gathering of family and friends, as I had so fondly dreamed there might be." Irene Stewart's experience was similar: "When I had left the Navajo country years before, I felt heartbreak; now I was disappointed in it. I could not make up my mind to stay on the reservation." A Hopi student who returned to her family wrote, "I didn't feel at ease in the home of my parents now."[56] Caught between two worldviews, value systems, and modes of life, many graduates of the boarding schools felt at home nowhere.

Part of the returning students' discomfort also came from new standards of living they encountered at school. After having electricity, running water, and indoor heating at school, many found that their family homes, even when sweetened by close relationships, were far less physically comfortable than their accommodations in the white world. Zitkala-Să (Gertrude Simmons Bonnin), a Sioux educated at an Indiana boarding school and the New England Conservatory of Music, told of returning to her mother's house and seeing it with new eyes. It was built of "naked ... unstained" logs, and had a sod roof. "Mother, why is not your house cemented? Do you have no interest in a more comfortable shelter?"[57] Perhaps her mother had no interest, but Zitkala-Să now did. As the standard of living rose in urban areas across America, many people of all races who had left home found that going back to a lower standard of living was difficult. They might long for return, but they had become modernized along the way, and their homes had not. The difficulties they encountered were those an entire generation of Americans of all races and backgrounds faced, as they tried to assign values to home and community, to self and success, but Native Americans confronted these dilemmas most starkly.

THE SPANISH-AMERICAN WAR

The goals of national progress and racial reinvigoration put pressure on young white men to leave home as well. The Spanish-American War required young men to take on a different sense of self, as they became the foot soldiers of colonial expansion. The war, which broke out in 1898 over the issue of Cuban independence from Spain, quickly involved other Spanish-held territories, including Guam and the Philippines. Although the original mission was the liberation of subject people from a colonial power, that mission gradually evolved, and America became an occupying force in countries far from the nation's borders.

Those promoting American imperialism embraced a new model of masculinity which required men to distance themselves from home. For most of the nineteenth century, white manliness and martial spirit had been tied to the love of home; by the end of the century, many national leaders suggested that home life was instead emasculating. Men could find true virility only away from home. They claimed that because the nation was growing beyond the confines of its traditional continental boundaries, men should venture beyond the domestic threshold as well. A congressman contrasted those who feared leaving home to fight in the war with the pioneers who had forged ahead, bravely and unhesitatingly: "In this day, some of us Americans have become so effeminate, either through wealth, or through excess of civilization . . . that they dread boarding a ship to go to the Philippine Islands, when their forefathers girded up their loins, saddled their horses, packed their mules, yoked their oxen to their wagons, and took their wives and their children . . . and they were not afraid." Theodore Roosevelt, a strong supporter of the war, tried to shame men who were hesitant to leave home and join the cause: "None of us respects the man whose aim in life is to avoid every difficulty and danger and stay in the shelter of his own home . . . unable to face the roughness of the world. We respect the man who goes out to do a man's work."[58] Those in favor of America expanding its sphere of influence through warfare suggested that sending men overseas was a sign of national maturation. By leaving the safety of their own shores, American men would show that they, and their nation, had come of age. Only the soft, weak, and immature would be tempted to remain behind when opportunities for individual and national advancement beckoned.

Yet despite the call for bravery, virility, and maturity, and despite the fact it was a short war in which many volunteered to serve, soldiers rather quickly expressed longings for the comforts of domestic life and strenuously complained of homesickness. Individual desires often ran counter to imperialist ideology. Soldiers' frequent complaints, and the fact that one of their number—Private Henry Atkins, of Company I, Second Massachusetts—succumbed to nostalgia during the summer of 1898, brought renewed attention to the disease. Reporters lavished attention, and a fair amount of praise, on the unfortunate Atkins.

The *Congregationalist* offered a sympathetic discussion of Atkins's death: "In the pathetic list of the dead . . . among cases of typhoid and yellow fever is found the record that Private—of the Second Massachusetts died of nostalgia." Atkins's touching death should remind female readers to make their homes deserving of such tragic yearnings: "An incident like this is a call to us to make home worthy of love which is an inspiration on fields of war and finds solace in loneliness by magnifying every grace of home and dear ones. We mothers, sisters, wives are proud of those whose thoughts come back to us from strange shores. It is for us so to live that there shall be no gulf between their ideal home and the reality."[59] The *Kansas City Star* attributed Atkins's death to the fact that he was a country boy, and thus had closer ties to and greater affection for his home than urban folk.[60] Rather than seeing homesickness as a weakness, as imperialist politicians often did, many Americans considered it a sign of character, morality, and innocence.

Dozens of more general articles appeared on nostalgia and homesickness during the war in Cuba and the engagements in the Philippines. Most of the articles dealt sympathetically with sufferers, noting that the condition was potentially fatal. Perhaps there was special compassion for the 126,000 soldiers stationed in the Philippines because they were so far from home.[61] And it was indeed a great distance: young men from the East Coast stationed in Manila were more than 8,500 miles from home, a great deal farther than most Americans had ever traveled from home. Newspapers attended to this point. The *Aberdeen (South Dakota) Daily News* reported, "There is a general epidemic of homesickness among the American troops in the Philippines, which appear to the poor fellows like being on another planet from that with which they are familiar, instead of only in another hemisphere."[62]

The war with Spain and then with the Philippines was portrayed in the press and in politicians' speeches as a chance for American men to become more manly, to escape the cloying confines of domestic life. Its supporters suggested that leaving home to fight was a necessary phase of both national and individual development. Yet for those engaged in extending the borders of American influence, such efforts often contradicted their inner desires, and significant elements of the American public sympathized with soldiers' sentimental longings for home. America was not just at war with Spain and the Philippines, but at war with itself when it came to the issue of how far from home the nation, and its armies, should wander.

MAKING ONE'S WAY IN THE CITY

This battle over the contours of modern manhood was being fought in civilian life as well. A modern economy was emerging during the late nineteenth century, and men were encouraged to leave home to find their place in the new industrial order.[63]

This new ethic of independence was evident in much of the literature on male homesickness. Increasingly, the emotion was linked to failure and backwardness, while the ability to sever ties was often considered a prerequisite for success. In 1900, the *Alaska Dispatch* described nostalgia as "a selfish disease" and maintained that "ardent, enthusiastic people, who continually look forward . . . have the advantage, if advantage it be, of remaining immune [to nostalgia]."[64] Other publications highlighted the fact that feeling too much homesickness could be a handicap in the modern world, and connected extreme forms of it to provincialism. One journalist suggested that the emotion "is peculiarly strong in all rural populations, largely because of their want of education, and consequent want of mental resources when taken away from their friends and native scenes."[65] In extreme cases, sufferers will "peril position, business prospects, honor, life itself, to fly to the only cure that can relieve them," wrote another editorialist. Yet overall, Americans were inured to such a condition, taught by their roving habits never to grow too attached to a particular spot. They did "not possess that affection for home which is characteristic of other nations. Then, too, they are migratory, and seldom have any fixed habitation that changes of business relations may not modify."[66] Such rootlessness was not a moral hazard, as it had been in the antebellum years; instead it was a national strength.

Some claimed that homesickness correlated not just with nationality but with the level of civilization that a people possessed. In the age of social Darwinism, commentators discussed the speed and ability of certain groups to adapt themselves to new environmental conditions, and concluded that it was the more civilized and educated populations that suffered the least amount of homesickness. One writer concluded, "The less the degree of civilization, the greater is the love for the native country. Savages, men of the grossest civilization, and the most desolate climates, quit their country with great reluctance."[67] Supposedly, whites were less prone to homesickness than either Native Americans or African Americans, for they were presumed to be more advanced and more adaptable, and hence more successful.

Practitioners in the emerging field of psychology sometimes merged their theories of the human psyche with social Darwinism as they tried to explain why certain personality types were suited to moving on, while others were more likely to stay put.[68] Clearly preferable were the individuals suited to movement. In his lengthy treatise "The Migratory Impulse vs. Love of Home," published in 1898, the psychologist Linus Kline tried to sort out the motives that animated both the homebodies and the wanderers. He recognized that many homebodies were prone to nostalgia, but offered a new theory of the condition which rested on the Darwinian idea of adaptability. The nostalgic individual who relocated had had "his 'psychical plane of reference'—composed of familiar scenes, friends, sense of security and the like—rendered uncertain and bewildering." Ideally, when an individual moved, he realized that "new adjustments must be made, old brain paths must be dropped and new ones formed. He must fuse with a new stratum." Nostalgia resulted when those who migrated "do not try to make a 'fusion' at all, do not seek a new 'plane of reference,' do not attempt to build new brain paths, but rather yield passively to their prison-world with wonder, timidity and fear." In such circumstances the nostalgic individual experienced a "shriveling" of the ego and lost his sense of self. Such people also were inevitably consigned to a lowly spot in the social world: "The lover of home is provincial, plodding and timid. He is the world's hod-carrier. His interests are identified with the conservative and microscopic affairs of society." Far more advanced was the individual able to leave home. "The migrant is cosmopolitan, has manifold interests, and finds profitable objects and kindred spirits in a variety of situations. He may be found in the commercial, speculative, daring, progressive, macroscopic interests of the world."[69]

As they looked for new explanations for homesickness, Kline and his fellow psychologists linked the condition to low intelligence, a lack of motivation, and a weak commercial orientation. They questioned the overall fitness and adjustment of those who suffered from acute or crippling cases of the condition. They repudiated past understandings of homesickness as a tender feeling, and now conceived of it as a hindrance to success. This perspective pointed toward the new view of the emotion that would emerge in the twentieth century. Life demanded change and motion.

Advice manuals popularized such ideas.[70] In *Manhood's Morning: A Book to Young Men between Fourteen and Twenty-Eight Years of Age*, Joseph Conwell told his readers that as they left childhood, they *"must leave home*. To leave the parental roof and go out into the world is the lot of most young men. The event with its accompanying experiences is entirely natural and should always lead to wholesome results." Conwell claimed that young men would benefit from leaving home, for they would learn self-reliance and independence: "By being thrown upon their own resources young men develop self-confidence, industry and independence; they learn to assert their own rights and to love what is theirs because they earn it, they become broad-minded and self-respectful and acquire moral courage." He warned that men who were too timid would never succeed: "Young men must not stand upon the brink of life's business channels and shrink and shiver into despair, but they must plunge in, and through their own industry, grit and brains overcome all obstacles and win success."[71]

Inspired by such ideas and hoping for material success, many young men left their rural homes in search of opportunities in America's growing cities. During the late nineteenth century and early twentieth, urban populations swelled and rural populations declined. In 1860, there were 6.2 million Americans living in what the U.S. Census Bureau designated as urban settlements, towns or cities of 2,500 or more; by 1900, there were 30 million.[72] A significant portion of the urban population was single men and women.

Some lived with kin, but many lived on their own in boardinghouses and apartments.[73]

While they did not face the isolation of living miles from their nearest neighbors, as often happened in farming regions, urban migrants discovered the new loneliness and isolation of living amidst hundreds or thousands of strangers. Clarence Darrow described his feelings when he moved to Chicago as a young lawyer:

> I rented a very modest apartment and took desk room in an office. . . . From the very first a cloud of homesickness always hung over me. There is no place so lonely to a young man as a great city where he has not intimates or companions. When I walked along the street I scanned every face I met to see if I could not perchance discover some one from Ohio. Sometimes I would stand on the corner of Madison and State Streets—"Chicago's busiest corner"—watching the passers by for some familiar face; as well might I have hunted in the depths of the Brazilian forest.[74]

Another young attorney, William F. Harding, born in North Carolina just after the Civil War, felt compelled to leave his hometown because there were too many lawyers there: "I decided to try my fortune in New York," but, after opening a law office there, "no clients darkened my door. My money soon ran low and I grew lonely and homesick. I was lost. The lonesomeness of a great city is worse than the lonesomeness of the wilderness."[75]

Thousands of other young men made the same transitions and came to similar conclusions. Leaving home seemed necessary, but it was not always easy to assume the identity of the modern, unfettered individual. The conflict between family and opportunity was visible in the letters of the Wilbur boys, George and Albert, natives of Belvidere, Illinois. They moved from home during the 1870s. George migrated mostly within Illinois, first to Flora, then to Champaign in 1872 to attend school, and then in 1875 to Chicago, where he became a lawyer. Albert studied at Champaign and then worked for various railroad and telegraph companies in the West. Both boys at times wanted to return to Belvidere; both expressed concern about their mother's condition, and occasionally spoke of permanently reuniting the family, yet that never occurred. They lived their adult lives away from their birthplace. Their letters reflect homesickness, guilt, ambition, and sibling rivalry, as each young man tried to suggest that the other should take better care of their mother, who remained in Belvidere.

Albert, who had traveled farthest from home, wrote to his brother that he missed his family, yet he did not propose returning home; instead he hoped they would move out west to join him. Writing from Carson City, Nevada, Albert told George, "Am getting very anxious to see you & mother again. . . . Am thinking some of leaving here. Want to go to San Francisco to work, where living is very cheap. If I get along here all right for a few months longer I will probably go there & arrange it so you and Mother can spend winter there with me."[76] Albert did not send for his brother and mother, but he did move on. He sometimes seemed little affected by homesickness and observed that parting got easier the more one did it. He left Carson for work in Reno, writing to his brother in the fall of 1876, "I hated to leave Carson as I have so many friends there It is almost like leaving home again but now that I am away it is very likely that I will never return there again to work."[77] He expressed his growing estrangement from Belvidere itself, noting that his only connection to the place was his family: "You do not write me any news from Belvidere, I would rather like to hear what is going on there, but I can see I am gradually losing my interest in the place. After mother gets away from there I will not care much for the place."[78] He was growing comfortable with unceasing movement.

When homesickness did strike them, Albert and George displayed an increasingly modern attitude toward distance, an attitude utterly dependent on new, fast transportation, on the transcontinental railroad recently completed, and the new branch routes that were spreading across the landscape. In 1875, George wrote his mother of his desire to return home: "I believe I am lonesome a little tonight. If it did not cost so much I would go out on next train."[79] Albert wrote a few years later to his mother of his hope that new trains would help him deal with his occasional bouts of homesickness: "You cannot realize how anxious I am to get home again and be with you and George. There is some talk out here that the overland trains are to be run faster in a few months. It would not be much of a trip to Chicago if I could get to Omaha in about two days time instead of nearly 4 as at present."[80] Two years later, after yet another move, Albert wrote to his mother, "I sent a letter to you several days ago via Santa Fe and Kansas City. By this route I am only 4 days ride from home and the two roads are very nearly connected so as to form another overland route."[81]

Relying on such modern transportation networks, the Wilbur boys moved farther from home rather than closer, in part because their sense of space changed as railroads became faster and lines proliferated, connecting previously isolated spots with the rest of the nation. Both felt drawn to home, and particularly to their mother, yet both stayed in their new locations and pursued careers in business. They counted homesickness as part of the experience of moving up in the world. Their journeys were becoming an accepted part of modern manhood.

When they moved to cities, young men frequently relied on new organizations to keep them connected to domestic culture. American religious groups created a host of institutions to shelter the homesick as they made their ways through the urban landscape. These institutions did not seek to return men home; rather they hoped to cushion their landing as they made the inevitable transition away from it. Branches of the Young Men's Christian Association, for instance, began to crop up in American cities during the 1850s, and their numbers grew dramatically during the late nineteenth century. By 1900, there were 1,500 branches with more than 250,000 members nationwide. The Y's motto was "A home away from home"; it hoped to reinvigorate home values and provide newcomers with a compass with which to navigate the city's moral and social geography. One early YMCA leader explained that the organization tried to "keep up the home feeling associated in his mind with the sweetest recollections." To that end, the Y created a domestic atmosphere within its walls, caring for sick members, sponsoring Thanksgiving dinners, and celebrating other holidays. Different branches elaborated on this mission in their own ways. The Boston YMCA carried more than forty local newspapers from small towns throughout New England so that each young man could have "a paper familiar to him and associated with the social remembrances of his early home and friends." YMCAs also offered a host of other domestic amenities designed to insulate men from the outside world. The Central Y in Chicago offered residents the use of four parlors, a restaurant that could seat a thousand diners, a library with 1,500 books, showers, baths, a swimming pool, and a barber shop.[82] A number of similar organizations sprang up in American cities, such as the Young Men's Hebrew Association, the first branch of which was founded in 1880, and the Fenwick Club, established to aid Catholic bachelors new to urban life.

These organizations represented an attempt to combat the disorienting effects of homesickness among urban youth, but their reach was relatively limited. By one estimate, only 1 percent of men in Chicago and Boston belonged to the Y.[83] Yet they were important symbols of how Americans envisioned young men away from home. Although their founders worried about men making their way in the cities, these organizations did not seek to send the men back home, for it was inevitable and commendable that they would migrate in search of opportunity. Instead, the YMCA and organizations like it hoped to facilitate the transition to independence.

The reformers and journalists who studied men's migrations in the late nineteenth and early twentieth century knew that they would experience homesickness. They believed men should master the instinct, and that the ability to do so was a sign of fitness. However, they did not believe that the love of home, in and of itself, was illegitimate, nor that sorrow at leaving it was to be denied.[84] Of course, young men would feel sadness as they set out for the city; if they did not miss home, there might be something wrong with them. Ideally, they should feel the emotion but not act on it during their careers. Popular literature supported this idea. For instance, *Zion's*

Herald, a Methodist journal, suggested that homesickness was widespread among successful men and that possession of the emotion indicated deep religious sentiments:

> Most of the prosperous business men who read this were born in the country and day and night they love to think of the time coming when they will be relieved of business responsibility; and then how they will fly back to the old home and restore its vanished charms as they once knew them. Not one of the homeliest details will be lacking. Even the old-fashioned flowers which they have not seen for twoscore years must be replanted where they once bloomed. What does it all mean? . . . Why does the love of the old home grow stronger rather than weaker with the flight of years?

The answer, the article suggested, was that love of home was akin to the love of heaven.[85] Only at the end of life could individuals return to God; only at the end of their careers could men return home. In the meantime, they should repress homesickness and continue on in their labors.

Unlike their brothers, young white women were expected both to feel homesick and act on the feeling.[86] While married women were still expected to repress their homesickness and follow their husbands wherever they went, single women read advice telling them that they should act on their homesickness and return to their families and their homes. This was a message shaped by demographic realities of the last decades of the nineteenth century, when hundreds of thousands of women were making the same transition to city life and independence as were their brothers. They found that moralists, psychologists, and advice columnists were less comfortable with their journeys, for they believed women were more naturally tied to home, more prone to homesickness, and more vulnerable to the perils of urban life than men. Consequently, if young women ventured to the city and felt homesickness, they should give in to the natural promptings of their hearts and return home.

From earliest childhood, girls received the message that they should have a strong affection for home and not leave it. The popular literature of the day painted females' homesickness as a virtue, for they should never be fully autonomous. The *Independent* printed a tale of two young sisters, Alice and Lotty, who insisted on leaving home to visit a nearby farm. Very quickly they began to feel homesick and were soon returned to their mother's home. "And when they got there—the cool shaded rooms, the smell of flowers, Mamma in her white wrapper, and the tea-table, with its raspberries and sponge-cake, its snow-white biscuit and cunning pots of butter, even the rustle of the ice in the milk-pitcher—how delightful it all was."[87] The ending of the tale vindicated the girls' decision to succumb to their homesickness and return, for their home was, after all, a very pleasant place. The

New York Evangelist told the story of "a little girl whose parents had moved from the country to a village. The child was very homesick, longing after her old home continually. So one time when some one was going there, she begged so hard to be taken with him, that her parents consented to have her go and visit an aunt, who lived next farm to the one that had been theirs." She was so eager to see her former home that she trudged through the drifting snow, risking her health and life to see the old place. The story praised her strong love of home and her valiant efforts to return to it.[88] Girls' love of their homes was noble, their efforts to return to them laudable.

Such attitudes shaped expectations about how young women should behave as adults. While young men should venture away from home, there was little consensus among social critics, ministers, and reformers that young women should. They were not yet deemed fully independent creatures, their desires for financial self-sufficiency not yet recognized as legitimate. When young women migrated from home, they left the protective circle of the family hearth and faced certain moral peril. Their inevitable homesickness left them exposed to false friends who would temporarily assuage their loneliness but ultimately exploit their trust. Margaret Sangster, a prolific author and frequent contributor to the *Ladies' Home Journal*, traced this logic: "Educators, professors and school masters and college presidents tell us that they found . . . that boys look forward to and prepare for this hour long before girls even think of it." When they did leave home, the positions that women found in cities were not consonant with their abiding natures. "If her flight from the home be a necessity, it is simply as a means to an end, in most instances. She makes her excursion into the office, or shop, or factory, but it is an excursion only, more or less experimental, and by and by, if she be among the happiest of Eve's daughters, she finds her mate, and settles down with him to home-building of her own." When women felt the press of necessity to leave home, Sangster counseled them to be careful and deliberate about their choices, for they would face challenges and hardships: "Do not come from the safe shelter of your own home, and from your mother's side, into a great town filled with strangers, where you have as yet not foothold, and where your chances are uncertain, where it may be next to impossible to procure employment at a rate of payment at which you can be self-supporting." Financial problems might be the least of the young women's problems. Sangster wrote, "My motherly heart yearns over homesick girls, waifs in a crowd of alien people, none of whom care for them."[89]

The specter of moral ruin hovered round her advice; other writers were far more willing to describe its horrors explicitly. An article in the *Youth's Companion* noted, "Loneliness, that begets homesickness, is the companion of the girl fresh from the country, and newly installed in some great city establishment." The typical girl in the city was "tired and depressed," friendless, and lived in a "cheerless" room in a boardinghouse. Such conditions had ruined a young needlewoman living on her own in Boston: "While suffering the horrors of homesick-loneliness, a fellow seamstress offered her sympathy. An acquaintance was established. The new friend was lively, and diverted her. Her sombre moods grew less frequent, and the acquaintance grew into intimacy." The new friend introduced the ingénue to a young man. "To her ruin she found that he was a libertine, to whom her false friend had betrayed her."[90] Although melodramatic, the story portrayed a common fear: young women on their own, away from home influences, might become promiscuous.[91]

To avoid such perils, observers suggested that working girls seek out the Young Women's Christian Association, the female coordinate institution of the YMCA. Designed to give working women in America's cities a safe place to socialize and live, they were moral oases in the dangerous and lonely metropolis. Margaret Sangster suggested that young country women head straight to the YWCA when they arrived in a new town. "Stay where you are until you have an assured position awaiting you, and through acquaintance or relatives, or the Young Women's Christian Association, make full and definite arrangements as to the home in which you will be received."[92] There were a host of imitators of the YWCA. Some targeted particular ethnic or racial populations; others were organized along religious lines. All offered women away from home some of the amenities of the idealized middle-class home: a piano, a parlor, a library, a sewing room. The Y and organizations like it self-consciously touted their homeyness. Y leaders in Chicago described their lodgings as "a house where [women] might come and feel at home in a city of strangers."

While they offered girls shelter, the reformers who founded the YWCA and similar organizations viewed young women's sojourns differently from young men's. The YWCA conceived of women as helpless creatures who ideally should be back home with their families. In contrast, the YMCA would help men develop their characters and become independent. Reformers believed that men could survive homesickness, but women would find it psychologically and morally debilitating because they were not equipped or designed for independent life.[93] Like African Americans who were supposedly constitutionally unsuited for a life away from the fields, young white women were incapable of living away from family. If either group left, they might suffer. Women were one of many dependent classes in America; their homesickness supposedly proved that this dependency was an inherent feature of their nature. White men's ability to conquer their homesickness showed that they were innately suited for an independent life, far from the parental home.

THE RISE OF NOSTALGIA

Many Americans who moved far from home and grappled with homesickness began to express a longing not just for the home they had left, but for a home they had permanently lost—in time.[94] This mood differed from homesickness in one important way. Homesickness contained a faith in the possibility of returning home because it was a place that still existed. The longing for lost times, on the other hand, carried with it the realization that home was truly lost because it existed only in the past. The homesick were separated from home by a gulf of geography; the nostalgic by a greater gulf—the gulf of time.

This new mood, which would come to be known as nostalgia, was in part a response to the new technologies that were reshaping American life. These technologies had caused some to yearn for lost times even before the Civil War, as men and women in the East and Midwest witnessed the transformations brought on by industrialization and the railroad.[95] After the Civil War, many more realized that these innovations, including the transcontinental railroad and steam-powered ocean liners, made it easier to return to a physical home and thus, at least theoretically, easier to assuage homesickness. Upon traveling back, however, they found they had not arrived, and never could, for the same technologies that had brought them home had also disrupted traditional ways of life. Home was gone, lost in the past. And while space could be traversed, time could not. This realization was at the heart of what we now call nostalgia.

This new mood was also a result of the trauma of the Civil War. The war tempered the widespread optimism that so many white Americans had expressed in the early nineteenth century, and made some sectors of the population long for a lost social order. As Lucy Buck of Virginia observed, "We shall never any of us be the same as we have been."[96] The war also undermined a belief in heaven and resurrection, given the dismemberment of so many soldiers on the battlefield.[97] The promise of heavenly reunion that had allowed the homesick to cope with their sorrows was being eroded by new doubts about heaven itself.

The mood of loss was also a response to changing social patterns. Many Americans began to worry that families were decaying and believed that mobility was the root cause of such decay. A French visitor to the United States wrote in 1895, "A thousand signs indicate ... [the] disintegration of the domestic hearth. ... The American family appears to be more than anything else an association, a sort of social camp, the ties of which are more or less strong according to individual sympathies, such as might exist between people not of the same blood. I am certain ... that the friendship of brother and sister, or sister and sister, is entirely elective." Another observer noted that the "American of Anglo-Saxon origin" did not seem to possess "that large family feeling which characterizes certain European peoples; he is not bound to folk of his own blood by any special connections."[98] Hamlin Garland, who witnessed the splintering of families firsthand when he left his family in the Midwest to seek success in Boston, likewise decried the process of moving on in the late nineteenth century, describing it as "the mournful side of American 'enterprise.'" Although he himself had left farm and family, he lamented, "Sons were deserting their work-worn fathers, daughters were forgetting their tired mothers. Families were everywhere breaking up. Ambitious young men and unsuccessful old men were in restless motion, spreading, swarming, dragging their reluctant women and their helpless and wondering children into unfamiliar hardships."[99]

As a percentage of the population, more native-born Americans had moved during the antebellum era than after the war.[100] Nevertheless, the migrations of the late nineteenth century provoked a new sense of concern, for widespread among those moving on was the conviction that they would never again be fully reunited with their families. The hope of reunion, either on earth or in heaven, that had consoled earlier generations was fading away in a secularizing society. The loss of home, the necessity of movement, and the impossibility of return were becoming facts of life, but they were still painful facts to accept. Consequently, for this generation of Americans, the longing for lost times was probably a more intense and poignant emotional state than it is today.[101]

During the Gilded Age, people spoke more frankly than they had in the past of the irreversible changes that families, homes, and towns experienced. There was a growing recognition that stability, if it ever had existed, was gone forever. A powerful example was the reaction to Thomas Hovenden's painting *Breaking Home Ties*, which won first prize at the Columbian Exposition in 1893.[102] Huge crowds flocked to see the painting, which portrayed a son about to leave his country home, presumably in search of opportunity. One observer reported that the area where the painting was displayed was "always jammed, and always will be till . . . the very last minute visitors are allowed in." Another claimed, "No picture ever painted in America . . . came so near to the common life of the common people. Strong men bared their heads and women wept before it." Thousands of reproductions of the painting circulated across the nation.[103]

Viewers responded to the painting because it portrayed a leave-taking they themselves had made. It caught the moment of change, when the past and home were left behind and the future embraced. While earlier artists had depicted such leave-takings as fraught with moral peril for the young man heading off to the city, *Breaking Home Ties* showed no such concerns, just sadness at the seemingly inevitable separation.[104] Joseph

Thomas Hovenden's *Breaking Home Ties* was, for a time, the most popular painting in America.
Source: Image courtesy of the Philadelphia Museum of Art.

Conwell in *Manhood's Morning* celebrated the painting for documenting an important transition that all white men must make. Conwell quoted an unnamed author who wrote, "More than a thousand boys like this one go out from their homes every day to make homes for themselves, to create new conditions, to acquire property, to marry well and establish other families, to become good citizens and valued members of new communities."[105] Conwell endorsed the idea of *Breaking Home Ties,* but the weeping and fascination the painting provoked in others suggests that many Americans had not yet learned to move forward in time and space without pain.

Across America, citizens sadly accepted mobility and permanent separation as the price of progress. Many poems of the era portrayed homesickness but seemed to signal a new acceptance of the fact that family separations might be permanent. In "Homesickness," published in 1899, Alice Turner Curtis told of living in the city, far from the familiar comforts of rural life:

> Adown the dark, unlovely street
> I watch the moonlight, far away
> I know how soft this same glow falls
> Upon a mountain-sheltered bay.
> I know the honeysuckle drifts

Its fragrant blooms about the door
Of that old house, where silence is,
Whose threshold I shall cross no more.
Lost, lost to me the care-free heart
That felt all fragrance, all delight,
That knew the moonlight as a joy,
And watched the dawn and loved the night.[106]

Despite the poem's title, the wistful longing could not be solved by simply going home. The world Turner remembered was "lost, lost" to her, as was her "care-free heart."

The idea that reunion and return were impossible came through even more clearly in poems that dealt with Thanksgiving, the traditional celebration of family togetherness. "Coming Home," published in the *Saturday Evening Post* in 1903, portrayed a new attitude toward leave-taking. In it, elderly parents rejoiced that their sons and daughter were returning to the farm for Thanksgiving:

They're comin' home! They're comin' home! They're comin'
    back to-day
To make the old place like it was afore they went away;
And Dan'll leave his Boston store and Ned'll leave his stocks,
And John'll stop a-drawin' plans for buildin' city blocks,
And Mary'll leave her New York house, with all its high-toned stuff,
And come down here and say it's Home and plenty good enough.
And there'll be boys and girls around jest like there used to be—
To make it real Thansgivin' Day for Mother and for me.

The celebration would mask the great changes the family had seen, allowing a blissful, if temporary, forgetting.

And we'll forgit that winter's come with all its snow and cold.
Forgit the next week's lonesomeness, forgit we're gittin' old,
And jest be young as when our heads weren't nigh so white
    as foam—
Thank God for His Thanksgivin' Day! The children's comin' home.[107]

But the family reunion was just for a few days, then all would return to their regular lives: the children would return to their prosperous careers in the cities, the parents would return to their lonely and forlorn days on the farm. True and lasting reunion was impossible. The children, after all, were never going to move back for good.

Given their realization that the past and childhood homes where all were together were gone for good, Americans often tried to temporarily recreate a sense of home and the past, even as they pushed forward. Through architecture, festivals, reunions, and songs, they tried to manufacture a connection to earlier times. The mere fact that they had to work to re-create the past was evidence of their knowledge that the real past was gone for good.

For instance, the creation of a mythology of the Old South and the Lost Cause was a manifestation of the desire for an older, rural way of life, when social and racial hierarchies were intact. In 1892, Thomas Nelson Page, one of the chief propagators of such imagery, wrote in *The Old South* of the idyllic conditions that had prevailed on the plantations of old: "Let me see if I can describe an old Virginia home recalled from a memory. . . . It may, perhaps, be idealized by the haze of time." According to Page, the home he recalled was a plain wooden structure, adorned with "quaint dormer windows" and "long porches," and was "set on a hill in a grove of primeval oak and hickories." Another southerner, George Bagby, ably filled in the details of this nostalgic idyll: "Sorrows and cares were there—where do they not penetrate? But, oh! dear God, one day in those sweet tranquil homes outweighed a fevered lifetime in the gayest cities of the globe."[108]

Southern whites not only waxed poetic about their own happiness in the antebellum era, but also described the contentment their slaves had experienced. They implied that African Americans were still loyal to their former masters and dissatisfied with the new social arrangements brought about by emancipation. To underscore the point, whites organized Old Plantation Days festivals, which featured scripted performances of Confederate soldiers and former slaves discussing the "good old days" of Dixie. However, the nostalgic mood of white southerners often stood in stark contrast to the actual memories of formerly enslaved blacks.[109]

White southerners were not the only ones beset by nostalgia. In Kansas, William Allen White's father, a prosperous doctor, so longed for simpler times that he moved his whole family out of town and into a log cabin in order to bring back to life his childhood memories of the frontier: "My father's idea was to duplicate exactly the cabin in backwoods Ohio where he was born and grew up. He thought he could go back to the golden days of his youth." He equipped it to look just as his childhood home had, even building a trundle bed for young William to sleep in. This romantic idyll did not sit well with White's mother, who seemed to prefer the refined and comfortable domestic life of the late nineteenth century to the rough and ready conditions of earlier years: "But clearest of all my recollections is the vast, continuous indignation of my mother at the sentimental tomfoolery of this whole business. Mary Ann Hatten had not spent ten years of her life toiling for an education just to go back to the blanket—two jumps behind a squaw." Nevertheless, his mother tried to indulge his father, for "she knew what a sentimental old codger he was. . . . She knew the thousand little joyous pricks and quivers of memory that came to him as he relived his childhood in his fifties. She tried hard to give him this pleasure." Eventually, however, her patience wore thin, and the family returned to town living and more modern ways.[110] White's father longed for lost times, but they were unrecoverable. Because the family had lived in a house with more modern amenities before moving into the cabin, Mrs. White was not long content with the rustic lifestyle her husband tried to manufacture. It was a fake, a pose. The effort to re-create it—and Mrs. White's impatience with this re-created hardship and rusticity—was also a tacit recognition that it was gone.

Other Americans, unwilling to put up with the inconveniences of cabin living, tried to recapture the past by moving into the romantic suburbs that sprang up across the United States in the mid- to late nineteenth century. Such suburbs embodied a longing for a simple, rural life; the people who moved to them were generally the affluent who were flourishing in the new economy and society, those who had learned to embrace change and break home ties.[111]

Prosperous families also traveled to historic places that resembled their visions of what a true home should be. Although they were merely traveling through space, some felt as though they were traveling through time as well. Emily Newell Blair, born in Missouri in 1877 to two easterners who still longed for home, wrote of her nostalgic travels in Maryland. During a trip to Annapolis, she wandered through the cobblestone streets of the city, admired its "old carved doorways," and concluded, "There is a wistfulness about the middle westerner's love of these old things not understandable to those who have always known them. . . . I have always understood the Kansan who moved the old Maryland house rock by rock to his prairie farm. He was trying to retrieve something he felt he had lost, not knowing that it cannot be done that way."[112]

Like Blair, many Americans toured older settlements on the East Coast that seemed unchanged by time. Vacations on Vermont farms or Nantucket Island offered a way to return to an idealized home and an earlier way of life. According to one commentator, Nantucket possessed the "dust of centuries." Many of the New England towns that became vacation destinations in the late nineteenth century were places that time seemed to have skipped; their quaintness was a result of their economic backwardness.[113] Although they would not want to actually live in such an economic order, prosperous urban vacationers flocked to these rural idylls to experience ways of living they had left behind. Such places allowed them to be at least temporarily connected to their old identities even while enjoying their new.

Americans also organized festivities to build a connection to their own particular pasts. As they came to recognize that social patterns and economic forces were splintering families permanently and that many would never live together again as intact kin groups, middle-class Americans created occasions designed to bring clans together, if only temporarily. Beginning in the 1870s, families began to hold reunions.[114] They were such novel events that major newspapers ran stories detailing the mere fact that they had taken place.[115] These reunions were meant to compensate for the lack of enduring familial ties in America. Many speakers at the gatherings pointed out how scattered families had become. One said, "Brothers and sisters are sundered for so many years, so far apart, they almost forget each how the other looks. Years go by, vast spaces intervene; and if their hearts are not parted they themselves are." Another reunion orator worried that families "not only lose sight of, but cease to retain any affection for their brethren." At the More family reunion in Roxbury, New York, in 1890, John More, whose father had migrated from New York to the Midwest, told his newly found cousins, "I have been long and widely separated from you. . . . This is the first time I have had the pleasure of visiting the old homestead, and of looking upon these grand old hills and lovely village, since that day." More lamented the effects of his father's migration on family life; over the course of forty years he had met only four or five relatives. "I am a stranger to most of you, and have been deprived of the good influences supposed to exist among families so large, and so intimately associated with each other."[116] Reunions addressed this problem, for they promised to bring together the scattered, if only briefly.

Often reunions took place at the site of an old homestead; during the celebration family members visited ancestors' graves, recited poems, and sang songs. At the reunion of the French family in Massachusetts in 1879, returning family members took the train to the clan's hometown of Dunstable. At the depot they were greeted with a brass band, then piled into a wagon and rode to the old homestead. As they neared the house, they broke into a chorus of "Auld Lang Syne" and then toured the home and its grounds.[117]

Families produced books documenting the events in an effort to capture the moment of family togetherness, fleeting though it might be. By including genealogies, family speeches, and recollections, they provided tangible portraits of family ties. Some clans might come together only at these brief reunions. On a family tree or a genealogical chart, however, they were all reunited, their relationships given a permanence and fixity on paper that they did not possess in reality.

In addition to family reunions, many displaced people participated in town reunions. At the turn of the century, dozens of New England towns hosted

Old Home Week festivals, designed to lure back former residents who had broken home ties. New Hampshire started the tradition in 1899 (although the town of Portsmouth, New Hampshire, apparently had tried out the idea in the 1850s).[118] Soon, other New England states followed suit. In 1902, the *Worcester (Massachusetts) Daily Spy* endorsed the festival and celebrated the fact that more and more towns were holding such events. New Englanders had migrated across the continent, but they had not forgotten home. "It is the dream of many of these emigrants to return to their New England birthplaces either for a visit or when they have retired from business.... We believe that this idea is going to strengthen the patriotism and develop the interest in local family and town history which is the basis of all history."[119]

In 1903, some estimated that as many as a half million Americans would return to the East to celebrate Old Home Week. Towns in every New England state save Rhode Island were holding such festivities, which one newspaper described as "a mammoth family reunion." The paper reported, "[Towns] have invited their wandering sons and daughters who went forth many years ago to make their fortunes ... back for a week on the old sod.... Thousands and hundreds of thousands will turn their steps eastward. Every boat and train will carry them, some of them across the whole breadth of the continent."[120]

Such events celebrated earlier times and associations and were thick with yearning for the past. In 1909, the town of Wilbraham, Massachusetts, held an Old Home Week celebration, where an orator talked of both the progress the town had made and the losses it had experienced along the way: "You probably had more people in 1839 ... but now you have greater wealth, more habitable houses, better furniture, more facilities for travel, better mails, better newspapers ... and on the whole an easier and happier life." However, the orator did not view the town's history as one of unmitigated progress: "But you look back to the earlier days with regret; a veil of pleasing romance hangs over those times of large families and housewarmings, of Thanksgiving reunions and great wood-fires.... Something has actually been lost, as well as much gained, during this transition."[121]

That wistful evocation of the past was common, and those who came to Old Home Week were hoping to recover what they had lost. Most made clear, however, that they knew this was but a temporary excursion into the past, not a permanent restoration of bygone ways and days. A poem composed for the town reunion of Westminster, Massachusetts, exclaimed, "How sweet in the midst of life's busy turmoil, To visit these scenes, tread our own native soil."[122] Old Home Week highlighted the fact that reunion was possible, but it would not be permanent. These festivals offered the chance to revisit native soil, not return to it. The trip to Massachusetts or New Hampshire was a vacation, not a permanent relocation.

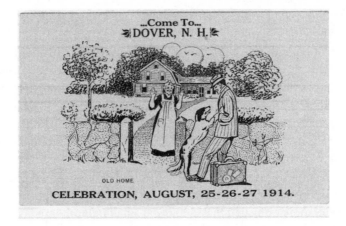

A postcard from Dover, New Hampshire, advertising the possibility of return and temporary reunion during Old Home Days.
Source: Image courtesy of Sam Allen, the Granite State Collection, Dover, New Hampshire.

While deep longings undergirded the return of the migrants, other motives may have been at work on the part of sponsoring towns, which hoped to recover not just lost residents, but lost revenues. For that reason, towns worked hard to lure back native sons and daughters and then tried to provide them with a warm welcome. Wilbraham held an Old Home Week in 1902: "Coaches were sent to every train at North Wilbraham yesterday morning and to the cars on the Southeastern electric road, and each train brought in a good number of people, while others from near-by towns, came in by teams. They congregated on the campus near the Methodist church, where they were greeted by the members of the reception committee."[123] The festival organizers hoped that returning migrants would spend money for improvements in the town. As the *Montgomery (Alabama) Advertiser* reported in 1903, Yankees always looked for profits and had "a reputation for practical hardheadedness which will put even sentiment on a practical paying basis." The newspaper suggested that the men and women who had left their hometowns as young adults in search of opportunity would now return, prosperous and eager to reestablish connections. Some might purchase old houses and make them into vacation homes; others might endow local institutions.[124] Old Home Week fulfilled the needs of the nostalgics and the pocketbooks of the homebodies. Money had often motivated men and women to leave their hometowns, and money motivated those who welcomed them back. Many Americans realized that the widespread longing for the past could be used to sell experiences, places, and objects. Old Home Week commercialized this yearning, setting a trend that would persist for years.

These nostalgic vacations and reunions in small old-fashioned towns and at "ancient" homesteads depended on modern transportation.[125] Whole clans and even whole towns sometimes chartered trains to visit their old homes.[126] Yet while new technologies made it easier to travel across space, these same technologies made it clear that time was the true barrier. When earlier generations had set off across the prairies in wagons, their thoughts of home remained unchallenged by visits back; they could hold on to memories of home as it had been. When they returned for Old Home Week, however, they found that life had moved on without them, towns had changed, new people had moved in, and familiar faces had departed. In 1906, the *New England Magazine* expounded on the feelings of those returning home: "Think what it would mean . . . if they could come back to their old home in the east in a fast-flying train of Pullman cars and find their townsmen waiting to receive them with open arms and brass bands, decorations, street parades, public meetings and banquets. There would be a note of sadness in it all, perhaps, for the changes in the place would be marked and the vacant chairs many; but the joy of friendly reunion would be the dominant key-note, after all, and the visitors from the far west would go back again feeling that the old home ties had never really been sundered." The journalist admitted that some returning migrants would not find any familiar faces; others would see dramatic changes. They had, after all, left in wagons and returned in Pullman cars.[127] When travel became easier, many came to realize that they had left behind an era, not just a place. In some ways, by making return easier, new technologies of travel reduced homesickness but increased what we now call nostalgia. Because they could go home again physically, many recognized that, in another sense, they could never really return. Across America, whether it was Native Americans returning to their tribes after time in boarding schools or middle-class men and women revisiting their rural hometowns, many came to this conclusion. They had no choice but to leave home, and the past, behind.

As individuals made such discoveries for themselves, the larger culture reinforced this outlook. Those far from home learned they should master their homesickness because it threatened individual and social progress. Homesickness, after all, encouraged the temptation to return home. As one author noted, those who suffered from acute homesickness would risk everything to return. They might "peril position, business prospects, honor, life itself, to fly to the only cure that can relieve them."[128] In contrast, the longing for a lost time, admitting its own futility, was less disruptive, offering a way to establish connections with the past that did not seriously undermine the present. Individuals could look backward wistfully, but ultimately must be willing to leave home and move forward. Progress came with movement; to stay put was to reject opportunity.

Earlier generations of homesick Americans had hoped that they might once again live together with their kin; this was often unlikely, given how far-flung they were geographically. Many therefore had also taken consolation in the fact that failing a reunion on earth they would have one in heaven. In either case, the homesick in antebellum America comforted themselves with the thought that sometime in the future they would all meet again and live together. After the Civil War, more Americans seemed resigned to the fact that their families would never again all live together. Instead, they would have to settle for short reunions, festivals, and vacations. These ritualized moments of coming together were a sign that families realized they would be permanently scattered. Middle-class Americans had gone from being homesick to being nostalgic.

CHAPTER 5

ᕉ

Immigrants and the Dream of Return

Between 1871 and 1920, 20 million immigrants journeyed to America. Coming during the era of the steamship and the international railroad, they regarded their migrations in a new light and experienced homesickness differently from earlier generations. Immigrants embarking for the United States before the Civil War had often stared into an emotional abyss as they left home, for they worried they might never return. Many understood the sorrow that Jacob Dunnink, a Dutch immigrant to Michigan, felt when he wrote his parents in 1851, "Now, my dear Father and Mother, it's as if we have buried each other before dying, because we will not see each other's faces again on this side of the grave."[1] In contrast, immigrants embarking in the late nineteenth century could console themselves that they need not wait until death to once more see their families, for travel was easier, making return more feasible. As a guide published in 1873 noted, "It is no longer either so dangerous or so toilsome a task to cross the Atlantic as it once was."[2]

Although steamships had been crossing the oceans since the 1840s, they became widely popular only after the Civil War. Both the number of steamships and the number of passengers on them increased dramatically in the late nineteenth century, and growing numbers of Europeans and Asians were able to purchase tickets to America because their prices were falling. In 1860, tickets from Liverpool to New York sold for $45; by 1880, that price had been cut in half. Even immigrants from Asia were paying only $35 to travel the great distance to San Francisco. Not only did prices fall, but the length of the journey decreased as well. In the early nineteenth century, the trip from Western Europe to America took between four and six weeks; by the end of the century, it took only seven days. By 1867, passengers could travel from Hong Kong to San Francisco in roughly twenty-three days.[3]

The spread of railroad lines also brought new immigrants. By 1853, rail had connected Canada and the United States, and by 1882, it stretched from the United States to Mexico.[4] In the 1920s and 1930s, immigrants from Canada and Mexico also had cars to aid their migration. These changes made leaving home easier and seemed to promise, sometimes falsely, that return would be easier as well. As transportation became cheaper, more rapid, and more aggressively promoted, immigration rates rose. In the half century between 1820 and 1870, roughly 7.3 million people migrated to America; over the next half century, nearly three times that number came.[5] This stream of immigrants diminished in volume only in the 1920s, when Congress passed tight immigration quotas that effectively turned the stream into a trickle.

Many who came to America's shores during the late nineteenth century and early twentieth considered their migrations temporary, knowing that faster and cheaper transportation would make going home easy. In fact, the conviction that they would eventually return motivated many to leave home in the first place. Immigrants who arrived between the Civil War and the 1920s came to America in pursuit of a dream: they hoped that success in the New World would enable them to return with money to enrich their homes and families in the Old. Consequently, their migrations should be understood not as individualistic efforts to break free of kin and community, but as actions often undertaken for the sake of long-term family unity and welfare.[6]

That many immigrants clung to dreams of return is evident from the way they spoke of home. Common among Chinese laundrymen in the United States was the motto *Fu-quai-re-quai-ku-shiung*: "To return to the native village with wealth and distinction." As one historian explained, Chinese immigrants envisioned "going home with presents—with perfumed toilet soap (*gum shan shee*—'Golden Mountain fragrance'), a sewing machine, and even a radio for their wives. They would be admired by the villagers.... They would swagger down the village streets and show off by speaking to one another in English ... would build a *Chuo-sai-kai* (wealthy home) and sponsor 'big affairs' like the weddings of their children."[7] In the early twentieth century, the sociologist Robert Park observed that Sicilian immigrants had the same hopes: "Most of the Cinisari in the Sixty-ninth Street group intend to return to Sicily. The town of Cinisi is forever in their minds: 'I wonder if I can get back in time for the next crop?'—'I hope I can get back in time for the festa.'—'I hope I can reach Cinisi in time to get a full stomach of Indian figs.' ... They expect to return. Whole families have the date fixed."[8]

The writings of immigrants themselves confirm this. Hans Hansen, born in 1859 in Ørsta, Norway, wrote from Seattle to his father in 1890, "It is just as much my intention now as ever before to come home to Norway, but I cannot fix the time just now as something could possibly hinder me. Yet I live with that hope that I once again will be seen in the first home of my life." Although he could not fix a date then, he did later, returning to Norway for good in 1895.[9] Umberto Dini, born in Lucca, Italy, in 1891, emigrated to the United States in 1908 and worked in a sweetshop. He recalled his decision to migrate as a rather casual one, believing that he would soon return home: "I decided because I heard quite a bit about the United States and so I thought I come over and look around. . . . In the beginning I thought I was going to go back but then after awhile I decide to stay."[10]

This casual approach to international migration was a sign of how technology had transformed conceptions of distance. In the new age of high-speed travel, going to America did not feel like a permanent or irrevocable decision, even if it became one. Earlier generations of immigrants who had left their families had invoked hopes of a heavenly reunion, placing their fate in God's hands, believing they might be reunited only after death.[11] But immigrants in the late nineteenth century and early twentieth, while still relying on God, also placed faith in Cunard, Hamburg-America, White Star, and other steamship lines.

Because immigrants thought of their time in the United States as temporary, they calculated gains in the New World in terms of what these would buy them in the Old.[12] A sojourner who eventually returned to his home in Italy recalled, "I dreamed of the land I would one day buy with my savings. Land anywhere else has no value to me."[13] Another Italian immigrant echoed the sentiment: "We brought to America only our brains and our arms. Our hearts stayed there in the little houses in the beautiful fields of our Italy."[14] A Filipino declared, "My sole ambition was to save enough money to pay back the mortgages on my land."[15]

These hopes for return retarded assimilation. Because they planned to stay in the United States only temporarily, many immigrants did not invest time or effort in becoming Americanized. Carlos Almazán, a Mexican immigrant born in Zamora, told an interviewer, "As I have always been with one foot in the stirrup, ready to go back to Mexico, I don't even have a decent little house to which to invite you."[16] In 1931, in his study of Filipino immigration, Bruce Lasker asked, "Why does not the Filipino create a satisfying home life for himself? For the same reason that other young foreigners who intend to return to their country make no such effort." This pattern was visible in immigrant communities of every description.[17] At least initially, immigrants made scant emotional or financial investment in the New World because of their ongoing and deep investments in the Old.

Their conviction that they were going home also made it difficult to improve labor and housing conditions, since immigrants were often focused on visions of life elsewhere rather than on the rough realities that were immediately before them.[18]

Yet even if many immigrants did not immediately invest in the American way of life because of their conviction that they would return to their native lands, what they ended up doing often differed from their initial plans. Some indeed went home, if only for visits; others returned home permanently. But a significant number stayed on, despite their deep hopes and best laid plans.

THOSE WHO WENT BACK

Immigrants returned home for a host of reasons, but contemporary observers and modern historians have concluded that homesickness was a primary reason.[19]

Many went home for visits, though not always as soon as they had expected. Some, like Caren Lundgren, who emigrated from Sweden in 1921, were able to return for a visit relatively quickly. Lundgren was homesick in America: "When I wrote home, I had to be so careful about getting tears on the paper." Trips home allayed her sadness, at least temporarily. "I went back to Sweden in 1926, 1930. I went back several times." Others, like Carla Martinelli, who emigrated from the small village of Pietragalla in northern Italy in 1913, had to wait decades to return to her home and her mother: "I wrote mama all the time, though. After I came here I wanted to go back. I wanted to see my *mamma mia*, and, in 1948, I went to Italy. I went back. To visit. For the last time."[20]

Others went back and forth repeatedly between their homeland and the United States. Some made multiple trips, motivated by pecuniary desire on the one hand, and homesickness on the other. For instance, French Canadians often journeyed between their rural villages and the mills of Massachusetts. Phillipe Lemay, born in Quebec in 1856, went to Lowell, Massachusetts, by train in 1864. Lemay's parents returned permanently to Canada in 1875, but many of their countrymen stayed and made annual visits home: "Each spring and fall, it seems, the older immigrants had a touch of homesickness. Most of them still had farms in old Quebec. 'I want to see if it is still where I left it,' they'd smilingly tell the boss when they asked permission to be away for five or six weeks. So they went back to Canada twice a year. . . . They were still farmers like their ancestors had been, and they wanted to get something out of those farms, some of which had been in the family for many generations." When they returned to Quebec in the spring they plowed and sowed; when they went back in the fall they harvested.[21] Coming to America was not an end in itself; it was instead a way of keeping the family homestead flourishing back in Canada.

Those immigrants whose native lands were across the ocean rather than just across the border nevertheless were known to travel back and forth repeatedly. Port records indicate that between 1899 and 1906, almost 12 percent of all immigrants had already landed at least once before on U.S. shores. Some immigrants made as many as seventeen round trips to America, essentially splitting their lives between two continents.[22]

A large number returned home for good after a period in the United States. Over the course of the nineteenth century, as fewer immigrants came with the intention of farming and more came in the hope of earning quick profits from industrial jobs, and as steamship travel became more accessible and affordable, reverse migration increased. Estimates vary as to the exact size of this return migration, and official records are incomplete. Nevertheless, there is ample evidence to suggest that in some decades close to half of the immigrants returned to their homelands.[23]

Rates of return varied enormously among ethnic groups, but all groups showed evidence of return migration. Some, like those from southern Italy, were reputed to be more closely tied to their native land than other groups, and indeed, 56 percent of southern Italians eventually returned home.[24] During the late nineteenth century and early twentieth, an estimated 50 percent of all Italians, 25 percent of Norwegians, 17 to 27 percent of Austro-Hungarians, 46 percent of Greeks, 10 percent of Irish, 20 percent of Lithuanians, 30 percent of Poles, 19 percent of Swedes, and 20 to 36.5 percent of Slovaks returned. Roughly 55 percent of Japanese immigrants to Hawaii went back to Japan. Before 1900, 15 to 20 percent of Jews sailed home to Eastern Europe; thereafter remigration fell off steeply due to ethnic and religious violence in their homelands.[25]

It is worth looking at this last group's return migrations in depth, because Jews were supposedly the least likely to go home. Historians once regarded them as single-minded in their determination to go to America and leave the oppressions of the Old World forever behind them; in reality, however, they often returned home to allay their homesickness. Their experiences and emotions defied expectations and indicate that despite persecution, people could carve out a home and sense of place in the midst of an oppressive society. Although they were treated as outsiders in Lithuania, Russia, and Poland, many Jews still considered such places home, and found that America, with its vaunted opportunities and liberties, was alien.

Rose Benjamin, who emigrated to the United States as a teenager, eventually brought the rest of her family to join her in Philadelphia. She longed for the familiar places she had left behind, however, writing in an essay contest, "Even though I live in glory and splendor I still have a yearning to see my home where I was born and raised at least once before I die."[26] The historian Jonathan Sarna has shown that such yearnings were quite common; many Jewish immigrants nursed hopes of return, and some made good on such hopes. It was only after the well-publicized Kishnieff pogrom in 1903 and a series of riots in subsequent years that Russian Jews showed a greater desire to stay in America. Before that, central and eastern European Jews resembled their gentile neighbors in the way they viewed America: many hoped for success in the New World that might enable a better life in the Old. Some ended up staying in the new country and returning for visits; others tried America and then rejected it.[27]

Even after conditions worsened in Europe in the early twentieth century, some Jewish immigrants indicated that they would rather be in their native land than in America. In 1906, in the wake of several pogroms, the *Dallas Morning News* ran a story titled "Homesick Russian Jews: Refugees Who Yearn for the Land of Persecution."

> "Would you think," said Dr. Maurice Fishberg, medical examiner for the United Hebrew Charities, "that any Jew who was lucky enough to be out of Russia at the present time would want to go back?" Dr. Fishberg picked up a bunch of record slips and selected half a dozen or so from them. "Here," he said, "are just one week's applications for transportation back to Odessa, St. Petersburg, Warsaw, Vilna—all the cities where the worst massacres have taken place. Some of the applicants are refugees who came here less than six months ago for the sake of safety. They are simply our regular quota of nostalgia or homesickness cases, which not even the news of massacres at home has had the power to kill."

Even on days when local newspapers carried reports of new pogroms, homesick Jewish immigrants lined up in Fishberg's office hoping to get tickets home. They went to the United Hebrew Charities because in earlier years the organization had funded journeys back to Europe, helping more than 7,500 Jews return to Russia in the 1880s and continuing those efforts throughout the rest of the century. In the early twentieth century, it temporarily suspended its repatriation programs. Nevertheless, nostalgic émigrés looking for a way home continued to appear at the office. Fishberg said they discounted the dangers they faced: "[They] would rather run the risk of massacre in Russia with friends and family and among familiar scenes than to die among strangers in a foreign land, for they are certain that they are going to die if they stay." Not all admitted to being homesick, but Fishberg could tell that they were. Many had common symptoms of nostalgia: they could not breathe the American air, could not eat or sleep, had bad dreams, felt nervous and enervated, and experienced random pains.[28]

Jews continued to display homesickness well into the twentieth century. In 1921, an immigrant from Poland lamented, "We Jewish immigrants from Bialystok suffer from an acute homesickness." Such sentiments were common throughout the 1920s and 1930s. The *Bialystoker Stimme*, a Yiddish newspaper, carried the reflections of another Bialystok native in 1926: "I have been away for many years. But I have not once been able to forget my dear city; I constantly contemplate your mountains. . . . Many years ago I have already left, my feeling should have also diminished but the miraculous power of my intimate-beloved-mother-land . . . prevents this from happening." Although long settled in the United States, immigrants from Bialystok continued to refer to that city as their *muter-shot* or *muterland* ("mother city" and "motherland").[29]

Immigrants coming from relatively less oppressive circumstances than these felt equally drawn to their homelands. Some were troubled because they had believed they would like living in the United States but did not; others were heartsick because they had always intended to return but could not find the means to do so. Out of sympathy and concern for such unhappy immigrants, a variety of charities helped pay for their repatriation. The Syrian Ladies Aid Society, founded in 1908 in Brooklyn, "helped return to the homeland" those Syrian immigrants "who could not, or would not withstand the many hardships" that newcomers to America faced.[30] The Japanese Benevolent Society negotiated discounted steamship tickets for members who wanted to return to Japan, and in the 1880s, the German community in New York helped homesick immigrants return home.[31]

Newcomers sometimes dreamed that their homelands would help them repatriate. Discontented Swedish immigrants hoped their government would send a ship to retrieve them from American shores; homesick Greeks must have found some satisfaction when their government subsidized return travel; Jews likewise asked the Russian government for aid in returning to that country. In 1912, the *New York Times* reported that it was quite common for foreign governments and foreign banks to assist immigrants wanting to go home, and estimated that on average 400,000 immigrants returned each year.[32]

There were, however, many who wanted to go home but could not. A Norwegian who eventually made it back to his native land recounted his eagerness to go home and his difficulty in doing so: "I was so disappointed. If I had had the money I would have gone straight back to Norway."[33] A Greek newspaper in 1908 reported on a group of returned citizens, "150 Greek emigrants disembarked from the land of gold. We met many of the returned ones who gave us a melancholy picture of the conditions among the Greeks there. . . . They assured us that there are many thousands of Greeks who wish to return to their homes, but do not have the means. . . . In general the returned portray the conditions among the immigrants in the United States as frightful."[34]

Frightful they were, but many immigrants blamed not the general economic conditions but their own characters for their success or failure in the New World, and worried that coming home with empty pockets would mean coming home in shame. Alhough they were homesick, they also were prompted by a sense of honor to stay until they could return home with pride. Twenty-eight-year-old Bonifacio Ortega, a native of Jalisco, Mexico, said that he had no complaints about his one and a half years in the United States: "[But] I love my country more and more each day and I hope to go back to it; but I want to go back with some little money so as to start up in business again." Until he had that money he would stay. A Polish immigrant, Anthony Jarzynkowski, felt the same way. In 1890, he wrote from Cleveland to his family in Rypin, "If you have the urge and the desire to absolutely be in America, then come at your own [expense], because if I had a few dollars, then I myself would return to my beloved old country."[35]

Despite low wages and harsh working conditions, a significant number of immigrants managed to save the necessary money and bought a ticket home. When they settled back in their native villages, they built houses that reflected their initial motivations for leaving. They had not abandoned their homes but had left so they might improve them. Across Europe, Asia, and the Middle East, returned immigrants built "American houses" with the earnings they saved. In small villages in Lebanon, returning migrants refurbished completely their ancestral homes, leading observers to comment on the proliferation of red tile roofs, an innovation in that region.[36] In Poland, they built fancy modern houses with tile or slate roofs, often adjacent to the small houses with thatched roofs in which they had been born.[37] In the Hungarian village of Mezőkövesd there were neighborhoods named "Money Pit" and "Dollar Mountain," where those who had returned from the United States built large homes.[38] Such houses were a testament to the successful realization of the American Dream—the dream of returning home rich—and a tangible payoff for the homesickness that so many had endured.

THOSE WHO STAYED

Millions remained in America. Some continued to nurture hopes of return; others eventually grew to like their lives in America and consciously desired to stay. And some looked homeward not at all. George Price, a Russian Jew, was of this last school: "Should this Jewish emigrant regret his leave-taking of his native land which fails to appreciate him? No! A thousand times no!

He must not regret fleeing the clutches of the blood-thirsty crocodile."[39] More frequently, immigrants experienced some homesickness, but it many cases it was transient, replaced after a time by other, more positive evaluations of the United States. A Polish immigrant wrote in 1891, "I, when I arrived in America, was very lonesome. But now, not at all. We are not even thinking about returning to the old country very soon."[40] In the same year, John Chmielewiski wrote his mother from South Chicago Harbor, "Nowhere do we have complete satisfaction, everywhere there is misery. It is not good in America, but at any rate it is better than in the Old Country."[41]

Other émigrés felt homesick for many years but realized that the United States offered better opportunities. Nikola, a Serb who had settled in Johnstown, Pennsylvania, regretted his migration and returned to his homeland after two years. Finding nothing to do there, he went back to Pennsylvania and began to work in a coal mine. "It was terribly hard work, coal mine, back-breaking, dirty, awful. But I still preferred it here, thought it was better. I saw here some future, and at home there was none."[42] In 1909, after six years in the United States, Emma Huhtasaari, a Swedish Finn living in Hancock, Michigan, felt both a longing for home and an appreciation for American life: "Ever-beloved Mother, far away in the dear homeland, I always think of Mother and tears come to my eyes when I think that the seventh year has begun since I left the dear home of my birth. I am not so attached to America that I should forget the homeland. One always feels such a strange longing. Though now I have it very good."[43] Those immigrants who stayed and flourished in the United States probably felt a jumble of emotions: pride at their success, guilt at their distance from home and their greater prosperity.[44]

While they missed many things, generally the hardest psychological adjustment for immigrants was their separation from family. They often had left to improve their family's life, but, in the short term, family life was sacrificed. What Robert Orsi said of Italian Harlem was true for most ethnic colonies: "Italian Harlem ... was a community in separation: men separated from their wives and children, men and women separated from their parents and grandparents."[45] Sometimes men came to the United States alone, with the plan of returning home or sending for their families later on. Until the early twentieth century this was a common pattern among Italians, Poles, Greeks, and Jews.[46]

Away from their families, immigrant men found their time in America lonely, particularly during holidays. Twenty-five-year-old Hans Øverland wrote from Montana to his father in Norway in 1889, "Dear Father, Received your letter of the eleventh today. It was most welcome to me, alone out here in the wilderness.... I wish I were home again, that is all, but I don't dare think too much about that, or I'll get sick from it, like I was at

Christmas time."[47] Some Jewish immigrants believed that the worst time was during Passover, when scenes of life back home, amidst kin and community, haunted them. Maurice Fishberg of the United Hebrew Charities noted, "Every spring, . . . as Passover draws near, men who during the previous months have been well and cheerful, who have worked steadily and have even laid up a little money toward the desired object of sending for their families, get to think of the Passover table and the Passover ceremonies, and of the wife and children gathered about the Passover dainties without them, and develop first class cases of nostalgia."[48] Holidays brought back potent memories of family gatherings and togetherness, of familiar rituals that seemed to transcend time but could not transcend space.

While the holidays could exacerbate homesickness, many men needed no special occasion to experience it, particularly during their early days in the United States. John Muszeński, an out-of-work Pole living in Bayonne, New Jersey, wrote his wife in 1891, "You are puzzled that I am so sad on the photograph. I have not yet been happy in America! I am always sad and lonely and I look forward to the day and the hour when God will assist me to get to my dear wife and my dear children."[49]

Some men sought to avoid loneliness by migrating with their wives, but while this may have made them happier, it often left their wives desolate. Most married women left home with less enthusiasm than their husbands. Barbara Di Nucci Hendrickson said of her grandmother, Virginia Reverberi, who emigrated in 1915, "She had never wanted to leave her home and relatives. . . . She said that she had no choice, that a woman had to go where her husband went. Somehow, I picked up some kind of myth from my mother about how both my grandparents wanted a better life for themselves and their children, so decided to emigrate to the New World. Now I understand that it was my grandfather who had that dream, not my grandmother."[50]

Immigrant women frequently resented the lack of control they had over their own and their families' migrations. Like American women on the frontier, they felt acutely their distance from kin and their powerlessness to rejoin them. Filomena Mazzei, whose husband went to the United States seven years before she did, was unhappy in her new home. She complained, "America—I didn't like it. . . . I couldn't speak the language, I had no relatives. . . . I had the little children. I stayed home, alone. My husband worked and I felt like a lost person."[51] Mrs. Revel, a Jewish woman living in Houston, recalled that marriage had compelled her to migrate: "I was married in Europe in 1910 and immediately after my wedding I came to America landing in Oklahoma. I found it very hard to get along with the people of Oklahoma for I could not speak the English Language. . . . The happiest day of my life will be when I see my parents again. I have not seen them for seventeen years. Some Day I hope to see them again."[52] Pasqua Sparvieri also went to America to join her husband, but longed to return to her hometown, Asoli Picane. Of her early years in America she recalled, "I told my husband I want to go home and he said—I was so many year here myself now I got married you want to go home." But Pasqua fell ill, and her husband was sympathetic to her plight. "So my husband says—my God, I don't want really anything to happen to you. If you want to go to Europe really . . . he says you can go—then four or five years I come back he told me. But you can tell my husband feel bad, so I says okay." And Sparvieri therefore stayed.[53]

Sparvieri's husband needed her to be with him in Chicago in order to allay his own feelings of homesickness. To him, she represented home and family. But for Pasqua, her husband was not enough. It was only when she became pregnant that she began to feel as though she had family ties sufficient to bind her to the New World. She described her feelings after her daughter Mary was born: "Then after that I never talk I want to go back to Italy because I've got my own baby here you know make me happy. My husband was so happy—since that time I was O.K."[54] It was by establishing a new family in America that immigrants frequently overcame their homesickness, abandoned their plans for return, and began to feel at home in their new land.[55]

Yet even when they were joined by their families or created new ones in America, immigrants missed other things from the Old World. Many longed for the beauty of their homelands and were dismayed by the industrial world they saw before them. Emma Huhtasaari contrasted the pastoral landscape she had left behind with her new location: "Nothing can be compared with that beauty. There is never a birdsong in America's dark nights. . . . Here the hills are so jagged and you don't see such pretty little islands and meadows filled with flowers. There is only coal smoke and dusty streets. Coal smoke from many factories so that the air gets heavy. It feels so bad when you have grown up in Norrland's fresh air."[56] A Polish immigrant wrote to her parents about life in New York, intimating that she found it crowded, alienating, and ugly: "Father should . . . not even dream of coming to America. Oh, how lonely I am! Here you only hear the noise of thousands of people walking, of the whistling of factories, of the bells of trolleys, of the whistling of traders in place of nightingales and larks. Instead of roses, tulips and lilacs [you find] barrels of garbage and covered wagons, and stench instead of fresh air."[57] Sophie Kosciowlowski had similar feelings about the noisome neighborhoods near Chicago's stockyards: "[It is] the stinkiest place in the world. We came from a city in Poland and you couldn't compare it with that, it was quite a shock, you know, to go to that place. . . . I made the trip . . . twice. I was here when I was nine years old and my mother couldn't bear this place and she left two children in Europe. So she insisted on going back." Eventually, however, Sophie and her mother returned to Chicago.[58]

In addition to longing for more pastoral landscapes, it was not unusual for immigrants to be homesick for the physical structures of their old houses and to regard American houses as inferior. To many, it was a shock that they might have enjoyed a higher standard of living in their homelands than in the United States, reputed tó be so wealthy.[59] Maria Valiani emigrated from Tuscany in 1911, when she was nine. She traveled with her mother to Chicago, and along the way she saw how her mother mourned the greater comforts they had left behind. "As we were crossing from New York to Chicago, we saw a lot of ugly . . . wooden houses. We always had stone houses in Italy. . . . My ma says . . . Oh, I'm sorry we came here. . . . Our little town was better. We could see that beautiful Viareggio, the ocean. . . . Mama mia, how we gonna live over here? What kind of a place is this?"[60] Pasqua Sparvieri, who emigrated in 1929 at the age of twenty-seven, had a similar first impression: "When I come to this country to tell the truth I don't . . . like it. I see all this frame house. I see all this like a shanty you know things like that. I say—my God, I say—this is called America? . . . When I come to this country it was so cold over here. In Italy it's not cold. . . . So I told my husband I want to go home."[61]

While immigrants settling in urban areas had to deal with the loss of pastoral landscapes, many who settled in rural areas believed that the deprivations they experienced were greater than those they had known in their native lands. Some talked about being too far from civilization in their frontier homes. A Basque immigrant, Maria Petra Mendiola Loisate, who emigrated in 1920, recalled her sinking mood as she contemplated the barren landscape of Rock Springs, Wyoming: "Gracious, I thought. I come to the end of the world. . . . I was used to all greenery and everything, and I get here, nothing . . . all dry and no trees and nothing, no paved sidewalks or main streets, and stuff like that. . . . I didn't like the looks of it."[62]

Given the hyperbolic descriptions of America that prompted men and women to leave their homelands in the first place, there was little chance the nation could measure up to the myths that circulated about it. Immigrants presumed the United States was brighter, cleaner, and richer than their homelands, yet the places most immigrants first saw, the neighborhoods they settled in, were often no better and frequently much worse than those from which they had come. Even when these new places could offer greater physical comforts, such as running water and electricity, they lacked the warmth of family life, the comfort of familiar architecture, the cushion of known custom.

ETHNIC COLONIES

To cope with this world turned upside down, immigrants struggled to create a sense of the familiar in the United States. In ethnic enclaves, homesickness took on a more communal face, for there immigrants found others from their native lands who also felt the difficulty of adjusting. To maintain a bond with past places and selves, newcomers established ethnic groceries, churches, fraternal organizations, singing clubs, and newspapers that offered familiar tastes, sounds, and rituals.[63] Many of the social institutions were created, at least in part, as a way to assuage homesickness.

Immigrants rarely settled in isolation from their ethnic group. Indeed where an immigrant chose to go generally was determined by where earlier migrants from the home village had settled. For instance, when they landed in America, most Italians from the town of Bagnoli del Trigno went straight to Fairmount, West Virginia, to join their townsmen at work in local glass factories.[64] In Chicago, Italians re-created their villages in urban neighborhoods. On Sangamon Street lived several hundred immigrants who all hailed from the same small town of Calvello; between 22nd Street and 25th Street were residents of Ricigliano; at the intersection of Archer Avenue, Clark Street, and 20th Street lived immigrants from Termini Imerese.[65] In Grand Rapids, Michigan, where so many Dutch settled, one historian has noted, "Even though each neighbourhood could easily be characterized as a 'little Holland,' it would be more accurate to identify each residential cluster as a 'little Zeeland,' 'little Groningen,' or 'little Friesland,' thereby affirming the provinciality of the particular settlements."[66] Village borders were maintained in American cities, particularly during the early years of settlement.[67]

Most immigrants clustered as close to their countrymen as they could. Robert Foerster, an early twentieth-century observer, noted that Italian immigrants displayed *campanilismo*, a "loyalty to that which falls within the range of the bell tower" of their native towns.[68] Such loyalty, intense in the Old World, was often equally if not more significant in the new, where people clung all the more tenaciously to the familiar because they were surrounded by so much that was strange. Salvatore Castagnola, born in Messina, Italy, in 1893, emigrated when he was ten. The adjustment was particularly hard for his mother, but their south Brooklyn neighborhood provided consolations, for there an immigrant "could live an ordinary life without hearing a word of English. One could purchase clothing, food, furniture, and all the other necessities of life as conveniently as though he were in 'the Old Country.' One could be married at the Italian church by an Italian priest, give birth with the assistance of an Italian midwife and be buried by an Italian undertaker."[69] In such neighborhoods, some felt that they had

re-created their old life anew. An observer noted, "One of the greatest sur-
prises of my life . . . is to hear from time to time, especially from Italian
women who have lived in America for years, a statement like this: 'I have
been down to America today,' meaning that they have gone a few blocks
outside the district of the Italian colony."[70]

Eleanor Rantanen, a Finn, found comfort by settling in a Finnish neighborhood in Chisholm, Minnesota. Born in 1888, she reluctantly followed
her husband to the United States in 1914. She found her new town more
hospitable than she expected: "There were so many Finns in Chisholm
when I came, it was like being in Finland. . . . There were even five sauna's
run by the Finns. We did not need any other language." So complete was
that Finnish community that even after more than sixty-five years in the
United States, Rantanen admitted in 1981, "I do not speak English too
well."[71] Ernesto Galarza and his family found comfort in their California
barrio, often forgetting they were in a foreign country: "Within the *barrio*
we heard Spanish on the streets and in the alleys. On the railroad tracks, in
the canneries, and along the riverfront there were more Mexicans than any
other nationality. . . . In the secondhand shops, where the *barrio* people sold
and bought furniture and clothing, there were Mexican clerks who knew
the Mexican way of making a sale. . . . In the family parties, the baptisms, the
weddings and the birthdays, our private lives continued to be Mexican."[72]

These ethnic enclaves helped homesick immigrants feel more at home,
although for many they never quite replaced what had been left behind.
Sophie Nadrowska told her parents in 1890 that the ethnic colonies were
reminiscent of home but still not the same: "Chicago is Poland in perfec-
tion. You can hear Polish hymns in Church. Lessons are different than what
you have there. It is very gay here, so that one can forget one's longing. And
I cannot regret those two years . . . but when I think about you I am a little
lonely. I am, as it were, still at home."[73]

In these Polonias, Little Italys, Chinatowns, Bohemian Quarters, and
Little Tokyos, immigrants reproduced much of the social life of their old
communities. The neighborhoods also became the site for procuring the
material goods of immigrants' native lands. The same revolution in transportation that made possible the mass migration of immigrants also made
possible the mass importation of consumer goods from afar. With faster
and cheaper overseas shipping and rail transport, and with breakthroughs
in refrigeration, it became possible to bring more of the amenities of home,
even the perishable ones, to a new location.[74] Sentimental symbols and mementoes of the Old World, as well as the familiar if sometimes mundane
items of daily life, could be more quickly and easily imported from abroad
than in previous decades. The immigrants who came to America in the late
nineteenth century and early twentieth were among the first to witness the

way new transportation technologies and the concomitant rise of a consumer economy could both carry them away from home and reconnect them to it.

Entrepreneurial immigrants were the first to pay attention to the market opportunities that homesickness represented. They found there was a substantial profit to be made by selling the sights and tastes of home to their fellow immigrants who hungered for them. For instance, Fritiof Colling, a Swedish artist, made his living off homesickness. Immigrants commissioned him to return to Sweden to paint pictures of their childhood homes. Colling traveled there at least eight times between 1885 and 1902 to create his paintings, probably producing hundreds of them. He must have been homesick himself, for he eventually returned to Sweden permanently. The historian Mary Swanson noted that other artists also saw a lucrative market in the homesick. She described G. A. Johnson of Winburne, Pennsylvania, who "advertised that he would take '*En Fotografisk Resa Genom Sveriges Bygder*' (a photographic journey through Sweden's sections). One dollar bought a postcard of the patron's childhood home or nearby scenery; six cards cost two dollars, and a stereograph view, three dollars. The advertisement instructed the would-be consumer to give his *landskap* (township), *län* (county), *socken* (parish), *jernväg* (railway line), as well as the name of his home (Swedish cottages normally had names) and neighbors."[75]

One of Fritiof Colling's farmhouse paintings, which he made for Swedish immigrants in America who wanted pictures of their native homes.
Source: Courtesy of the Swedish Emigrant Institute.

While only a relatively small number of immigrants could afford such pictures, entrepreneurs found a large and profitable market in filling the stomachs of their homesick compatriots. In the diaries and letters they left behind, immigrants made it clear that next to their families and their family homes, they longed most for their native foods.[76] Because of the difficulty of acquiring these in the United States they regarded what would have been everyday meals in their homelands as special treats to be savored and treasured. Ida Lindgren, a homesick Swedish immigrant living in Kansas, wrote her mother in 1870, "Do you know what I miss here most in the way of food? Really good sour-sweet rye bread and a glass of fruit drink, for such things do not exist here."[77] In 1886, Berta Kingestad had a similar complaint. She wrote to her sister in Norway that although her stomach was quite full in America, she was still hungry: "I often wish I were at home and could sit at the table with you and eat those delicious fresh potatoes and fish. Here they eat only pork, and I cannot stand to eat the wheat bread that they use. . . . I have not suffered for lack of food, as I am allowed to fry pancakes for myself." Over the next few years, Berta continued to long for Norwegian dishes, writing of her yearnings for a holiday treat in 1893: "How I wish I were close enough to go home and have Christmas in Bjørvåg and taste your delicious Christmas porridge. What I wouldn't give, Mother, for a few spoonfuls of that porridge and a little of your good pickled pork."[78] Many homesick immigrants yearned for and remembered the simple repasts they had enjoyed at their mother's table.

Some immigrants, particularly those in urban areas, could more easily satisfy their hunger for the foods of home than Kingestad because they were able to purchase familiar dishes from a range of businesses springing up in immigrant districts. Entrepreneurial newcomers frequently opened restaurants, hoping to drum up a trade among their homesick countrymen. Often it was single men who had come without wives, mothers, or daughters to cook for them, who frequented such places, trying to satisfy their hunger for homeland and home cooking. In *Greeks in America*, published in 1913, Thomas Burgess described a Greek restaurant that opened its doors in 1885 in New York City: "It was a poor, forlorn affair; yet to the lonely immigrant it meant comradeship and a breath of home. This the peddlers made their rendezvous. Here they found the cooking of home, and here they could discuss their present interests and the affairs of the fatherland."[79] Other ethnic groups also established restaurants to serve their countrymen; by the 1930s, there were ten thousand Italian restaurants in New York City catering to homesick immigrants' tastes.[80]

Those who wanted to cook the traditional dishes of home for themselves came to rely on immigrant-owned stores, many of which imported goods from overseas.[81] Immigrant grocers offered their customers a rich array of foods that might slake the hunger of the homesick. In the Sicilian neighborhood in Chicago that the sociologists Robert Park and Herbert Miller studied, "there was no food for sale that was not distinctly foreign; it was impossible to buy butter, American cheese, sweet potatoes, pumpkin, green corn, etc., but in season artichokes, cactus fruit (fichi d'India), pomegranates, cocozella, and various herbs and greens never sold in other parts of town were plentiful."[82] By the late nineteenth century and early twentieth, there were countless ethnic grocery stores, bakeries, and restaurants selling such items. A study from the 1930s showed that New York City boasted around ten thousand Italian and ten thousand Jewish grocery stores. Collectively, such businesses sold an impressive quantity of imported foods: millions of gallons of wine, thousands of gallons of olive oil, and tons of figs. Non-European immigrant communities displayed the same pattern. Chinese in California imported millions of pounds of rice each year, Japanese imported thousands of pounds of red pickled plums, and Mexicans supported a lively trade in imported green chilis.[83]

These consumer patterns had implications not just for the homesick, but for merchants as well. As a result of their reliance on local ethnic grocers, immigrant communities were much slower to admit chain stores into their neighborhoods because they offered only "American" food rather than Greek or Italian or Polish delicacies to which they were accustomed.[84] The corporations that owned the chain markets did not yet realize the profits to be made by catering to the homesick, but ethnic entrepreneurs, who often experienced the emotion themselves, certainly did.

Entrepreneurs were most likely to set up shop in urban areas, and for that reason the bounty of the consumer economy was most available to immigrants who settled in cities. These immigrants were the first to fully taste the fruits of a global consumer economy; their emotional experience differed from that of earlier generations who, because of slower ships and more expensive freight rates, could not as easily acquire Old World staples in the New World. The ability to import the goods of home relatively easily was a feature of immigrant culture and social life that emerged only in the late nineteenth century. It became a pattern that would be commonplace for succeeding generations of immigrants, who looked to the consumer economy to provide them with a connection to home.

In these ethnic neighborhoods, immigrants could find not just the tastes of home, but news of it, for immigrant newspapers flourished. Most often written in the immigrants' native languages, they carried updates on the events of small villages overseas. No matter how long they had been in America, many immigrants still wanted to know what was going on back home and subscribed to such papers for years. In 1907, a Swedish immigrant living in Minnesota reported, "Although I have now been in this country for sixteen years I still follow the course of events back home and take great interest in the welfare of my homeland." He read a half dozen Swedish American newspapers because they "include[d] a couple of pages of news from Sweden as well as special correspondence on the events of the day.... I feel a deep love for the land where my cradle stood, where my old father lives, and where my mother's remains lie at rest."[85] So popular were such papers and so eagerly did immigrants seek out news of their former homes that Emily Greene Balch, who studied Slavic communities, found that there were more Slovak-language newspapers in America than in the Old World. Many carried features designed to inform "homesick exiles of happenings, big and little, in the old country." Often it was the little happenings that held most interest for the readers: "No village occurrence is too small to be reported. Especially in Slovak papers I have noticed the columns of quaint individual happenings, arranged country by country."[86] Just as Boston newspapers gave New England Forty-niners in California a feeling of connection to their home communities, so foreign-language papers offered that same sense of connection. And with faster means of communication, from the telegraph to transoceanic steamships, one might know the news from home soon after it had occurred. These papers helped keep immigrants invested in their homelands and fostered the growth of nationalism.[87]

Ethnic colonies offered other connections to home, as well. Immigrants built churches and temples that blended old traditions with new realities. The historian Timothy L. Smith noted that for many immigrants, religion became more important in the New World because of the very "acts of uprooting, migration, and repeated resettlement." Newcomers experienced not only loneliness and homesickness but also guilt at having left home, and often their feelings coalesced around the imagined order and purity of their village congregation. For that reason, Smith suggested, "migration was often a theologizing experience." While immigrants might believe they were just being faithful to old ways, America increased their faithfulness and often their level of orthodoxy and observance.[88] Religion offered immigrants the (sometimes false) sense that they were participating in the very same rituals their ancestors had. It gave them a feeling of continuity both with their forebears and with biblical times, comforting them at a time when so much of their experience was discontinuous with that of their ancestors. Religion gave immigrants a sense that they were part of an unbroken chain that stretched across generations and across oceans.

Congregations also offered a connection not only to the past and to home, but to fellow countrymen who had settled in America. This too soothed homesickness and was a reason religion took on even greater importance in America than in the immigrants' homelands, where such opportunities for community might be taken for granted. As one Norwegian immigrant recalled, "The church was overcrowded because there was no Sons of Norway where we lived. It was a place to meet." Another noted, "People at church lived on memories. It was a social club rather than a church."[89]

Some immigrants desired to reproduce not just the bonds of kinship and the ambience they had known in the Old World, but also as much of the worship service of their home churches as they could. For instance, Dutch immigrants in Grand Rapids often sent for pastors from their home villages in Holland to minister to their reconstituted congregations in America.[90] Italian Catholics likewise tried to re-create traditional religious practices, frequently requesting priests from their particular province.[91] Many Italian neighborhoods also adopted the saints of their home villages and imported statues of them. These became the focal point of religious festivals held on the gritty streets of American cities.[92] Jewish congregations re-created the conditions of Old World worship. One observer noted that synagogues on the Lower East Side of Manhattan were "organized on the basis of common origins in Europe. The name of such a synagogue or aid society indicates that it has been formed by a group of persons who emigrated from the same village or city in the Old World."[93]

That immigrants gravitated toward religious ritual for emotional reasons as well as spiritual was evident to many. Bishop Scalabrini, an Italian bishop and advocate for immigrants within the Catholic Church, noted that men and women loved God and loved family. "Both, together with some other elements, form the idea of nationality. Thus, as long as a person, even passively, remains faithful to the religion of his forebears, he feels the love of family and with it the love of country. . . . Faithfulness to religion takes along faithfulness to fatherland."[94]

Congregants often attended services in search of just such a connection, as a young Russian immigrant confided to the "Bintel Brief," the advice column of the *Jewish Daily Forward*. He had joined the Progressive Society, which eschewed religion, yet he nevertheless was drawn to synagogue during the High Holy Days, when he felt melancholy: "My memory goes back to my happy childhood years. I see clearly before me the small town, the fields, the little pond and the woods. . . . I recall my childhood friends and our sweet childlike faith. My heart is constricted, and I begin to run like a madman till the tears stream from my eyes and I become calmer. These emotions and these moods have become stronger over the years and I decided to go to the synagogue." He went to salve his homesickness, he admitted: "I went not in order to pray to God but to heal and refresh my aching soul with the cantor's sweet melodies, and this had an unusually good effect on me." Services transported him away from the

dreary condition of his present life to a happier place: "Sitting in the synagogue among *landsleit* and listening to the good cantor, I forgot my unhappy weekday life, the dirty shop, my boss, the bloodsucker, and my
pale, sick wife and my children. All of my America with its hurry-up life
was forgotten."[95]

Salvatore Castagnola offered another account of the psychological comforts of religious observance. His mother, who had traded her high social
position in Messina, Italy, for the less exalted station of a laborer's wife in
Brooklyn, found her sense of self restored at church. "She prayed constantly
and burned votive candles to her patron saint, La Madonna del Carmine,
who had been . . . [her] protector since early childhood. . . . No longer was
she in a far away land, strange and desolate. . . . Here, distance was not [a]
barrier, she was no longer alone as she had always felt, away from her sisters
and relations. The Good Madonna who knew her well spoke to her in her
native tongue."[96] The pews of many churches were filled with parishioners
seeking such comfort. A Catholic priest noted that aged Irish transplants
found their chief solace in religion: "The familiar scenes and associations of
from fifty to seventy years are lost; and no amount of novelty in the change
of circumstances can fill up the blank caused thereby in the affections of the
heart. If it were not for the deep religious sentiment which seems to be inherent in our race, much more discontent and despondence would prevail
among old people who emigrate than we now meet with."[97]

A host of secular institutions also helped immigrants make their way in
America and stay connected to ethnic and even hometown communities.
Thousands of fraternal and mutual benefit societies emerged in immigrant
neighborhoods. By the second decade of the twentieth century, an estimated 75 percent of Poles living in the United States belonged to a fraternal
organization—800,000 immigrants in more than seven thousand societies.[98] By the early twentieth century, Italian immigrants in Chicago had
created 110 mutual aid societies with 150,000 members; nationwide there
were more than 1,110 Italian organizations in thirty-five states.[99] A study
completed in 1917–18 estimated that members of Jewish fraternal organizations numbered close to 1 million. By the 1940s, in Chicago alone, there
were more than six hundred Jewish *landsmanschaftn*, societies of immigrants from the same hometown.[100]

Their purposes were multiple. One historian described such groups as a
"brotherhood of memory" that looked back to the traditions of the homeland. At the same time, such organizations helped immigrants find their
bearings as they moved forward in the New World.[101] At least in the early
years of their existence, most were based on village and provincial ties and
helped to reinforce and re-create the web of relationships that had existed in
the homeland. In 1894, for instance, *L'Italia*, an Italian-language newspaper

published in Chicago, announced, "The people from a town in Italy called Arizi are founding a society. . . . In Chicago there are 50 people from Arizi Province Basilicata Italy. A society was founded and called the Arizis Society of Mutuo Soccoroso (Arizi Society for Mutual Assistance). . . . The rest of the Colony are wishing this society and its members loads of success."[102] Small groups like this were common, for most desired to re-create intimate village ties in growing American cities.

An important function of these organizations was to provide immigrants with burial services and benefits. Time and again, and regardless of their country of origin, immigrants expressed a fear of dying away from home, amidst strangers, and being buried in unmarked or unsanctified grounds. Whether they were Italian, Greek, Chinese, or Russian Jews, most newcomers to America harbored similar fears. An Irish ballad, "The Shores of Americay," spelled out the dark worries that plagued immigrants:

> And if I die in a foreign land,
> from my home and friends far away,
> No kind mother's tears will flow o'er my
> Grave on the shores of Americay.[103]

In the face of such misgivings, burial societies offered an assurance that immigrants' kinsmen and fellow villagers would safeguard their souls and bodies. If they could not die where they were born, they could rest easier in the knowledge that they would not die uncared for in a strange land. In Peoria, Illinois, immigrants from Itoo, a hamlet in Lebanon, formed the Itoo Society in 1914. According to records of the group, "A fatal accident of one of their fellowmen who had just arrived required them to raise money for his burial. It was then they decided to organize the society for charitable purposes in aiding their fellow Itooians in times of misfortune."[104] Such a pattern was consistent across ethnic groups. A resident of Italian Harlem confided to an interviewer. "Preservation of funeral rituals is sacred to the old folks. . . . And so the Mutual Aid Societies are fulfilling their probably most important role in assuring a member of a dignified funeral."[105] If they were not laid to rest at home, members might die confident in the knowledge that they would be cared for by and interred alongside their fellow villagers.

The organizations also offered comfort in daily life. The *Sunday Jewish Courier*, a Chicago Yiddish newspaper, described early fraternal lodges in America. They had been founded "to overcome that strangeness and loneliness which existed among the Jewish immigrants, who had been torn away and driven from their homes, their surroundings, and everything dear to them. During the period of distress and misfortune, the Jewish immigrant was particularly in need of a helping hand and the lodges promised to extend such aid. It is no wonder, therefore, that large numbers of Jewish immigrants joined these lodges."[106] The editorialist supposed the feelings of anomie were particular to Jewish immigrants, but these emotions cut across ethnic lines. A German newspaper published in Chicago, the *Abendpost,* described immigrants' reliance on such organizations. After the initial years of "gnawing homesickness," immigrants became "acclimatized" as "their adopted country shared its wealth and freedom with them. . . . But still they carried the memories of their old home town in their hearts. In their 'Schwaben Verein' [clubs for natives of Swabia], in their 'guilds,' in Singing Societies or 'Turner-Vereins' [gymnastic clubs], in German churches with German Pastors and with the harmony of German church songs, they found, in the city, as well as in the rural districts, their little old home village again."[107]

Immigrants eagerly flocked to the social events sponsored by these groups. Sometimes they were informal in their structure and their activities. Marietta Interlandi, born in Sicily in 1898, came to Chicago in 1906 and eventually married a young man from her hometown. She recalled of her life in Chicago, "Well, we had like a bunco club from our town, all women from our town. . . . From Acate, that's right, all from our town, and we organized it and there used to be about 14 of us and we used to meet at each other's house, you know, have lunch, play bunco, talk and have little parties once in a while, you know, stuff like that."[108] Such clubs kept village ties alive.

Many groups, however, were more formal in their programs and more focused on the larger homeland. In 1900, the *Skandinaven* reported, "A Norwegian concert was given last Sunday afternoon and evening at Humboldt Park House. . . . A number of works of Norwegian composers were presented, such as . . . 'Norway Home echoes.'" The Chicago Lithuanian newspaper *Lietuva* reported in 1905, "A branch of the Lovers of Fatherland Society was organized on Sunday, January 15, on the North Side of Chicago. The first meeting was held with songs and declamations. . . . Miss Aldona Narmunciute recited the poem, 'I am a Lithuanian Child' and sang 'I am Reared in Lithuania.' Miss Antigona Aukstakalniute recited the poems: 'Wake up Brother Ancestor' and 'As Long as You are Young, Loving Brother, Sow the Seed'; she also sang two songs 'Hello Brother Singers' and the 'Love of Lithuania.'"[109]

The ethnic neighborhoods and the fraternal lodges that flourished in them provided immigrants with a sense of their old selves. What many immigrants longed for was a lost "social order," in which they had a role and a place.[110] Some had lost status in their migration to America, and mutual benefit organizations helped restore to them a sense of significance. As a historian of the Sons of Norway organization noted, "The immigrant, in associating with people of his own race, who understood his language and were able to appreciate his national characteristics, was given recognition for his own worth. Had he not mingled with his own, he would have been constrained for an indefinite period to pass as the 'ignorant foreigner.'"[111] Salvatore Castagnola witnessed the social value that immigrants found in mingling with their own and joining such organizations. His parents had been prosperous and respected citizens in their hometown of Messina, for his father had been the captain of a schooner. In America, the family suffered a loss of status and a change in their identity. While there were many things they missed about life in Italy, one of them was their position. Castagnola's father found his dignity at least partially restored when he became president of the Messinese Society: "Here within the walls of the Society [they] were no longer the slaves of unmerciful exploitation. They were not icemen, longshoremen, diggers, and scavengers,—they were secretaries, treasurers, and masters-at-arms."[112]

These organizations also helped immigrants stay tied to the Old World. Many sponsored trips home. In 1895, the *Sioux City Journal* described the departure of five hundred Swedes, Danes, and Norwegians who were going home for a Christmas visit. While loyal to their new country, many "from the time of their landing look forward to a visit to their homes on the other side of the Atlantic about Christmas time." Departing from Chicago's Dearborn Station on a train bound for New York, the travelers were seen off by friends: "As the train pulled out the bands struck up the Swedish national anthem and a thousand voices joined in the chorus."[113]

The neighborhoods, the churches, and especially the fraternal organizations crystallized immigrants' sense of nationality. Often, foreign governments collaborated with these groups to keep alive among immigrant populations a connection and sense of obligation to home.[114] The organizations tried to tie memories of the family house and native village to memories of the larger nation. The connections between nationalism and homesickness were evident in many of the groups' activities, which frequently invoked the idea of a common past, a shared blood, and a bond to the soil of a distant land. For example, in 1922 a Chicago immigrant group, the Ceskoslovenská Národní Rada v Americe (Czechoslovak National Council in America), tried to foster support for Czechoslovakia, a new nation created in the wake of World War I that incorporated diverse ethnic groups. The organization attempted to bridge such differences, as it called upon "all the Czechoslovaks of Chicago and vicinity, regardless of their political or religions affiliations, to attend a festival in which an urn, containing the sacred soil of places very dear to all of us will be received.... The shipment of the urn was accompanied by the following letter: 'May you, our brothers ... be inspired whenever you look upon this urn. May the secret whispers of the symbolism of these three clods of native earth become audible to you.'"

In the same year, another Czech organization in Chicago sponsored a trip back to Czechoslovakia. In describing the journey, an officer of the organization mixed memories of home with references to the nation as a whole: "In a few days you will be on your way to the land where your cradle stood, the land which you left ... while still young. . . . You may consider yourselves lucky to have the opportunity of seeing the thresholds of your native homes, to look at the roofs under which you spent your childhood days. . . . Many of you will still find under the same roofs your aged fathers and careworn mothers who will clasp you in their embrace and tell you about their sorrows and their pleasures while you dwelt abroad. Only a few days more and you will see that dear beloved homeland." The speaker associated the intimate and familiar details of home life with the national life; as one historian has observed, "hearth and home, rather than sceptre and sword," came to symbolize national identities. Such ceremonies and expeditions excited feelings of sentimentality and homesickness, endowing them with a public and communal meaning. Irish, Italians, Slovenians, Greeks, Hungarians all developed a bond not just to their home villages but to their nations while living in the United States. Even eastern European Jews who had fled oppression and pogroms sometimes romanticized not just their families, but the nations they had left.[115]

This sense of ethnicity and nationalism grew out of homesickness and, in many cases, was able to develop only after immigrants had left their homelands. In 1879, a Polish government official noted that in Poland, citizens were indifferent to their national identity; when abroad they were not: "Every Polish peasant, from whatever Polish province he comes, ... when transferred to a strange soil among foreigners develops a Polish sentiment and a consciousness of his national character. . . . National consciousness originates in him spontaneously in a foreign country in consequence of the feeling of the striking difference between his speech, his customs, his conceptions, from those of the people who surround him."[116] Another observer of the era, Emily Greene Balch, suggested in 1910, "When men are scattered in a strange country, the 'consciousness of kind' with fellow countrymen has a very special significance. . . . To many an immigrant the idea of nationality first becomes real after he has left his native country; at home the contrast was between village and village, and between peasants as a class and landlords as a class. In America he finds a vast world of people, all speaking unintelligible tongues, and for the first time he has a vivid sense of oneness with those who speak his own language, whether here or at home."[117] Among immigrants, a sense of ethnicity and nationalism grew in the fertile soil of memory and longing.[118]

MASTERING EMOTIONS

Coping with homesickness through ethnic festivals, nationalist sentiments, or religious services were strategies that worked for some newcomers, but not all. Émigrés sometimes found their emotions overpowering and succumbed to them. In 1901, Yadro Espier, a Puerto Rican, used a double-barreled shotgun to kill himself in San Jose, California. The San Jose newspaper announced, "Nostalgia drove lonely native to meet awful end."[119] "Self-slain Irish girl was homesick—Katie Clark cuts her throat in hour of despondency," reported the *Boston Sunday Journal* in 1903. A month later, that paper carried the news that a Swiss immigrant, "homesick for alps," had used the same means to end his life.[120] In 1907, the *Tucson Citizen* reported, "Two homesick Greeks end their lives with gas." The men had lived in Chicago, and one of them left behind a suicide note that read, "America is not as great a country as my own."[121] The same year, newspaper readers also learned that a seventeen-year-old Hungarian bride swallowed laudanum and died in her husband's arms after declaring that she was "so lonesome and homesick that she did not desire to live."[122] Readers of the "Bintel Brief" read a desperate plea from a suicidally homesick newcomer: "I am lonely here in the country where I have been for five years and I believe that's long enough, that it's time I should free myself from my troubles. My 'freedom' is already standing on the table in my bedroom. I beg forgiveness from my friends. Good-by. Respectfully, The Unfortunate One from Stanton Street, New York."[123]

Not all used such dramatic means. Some seemed to waste away, victims of depression. J. M. McHale, an Irish priest new to Brooklyn, died of starvation induced by nostalgia in 1887.[124] After eight months in the United States, Cal Abraham, a seventeen-year-old Assyrian, wasted away and died in 1896. The *Daily Charlotte Observer* reported, "His friends say he was homesick all the time, and would sometimes sit for hours thinking of home. When he took sick he had no hope nor seemed to want to live."[125]

The suicides, though dramatic, were relatively rare. Mental breakdowns, however, were not, and many social scientists at the turn of the century observed with concern that within the United States there was a higher rate of insanity among the foreign-born than the native-born.[126] The Census Bureau repeatedly arrived at such conclusions, as did a variety of physicians and psychologists.[127] Many supposed that this was caused by the great gulf that separated the old life and the new. As the Committee on Lunacy reported to the Pennsylvania Board of Public Charities, the high incidence of insanity among immigrants might be attributed to "the sundering of home ties without an abandonment of home affections. . . . It must be recognized that the daily prolific cause of insanity, Nostalgia, finds among the foreigners a harvest field."[128]

As they examined foreigners' elevated insanity rates, psychologists, reformers, and immigration critics searched for patterns. Some studies indicated that women fared worse than men, perhaps because they did not get
to make the decision to migrate for themselves.[129] There were other patterns
as well; observers frequently maintained that nervous disorders associated
with homesickness and nostalgia were particular to one ethnicity or another. In 1888, doctors at the Illinois Eastern Hospital for the Insane
claimed that although nostalgia and disappointment made all immigrants
vulnerable to insanity, Germans and Scandinavians were especially susceptible to depression.[130] Edward Steiner commented on the large number of
pathologically gloomy Swedes, Danes, and Norwegians, "The asylums
of the Northwest are full of Scandinavian men and women who have sunk
into hopeless melancholia because of homesickness."[131] Maurice Fishberg
of the United Hebrew Charities believed Jews had a "natural tendency . . .
toward nervous disorders," which led to the "morbid conditions of nostalgia," and culminated in "melancholia and insanity," and even death.[132]

Dr. Allan McLaughlin of the U.S. Public Health Service did not single
out a particular ethnicity as especially vulnerable to mental and physical
breakdown. He maintained that all of the southern and eastern Europeans
flooding into America represented degraded racial stock, claiming he could
see a "pronounced deterioration in the general physique of the immigrants
and a much higher percent of loathsome and dangerous disease." He was
worried about contagious physical ailments they might carry, such as tuber-
culosis and trachoma; he also fretted about their supposedly higher rates of
insanity, suggesting that while most who became insane were sane when
they landed, they carried with them a predisposition to mental instability
that was provoked by "nostalgia or homesickness, or other exciting causes,"
all of which served to "unbalance" such aliens.[133]

These ideas were typical of the era, for racial and ethnic theories
abounded in the late nineteenth century and early twentieth, and most of
the theories carried the imprint of social Darwinism. Social scientists, reformers, and nativists often divided populations into pseudo-racial categories, conceiving of Slavs, Jews, and Italians as different races.[134] Implicit in
such categories and explicit in their theories was the belief that some races
and individuals were superior to others. Nativists believed Anglo-Saxons to
be the best race and worked assiduously to limit the in-migrations of southern and eastern Europeans, Asians, and Africans. Immigrants' perceived
mental instability and vulnerability to the ravages of nostalgia provided
them with ammunition, for they could point to the newcomers filling
America's asylums as a threat to national strength and racial purity.

It was not just the insanely nostalgic who elicited concern, however. Many
native-born Americans believed that even mildly homesick immigrants

undermined the nation in other ways. Those who came as "birds of passage," with every intention of going home, were financial drains on the U.S. economy. They added little and extracted much.[135] In *The Immigrant Invasion*, Frank Julian Warne railed against sojourners who were only in the United States so that they could get rich and return home: "Every mail takes thousands of dollars to Italy, Austria-Hungary, and Russia where they are placed as savings in the banks of the principal cities in the emigration districts, these having on deposit millions of dollars earned in America. This immigrant earns and saves and in a few years returns home." In the meantime, he carried on life in "degraded" living conditions in the United States and drove down conditions and wages for others.[136] Homesick immigrants were improving their old homes at the expense of their new.

Ethnic colonies and their ties to foreign countries were similarly vulnerable to criticism. If immigrants were going to come to the United States (and many critics were convinced they should not), they should at least work to integrate themselves into American society. Their continued isolation in foreign enclaves and their participation in fraternal organizations, which often were supported by foreign governments, were troubling signs that this generation of immigrants might remain outside the mainstream of American life.[137] Their stubborn refusal to "melt" in the vaunted melting pot worried some observers and inflamed others. In the context of World War I, this became an even greater problem. "Hyphenated Americans," who clung too tightly to an ethnic identity, were seen as having dubious loyalty to the nation. They should be single-minded in their commitment to their new home, not harkening back to memories of their old one.[138] Homesickness and its cultural manifestations were troubling stumbling blocks on the route to assimilation and national unity.

These various critiques of homesick immigrants represented two competing conceptions of immigrants and race. The historian John Higham noted that for much of the nineteenth century, native-born Americans (particularly those of English or German extraction) had confidence that Anglo-Saxon culture defined America; this culture was powerful enough to transform diverse peoples into Americans. This was a vision based on race, but it was loosely defined, allowing outsiders to join the American race so long as they assimilated. Scientists like Charles Darwin and social theorists like Herbert Spencer gave this idea support, suggesting that immigration was an extension of Darwinian selection, often holding up America as the destination for the best men and women. In such a schema, immigrants would naturally self-select and come, filled with energy, to the United States. The nation would be enriched by their presence.[139] Consequently, to proponents of such a vision of America, the homesick "birds of passage" who wanted to return to their native lands were worrisome, for they refused to assimilate. Even when sojourners decided to settle permanently in the United States, their tendency to remain in ethnic colonies, to cluster amidst reminders of their foreign homes, posed a challenge to prevailing definitions of national culture.

In the late nineteenth century, some began to doubt the assimilative power of Anglo-Saxon nationality, and instead attacked immigration from a new angle. They regarded the foreigners coming to the country as biologically weaker races who should not be admitted into the nation, for they would dilute its power rather than augment its strength.[140] To those who thought in these terms, the alleged temperamental weaknesses of the newcomers, evident in their patterns of homesick insanity, were one of many telling indicators of their racial inferiority.

Newcomers had to contend with such perceptions, and consequently immigrant leaders worried about the homesick in their own communities. Those who favored assimilation saw their compatriots' homesickness as a weakness that rendered them unworthy of America's bounty. For instance, Maurice Fishberg wrote, "Nostalgia . . . is the first and most effective aid to the natural selection of desirable immigrants. It is only the immigrants who are least capable of assimilation that develop the worst symptoms of homesickness. Just in so far as the immigrant is unable to adjust himself to conditions of life in America will he be afflicted with nostalgia. The hopeless cases are eliminated—by death, suicide, insanity, or by the less heroic method of returning to their native country. The desirable element is assimilated and produces good citizens for its adopted country."[141] In keeping with this view, the United Hebrew Charities, for which Fishberg worked, sent thousands of homesick immigrants back to their homelands during the late nineteenth century, fearing that those who could not adapt to the United States would be a burden on the community.[142]

Not all immigrant advisors spoke in such explicitly Darwinist terms, yet they nevertheless shared the belief that homesickness was a sign of weakness and must be mastered. Those who did not recognize the opportunities that America afforded were fools. This advice was most visible in the Jewish community, where homesickness was often widespread but home itself less than hospitable. An advice book for Russian Jews published in 1891 counseled those making the journey to focus on assimilating into their new culture: "Forget your past, your customs and your ideals. Select a goal and pursue it with all your might. No matter what happens to you, hold on."[143] The "Bintel Brief" repeatedly reminded readers of this emotional imperative, telling the homesick they should recognize America's superiority to their homelands. In 1911, a despondent immigrant wrote in to the column, "A long gloomy year . . . [has] gone by since I left my home. . . . My homesickness and loneliness darken my life. Ah, home, my beloved home." He asked whether he should return. In reply, the editor compared immigrants to "plants that are transplanted to new ground. At first it seems that they are withering, but in time most of them revive and take root in the new earth. The advice to this young man is that he must not consider going home, but try to take root here. He should try to overcome all these emotions and strive to make something of himself so that in time he will be able to bring his parents here."[144] Newcomers should develop traits of hardiness and adaptability. Those who could not adapt and evolve to fit new circumstances would perish. The idea of adaptability was especially celebrated by Jewish immigrant leaders, who, after the Kishnieff pogrom, wanted to discourage reverse migrations because of the dangers of the homeland. They believed the failure to adapt had life-or-death consequences.

Other émigrés who faced less perilous returns nevertheless encountered similar advice. They should force themselves to adjust to American life or face failure. An Irish immigrant told his brother, "Never . . . come to this Country wile you are undecided whether it would suit you better than Ireland, for no body prospers Here that thinks they could do better at home. When you make up your mind to leave Ireland, do it for good and all."[145] A French Canadian woman living in Manchester, New Hampshire, worked hard to put memories of where she came from behind her. Early on she resolved to look "forward": "I was always proud of my French ancestry, but I 'acclimated myself artificially.' I did not wish to live in the past; you cannot go very far nor advance very fast if you look behind you."[146]

Some immigrants tried to accomplish this emotional feat by emulating earlier Americans who had faced similar challenges. On occasion, newcomers likened themselves to pioneers who had headed west, using them as models of emotional comportment. Amadeo Yelmini, who was born in 1903 in Milan and emigrated in 1921, was sorely tempted to return home but ultimately did not: "As a pioneer I stuck to it. One thing my mother did when I came here, she gave me sufficient money, cash to return. If you don't like it, you come right back. But after I got there, I figured well, this country was developed by people with courage so I'm going to stick it out."[147] Other immigrants referred to their early years in America as their "pioneering era."[148]

Although the pioneers themselves had often been homesick, they were mythologized as brave men and women who set forth and never looked back. Few seemed to realize that pioneers had struggled with their emotions in the antebellum period, that many had wanted to and sometimes did go back to their homes in the East. Nor did they realize that being a bird of passage was a long American tradition, dating back as far as Jamestown, that having one's eyes focused on some other place was nothing new. Although homesickness had long been a part of the American experience, this history was suppressed. Immigrants at the turn of the century felt increasing pressure to master the emotion if they wanted to fit in to their new community. Eventually, their own migrations to America would be idealized and their profound homesickness forgotten. They too would be installed in the pantheon of American heroes alongside the pioneers, portrayed as people who had bravely moved forward and embraced the future.

Yet, in reality, most immigrants did not completely shed their pasts or free themselves from homesickness. They faced forward but also looked backward, gradually integrating themselves and their families into American culture while still holding on to Old World traditions, customs, and connections.[149] Many felt homesick their whole lives, and while social critics increasingly saw the emotion as quaint at best and a sign of maladaptation at worst, for most it served a useful psychological purpose. Feeling homesick allowed immigrants to express fidelity to old lifeways and family relationships even as they sought new social statuses and opportunities.[150] It was a bridge that connected their old identities with their new, and preserved a sense of self in an alien environment.

THE PROBLEM WITH GOING HOME

Throughout their lives, a significant number of immigrants wanted to cross that bridge, go home, and assume their former identities. Some who went back soon after they left successfully reintegrated themselves into their old worlds. Those who waited longer, however, often had a more difficult time. Despite the fact that they had been homesick for years, they discovered they could never really return home. When they arrived in their native lands, they found them different than they remembered.[151] In 1920, Marcus Ravage, a Romanian immigrant, and his French wife had such an experience when they decided to visit their childhood villages. Ravage wrote of their journey home, "As for the old place, why it was the one thing in all the world I wanted to see. It was the thought that some day I would go back that had kept me alive. Only I had been dreaming of it so long that the craving had come to seem more agreeable that the realization. To return to Rumania was like going to heaven." Upon their return, however, the couple was disillusioned, for what they found when they arrived in Europe did not match their memories. Arriving at his village, Ravage discovered that his brightest classmate, never having moved, lived an impoverished, unstimulating life. He concluded that his move had been for the best. An interaction in America solidified his new attitude: he asked the man who shined his shoes, "'Why don't you go home for a while? Aren't you homesick for Italy?' 'No, sir' said Tony with conviction. 'No Italy for me. No good there.

America fine enough for me.' 'You are a wise man, Tony,' said I, 'and you've got a better memory than I have.'"[152] Ravage had been homesick for a home that no longer (and perhaps never had) existed.

Other immigrants made the same discovery. Ellen Raatikka wrote of her grandparents, "In 1901 my grandparents . . . left for America and settled in Brantwood, Wisconsin. . . . They bought a small farm and worked in lumber camps. . . . In 1910 they sold their farm . . . with the idea that they would move back to Finland to live. After being only six weeks in Finland, they decided to return to America."[153] John Lindberg found the same pattern among Swedish immigrants who sometimes yielded to the "consuming longing" to return home. Once in Sweden, however, they received a shock: "Old friends and relatives are dead; the remembered idyll vanishes with the advance of a new age, and the returned emigrant feels himself deeply disillusioned." Such repatriated migrants felt isolated and homesick for the United States and could not fit back into their old lives. "After a time [they are] glad to return to America."[154]

Countless immigrants who returned home had similarly jarring encounters. Emma Matko Planinsek, who migrated from Slovenia in 1921, revisited her native village after many years: "I was home again, visiting and speaking endlessly with people, who were part of my past . . . but at the same time realizing with each passing day, that I was no longer tied to my homeland as I had imagined. My heart, which had carried the weight of loneliness for four decades, suddenly was lightened and relieved from fantasies of what might have been. . . . It was evident how much Trbovlje had changed; how much I had changed, and how impossible it was to go back in time and expect everything to be the way I had left it." The realization that she was separated from her childhood home not just by distance, but by time, cured her of her homesickness. "Those early years in Trbovlje and Zagreb became cherished memories of a beautiful but distant youth. America—my new home—was my real home. My roots were firmly transplanted from the 'old country' to the 'new country.' My heart was now at peace."[155]

These immigrants' painful homesickness finally had been replaced by nostalgia, as they realized that true return was impossible. Such a sensibility could become widespread only in an age of rapid and affordable travel, when it became easier to go back to places one had left and to learn how they had changed. At the same time that native-born Americans returning home for Old Home Week realized that home was unreachable, immigrants who went back to their native villages came to the same conclusion. Recognizing that the old life for which they had longed was unrecoverable, many headed back to the United States, convinced that their true home was in America.

Even those who returned to their native lands and stayed there permanently often had mixed feelings about their homes. Many were ashamed that they had succumbed to homesickness. They insisted that interviewers give them pseudonyms if they wrote about their lives. Men on occasion blamed their wives for their return, suggesting that it was the women's homesickness rather than their own that had prompted their homeward voyages. These repatriated immigrants felt they had failed by coming back; their return was a sign that they had not made it in America. Yet they also felt that they did not fit in their old lands. Betty Boyd Caroli interviewed Italian immigrants who had gone back and forth between continents. One had migrated to West Virginia before World War I, returned to Italy, and there "he was surprised to find himself dissatisfied with life in the small town. . . . After a year he set out once again for the United States, and for the next 38 years he continued this back and forth migration between the two countries." When Caroli interviewed him in the late 1960s, he had finally returned for good to his hometown of Bagnoli del Trigno. "'It's difficult to come back,' Foglia said. 'You miss the conveniences. All the friends I once had here [in Bagnoli del Trigno] are dead or they have emigrated. Nobody is here to discuss with me the things I have seen and want to talk about. I have had many experiences that I cannot share with them. But . . . the only family I have . . . are here and I want to spend the last days of my life with them.'"[156]

Theodore Saloutos found mixed emotions among repatriated Greeks. He wrote of Mr. A., who longed for Greece while in America, and once back in Greece longed for America: "He never realized how contented he had been in America until he went to Greece to live. Today America is but a dream, and he tries to capture some of its spirit by glancing through discarded copies of *Life* magazine. When asked for a final comment, Mr. A responded with the title of a once popular tune: 'I Wish I Was in Peoria Tonight.'" Other immigrants shared Mr. A's ambivalence. According to Saloutos, "Some repatriates frankly admitted that they were unhappy in Greece during the first few months or years. A Peloponnesian who had lived in the United States from 1899 to 1913, and then had returned to the same general part of Greece, commented: 'Life was empty. It didn't appeal to me. It was almost zero existence. . . .' Said another who returned in 1927: 'Life appeared peculiar. This wasn't what I had grown accustomed to in the United States. It took me three or four years to adjust myself.'"[157]

Part of the problem was that immigrants had gradually and often unwittingly become accustomed to another standard of living during their time in the United States. Even while preoccupied with thoughts of home, they were enjoying more material comforts than they had grown up with in their native villages. When there was a more uniform standard of living on both sides of the ocean—when no continent enjoyed electricity, heating, running water—the difference between one place and another might not have seemed so great. Yet after being exposed to new conveniences in the United States, immigrants found it difficult to return to places that had none. After emigrating in 1946, Sam Ori, a native of Modena, periodically returned to Italy: "After three weeks, I was ready to come back, you know. God bless America. . . . Things are a little bit different and since I've been here—I've been here so many years, I'm Americanized. . . . I can't go back to the old primitive ways. It's hard. You know, we're spoiled. You get used to all the switches and all the automatic and over there it wasn't quite . . . that way yet and so after a while, you kind of want to come back."[158] Returned Greeks whom Oscar Handlin interviewed in the 1950s had similar misgivings about their old homes: "Almost all who return nowadays are elderly and have imperceptibly become accustomed to American standards of comfort, sanitation, and medicine; they are distressed by the deficiencies of the Old Country."[159] A returned immigrant explained, "I decided to come to Athens to live. Life in Tripolis and in the villages was unappealing. I preferred the city life I knew in the United States. The people seemed untidy. The stores were poorly kept. The food was unappetizing. Sanitation was lacking. . . . It took me about one and a half to two years to adjust myself to Greece. . . . We should have returned to the United States then. But we bought a new home that was completely modern. This made me more content."[160]

Many tried to re-create the texture of life they had enjoyed in the United States. Some imported building styles and appliances; others brought back American foodstuffs and flora. Across Europe, returned immigrants introduced cherries, almonds, lettuce, tomatoes, sewing machines, bicycles, and phonographs to their hometowns.[161] In the United States, they had eagerly sought out reminders of their home villages. Once back home, they sought out mementoes of their life in the United States.

Others who returned tried to re-create some of the culture. Mark Wyman notes, "Danish newspapers as early as 1876 reported formation of a 'United States Club' to unite 'all Danes returned from the United States.'" A raft of other groups was established in Sweden, Greece, Yugoslavia, Finland, Norway, and Italy, bearing such names as the America Club and the Western Wayfarers Club. Veterans who fought for the United States during World War I established branches of the American Legion across Europe.[162] In Greece repatriates founded a George Washington Club to commemorate their years abroad. Its president was a man who had sold fish on Cape Cod for years before finally going back to Greece. Oscar Handlin wrote of him, "It was curious, over in the States he kept being reminded he was a Greek; here he could not forget that he was an American."[163]

From these back-and-forth migrations, immigrants learned that though they could travel across the ocean, they could not really go home again. The home they remembered no longer existed; it had changed and so had they. Certainly those who had returned in earlier years might have experienced such emotions, but the mass migrations and repatriations of the late nineteenth century and early twentieth, and the rapid technological changes that made them possible, highlighted this sense.

Out of these circumstances emerged nostalgia as we know it today: the longing for an unrecoverable time. Before it was so easy to return home, many thought they were longing for a place. However, once they were able to go to that place, they realized that what they yearned for was a lost era. As a writer noted in 1935, "People talk so much about homesickness and such, but I'm not so sure there's any geography involved at all. The country one left, the name of which is childhood or youth—that nobody can return to. We who go on living in the same place don't notice it the same way as those who leave. People don't understand that it's their own youth or generation they have left behind, and so they confuse it with something geographical—when it's rather something inside us."[164] Those who traveled back and found their homes gone gradually came to this same realization. Nostalgia and homesickness became more distinct from one another, both as emotions and as words in the early twentieth century.

A second new sense that emerged during this era was placelessness. If Italians missed Italy when they were in America, and missed America when they were in Italy, where did they belong? If they moved back and forth, where was home? Where and what was one's true self? These were questions born of multiple travels and repeated adjustments. The experience of a German newspaper publisher in Chicago suggested the complexities of immigrants' emotional lives. The man had decided to return to Germany for a visit of at least six months, yet he was back in Chicago within five weeks. He explained that he had gone to a "drinking resort" in Berlin that featured "one of those automatic electric banjos." The machine began to play "Way Down upon the Sewanee River." Upon hearing the song, "tears came to my eyes. Think of it! A German, born in Germany, crying over a negro melody, which I had never heard until I came to America. The plaintive old tune made me homesick for Chicago, and I could no more shake it off than I could fly. . . . That is why I came back so soon."[165] Another German, Martin Koster, who migrated from Amrum in 1922, when he was seventeen, noted that after a time he didn't quite know where home was. He and his wife tried returning to Germany repeatedly but always came back to America. He told an interviewer, "It's hard to explain, because . . . when we were here . . . you were homesick, you wanted to go back to the island. When you were on the island you were homesick for this country."[166] A repatriated Norwegian noted, "Everybody wants to go back, but you end up not knowing where you want to live."[167]

Born of mobility and modernity, this sense of not quite being a native of anywhere was to be increasingly the norm for Americans, both immigrants and native-born. The emotional rules of immigration—that migrants should adapt and adjust, shed the past, and face forward—were guidelines that supported placelessness. Not all immigrants fully accepted such dictates, as America's rich ethnic landscape testifies. Instead, they developed new ways of coping with homesickness. Faced with feelings of not being at home anywhere, they tried to make everywhere home. They maintained ties with their families and native lands, moved back and forth between Old World and New, and imported reminders of their homelands to the United States and mementoes of the United States to their homelands.

CHAPTER 6

⌒∿⌒

Transferring Loyalties

World War I broke out in Europe in the summer of 1914. Americans looked on, but a significant portion of the population was eager to avoid involvement in the conflict, believing that the United States had no role to play in it. Many showed their reluctance to join by singing "Don't Take My Darling Boy Away" and "I Didn't Raise My Son to Be a Soldier."[1] Such songs stressed the importance of the family's claim over the demands of the government. Yet by 1917, after the United States had entered the war in response to Germany's resumption of unrestricted submarine warfare, many began to learn different tunes, most notably "Over There":

> Johnnie, get your gun,
> . . .
> Take it on the run,
> . . .
> Pack your little kit,
> Show your grit, do your bit.
> Yankee to the ranks,
> From the towns and the tanks.
> Make your mother proud of you,
> And to liberty be true.[2]

Some heeded this message willingly, others less so. Young men and their families had to adapt to the new role the nation was playing overseas and the new institutional culture developing at home. Both made demands on

Songs popular in the lead-up to World War I asserted the family's claim over the government's. Historic American Sheet Music, "Don't Take My Darling Boy Away!" (1915), Music A-6074, Rare Book, Manuscript, and Special Collections Library, Duke University.

Americans and required them to establish their identities as members of a bureaucratic society and not merely local communities.[3] This change was visible in attitudes toward homesickness. By and large, men and women, boys and girls, learned that they needed to conquer homesickness, not so they could be rugged individuals, but so they could leave home and fit into the large bureaucracies taking shape across America.

WAR

During World War I, approximately 3.9 million men were in the armed services, 72 percent of whom had been drafted under the Selective Service Act of 1917. This was the first time that draftees made up a majority of the fighting force and was a sign of the new and expanding role of government and the rise of a mass society.[4] In the army, both conscripts and volunteers were channeled through a growing bureaucracy. After appearing before draft boards, those selected for service were sent to training camps across the country. There they encountered psychologists who further assessed their fitness for service. Eager to aid the nation, the American Psychological Association (founded in 1892) organized a number of committees to assist the military. They hoped to use psychological theories to select the personnel most suitable for each position within the armed forces, address the emotional problems of soldiers, and elevate morale.[5] They attempted to screen out men with mental or emotional disabilities, for they believed that even mild problems in civilian life might become serious hindrances during wartime. Psychologists believed that the hardship of war, "with its unavoidable homesickness, loneliness, and depression," as well as its "actual physical dangers and hardships," could lead some men to break down. Such vulnerable individuals would better serve their country by staying home and working in civilian positions that supported the war effort.[6] Through careful screening, psychologists could ensure that the army was filled with well-adjusted individuals, suited to its demanding institutional life.

Those who made it through the various screenings were trained at camps across the country. It was during World War I that U.S. soldiers first received standardized, uniform training, designed to teach them total obedience. In the past, local military divisions had trained men as they saw fit, but beginning in 1917, this process became centralized under the War Plans Division, which maintained that training should follow standard processes and procedures. As a result, men from the same community were often sent to different units across the country, prompting Arnold Rumbarger to complain to his mother that he would tell her "of the feelings of the most homesick and forlorn boys in camp." The army began "separating . . . us Dayton fellows. Today, approximately one-half of the Dayton bunch has been sent away. Some were sent to Louisiana. Some to Florida and some to Washington D.C."[7] Such scattering broke down the comforting localism of the units and transformed them into national entities. The army tried to strip soldiers of local connections in other ways as well. One observer recalled that at training camps, officers required newly drafted men to give up the flags their home communities had given them as they left.[8] Such homey memorabilia had no place in a streamlined bureaucracy.

The army's effort to break down local ties accentuated the divorce between home life and camp life, and led many soldiers to feel lost in these new institutions. One key change soldiers had to grapple with was their diminished autonomy. Compared to earlier wars, the discipline during World War I was stricter, and soldiers' independence more limited. Paul Murphy, a corporal in the 309th Infantry, 78th Division, wrote, "Soldiering meant a complete new life for all of us and it was pretty hard to become adjusted to taking orders and having your whole life regulated by authority other than your own." This was a profound change and not an easy one. At Camp Meade in Maryland, while some draftees appeared lighthearted, others did not. An officer reported, "Others, (many, many of them) were sullen, subdued, sad—and I saw a good many of them who were having a hard time (and not always successfully) in keeping the tears back."⁹

That many men did not like the rigid discipline, standardized training, and bureaucratic atmosphere of camp life was clear. The army hoped to create a fighting force that was completely obedient to it, but this proved more difficult than expected. While still stateside, some young men missed home so much that they asked for furloughs; if and when those were refused, they simply deserted.¹⁰ At training camp, twenty-three-year-old Sherman Thomas witnessed desertions, and said of them, "One or two of the boys from the South went home without permission, but they had never been away from home and were homesick."¹¹ A deserter from Camp Gordon in Atlanta confided, "I was terribly homesick. . . . It is awful when that feeling comes over a fellow, especially one like me who had never been far away from my home in Henry Country. . . . I found myself unable to resist the craving to go home."¹²

Desertion merited execution, but Secretary of War Newton Baker favored suspending the death penalty in desertion cases, at least if they occurred stateside. Others supported his call for leniency. A judge advocate believed the root of the desertion problem was that young men were having difficulty shifting from their roles as private individuals to members of a vast, national bureaucracy: "The army now being assembled is made up of young men . . . many of them mere boys, who, perhaps, have never been absent from their homes. Many are undisciplined in mind and body. Undoubtedly for a time they will find it difficult to distinguish a call into the military service from the contractual obligations of civil life."¹³ The shift from individualism to a corporate existence was emotionally taxing and required the subordination of one set of loyalties to another.

While the war required men to subsume their identities into the institution of the army, and in so doing, conquer or at least conceal their homesickness, there were new organizations created to help them do just this. On both sides of the Atlantic, soldiers found a host of coordinated efforts designed to lift their spirits and assuage their homesickness. The army itself created a new agency, the Morale Division, in 1918, which worked to sustain enthusiasm for wartime service.[14] Some training camps also took extra steps to help soldiers adjust. At Fort Oglethorpe in Georgia, form letters designed to be sent to parents enlisted their help in raising their sons' morale. The letters explained, "You, too, are a part of the Army—you are the Army of Encouragement and Enthusiasm. Write letters filled with these things to Your soldier, and you will help us to help him." The government was using families as informal extensions of its bureaucracy, offering parents advice on how to use private, domestic feeling to achieve national goals.[15]

Another innovation designed to raise morale was the army newspaper, *Stars and Stripes*. Created by the Intelligence Bureau of the American Expeditionary Force, the first issue rolled off the press in February 1918. Edited by a handful of soldiers, the paper proved to be an efficient way to strengthen bonds between members of the AEF.[16] Soldiers had routinely asked for hometown newspapers in order to feel connected with the communities they had left behind; *Stars and Stripes* endeavored to forge a new community within the army to which soldiers could transfer their loyalties.

Commercial institutions also got involved in lifting soldiers' spirits. In December 1917, Pvt. Evan Miller, who was working at a base hospital in France, reported on a package he had received: "On opening it I found it was from Aunt Lill. It contained canned goods of different sorts, some candy and some chewing gum. Aunt Lill had ordered it through Gimbels and it has been sent over to me from England." Affluent families like Miller's used department stores to supply their sons with reminders of home, for in the expanding consumer economy, connections to home might be fostered and maintained with the help of merchants offering mass-produced goods.[17] Indeed, sometimes what young men seemed to miss most were particular branded products. Miller wrote from France to his father in 1918, pleading, "If it is not too much trouble you might send me a box of Hershey bars, about once a month, for we can't buy any good chocolate over here."[18] Thoughts of home centered not just on families and places, but on stores and products as well.

In addition to the for-profit efforts of Gimbels and other department stores, a number of nonprofit groups volunteered their services to help soldiers adjust to army life. While much of their work centered on maintaining virtue within the army, they also worked to transport some of the comforts of home, including consumer goods like candy and cigarettes for which soldiers longed.[19] Among the groups offering such items were the YMCA, the Red Cross, and the Salvation Army. In France, these organizations set up "huts" near the front and offered the young men stationed there a bit of rest and recreation. Herbert Pratt, a Standard Oil executive who organized the YMCA's efforts in France and Italy, saw his work as assuaging "that lonesome feeling . . . that inexpressible longing for familiar things." The Y, he believed, would help men relax and fight the destructive effects of melancholy.[20]

To accomplish this, the huts featured a variety of attractions. Frequently, young women staffed them, serving as hostesses. As the Salvation Army newspaper, the *Mess Kit*, said of its huts' female staff, "The Salvation Army lassies, together with the older women, were the touch of home which comforted the soldier on the front line. . . . Stories have come back to our headquarters of great husky lads who called nineteen year old girls 'Ma.' It was not funny, it was perfectly natural, and the girls and the men understood the great instinct which prompted the affectionate greeting."[21] These hospitality centers also offered letter-writing paraphernalia, signs reminding young men to write home, pianos, gramophones, shoestrings, soap, and cookies. They also offered pies, a fact celebrated in the *Mess Kit*:

> "Home is where the heart is"—
> Thus the poet sang;
> But "home is where the pie is"
> For the doughboy gang!
> Crullers in the craters,
> Pastry in the Abris—
> This Salvation Army lass
> Sure knows how to please![22]

Deployed to France, Pvt. Perry A. Yost wrote in his diary during the spring of 1918 of the other comforts such groups offered: "Received Piano & Y.M.C.A. Hut to-day. A piano surely does wonders among a lot of men like this." An ambulance driver, Addison H. Smith, wrote to his mother, "I am writing from the Y.M.C.A. which consists of a tent containing desks and supplies. . . . There is a fine Italian piano which is in use most of the time. Here also is to be found a canteen where we can buy all kinds of eats and smokes. Believe me the Y.M.C.A. is the greatest thing the soldier finds at home and a great deal more so abroad when it's the only place where you can find your own speaking people and home surroundings."[23]

Not all shared this evaluation of the Y's activities.[24] Some critics believed that such homey reminders ruined men's fighting spirit. Hervey Allen, a member of the 111th Infantry regiment, encountered volunteers selling jelly, cigars, chocolate, and cake to hungry soldiers. Of them, he wrote, "The harassed 'Y' men were for the most part very patient, but the nature of their business, selling gum drops and cakes when civilization hung in the balance, was so petty that they were bound to be despised by the very men for whom they labored. . . . A religious organization that found its greatest field in purveying stationery, jelly, and ginger snaps behind the lines of battle merited the contempt which it so often received." Allen believed that rather than indulging in the soft and softening comforts of home life, the soldiers would be better off if they submitted themselves to the discipline of the army. When spirits flagged, "it is only the great machine of the army that . . . lays its iron touch on mind and body and makes it possible to go on."[25] To stay committed to their aim, men needed the "iron touch" of hard discipline, not piano music, gingersnaps, and chocolate.

The army did show a new toughness in dealing with the homesick, using an approach that differed from nineteenth-century techniques and that laid the groundwork for later policies. Whereas in earlier wars, the homesick had been sent to hospitals away from the front or even back to their homes, during World War I, physicians and psychiatrists did not consider soldiers with mental disturbances physically ill and instead offered them new kinds of psychological treatment. These treatments took place close to the front, reminding soldiers that they were expected to return to service. Often the men were told of their unit's success and reminded of the necessary functions they performed. Rather than being separated from their comrades, homesick men were kept close to them, in the hope that this would hasten their return to active duty.[26] Implicit in such treatments was the message that loyalty was to be directed toward the army, not the home; the importance of civic obligations and institutional affiliation was thus reinforced.

One sign of this new approach was the decreased incidence of nostalgia as a diagnosis. Although the armed forces reported a handful of cases, Pvt. George Arnett's appears to have been the only known death from nostalgia.[27] One newspaper reported, "In France there is perhaps less moral excuse for the homesick condition. The magnitude of the crisis, of what the boys call 'the big job,' should clear their hearts and their minds of all lesser things, and make them forgetful of hardships, of danger, of the long, fierce roar of the unceasing guns, and of the thousands of miles that intervene between them and the folks at home. It seems to work that way. Note that but one case of fatal homesickness has been recorded in France."[28] Perhaps there were fewer cases of fatal nostalgia because the army diminished its legitimacy. A growing impatience with nostalgia was manifest in the *Stars and Stripes*. The paper admonished, "Homesickness Is Not Rheumatism So Don't Try to Make the Army Doctor Believe It Is." The article noted that "sympathetic but professionally skeptical medical officers" were encountering "daily increasing parades" of men suffering "elusive pains and baffling spells of dizziness."[29]

While the growing skepticism about nostalgia may have limited the number of individuals diagnosed with it, there were also new labels used in place of it. Some psychologists and military officials believed there was a connection between homesickness and the newly identified condition of shell shock. A War Department memo from 1918 explained that often there were warning signs before a man succumbed to shell shock: "Reports from abroad indicate that a large number of the soldiers who break down nervously (shell-shock) had, for several days before their final collapse, given evidence that they were fast approaching the limit of their nervous endurance." The warning signs included "persistent homesickness, nervousness, depression, self-reproach, unreasonable fear . . . and general complaints of ill health." An army psychiatrist likewise stressed the importance of keeping the army "as cheerful and contented, mentally, as is possible." Men who had plenty of recreation and "good diversion," who were not haunted by thoughts of home, were unlikely "to suffer from the purely mental kinds of shell-shock."[30]

Although shell shock and nostalgia were related phenomena, there was an important difference between them. During the Civil War, many Americans believed that one of the greatest traumas of war was that it removed soldiers from their home and families. In World War I, it was the exposure to hellish battle scenes that traumatized men.[31] Presumably they were already used to leaving home, and that aspect of soldiering was no longer wrenching or psychologically wounding.

As it dealt with the perennial problem of homesickness, the military envisioned men's service differently than in earlier conflicts. Whereas honor was the attribute that soldiering might confer during the Civil War, and emotional maturity and masculinity the virtues emphasized during the Spanish-American War, the imprint that military service would leave on soldiers in World War I was the ability to fit into a bureaucracy, an ability that would be in demand in civilian society. Edgar Garland, who enlisted in Colorado in 1918, when he was twenty-one, recalled of his field artillery unit, "Morale was great as a whole. . . . Homesickness, well that is different. It happened to all, sometimes." Yet despite the waves of homesickness that beset soldiers, they learned to cope with the emotion and conquer it. Garland wrote that army life taught him to master such feelings and focus on larger goals: "It was a great benefit, because I had learned to take orders in the Army, Believe me it helped in civilian life."[32] Men and women in the twentieth century increasingly needed to conquer their homesickness in order to be members of a well-functioning bureaucratic team.[33]

CIVILIAN LIFE

The imperative to repress emotions and be an efficient team member was also apparent to workers across America. In the early decades of the twentieth century, companies began to create corporate welfare and industrial relations departments to help their workforce adjust to office and factory life. One study from the 1920s found that 80 percent of the largest corporations in American had welfare departments.[34] By the 1930s, nearly a third of all companies had industrial relations departments.[35] They tackled a range of social and emotional problems that might crop up in the workplace. Their main goal was to defuse anger and improve morale. Homesickness was often a secondary concern; nevertheless, these departments taught workers how to cope with the feeling, for it could interfere with their efficiency.

These departments were established to ease individuals' adjustment to work life. Young men and women might leave home, go to the city, and find lodging at the YMCA; at work they might find a familial, homey atmosphere over which welfare workers presided. An employee of Metropolitan Life, new to New York City, described the beneficial influence of the homelike atmosphere and nurturing touches that welfare workers brought to corporate life: "I came to New York City about six months ago, quite alone, and found both the people and the ways of the city strange to me. One day I woke up to the fact that I very much needed advice. . . . Please, Mr. Fiske, accept my sincerest thanks for providing us such a 'Mother' as I have found . . . Mrs. Brockway to be." Corporate welfare workers in these years were often women and frequently were perceived as motherly figures. In turn, many corporations began to present themselves as families. A corporation that did this was American Telephone and Telegraph, which, one historian notes, "redefined itself as the 'Bell Family' and claimed that restrooms, matrons, and pleasant surroundings helped to create a family feeling among its employees."[36]

The Michigan State Auto School in Detroit created a welfare department to counsel homesick farm boys who enrolled in its training program for mechanics. When a country boy first arrived in Detroit, "naturally he is homesick. The bright lights and the crowds bewilder him." To combat such feelings, "the minute a student shows signs of becoming discouraged, or a desire to break away, a welfare worker takes him in hand and chums around with him. He gets him over the rough spots, and the student begins to take an active interest in his work."[37] Workers could be successful only when they focused on the task before them rather than on visions of home.

The federal government also endeavored to help its civilian employees cope with homesickness. During and immediately after the war, the federal payroll expanded. According to a government report, many of the new employees "were drawn from all parts of the United States," and many were young women who were leaving homes for the first time. To help them adjust to their new lives in Washington, the War Department established a welfare agency for workers, for "on grounds of pure efficiency it also became clear that clerks homesick, lonely, uncomfortable, sick, and otherwise suffering, could not . . . give the sort of attention to their work which was needed in the emergency."[38] Welfare departments, or personnel departments, as they were later called, were designed to ease the transition to work life and help workers adapt to their new environments.

Not all workers flocking to urban jobs during the 1920s received the counsel of such departments, nor did such efforts always succeed at diminishing homesickness. Corporate attempts to manufacture a contented workforce had their limits, after all. Frequently, workers learned to suppress homesickness on the job, but continued to display their often intense longings for home during their free time. Many writers have stressed the modernity of urban life in the 1920s, but those participating in it did not unambiguously embrace the new and novel. City dwellers worked in offices and on factory floors; they walked down city sidewalks amid automobile traffic and dense throngs of people and could wander into movie theaters, restaurants, and jazz clubs. They seemed to embody the modern temper, but in their leisure hours they still clung to older identities and affiliations.

This pattern was apparent in the towns and cities of southern California, one of the fastest growing areas of the United States. Arriving by automobile, most of the migrants during the 1920s came from Illinois, New York, Ohio, Missouri, Pennsylvania, and Iowa.[39] The easterners and midwesterners who settled in southern California found that their adjustment was not always easy. The cultural critic Carey McWilliams, describing life in Los Angeles in the early decades of the twentieth century, sketched a portrait of a town beset by a mood of "aching loneliness—the really terrible loneliness—that for years has been so clearly apparent in the streets and parks, the boarding houses and hotels, the cafeterias and 'lonely clubs' of Los Angeles." To find relief from such anomie, many transplants turned to state associations, which had begun to form in the late nineteenth century. By 1913, all forty-eight states had such organizations in southern California. C. H. Parsons, a transplant from Iowa and the driving force behind them, claimed that the groups "liquidated the blues." In 1913, he founded the Federation of State Societies, which by the 1920s had 500,000 members. According to McWilliams, Parsons had been inspired to organize these groups because "he had so frequently heard the expression, 'If I could only run into some one I know,' in the streets of Los Angeles.'" For decades, the state associations in California allowed Iowans, South Dakotans, and other midwesterners to sustain old ties and aid their fellow migrants.[40]

The state associations held frequent meetings, shared information with newcomers, and, most visibly, sponsored picnics at least annually and often more frequently. Iowa picnics were widely recognized to be the largest. In 1900, the Iowa picnic boasted an attendance of 2,000 to 3,000 Hawkeyes; in

An Iowa Picnic at Highland Park, Los Angeles. Security Pacific National Bank Collection, Los Angeles Public Library.
Source: Photo courtesy of the Los Angeles Public Library.

1913, picnic organizers claimed that close to 20,000 had shown up. There were 25,000 to 30,000 in 1917, 45,000 in 1926, more than 100,000 in 1935. Indeed, so popular did these festivities become that sometimes Iowans still living in Iowa would journey out for the events. Often the governor of Iowa attended and spoke, or at least sent a message to be read at the gathering. Picnickers were arranged by county to form a living map of Iowa.[41] Designed to mitigate the feelings of rootless anonymity that attended life in a mass society, they became mass events, testifying both to the new scale of urban life and to the widespread hunger for community within these bulging metropolises.

THE GREAT MIGRATION

On the other side of the continent, in Brooklyn, another group gathered for a picnic in August 1918. The Sons of North Carolina was an organization of black southerners who had relocated to Gotham. The picnic attracted a large crowd and concluded at one in the morning when the band struck up the tune "Home, Sweet Home." Founded in the 1890s to bring "together the natives from the old states, with the object of offering to each other . . . friendly and brotherly aid," the group attracted new members in the twentieth century, as more African Americans migrated north.[42]

Between 1917 and 1929, unprecedented numbers of African Americans took the train north for industrial jobs newly open as a result of the war and the accompanying decline in immigration. On average, five hundred men

and women left the South each day; by 1930, half a million had migrated to New York, Chicago, Philadelphia, Detroit, Cleveland, St. Louis, and a host of other cities across the North. With jobs available, and with active encouragement from the widely circulated African American newspaper, the *Chicago Defender*, many blacks decided the time had come to make a break with the South, the past, and most of all the Jim Crow system of segregation, which denied them social equality, civil rights, and economic opportunity. Blacks continued to move north during the 1930s as a result of worsening agricultural conditions; even more came during World War II to fill war jobs.[43]

In the South, many African Americans formed migration clubs and through them obtained discounts on their railroad fares. These clubs, based on town affiliations, allowed travelers to leave en masse, often in the face of opposition from local whites who hoped to prevent their exodus and thereby preserve their workforce. Club members together coordinated the details of the migration.[44] The migration clubs gave order to the process; so too did the railroads that carried their members north. Train lines directly linked southern communities to northern destinations. Mississippi migrants ended up in St. Louis, Chicago, Milwaukee, and Minneapolis. Alabama and Kentucky migrants took trains to Cleveland, and South Carolina migrants settled in New York and Boston. Train lines endowed the black migration with predictability and familiarity, making for more cohesive communities north and south.[45]

Many African Americans predicted that they would feel little sadness at leaving the South, and their sons and daughters generally believed their parents' journeys north were characterized by gain, not loss. Timuel Black, for instance, wrote, "For one reason or other our parents had no urge to go back south. For most of the people I've talked with whose families had left the South, there was no attraction to return. I think the reason was based on the fact that they had left the South because things were not good for them down there."[46] Migrants often discussed their motivations for leaving the South as wanting to "better their condition."[47]

Relatively few blacks were so homesick that they returned permanently to the South during these years. Nevertheless, they did experience the emotion. Richard Wright summed up the mixed feelings of many:

> We are leaving our homes, pulling up stakes to move on. . . . We look out at the wide green fields which our eyes saw when we first came into the world and we feel full of regret, but we are leaving. We scan the kind black faces we have looked upon since we first saw the light of day, and, though pain is in our hearts, we are leaving. We take one last furtive look over our shoulders to the Big House—high upon a hill beyond the railroad tracks—where the Lord of the Land lives, and we feel glad, for we are leaving.[48]

Wright's account of his own journey makes clear, however, that once migrants arrived at their northern destinations, their feelings often were tinged with despair. Of his arrival in Chicago in 1927, he wrote, "My first glimpse of the flat black stretches of Chicago depressed and dismayed me, mocked all my fantasies. Chicago seemed an unreal city whose mythical houses were built of slabs of black coal wreathed in palls of gray smoke, houses whose foundations were sinking slowly into the dark prairies."[49] His initial reaction was shared by another famous migrant to Chicago, Louis Armstrong. Of his first view of the city in 1922, he wrote, "I saw a million people. . . . I never seen a city that big. All those tall buildings. . . . I said, no, this is the wrong city. I was fixing to take the next train back home."[50]

In letters, surveys, and interviews, migrants praised their new lives in the North but admitted there were losses as well. Joining a mass society was difficult. A migrant to Pittsburgh wrote her pastor of her new life in the North, "I like the money O.K. but I like the South bettern for my Pleasure this city is too fast for me." Another wrote from Cleveland, "i have seval nochants of coming back, yet i am doing well no trouble what ever except i can not raise my children here like they should be this is one of the worst places in principle you ever look on in your life but it is a fine place to make money."[51]

Again and again, migrants made it clear that they missed the close-knit social life of the rural areas and small towns they had come from, for modern urban life was anonymous and alienating. Yet migrants could generally find oases in the social landscape where they felt at home, where they could find people from their hometowns. In one Chicago neighborhood was a cluster of more than 150 families from Hattiesburg, Mississippi. In the northern section of Philadelphia, South Carolinians from Greenwood formed a small enclave. In New York and other large cities, researchers found that Sea Islanders hung together.[52]

In an effort to solidify social and familial bonds and to offset homesickness and feelings of alienation, migrants in these communities founded fraternal societies. Some, like the Sons of North Carolina, had been established by earlier waves of black migrants. These older groups were joined by new ones, created during the 1920s and 1930s. In Chicago, there were at least nine state clubs that offered migrants a link to their homes in the South. (Many of them continue to exist today.) As two observers noted, "Though they had been glad to escape from oppression, nostalgia for the more pleasant associations of the homeland assailed the exiles. Homesick for familiar speech, faces, and scenes, they banded themselves into social and fraternal clubs named for the States and localities from which they had emigrated. There was the Alabama Club, the Mississippi Club, the Vicksburg Club, the Louisiana Club, the Arkansas Club."[53] Often state organizations took root in churches. In the Mother Bethel Church in Philadelphia, there was a South Carolina society as well as Virginia and Georgia societies. Members of New York City's Abyssinian Baptist Church formed Alabama and South Carolina clubs.[54]

Migrants worked hard to re-create ties not just to their state, but to their hometowns, and again churches provided a way to rebuild southern communities in the North. Migrants established branches of the churches they had left behind and gave them the same names. African Americans who moved from Greenwood, South Carolina, to Philadelphia in the 1920s started a branch of their church in their new city, giving it the name of their old church, the Morris Chapel Baptist, and sent for a minister from home to preside over the services. As members migrated from south to north they brought with them "letters of transmittal," establishing that the bearer was recommended by the old congregation.[55] Across the North, similar patterns could be found. Sometimes ministers from the South traveled north for visits; sometimes they were induced to leave the South and rejoin their congregants in the North. Had they not, they might well have been preaching to empty pews in the South.[56]

Those congregations that remained in the South received yearly visits from at least some of the migrants during "homecoming" celebrations. According to one historian, "Sponsored by the church and usually taking place in mid or late August, homecoming brought together present and former church members. . . . Many family members and friends who had left returned to renew old ties and show their successes."[57] Migrants who never planned on returning during their lives also relied on southern religious communities, requesting that their bodies be sent south after death. In a study of migrants from the Sea Islands to Harlem and other cities, researchers in 1932 found, "Almost invariably Islanders in New York expressed the desire of being returned to St. Helena for a permanent resting. 'Eart' det bears you lies lightest on your bones.'"[58]

In the meantime, they re-created and maintained a southern culture while living in the North. In Chicago, migrants could patronize the Florida East Coast Shine Parlor on State Street or visit the Carolina Sea Island Candy Store on Wabash Avenue.[59] Numerous restaurants advertised southern cooking.[60] Clubs and bars provided patrons with music that reminded them of home. The scholar Farah Jasmine Griffith tells of James P. Johnson, a pianist in New York City. Some nights patrons would say, "Let's go home." "Johnson knew this to be a request for a more Southern style of music and he would oblige them. For those few hours that the migrants danced to a familiar Southern style of music, they recreated the South right in the middle of Manhattan."[61] Often blacks in the North could hear the same musicians they'd listened to in the South because the local music scene had been transplanted along with the rest of the town.[62] Migrants in the North embraced their southernness; it was not something to be shed.[63] It was also increasingly available in northern nightclubs, dance halls, and candy stores.

Like foreign immigrants and other internal wanderers within the United States, some African Americans dreamed of returning home, but their dreams were complicated by the reality of Jim Crow. Some returned for visits, but preferred life in the North; others hoped to be able to move back at some point in the future, if social conditions improved. One migrant wrote to the *Defender*, explaining why he would not go back home. In 1918, he returned south to visit his mother, daughter, and brother in Selma. His time with his family was "most delightful." "But here is the rub. I had to get there. As every one knows, there is a line known as the Mason and Dixon going south. The trip was lovely until we arrived in Evansville, Ind." At that point he had to change railroad cars and sit in a segregated compartment. Once home, he was insulted by whites. Consequently, he vowed not to return again.[64] There were people who drew him south, but there were also people who repelled him. Willie Mae Cotright, a Louisiana native who left her home for work in the shipyards of Richmond, California, during World War II, told an interviewer, "When I left there, I had the feeling I never did want to go back to live. I'd like to go to visit, like I do now, but never to live. I never wanted to go back to live."[65]

Yet despite the segregation they faced in the South, others still longed to return permanently. James Plunkett, a migrant from Danville, Virginia, said, "I came up North to see it, but sometimes I wish I had gone back to Danville. They treat you fine and dandy if you stay on your side of the fence." Many of the black women who left for California during World War II likewise did not always see that state as their permanent destination but as a place where they could make money for an enriched life back in the South.[66]

Some did return for good. During the New Deal, writers for the Works Progress Administration interviewed a black farmer from Edisto Island who had migrated to Harlem in 1924 and found a well-paying job as a stevedore. "After nine months he returned to South Carolina. He liked New York well enough but he said that he was homesick for . . . family and the farm, and the creek filled with good free food." He told the interviewers, "My traveling day done over. . . . I too old for flutter 'round now. I rather stay gradually and nicely at home."[67] He seems to have been the exception rather than the rule. The historian James Gregory suggests that one out of five black southerners returned to the South during the Great Migration of the first two decades of the twentieth century.[68] Those who stayed on in the North harbored at least some fond thoughts of the South but did not want to go back to the segregated conditions of southern living.[69] It would only be in the 1970s and 1980s, after Jim Crow was dismantled, that large numbers of blacks would begin a reverse migration to the places their parents and grandparents had left behind.

African Americans maintained ties and connections to the South, but by remaining in the North they shed the reputation of being premodern, emotionally tethered to the soil, and vulnerable to homesickness. Instead, they came to be seen as urban, modern individualists. Migrants confounded those who thought they had limited ambitions and therefore would stay contentedly in the South. They refuted those who believed that even ambitious blacks were unsuited for urban life or industrial work and discipline. They were homesick, but they also proved they were not tied to the land. By traveling north, they adopted the modern identity of the footloose worker, willing and eager to change jobs and locales in order to maximize profit and opportunity.[70]

THE DEPRESSION

If homesickness afflicted Americans who had left home by choice in the 1920s, during the 1930s, it struck with a vengeance those who were pushed out of their homes by necessity. Overall mobility rates declined during the Great Depression, as fewer individuals ventured away from the relative security of home. Yet some had no choice but to move.

Britomar Lathrop, born in 1921, described what life was like for her family when they were forced to leave their house. In 1931, after her mother lost her job and the rent came due, the family decided to leave. She wrote of her father's reaction, "After supper he sat in the straight-backed chair, smoking his corncob [pipe]. His eyes wandered around the dark walls, took in the blue and white curtains that he had chose himself, took in the fire-place we were all so proud of. 'It's the last smoke in the old house,' he said in a down voice, and closed his eyes for one last puff." The family spent five years on the road, living in abandoned houses, under bridges, and in the open air. During that period, Lathrop kept a diary, charting the family's pro-gress across California. In 1935, she alluded to the psychic toll of being without a house: "Why in the name of all anything, do we have to be on the road? Why not in a cozy house, or at least some other place better than this old shed?" Occasionally the family set up housekeeping for a few days in an empty house, and sometimes Lathrop felt a longing to settle there perma-nently. Of one house, she wrote, "I love this little cabin. It is in an ideal loca-tion. And it could be fixed up so nice. . . . I want it, and I can't have it." In another entry she tried to sum up her feelings: "I feel unaccountably lonely and—I'd say homesick only I never had a home so I can't be homesick. I feel like gloom itself."[71]

More visible and countable than families like the Lathrops were those who left the Great Plains. The most famous migrants of the 1930s were the Dust Bowl refugees, often referred to as Okies. Displaced by a decade-long drought, traumatized by dust storms that killed their crops and hard economic conditions that led to farm foreclosures, they found themselves with few alternatives other than moving on, often to California. Those who went to California during the 1930s were more desperate and less willing to leave their old homes behind than earlier migrants to the Golden State. They came from all over, from Mexico, Oklahoma, and Arkansas, and relied on cars to take them to what they hoped was a sun-nier future. Officials who studied the conditions of migrant workers in California wrote, "The refugees travel in old automobiles and light trucks, frequently with trailers behind. All their worldly possessions are piled on the car and covered with old canvas—ragged bedding, bedsprings some-times, a small iron camp stove, a lantern, a washtub. Children, aunts, grandmothers, and a dog or two are jammed into the car, stretching its capacity incredibly."[72]

Upon arrival, they found few opportunities in California and felt at sea in the mass, mobile society they were joining. As an Oklahoma mother of ten told interviewers, "This movin' from one place to another ain't what it's cracked up to be."[73] Another Oklahoman remarked, "I sure do like my country better than your country. . . . [At home] they won't look on people . . . as if they were under their feet. There're clean, pure hearts." Many migrants discussed their dissatisfaction with their employers—how impersonal those relations were, how different they were from those at home. "Here the people don't care for you. There the people'll do anything for you. Here they hire you to work and that's all. They treat you just like a working hand. They don't pay you no mind. There they take you in with the family if you're working for 'em."[74]

The poor living conditions were also troubling. Many migrants lived in temporary camps, some erected by growers for whom they worked, others by the government, and still others by entrepreneurs eager for profit. The impermanence, and in many cases the squalor, of these dwellings represented a come-down for migrants. One noted, "I never even knew there was people livin' like this before. I had a six room bungalow, all furnished, in Arkansas. It is a new thing for me."[75]

In these California camps could be heard the lively songs migrants wrote and sang to cope with such feelings. Jack Bryant, a Dust Bowl refugee, composed a song warning other would-be sojourners against making the trip to California:

A photo taken in 1939 by Dorothea Lange of a Farm Security Administration Camp for migrant laborers in Imperial Valley, California. The tent was occupied by a family with eleven children from Mangrum, Oklahoma. The mother hoped to return home, telling interviewers, "I want to go back to where we can live happy, live decent, and grow what we eat."
Source: Photo courtesy of the Library of Congress.

> You people in Oklahoma,
> If you ever come out West.
> Have your pockets full of money,
> And you better be well-dressed.
> If you wind up on the desert
> You're gonna wish that you were dead;
> You'll be longing for Oklahoma
> And your good old feather bed.[76]

One observer of camp music noted that there was a wide variety of melodies that touched on these themes, for instance, "'homesick' songs about the good things to eat back in Arkansas: 'peanuts, pumpkins, buttermilk and good old turnip greens.'"[77]

Fond memories of home and complaints about California often sent residents packing for home. Ernest Atchley, a Texas native, wrote in a letter, "California is all right for Californians but we're going back to . . . where the long-horn cattle roam, where the 'gen'ral sto'keeper treats yo' all lak humans,' and where hospitality reigns. A fellow don't appreciate home until he comes to California."[78] The *Weed Patch Cultivator*, published by residents of a migratory labor camp in Arvin, California, reported under the headline "Oklahoma Bound," "Arlay Terry left for Oklahoma last Sunday. . . . Tom Shepard and his wife left for Missouri last Sunday."[79] A report on residents of migratory labor camps calculated that one-third of those interviewed hoped to return to the states from which they had originated, chief among them Oklahoma and Texas, although many were not sure how soon they could make good on these plans.[80] By the end of the 1930s, observers at the California state line recorded significant car traffic heading east, toward home.[81] Those who stayed on in California continued to long for Oklahoma. That longing was visible in their Southern Baptist religious services, their lodge affiliations, their bars and roadhouses, and most particularly their music—all of which consciously evoked homes left behind.[82]

Another powerful symbol of the Depression was the tramp. Hundreds of thousands of tramps and hobos rode the rails during the 1930s. Grace Abbott, the chief of the federal government's Children's Bureau, wrote, "We found that there was a new army of transients moving across the country, going by railroad—riding the freights—and hitchhiking, by automobile. . . . We found the railroads overwhelmed by the problem." Abbott reported that in some small railroad towns, two hundred men and boys arrived each day, and "the railroad men in Kansas City, when interviewed last spring, estimated that every day approximately 1,500 men and boys went through that city riding the freights."[83]

Many of these transients were very young. During the worst years of the Depression, perhaps a quarter of a million teenagers left home in search of opportunity, adventure, or escape. Some left of their own volition, others because their parents could no longer support them. Clarence Lee, born in 1913, left home at his father's prompting when he was sixteen: "I wanted to stay home and fight the poverty with my family. I didn't have it in my mind to leave until my father told me, 'Go fend for yourself. I cannot afford to have you around any longer.' Until today it hurts when I think about it but there was nothing I could do." He rode the rails across his home state of Louisiana for a year and a half: "I got homesick many nights as I lay in the total darkness." He eventually found a job and then returned home with money in his pocket to help his family. Arvel Pearson of Arkansas started to ride the rails in 1930, when he was fifteen. He hoped to find well-paying work: "You leave home with good intentions and tell your folks you're going to come back a millionaire. You return with your head between your arms." Although he was elected King of the Hoboes in 1939, Pearson did not find the wealth he expected to as he crisscrossed the nation in boxcars; instead he found a fair amount of misery. "There were nights I'd get homesick waiting for a train with nobody to talk to, sitting alone on a pile of ties under a water tank. . . . You're only a kid and you get to dreaming about that warm bed back home and seeing the folks."[84]

Some applauded the gumption of these youth on the move, but many others worried.[85] A number of social reformers were concerned that these homeless young people were out of control, that they were wandering too far, and might become a dangerous horde, an unsocialized mob. Others worried more about the psychological changes tramps underwent during their wanderings. Margaret Ford of the Travelers' Aid Society observed, "The boys for instance are growing harder and more difficult to adjust. They are joining the professional group of homeless men; they are becoming diseased; crippled; are growing accustomed to the road and if employment were offered many of them would not accept it."[86] Perhaps most worrisome was that these young men, while displaying their independence by leaving home, were finding that independence did not pay off. Reformers might applaud young men's willingness to leave home if they sought employment and income, but they worried when those journeys proved fruitless, and men and boys continued to wander across the country without a destination or purpose. Gen. Pelham Glassford said of those who had been on the road a long time, "They appear to have lost ambition."[87] These men were independent, but they were at sea, separated from their families and from all institutions of society.

In response to the problem of unemployed youth, as well as the fears about their purposeless mobility, the federal government created the

Civilian Conservation Corps to channel them back into ordered social life. The program was responsible for conservation work across the country, including flood control efforts, soil conservation, tree planting, and park improvement. It deployed young men to camps across the country. In the first year 300,000 men enrolled and received $30 a month, all but $5 of which they had to send to their families.

Like tramping, the CCC separated young people from their families, but it also guaranteed them an income and room and board and gave structure to their youthful labor and peregrinations. The CCC also acclimated youth to institutional culture. Jim Mitchell, who had been wandering the country by train since his sophomore year in high school, recalled what a change life in the CCC represented: "Out on the road you lived for yourself and to hell with everyone else. In the CCC you not only learned to live with other guys, you had to go out with a crew and haul logs together. You learned to work as a team."[88] In place of the random, highly individualistic wanderings of young tramps, the CCC offered order and structure.

While Mitchell seemed to appreciate this introduction to institutional culture, others involved in the program found its quasi-military organization unsettling. From its inception, the program lost recruits to homesickness. Within a week of arriving at Fort Slocum in New York, 257 of the 1,791 men sent there had dropped out of the CCC. A reporter explained, "Of those who returned to their homes, fewer than thirty were rejected because of physical defects. Others became homesick and some were sent back at the request of their parents."[89] An article published in 1933 explained that young men used to city life found the emptiness of the forests lonely: "To a man, almost, they were homesick."[90] Some survived but would not reenlist because of their homesickness; others quit after just a few weeks. Willard Mitchell of Florida confided to an interviewer, "I did go to CCC camp, but they sent me way out to western Louisiana and I got homesick, so I quit and come back after six weeks."[91] In 1935, administrators sent "a young CCC worker to his North Carolina home to recuperate from 'acute nostalgia.' Informed by letter of her son's ailment, his indignant mother filed claim against the corps for damages, declaring that her boy never had trouble with nostalgia until he left home."[92] The federal government, the epitome of the new institutional culture, took care of its citizens but required them to subsume their desires and their movements to larger civic and organizational goals.

PSYCHOLOGISTS AND CHILD-REARING EXPERTS WEIGH IN

As new government agencies, an enlarged military, and powerful corporations emerged in the twentieth century, many Americans might have agreed with the insights of the sociologist Ernest Groves, who wrote that institutions were taking on what had formerly been the exclusive functions of the family. Schools, social workers, and ministers were all assuming roles and tasks previously the domain of parents. Groves maintained that this was nothing to worry about if families managed the changes well: "There is no danger of the family's crumbling just because it gives up some of its old time functions, if it keeps its directing power."[93] The key was to have families delegate some of their less important functions to the many institutions, from schools to social workers, that were shaping social life and preparing individuals for the bureaucratic society.

Experts seemed to suggest, in fact, that children would benefit from more time away from their parents and greater exposure to social institutions, for they would eventually have to function efficiently within them. Social workers, mental health experts, and child-rearing advisors all manifested an interest in helping children adapt to the organizations they would join as adults. Part of that adjustment process meant coming to grips with life away from home and family.

Experts agreed that the way to have an adaptable workforce and citizenry was to improve parenting techniques. The behaviorist psychologist John Watson, who exerted tremendous influence on twentieth-century child-rearing practices, maintained that all human traits were learned and all people were products of their environment. One of society's key problems was that parents, and particularly mothers, were too affectionate and created the wrong environment. They had "become overly devoted to their children. The earth revolves around them. . . . The children are not allowed to draw a breath unscrutinized. These mothers are prodigal of their affection." According to Watson, parents trained their children to be unduly attached to them through cuddling, kissing, and hugging. "Mothers just don't know, when they kiss their children and pick them up and rock them upon their knee, that they are slowly building up a human being totally unprepared to cope with the world it must later live in." Families might function in an affectionate and indulgent manner, but "society doesn't do this": "We have to stick to our jobs in commercial and professional life regardless of headaches, toothaches, indigestion and other tiny ailments. There is no one there to baby us." Watson believed that children raised in such households would try to return to them. To avoid such a calamitous situation, he suggested that parents treat their children "as though they were young adults. . . . Let your behavior always be objective and kindly firm. Never hug and kiss them, never let them sit in your lap. If you must, kiss them once on the forehead when they say good night. Shake hands with them in the morning. Give them a pat on the head if they have made an extraordinarily good job of a difficult task."[94]

Watson's jaundiced view of the overly affectionate family became widespread, and many child-rearing experts urged parents to help their children separate from them. Ernest Groves observed in 1934 that children were all too eager "to cling to infantile patterns," which ultimately impeded their emotional development and kept them bound to their parents. "Smother love" was the name Sidonie Matsner Gruenberg gave to the phenomenon; "momism" was the term Philip Wylie invented for the problem. Social workers, child-rearing experts, and cultural critics all concluded that homesick, needy individuals were the products of the overly loving, tightly bonded family.[95]

While in the nineteenth century, mother love was considered a positive force that could shape morals and order families, in the twentieth century, in a corporate society that relied on other institutions for socialization, maternal affection was dangerous, for it kept the young too closely tied to hearth and home and squelched their autonomy and initiative.[96] Given these views, it is perhaps not surprising that this generation of child-rearing experts counseled parents to send their children away from home in order to prepare them for adulthood and modern social life. For instance, in *Principles of Adolescent Psychology* (1935), Edward Conklin urged parents to prepare their children for inevitable, and ultimately desirable, separations: "Through an early training in independence and self-reliance, through much changing about, through occasional absences from home at summer camps ... through a careful avoidance of that excess of petting and coddling which develops parental fixations, the conflicts which produce homesickness with all of its distressing effects might be avoided."[97] Likewise, in 1941, the psychologist W. H. McCann recommended "that the child be allowed to make frequent visits away from home and that everything be done to prevent a strong emotional fixation or attachment to the home situation or to any item in it."[98]

One way to teach children how to adjust to absences from home was to send them to summer camps. In the 1920s and 1930s, many parents used camps not only as a way to show their children the natural world, but also as a place where children could overcome their homesickness. To inculcate habits of independence, they sent their sons and daughters to live as nineteenth-century settlers had, in an effort to at least partially re-create frontier conditions.[99] In such places, parents hoped their children would learn some of the values and virtues of the pioneers, national symbols of courage and adventure.

When they sent their children to camp, parents often explicitly embraced the goal of making them more independent, for camps offered a safe place for children to practice for later and longer separations. When children became homesick, parents told them to tough it out. One mother wrote her homesick son at Camp Dudley in upstate New York, "Don't let anybody know you are homesick.... Men never show their feelings like this and you would be a 'SISSY' if you came home. Buck up and be a sport and the answer is YOU CAN *NOT* COME HOME."[100]

Of course, not all parents could maintain such an attitude, and camp directors and child-rearing experts warned that they must take care not to undermine the mission of the camps. Through well-intentioned but overly affectionate gestures they might sabotage the lessons of independence. Catherine MacKenzie, a *New York Times* columnist, told parents to avoid writing letters that would induce homesickness in their children. She provided an example of what not to write: "Dear Billy: I hope you are not too homesick at camp. It is certainly lonely here without a little boy to tuck in at night. Daddy misses you terribly. We are driving up to Lake George next week-end, and wish you were coming with us.... Would you like to come home? Be sure to write to tell us. Lots of love from MOTHER." MacKenzie noted that while this was a fictitious letter, it was typical of what parents sent their children.[101] Parents interfered in camp life and impeded separation in other ways as well. When they visited too much or were overly sympathetic to their children's laments, they undermined the very purpose of the camp experience. In *Maternal Overprotection* (1943), David Levy recounted the case of a thirteen-year-old boy whose mother had delayed his schooling "because she did not like him to leave her.... When he was sent to camp at 14, the mother visited him on the second day, found that his feet were wet and took him home."[102]

A variety of parenting experts suggested that the psychologically sound approach to child rearing was to let children and teenagers stricken with homesickness tough it out. Just as the armed forces during World War I had insisted that soldiers stay close to their units and return as quickly as possible to them, so parental advisors suggested that crying, unhappy, homesick children remain at camp and overcome their feelings.

Camps were becoming an acceptable place for children to wrestle with their homesickness. Colleges and universities became another site for exercises in independence, and many institutions in the 1930s publicly acknowledged the emotional battles their students faced when they left home for school. A number of colleges began to offer freshman orientation weeks, designed to ease young people into their new surroundings. Antioch, Brown, Columbia, Cornell, Chicago, Dartmouth, Johns Hopkins, Stanford, Missouri, Princeton, Reed, Rutgers, Williams, and several other schools established orientation programs to help homesick students adjust to college life. The *New York Times* reported, "About half a million young men and women will enter the 1,500 colleges, universities, normal schools and junior colleges of the nation within a few days." Based on past experience, perhaps as many as a third would drop out. The problem was that the entering student was "torn from the familiar setting of home and high school. He is set down in a strange town and lives with strangers in a dormitory or in a rooming house." The size and scope of college life had changed as well. "The educational plant is larger than any he has known before. . . . The problem today is aggravated by the huge size of entering classes." But orientation week could solve this, giving young students "confidence and poise. . . . They have been too busy to become homesick." Ultimately, colleges should not "coddle" students, but instead should "act as a parent who bends every effort to make his offspring strong and self-reliant."[103] Colleges asked students to transfer their loyalties from the home to the institution, promising to act as surrogate parents for young people on their own for the first time.

While affluent families sent their children to camps and colleges where they learned to separate themselves from home, those who had wandered into hobo camps or rode the rails during the 1930s made these emotional adjustments on their own. Many reformers regarded the experiences of the tramps and wanderers as less useful than those of the campers and collegians. Despite the fact they had mastered homesickness, these impoverished young men and women were troubling symbols of isolation and disorder, for they bucked convention and stood outside of social institutions. While they had proven their grit and rugged individualism and displayed their ability to conquer homesickness, their lonely independence was out of sync with the emerging bureaucratic culture.

WORLD WAR II

The social imperative to leave home and affiliate with a group or institution was emphasized during World War II, as large numbers of soldiers had to adjust to the regimen of army life. With President Franklin Roosevelt's support, Congress passed the first peacetime draft in U.S. history, the Selective Service Act of 1940. Within a month, more than 16 million men had registered with the government, and those who passed examinations by draft boards were inducted for what was originally a twelve-month term of service. In the summer of 1941, Congress extended that tour of duty an additional eighteen months. After the bombing of Pearl Harbor on December 7, 1941, the new, massive fighting force was called to action. Over the course of the war, roughly 16 million men served in the armed forces, most of them draftees. More than half a million women served in auxiliary units.[104]

Far from home and faced with danger, soldiers felt tremendous home-sickness. A number of journalists chronicled the problem, most famously Ernie Pyle, who wrote, "Ten minutes hardly ever goes by without some nostalgic reference to home, how long you've been away, how long before you get back, what you'll do first when you hit the States, what your chances are for returning before the war is over."[105] The psychologist W. Edgar Gregory was "amazed at the power of the average man to idealize the home town and his home folks. No matter where he is—even in Hawaii, 'the Paradise of the Pacific'—he has considered his being there nothing but an imposition. Podunk is heaven, compared to 'the pineapple island.'" Gregory offered some laments representative of those he had heard from soldiers: "'Gee, what I wouldn't give for a banana split' . . . 'Sure wish I could set down to a glass of cold beer at Tony's again.' . . . 'Oh, for a nice New England snowstorm instead of this African sand.' 'I'll sure be glad when I don't have to look at water any more. Those Dakota prairies'll look pretty good.' . . . 'Sure wish I could taste a coke again. It's been two years since I even saw one.'"[106]

Some observers hoped that such feelings would motivate soldiers to fight harder so that they could return home more quickly. A reporter accompanying U.S. troops in Sicily in 1943 noted, "The Lord knows they are all homesick. . . . Properly considered, it is an asset, because it leads to the logical conclusion: 'Let's get this blankety blank war over with and go home.'"[107] Ernie Pyle wrote from Italy that the morale in the battery he was accompanying was "excellent." "The only thing is they're impatient for movement—they'd fire all day and move all night . . . if they could only keep going forward swiftly. Because everywhere in our army, 'forward,' no matter what direction, is toward home."[108] Even Secretary of War Henry Stimson admitted that soldiers were homesick; he too thought this was an asset, not a liability, for it showed Americans' reluctance to become occupiers once they had won the war. Stimson proclaimed in December 1944, "No country need ever fear a United States Army of occupation—our boys want to get home. . . . The American soldier is not afraid of anything, but he's the most homesick creature when he's at war in foreign land."[109]

To men who experienced it, however, and to officers and doctors who treated it, homesickness was a problem. Doctors and reporters at the time noted that concerns about what was transpiring on the home front, from romantic issues to financial woes, fueled soldiers' desire to return. As Army Medical Corps officers explained, "The thought of home intrudes itself disagreeably on the soldier's mind, when there are special causes for worry which increase his preoccupation with the subject and decrease his fighting efficiency. Lack of mail, worrisome letters, suspicion of wives' unfaithfulness, broken engagements, financial troubles," all made soldiers preoccupied with home.[110]

If soldiers were unduly preoccupied with such worries, their morale and fighting efficiency suffered. To combat this, the military tried to make men forget their pasts, in particular, memories of their domestic life. Two sociologists who evaluated military service wrote, "The essential fact about induction, reception-center, and basic-training experience is the knifing-off of past experience. Nothing in one's past seems relevant unless, possibly, a capacity for adaptation and the ability to assume a new role."[111] Another observer commented that upon induction, the soldier should give up his individualism and instead become "identified with the institution and dependent upon it for direction and stimulation." The goal was to create a well-adjusted soldier who would cease to be the child of his parents and instead become "a military dependent who looked to the institution for all his personal, social, and emotional satisfactions. . . . In psychiatric terms, the military institution becomes a substitute parent for an adult who has been reduced to infancy by the training it has given him." The infantilized soldier was utterly independent of his family, utterly dependent on the army, and consequently willing to subordinate his own needs to "institutional ends."[112] That the armed services had such aims was widely recognized by soldiers at the time.[113]

To accomplish this transformation, the military relied on psychiatrists and psychologists even more than they had during World War I. About 1,500 psychologists served in the armed forces during World War II, representing a quarter of all psychologists in the country. These experts took their insights about personality development in civilian life with them into the military.[114] David Flicker and Paul Weiss of the Army Medical Corps, for instance, believed that those who suffered from extreme cases of homesickness were emotionally immature. Reprising the critiques of homesickness that child-rearing experts had offered in the interwar years, they wrote, "Induction into military service calls for an emotional emancipation from adolescent and infantile ties. It requires mature emotionality. If too great a dependency on home or on any member of the family is present, psychic and somatic difficulties often arise." Homesickness was a sign of immaturity and, the doctors believed, a "weakling emotion." Those most prone to it were poorly adjusted to the demands of modern life, but if offered "kindly attention," they would become reconciled to the necessity of leaving home. Those immune to homesickness were, in contrast, "the most social, the most educated and the most intelligent persons," with "the most adaptability."[115] Unlike the homesick, they were equipped for success. Maj. A. Eisendorfer, another contributor to *War Medicine*, described the problem of the "acute nostalgic state" that seemed to strike "shy, passive persons" prone to patterns of "infantile dependence," and unemancipated from "their parental ties." Reflecting the new emphasis on organizational and institutional needs, Eisendorfer wrote that doctors and commanding officers needed to teach homesick men to transfer their loyalties from home life to army life. "We simply attempt to substitute one type of dependency for another; we initiate a process of emotional conditioning which if continued leads to a satisfactory adjustment in the Army."[116] Whereas a century before, many Americans had considered soldiers' love of home to be a source of martial strength, by World War II, strong attachments to home were seen as detrimental to the conduct of the war.[117]

This insight undergirded the military's general approach to psychiatric problems. The army resumed the World War I practice of treating those beset with emotional problems as close to their units as possible, although it took until 1943 to firmly establish this as the reigning policy. Once in place, the approach proved very effective at returning men to service. Before the policy was put in place, men stricken with emotional disturbances (including but not limited to nostalgia) were returned to full combat at a rate of 45 percent. After the policy was implemented, that number rose to 70 percent. The key to this success was a four-pronged strategy: (1) mild, short-term sedation; (2) reassurance that feelings of homesickness were normal and would be fleeting; (3) suggestion that the soldiers would soon rejoin their units; and (4) "exhortation," warning soldiers not to abandon their units.[118] The goal was to reinforce a soldier's sense of loyalty to the institution of the army and to the band of brothers in his unit.

To prevent nostalgia, raise morale, and keep soldiers loyal to the cause, the armed services and civilian groups created new agencies. If soldiers were expected to submerge themselves in large institutions, those institutions needed to provide them with resources to aid their adjustment. The Red Cross provided some facilities for soldiers; in the Asian theater it offered Service Clubs, which it had established with Army Special Services. There, soldiers could find "a little American oasis," "a touch of home for the most homesick army the world probably has ever seen." These clubs contained places to read and write as well as Ping-Pong tables and playing cards, "a large cozy room with a fire in a great fireplace on cool evenings and chintz curtains at windows." Service Clubs promised soldiers, "You will smell the pungent aroma of boiling coffee and of frying hamburgers, and you will hear the raucous strains of boogy-woogy mingled with nostalgic ballads coming from the radio-phonograph." Most appealing were the "nearly 100 girls [sent] into the China-Burma-India war theatre to staff these clubs and give them that extra touch needed to make them most like home." For those men stationed some distance from clubs, the Red Cross created five "club-mobiles," which traveled to the men and offered them familiar food and good conversation.[119]

Even more important, the United Service Organizations, founded by six organizations—the YMCA, the YWCA, the National Catholic Community Service, the National Jewish Welfare Board, the Traveler's Aid Association, and the Salvation Army—created "a home away from home" for servicemen. Incorporated in 1941, the USO worked to combat homesickness and often mentioned that emotion in its appeals for civilian support. A. H. Giannini, the chair of the Los Angeles–area board of the USO, said in a fundraising speech, "You have to remember that no matter how busy these boys are in the camps, sooner or later all suddenly are pierced with an intolerable feeling of homesickness." Dr. John Millet, chairman of the morale committee of the American Psychoanalytic Association, noted, "[The] USO helps relieve the natural anxieties of the new soldier, his homesickness, his boredom."[120] USO centers offered bathing facilities, lounges for meetings, space for letter writing, and sewing services.[121] The USO maintained 2,779 facilities in the United States, Alaska, Newfoundland, Bermuda, the Caribbean, the Canal Zone, South America, and Hawaii. By 1944, USO clubs worldwide counted 30 million visits from soldiers each month.[122]

At stateside centers, young women in their late teens and twenties served as junior hostesses and socialized with the servicemen in the hope of raising their spirits. A former junior hostess from Point Richmond, California, recalled that she would head to the local USO after a troop train had arrived: "We'd have our big baskets and we'd have gum and we had cigarettes and we had candy. . . . We'd mail letters for them." Other activities included dancing and socializing with the soldiers. "We just went there and danced and it was entertaining for everybody, and we were asked to do that so we did. . . . They came to dance. They just wanted somebody to talk to I guess, just as though they were home." She said of the soldiers, "These boys were lonely and it [the USO] gave them something to do, a place to go right?" She felt sympathy for them: "They were young kids just like us, away from home, probably for the first time. It's scary."[123] Earl Schneider, a New Jersey native who joined the navy, recalled how comforting such hostesses were. He was sent to San Diego for naval training. "Most of us . . . never had been out of our home state or home city." Schneider reveled in the opportunity to see more of the world; at the same time he wanted something familiar, so he headed to the USO: "They had young ladies there that would sit with you and have coffee . . . nothing sexual or anything like that. They were just friendly, you know, wanted to talk to you and make you feel at home or a home-away-from-home."[124]

Norman Rockwell celebrated the care the USO bestowed on soldiers away from home in this cover for the *Saturday Evening Post* in 1942.
Source: Image courtesy of Curtis Publications, with permission of the Norman Rockwell Family Agency.

Married women over thirty-five filled the role of senior hostesses. They were supposed to be surrogate mothers to the young men. Soldiers confided their worries to these women and frequently discussed their fears and their homesickness. Daniel Wilson, a Mississippi native stationed in Los Angeles, said, "Lots of evenings I don't even dance with the junior hostesses. It's sort of restful to talk with the older women who come to act as senior hostesses. You can talk about the war and home and things with them." The USO encouraged this type of relationship. An official from the Salvation Army, one of the constituent groups of the USO, said,

"Servicemen appreciate the presence of these mature, sympathetic women. Lonely boys, homesick boys, troubled boys with personal problems will talk by the hour to them."[125]

In addition to talking with the young men, USO volunteers cooked homemade goodies to remind soldiers of home.[126] Sometimes the centers held "state parties," where the cuisines of different regions were served. The USO also implored women to invite soldiers to their houses for home-cooked meals: "Your home contribution often may be one of the most valuable of all, for 9 out of 10 of those boys are desperately homesick . . . [and] hungry for home atmosphere . . . little attentions that a mother, perhaps a thousand miles away, would want you to give her boy."[127]

Significantly, some critics within the military contended that many of the young men who came to the USO out of homesickness did so because they had been brought up to be overly dependent on their families, particularly their mothers. The USO itself warned senior hostesses against engaging in "momism" and becoming too possessive or attached to the young men they served.[128] In 1942, James A. McCaffrey, who was leading the campaign for the USO war fund in Los Angeles, discussed the fine line the organization walked: "It's not the purpose of U.S.O. to coddle our fighting

Members of the Tacoma, Washington, USO provide motherly attention to soldiers in 1943.
Source: Image courtesy of the Tacoma Public Library Northwest Room, Richards Collection.

men. . . . Make no mistake about it, the Army, Navy, Marine Corps and Air Corps give them the kind of training and discipline that toughen them for the man's work they have to do." However, he continued, "the one thing military life cannot give them is home. Their mode of life is entirely changed. This abrupt change from home and the complete freedom of civilian life to the institutional, regimented life of military services necessitates psychological adjustments." During this process of adjustment, the USO offered the young soldier "scenes and things that remind him of home, the folks and associates he has left behind."[129]

Among the scenes that reminded soldiers of home were the USO shows—starring the Andrews Sisters, Bob Hope, Bing Crosby, and other celebrities—and movies. Both forms of entertainment carried troops back to civilian life and normalcy, at least for a few hours. Soldiers saw movies more frequently than live shows, and many relied on them to transport them mentally to other places. Some movies were homemade. For instance, in 1941, the citizens of Rutland, Vermont, sent their sons and husbands stationed at Fort Meade two hundred feet of movie footage of their hometown. One commentator said, "Rutland boys saw the film in their company day room. Excitedly they identified the familiar landmarks, familiar town characters moving across the screen. The pictures lifted them out of the mental bog."[130]

More common were commercial movies made in Hollywood. Although they did not show the intimate scenes of hometown life, they connected Americans overseas to the national mass culture of which they had been a part. Ernie Pyle reported that the army imported movies as part of its strategy to raise morale. In the Marianas Islands, soldiers could watch a wide selection of films that the army hoped would prevent the onset of "island neurosis" or "pineapple crazy," conditions born of boredom, isolation, and long bouts of inactivity. "These three Marianas islands have a total of two hundred thirty-three outdoor movies on them. And they show every night. Even if it isn't a good movie, it kills the time between supper and bedtime. The movies are usually on the slope of a hill."[131] Anne McCaughey, who worked as a Red Cross aide at the U.S. Army's 50th General Hospital, wrote in her diary in 1944, "Seeing GOING MY WAY last night was one of the pleasantest things that have happened since being in the army." A sheet served as a screen, and she watched the movie while sitting on a hill: "But still and all I loved it. . . . [Watching Bing Crosby] fills me with a feeling of happiness and contentment and being at home and at ease and having a helluva good time."[132] The diaries of others deployed overseas were likewise filled with references to movies recently seen and the cheer they brought. William Askin, yeoman second class on the USS LST 246, wrote that he had again received no mail from home. Luckily, however, there were other reminders of the life he had left behind: "Had movie in eve. 'Wintertime' Sonja Henie. Beautiful. Nice to see a movie now and then."[133] One marine explained the importance of the movies in connecting him to home: "I know what it is to be cut off from everything. . . . Those hours can stretch into centuries—and would, if it weren't for a movie now and then. Movies that stop us from thinking of ourselves and our surroundings. Movies that remind us that there are such things as pretty girls, gay music, and a civilization worth fighting for."[134]

In addition to bringing commercial entertainment to troops, the army brought them commercial products, with the help of the Post Exchange, variously called the PX or the Army Exchange Service. The modern PX, created in 1941, was crucial to maintaining morale among soldiers. It provided them with many of the material goods for which they longed, taking on a role that families had filled in previous wars.[135] The nearly 8 million soldiers who flocked to the PX during World War II eagerly sought brand-name consumer goods, from soft drinks and candy bars to *Time* magazine, for they were potent reminders of home. The journalist Meyer Berger reported, "These AES [Army Exchange Service] men know better than anyone else what name brands do for a homesick Yank in tropical or Arctic wilderness thousands of miles from Jenkins Junction, the Loop, or Broadway. Mere sight of a popular brand of cigarette, tomato juice, chewing gum, candy-bar or toothpaste touches off eager discussion of peacetime days in the village drug store, of home-cooked meals, of long-remembered dates." Brig. Gen. Joseph W. Byron, who oversaw the Army Exchange Service, believed, "[The soldier] gets a lift just out of seeing his familiar American label."[136]

Reminders of home were being mass-produced and commercialized. One showed one's sense of place and connection by purchasing and enjoying consumer goods rather than by receiving home-made objects. The armed services demanded that soldiers transfer their loyalties from home to the military; to aid this process it provided them with some of the commercial comforts of home that might assuage their homesickness.

BEHIND BARBED WIRE

Although the U.S. government and the American public showed sympathy toward homesick soldiers, there was little to spare for another group displaced by the imperatives of the national government. As a result of Executive Order 9066, issued by President Franklin Roosevelt in early 1942, 120,000 Japanese immigrants and their American-born children living close to the Pacific coast were forced to relocate to internment camps scattered across California, Utah, Arizona, Colorado, Wyoming, Idaho, and Arkansas.[137]

After being evicted from their West Coast homes, they were first sent to racetracks, fair grounds, and other large facilities that had been quickly converted into temporary relocation centers.[138] None were designed for comfort. At the Tanforan Camp, a former racetrack, internees lived in horse stables while awaiting relocation. At another relocation site, the Tulare Assembly Center, an internee wrote, "Our quarter is something awful. In a space by 20 by 25 feet we eight live together where there are 8 single beds, suit cases, big and small, clothes, hats coats and every thing of the kind hang all about enmeshed." A commentator reported, "Each evacuee made his own mattress of straw, took his place in the crowded barracks, and tried to adjust to his new life."[139]

In such an atmosphere, internees felt profoundly anxious, depressed, and angered. Many missed the homes they had been forced to leave in California or Oregon or Washington; the crisis situation of the camps made some long for Japan as well. Keikichi (K. A.) Imamura, his wife, Toshiko, and their son, Keichi, were forced to leave their home in California. First relocated to the Tulare Assembly Center, they eventually were moved to the Gila River Relocation Center in Arizona. Throughout their internment, they corresponded with Walter Millsap, a friend from California. K. A. Imamura wrote despondently to Millsap in the summer of 1942 from Tulare, "Frankly, I want to tell you, my friend, for the first time in my American life, my mind turned toward the homeward." Although Imamura had been in the United States for over a quarter-century, he felt rejected by his adopted country and resolved to return to Tokyo. In a letter written a few weeks later, his wife discussed her similar feelings: "Are you telling me that I am getting homesick? . . . I do not flatly deny that it isn't true. . . . I seldom homesicked for Tokyo [before the internment]." Now, she admitted, she did miss Japan.[140] Their son, a native of the United States, missed distinctly different things. He also wrote Millsap of conditions in Tulare. There was a baseball diamond at the assembly center, which led him to confide, "Things are going pretty good around here, but I like Pasadena better than here." He longed not for Japan but for the civilian world of the United States in which he had grown up.[141]

After a few months, the ramshackle and uncomfortable surroundings of the relocation centers became familiar, and when it was time to leave them for the internment camps many evacuees expressed regret. Yoshiko Uchida's family was evacuated from their home in Berkeley, California, to Tanforan, and finally to the Topaz Internment Camp in Delta, Utah. Uchida wrote of Tanforan, "It had only been a crude community of stables and barracks, but it had been home for five months and we had grown accustomed to our life there. Now it was another wrench, another uprooting, and this time we were bound for an unknown and forbidding destination. Those who remained seemed to watch us go with the same apprehension we felt. Neither side quite wanted to let go. We waved to each other as long as we could, and those of us on the train pressed up to the windows, holding close the final sight of all that was familiar."[142] At the relocation center in Santa Anita, an editorialist for the *Santa Anita Pacemaker*, a newspaper that camp residents produced, wrote:

> We'll all miss the magnificent Grandstand, the dances there . . . the tree lined walks . . . Anita Chiquita field and the many activities going on there at all hours of the day . . . the Sunday evening concerts with the Sierra Madres growing even darker and somber in the crepuscular moments . . . watching the trains and busses pull in with strangers and getting to know them and becoming friends and then watching the trains pull out again in the bleak hour after breakfast carrying new friends away to scattered destinations. . . . Santa Anita was all this and more, too. It was home to us for six months—and it always hurts to leave home. So this is goodby—with a tear or two but looking forward to Arkansas.[143]

In these most trying circumstances, the editorialist showed both homesickness for his temporary lodging and the increasingly common emotion of cheerfulness, more and more a requirement of public deportment in America.

Despite the upbeat tone of the editorial, what internees longed for was not the relocation center, but their real homes, left behind on the West Coast. Jeanne Wakatsuki, a young child when she was interned at the Manzanar Camp, missed family life and disliked her new institutional setting: "Before Manzanar, mealtime had always been the center of our family scene. In camp, and afterward, I would often recall with deep yearning the old round wooden table in our dining room in Ocean Park." At the camp, however, things were different: "Not only did we stop eating at home, there was no longer a home to eat in."[144]

Some missed family life; others pined for the American culture they had been a part of until the war. According to a government estimate, over 70 percent of the Nisei had never been to Japan.[145] In a booklet published in 1943 to commemorate their first year at the Gila River Relocation Center in Arizona, residents recalled the difficulties they had adjusting to camp life: "Many of these people previously lived in communities where the majority of their neighbors and friends were of the cross section of the American public. To them, it seemed strange to live in a strictly Japanese community. In fact, some of them do not speak Japanese."[146] A young evacuee captured this mood when he told his mother after moving to an assembly center, "Mother, I don't like Japan. I want to go back to America."[147] An older internee, Charles Kikuchi, wrote that he too felt culture shock when he first arrived at Tanforan, for he found himself surrounded by so many Japanese who were less assimilated. In the spring of 1942, he wrote, "Sometimes I feel like a foreigner in this camp hearing so much Japanese although our family uses English almost exclusively." A few days later, he complained about "all those Japanese old men . . . jabbering away." He was even more critical of those who tried to create bits of their native land in the concentration camp. He reported that one of the internees had created a garden that was "laid out beautifully. . . . The whole thing looks like Japan. Some people just can't divorce themselves from Japan and cling to the old traditions and ways."[148] While he was homesick for his assimilated lifestyle, his neighbors at the camp missed their Japanese roots. The garden his neighbors had created, and Kikuchi's reaction to it, showed the complexity of homesickness in the internment camps. Some found their longings for Japan heightened by the poor treatment they received at the hands of the U.S. government; others longed to return to their assimilated lives within American society.

Those who longed for their lives before the war worked to re-create them as best they could. Jeanne Wakatsuki and her peers tried to replicate the American institutions they had been a part of outside the camps: "In such a narrowed world, in order to survive . . . you try to re-create, as well as you can, your normality, some sense of things continuing. The fact that America had accused us, or excluded us, or imprisoned us . . . did not change the kind of world we wanted. Most of us were born in this country; we had no other models." Accordingly, the internees at Manzanar reestablished the American life that existed on the other side of the fence. There were "schools, churches, Boy Scouts, beauty parlors . . . fire and police departments, glee clubs, softball leagues, Abbott and Costello movies, tennis courts."[149]

As the internees looked back on their early days in the camps, they admitted that they had experienced "feelings and attitudes resultant from forced changes in their own lives—unrest, heartaches, and anxieties."[150] But as they thought about those experiences, rather than admit heartache or discontent with the harsh living conditions, some stressed their adaptability to their new environment. The *Manzanar Free Press*, another camp newspaper, opined in 1942, "Time will report that we met those problems with the same resolution which characterized the pioneers settlers."[151] Residents of the Gila River Camp adopted a similar tone, claiming that they had transformed the camp into a place that, in some respects, was "comfortably home-like. A home, yes, but one they know they will leave behind for homes in normal American communities." While internees congratulated themselves on making the camp comfortable, they also showed in their public pronouncements a willingness to embrace the future and forget about their past. "The whole tone of the camp has changed. No longer do they look backward to the 'good ole days.' The future stretches ahead of them. They know that their lives belong to the future and not to the dead past."[152]

Such attitudes, forged in the distinctive crucible of injustice and deprivation, nevertheless reflected far-reaching trends in American emotional culture. Internees knew that whatever their true feelings, they could not show undue homesickness, grief, or anger publicly, that instead they must display sunny optimism.[153] While some in America doubted their loyalty, internees showed in their writings just how American they had become in their mode of public emotional expression. In public pronouncements and papers, they minimized their homesickness and emphasized their cheerful willingness to accept the demands of the U.S. government. This new emotional conformity and the desire to fit in was symptomatic of what the sociologist David Riesman termed the "other-directed" personality type. All across America, individuals felt new pressure to tailor their emotions to the needs of the crowd—the army, the college, the company—rather than follow the inner promptings of their own spirit. Riesman wrote, "The other-directed person learns to respond to signals from a far wider circle than is constituted by his parents. The family is no longer a closely knit unit to which he belongs but merely part of a wider social environment to which he early becomes attentive."[154] Eager to fit into American society, internees displayed the upbeat personality that was rapidly becoming the national norm.

Between World War I and World War II, the contours of modern American culture began to appear. Citizens adjusted to bureaucratic life as they witnessed the rise of large corporations and the extension of government agencies and military forces. Experts did their best to encourage individuals to separate from their families and develop loyalties to new organizations and institutions. Sometimes, as in the case of drafts and internment, citizens had little choice in the matter. To ease this transition, those institutions offered tokens of home. Cookies, candies, slippers, and socks that used to be made by mothers, as well as countless other reminders of home, were now produced in factories and could be purchased at the PX and stores around the world. A sense of home could be found in commercial products, and since they were widely distributed, leaving home and reestablishing it elsewhere became somewhat easier. The Hershey bars, the Cokes, the movies, the gift packs from department stores that soldiers enjoyed, civilians did as well. The Abbott and Costello movies shown in internment camps and army camps, the sweets available at the Carolina Sea Island candy store in Chicago, all were objects from home that could now be bought far away from it. The imperative to leave home, to adjust to new institutions and make a strange world familiar with consumer goods became even more significant after the war.

CHAPTER 7

cVᔆ

Mama's Boys, Organization Men, Boomerang Kids, and the Surprising Persistence of the Extended Family

A s social commentators considered the postwar world, they concluded that a new personality type had taken shape. In 1956, the writer William Whyte described the "Organization Man" in *Fortune* magazine. "Organization men" not only worked for "the Organization"; they "belong[ed] to it as well. They are the ones of our middle class who have left home, spiritually as well as physically, to take the vows of organization life, and it is they who are the mind and souls of our great self-perpetuating institutions."[1] In a similar vein, David Riesman and his colleagues described the "other-directed" behavior of individuals who desired to fit into the mass society— men and women who took their cues for emotional comportment from those around them and could consequently fit in anywhere.[2] Whyte and Riesman were only two of the many commentators who observed (with alarm) that the postwar world required individuals to limit their emotional connections to home, family, and place, and to merge themselves with larger social bodies.

Other influential social scientists documented similar patterns in American life. The sociologist Talcott Parsons observed, for instance, that the extended family structure and all of its emotional entanglements were ill-suited to the circumstances of industrialized societies. He noted that the only type of family relationship suited to modern conditions was a "conjugal" tie, "which interferes relatively little with an industrial economy."[3] Parsons was describing the world he saw around him. In 1940, half of all

Americans between twenty and twenty-four lived with their parents; in the 1950s, this cohort was moving in increasing numbers to establish households of their own.[4] Between 1940 and 1980, the number of Americans living in multigenerational households fell by 50 percent (only to begin slowly rebounding after the 1980s).[5] In the wake of World War II, young men and women were forming relationships that were portable and discrete, and were separating themselves from extended family connections.

As the mental health expert William Henry explained in 1963, this trend rendered individuals free agents, outfitting them for success. The society and economy demanded "the ready transferability of person and of loyalty . . . a sensitivity to the values and actions of the system or organization . . . and, above all, a sense of personal autonomy."[6] The sociologist W. Lloyd Warner came to similar conclusions, describing the new personality type most useful to business. He suggested that being socially, occupationally, and geographically mobile required that individuals become accustomed to "adjustment, readjustment, and adjustment again. . . . Fluidity of position can only exist where it is possible for the family to relate itself to an emergent society and where it can permit its individuals to be trained in such a way that they move from position to position and place to place without difficulty." To form this type of personality, "families cannot be too closely attached to their kindred (extended kinship system) or they will be held to one location, socially and economically maladapted."[7] Individuals needed to be free of family ties and emotional claims in order to advance within the governmental systems and corporate bureaucracies that were everywhere in the 1950s and 1960s.

To be autonomous of one's family was not easy or natural, but a learned emotional style that required the repression of love and longing, the separation of private life from work life, and the masking of feelings.[8] These were the demands that Americans in the postwar years faced. Not all found the imperative easy to follow, and many quietly chafed against their bonds.

THE COLD WAR

Americans experienced the conflict between their feelings and the needs of the larger society during the cold war, for military officials and mental health professionals asked young men to transfer their loyalties to the military-industrial complex and aid the nation in its fight against communism. Ideally, strong men would defend the nation, supported by women who stayed at home and kept their emotions, affections, and sexuality in check.[9] Some cold warriors feared that this emotional ideal was out of reach for many who were trapped in patterns of overly affectionate family life, but they nevertheless continued to pressure men to subordinate family ties to national needs.

A telling moment came in the wake of World War II, after fighting ceased and soldiers still abroad were eager to come home. When a U.S. Senate committee visited the Philippines in January 1946, thousands of soldiers showed up to lobby for their quick demobilization and asked their families to exert pressure on the government as well. They circulated a handbill:

> Attention All Homesick G.I.'s Apparently you don't want to go home—or you feel as though you have one foot on the boat already.
>
> Don't accept APPEASEMENTS, or such words as ESSENTIALITY as meaning that you are going home.
>
> KEEP WIRING
>
> KEEP YOUR FOLKS WIRING
>
> KEEP YOUR BUDDY WIRING
>
> KEEP THE BALL ROLLING
>
> WE HAVEN'T WON YET[10]

For these soldiers, returning home would be the sign that they had won the war; securing the government objective of a structured peace was only a secondary concern.

The government eventually responded to such protests. Gen. William Styer, commander of troops in the Philippines, defended his unruly soldiers, noting that their actions were prompted by "acute homesickness aggravated by the termination of hostilities." Later in January, Gen. Dwight Eisenhower worked to step up the pace of demobilization so that the soldiers could go home. The U.S. Army recognized that soldiers and their families were experiencing fatigue and impatience after the long war, yet military officials hoped troops would conquer these feelings and work for the good of the nation, even if it involved sacrifice. A Charleston, West Virginia, newspaper reported, "Gen. Dwight D. Eisenhower promised homesick GIs and their families tonight that the revised demobilization schedule will be 'carried out to the letter.'" Eisenhower worried, however, that too many men would succumb to homesickness. "I know how homesickness and boredom may fill a soldier's letters with a disturbing sense of his own unimportance in the pattern of Army life. . . . But our Army is playing a great role in a troubled world. . . . The urgency of war has gone. But we have a new urgency—the necessity of building a secure peace." He hoped that "the practical commonsense which is America's birthright will conquer the sharp pangs of disappointment when the loved ones are delayed in coming home."[11] Americans should learn to endure separations in order to safeguard the world. Yet despite Eisenhower's cautions, the government brought troops home and, sensitive to the complaints of soldiers and their families, suspended the draft in 1947.[12]

This represented only a brief hiatus from military demands on the populace, however. In 1948, President Truman amplified the message that the family claim had to be subordinated to national needs when he reinstated the draft in response to flaring cold war tensions. It remained in place until 1973. During that quarter century, the reach of government and organizational life extended further than it had in earlier years.

Soldiers were called up in large numbers after the outbreak of the Korean War, and not all of the 1.5 million men inducted into the armed services over the course of the war served happily or willingly.[13] A debate arose anew over just how closely tied men should be to their homes and families, and whether such attachments were impeding the war effort. During the conflict, families still felt sympathy for the homesick, but many military officials did not. They sought to hasten men's separation from their homes, and in particular, their mothers, for once freed from home, these mama's boys would develop into organization men.

Soldiers found this vision less appealing than did the military commanders. In early 1951, Pvt. Bob Lloyd, a nineteen-year-old marine stationed in Korea, sent a letter home to El Paso. Writing from Munsan, at the southern tip of Korea, Lloyd told his parents:

> If you have been reading articles that say the marines are eager to return to battle, you can just tell the authors of those articles, that I said they are big, fat fibbers. I speak for myself, and all the men I know. All of us are infected with a very old, common sickness with only one cure—Home.
>
> I think if we stay here much longer we will all have to be put in padded cells. There is nothing to do except eat and sleep and sit and stare at the four corners of the tent. . . .
>
> It was O.K. for the first week, but since then, the monotony has been rising until all of us are on the verge of cracking. . . .
>
> I'd give my eye teeth along with the rest of my teeth if I thought it would help me get home for a while.[14]

Writing from Korea in the autumn of 1952, Melvin Horwitz, a MASH surgeon, similarly lamented to his wife, "My heart aches for a normal life—to be opposite you at the end of the day—eating, talking—what to do with this evening—what do you want to hear on the victrola—the newspapers—looking through the New Yorker—going downtown—New Haven—Willimantic—movies, shows, window shopping—watching the college students walking along quiet streets."[15]

During the Korean War, the girlfriends, wives, and parents of those stationed overseas worried about their menfolk and had compassion rather than contempt for those who suffered from homesickness. They did not want them to be organization men; they wanted them to be family men. Through gestures large and small, American parents, wives, and children tried to strengthen the bonds that tied them to their sons, husbands, and fathers in Korea. The most common way to comfort soldiers in distant lands was through letters, and a voluminous correspondence between parents and sons, husbands and wives, traveled back and forth across the Pacific. But some went to greater and more unusual lengths.

In 1950, 450 relatives of servicemen launched "Operation Homefolk." They set off from Scranton, Pennsylvania, to visit their sons, husbands, and boyfriends in the 109th Infantry Regiment of the Pennsylvania National Guard, now in federal service and quartered at Camp Atterbury in Indiana. With the help of the army, the group chartered a special train and then traveled by bus to the camp. One journalist reported, "'Operation Homefolk' gets under way tonight and by tomorrow noon will be battling homesickness. The commanders are confident of complete victory." The brief visit with kin went off with only a few hitches, and soldiers' spirits were lifted, at least temporarily.[16]

Even those who did not know the soldiers tried to bring them comfort and make personal connections to troops. The advice columnist Dorothy Dix told Agatha, a fifteen-year-old girl who was considering writing letters to soldiers in Korea, that if her parents assented, and if Agatha was not trying to start a romance with a soldier, it would be perfectly appropriate for her to initiate a correspondence with a serviceman overseas: "A boy away from home is a homesick boy; nothing means more to our young servicemen than cheerful letters, the more newsy the better. Many boys do not have large families, or a large circle of friends and they look to strangers to fill their need for mail." Dix suggested that Agatha consult with a local servicemen's club to find a suitable pen pal.[17] Civilians worked to maintain, and in some cases enhance, emotional ties with troops rather than sever them.

The military also tried to bring comfort to soldiers, and in some cases, abetted communication with families stateside. For the first time, the military offered a way to call home using the Military Affiliate Radio System. This system relied on radio operators in the army who would contact ham radio operators in the United States, who would then call a soldier's family collect. Conversations could not exceed five minutes, and connections were not always available or clear.[18] Although crude by modern standards, this telephone infrastructure represented more direct contact with the home front than any previous generation of soldiers had enjoyed.

Often, however, the military's efforts focused on making men content, or at least more content, with military life itself. This was particularly apparent during holidays, when soldiers yearned most for their families. Unlike the civilian efforts to combat homesickness, which seemed designed to connect men to their homes, these efforts were focused on reproducing home experiences within the military. In 1951, helicopters delivered a complete Thanksgiving meal to men on Heartbreak Ridge and Bloody Ridge in an effort to "make them a little less homesick on what has become the main nostalgic United States holiday."[19] A year later, the government flew Cardinal Spellman of New York to Korea. There he "celebrated mass for 800 men of the Second Division in an enormous chapel tent not far behind the lines. . . . Helen Traubel, the opera singer, went by jeep under brittle stars from one encampment to another on Christmas Eve to sing hymns and carols for homesick soldiers from all the United Nations divisions."[20]

When such measures proved unequal to the need, when men's homesickness was so great that it conflicted with national or bureaucratic goals, they received a fair amount of scorn and condemnation. Some military authorities, civic leaders, and psychologists ratcheted up the criticism of homesickness that had emerged during World War II and suggested it hinted at effeminacy and cowardice. In his book *Their Mothers' Sons*, Edward Strecker, a professor of medicine at the University of Pennsylvania and an army consultant, accused "Moms" of keeping their "children enwombed psychologically," and failing to "untie the emotional apron string—the Silver Cord—which binds her children to her." As a result, he considered "Moms" to be America's "gravest menace."[21] During the 1950s, a host of similar books and articles discussed the softness of the American male and the implications of this for society and international politics.[22] Some claimed that an army composed of emotionally immature men, afflicted with nostalgia, would doom the nation's international relations.

In September 1950, a Missouri newspaper editorialized on the "problem of homesick G.I.'s." The paper recounted the efforts of the homesick soldiers at the end of World War II, who had lobbied to be demobilized so that they could return to the States. The author worried that the same might happen again in Korea.

There are people who are convinced that much of the world's trouble today is due to the overly-hasty demobilization of the United States army following the last world war. At that time we had the military power to get just about whatever sort of peace terms we wanted, but American mothers wanted their boys home, their boys were anxious to come home, and they let the fact be known so emphatically demobilization possibly was hurried more than it should have been. . . . One wonders whether similar natural impatience following the end of the Korean war will lay the basis for more trouble later on. Defeating the North Koreans isn't going to end the menace of Russia.[23]

Later that year, when army morale dipped dangerously low, Mrs. William C. Reed, the national president of the American Legion Auxiliary, told women to avoid "momism," which, she claimed, had "wrecked the peace" at the end of World War II: "Many unthinking and uninformed women joined in the cry, 'bring the boys home' in 1945. This resulted in demobilization at a time when American might in Europe would have held the Iron Curtain back."[24]

Other commentators agreed that giving in to homesickness ultimately meant capitulating to the nation's foes. In 1952, Col. Anthony Standish, a combat commander during World War II, wrote an article for the army's *Combat Forces Journal* that was picked up by the popular press. "Dipping into psychology and psychiatry," one reporter wrote, "Col. Standish said the reasons for so poor a showing of courage lies in a man's childhood. Without a father's discipline, he opined, most men are raised under the influence of 'momism' and conditioned for a soft life without responsibility." Standish believed that America was in crisis. Referring to "momism," he noted, "We joke a lot about all this. But when the faulty upbringing of our manhood reaches the point where only a small fraction has the courage needed to fight for their country, it's not at all funny! It becomes a military problem." To resolve the crisis Standish suggested that both families and the military change the ways they dealt with the nation's young men. It was necessary to "get the father replacing the mother as head of the family and bring masculine disciplinary influences back into the rearing of children." The armed forces also could do their part to toughen up soldiers. Ideally, "camp followers are left at home or at least constrained from interfering with officer and noncom schools and other training preparation. U.S.O. activities are encouraged only to the point of providing recreation and relaxation so that all men are kept at the peak of mental and physical alertness and receptivity." Such measures were necessary, for, Standish claimed, the Eighth Army stationed in Korea was demanding, "Stop the mollycoddling—send us disciplined soldiers!"[25] While few went as far as Standish, with his call for severe restrictions on the USO, many shared his underlying concern about the weak men who seemed to populate the armed services.

Some commentators believed that with the right help, troops' character defects could be cured. With the aid of psychologists and psychiatrists, homesick soldiers could be trained to replace their ties to home with an attachment to the new organization they had joined.[26] In late July 1950, a month after the North Korean invasion, Sam Boal, a reporter for the *New York Times*, visited Fort Dix to see how this transformation was accomplished. Boal claimed that the military was creating a "new army" that was heavily reliant on psychological theory as it worked to convert "rawcruits," fresh from home, into capable soldiers. Soon after the young men arrived,

Boal reported, they listened to a lecture by Maj. Gen. John M. Devine on proper emotional comportment in the army.

> There will be the mama's boys who get homesick and take off. . . . There is nothing to be ashamed of in being homesick. It's a feeling many people have, and it can be pretty bad at times. . . . Homesickness is one of those things you just have to overcome. You've simply got to endure it by keeping busy, by working harder, by mastering yourself. It will soon disappear, the apron strings will be cut—they've got to be cut some time—and you'll be a man. Then, I assure you, mama will be very proud that her boy is not a mama's boy any longer.

Boal continued, "The new Army is strict without being nasty; it tends to be fatherly, but not motherly." Eventually, the army hoped, such training would teach soldiers to give "total obedience" and allegiance to it, rather than to their families.[27]

To help men still struggling with transition in Korea, combat psychiatrists were deployed overseas very early, and once there, they employed the same techniques that had been developed during World War I.[28] Division psychiatrists attended to homesick or emotionally troubled men near their unit and reinforced the expectation that their patients would return to their comrades rather than be sent home. As one observer noted, the military hoped that treating a homesick or depressed soldier near his unit would cure him of his symptoms and "preserve the group identification."[29] A news correspondent described the army psychiatrist's approach: "His attitude never is that you have left your outfit forever. Instead, 'Of course you're going back. Tell me when you're ready.' . . . Constantly he talks about your old outfit. Sure, it's tough up there, but the other guys are taking it. . . . The closer you are to your outfit, the easier it is to persuade you to return."[30] This approach was fairly successful, for a large number of soldiers suffering from a variety of psychological maladies, including homesickness, were returned to their units. Whereas 70 percent of neuropsychiatric cases were returned to battle by the end of World War II, during the Korean War, 88 percent of soldiers with neuropsychiatric problems were returned to their divisions, and 97 percent were returned "to duty somewhere within the combat theatre."[31]

Psychiatrists were in Korea to teach men how to cope with the trauma of war and the pain of separation. Rather than sanctifying the love of home and mother as noble sentiments and a source of civic virtue and martial motivation, military officials and psychiatric experts during the Korean War considered such feelings enervating and emasculating—a threat to military discipline and order. The discourse on "momism," which had developed during World War II, expanded during the Korean conflict and decisively severed the connection between love of home and martial valor. Homesickness was the sign of a sissy rather than the mark of a loving family man. Men needed to free themselves of home and Mom and integrate themselves into the spreading bureaucracies of postwar society. Yet despite this advice, the experience of soldiers during the cold war suggested that many found it difficult to live up to this ideal.

ORGANIZATION MEN

Like the military, expanding corporations required their employees, especially their white-collar workers, to manifest a willingness to relocate if they hoped to advance. Many complied. A common joke among IBM employees during the 1950s and 1960s was that the company's name stood for "I've Been Moved." IBM employees were hardly alone. William Whyte wrote that while business corporations demanded mobility, so too did most sectors of the economy, even nonprofit entities like churches and universities.[32] Moving was becoming less an option and more a necessity for advancement; during the 1950s, roughly 20 percent of the U.S. population moved each year.[33]

White-collar employees unwilling to move risked stalling their careers or losing their jobs. In *The Organization Man,* William Whyte reported, "'We never plan to transfer,' as one company president explains a bit dryly, 'and we never make a man move. Of course, he kills his career if he doesn't. But we never *make* him do it.'" Whyte noted, "The fact is well understood; it is with a smile that the recruit moves—and keeps on moving—year after year." Such moves, he conjectured, were good for corporations: "By deliberately exposing a man to a succession of environments, they best obtain that necessity of the large organization—the man who can fit in anywhere. 'The training,' as an I.B.M. executive succinctly puts it, 'makes our men interchangeable.'"[34]

Some felt distressed by this compunction to move. A wealth of studies showed that the constant relocation of white-collar workers in fact exacted a psychic toll, both on the predominantly male workforce and, even more so, on their wives. A report published in 1961 concluded, "There are many newcomers who have a difficult time uprooting themselves and beginning again elsewhere, even when the move brings higher status, a more attractive environment, and better schools."[35]

During the 1950s and 1960s, these moves seemed particularly trying for the wives of relocated workers. Men typically felt more excitement about their relocations, for they were moving up in a hierarchy, meeting new colleagues, and functioning within an organizational culture that gave them at least some emotional succor. Their wives faced a different reality. Like their mothers, these women expected, and were expected, to follow their husbands cheerfully, wherever their careers might take them. Cheerfulness, however, did not come easy. A study published in 1958 compared residents in Bergen County, New Jersey, a rapidly growing suburban area filled with middle-class relocated families, with residents of rural Cattaraugus County, in western New York, and found a higher rate of mental distress in the New Jersey suburbs. The authors concluded that "the strains of geographic, socioeconomic, and cultural mobility are associated particularly with the emotional disorders of childbearing women." This was because "the couples often have moved away from the homes of their childhood and are breaking up close ties with their families." Husbands conceived of such moves as a sign of success, and their wives sometimes did too. However, "in susceptible persons it creates stress to the extent that they suffer an emotional disorder and need a psychiatrist. The wife usually becomes the patient."[36]

Not all ended up on the psychiatrist's couch, but many women shared a sense of trauma when they found themselves uprooted. In 1967, Phyllis LaFarge confessed that she had been feeling homesick ever since moving from Brooklyn to New Haven to forward her husband's career. There were many things she missed, and she complained of the social isolation she felt in New Haven. "It did no good to go outside. Around me was the kind of staid suburban neighborhood in which I had never lived, the sort of place where people over the age of three never seem to go out of doors except to get into their cars." She longed for her Brooklyn life: "New York was filthy, noisy, and violent. But it was where I had lived for more than 20 years; where, once married, I had woven with my husband the humble web of acquaintance and habit that is a sense of home." She tried to tough it out, but her "homesickness did not get much better." She met other wives new to the area, and though they tried to put on a brave front, she realized that they too were homesick. Perhaps, she speculated, relocation was harder for women than for men "because home is usually their greatest 'creation.' A sense of 'place' is an important ingredient in making a home."[37] While the men encountered new opportunities that could offset the pain of pulling up roots, the women experienced social isolation and considerable loss.

THE ROOTLESSNESS OF SUBURBAN LIFE

This was particularly true of women who moved to the suburbs, far away from their families who remained in older urban neighborhoods. The suburbs, which had begun attracting large numbers of Americans in the years before World War II, grew even faster in the years after the war. It was not just their location that differentiated suburban houses from past housing stock; what also distinguished them was that they were designed for single families. As opposed to the apartment houses or even row houses that characterized much urban living, suburban living glorified the isolated nuclear family.[38]

Families moved to suburbs for a multitude of reasons. Some took advantage of the new government loan programs that encouraged settlement outside of older downtown cores. Others moved because they were following their jobs or because they accepted the popular wisdom that touted the suburbs as the good life. Many of the suburbs of the 1950s became famous; Park Forest, Illinois, was developed in the late 1940s, and the Levittown developments in Pennsylvania, New Jersey, and New York were constructed during the 1940s, 1950s, and 1960s. These developments and others like them were notable for the speed with which they were built, the mass-production techniques on which such speed depended, and the fears they inspired.[39]

Suburbs attracted a great deal of attention in the 1950s and 1960s. Some critics worried that they bred social isolation and discontent; others were more sanguine. Yet what emerged from the wealth of literature on these places was the sense that a significant portion of suburban residents experienced feelings of anomie, loneliness, and melancholy. In Park Forest, William H. Whyte found residents who felt unsettled. The suburb, situated roughly thirty-five miles from Chicago, marketed itself as a new hometown. Its advertising copy read:

> You *Belong* in PARK FOREST!
> The moment you come to our town you know:
> You're welcome
> You're part of a big group
> You can live in a friendly small town
> instead of a lonely big city.
> You can have friends who want you—
> And you can enjoy being with them.
> Come out. Find out about the spirit of Park Forest.

As he interviewed families, though, Whyte discovered a pervasive sense of dislocation. "Are the transients a rootless people?" he asked. "If by roots we mean the complex of geographical and family ties that has historically knitted Americans to local society, these young transients are almost entirely rootless. They are very much aware of the fact; surprisingly often they will bring up the home town, and though they have no intention of going back, they dwell on what they have left behind."[40]

Families also left these new neighborhoods with great frequency. Suburbanites living in the New York area moved so frequently that in 1960, only 6 percent still occupied the same house they had lived in five years earlier. Every year, one sixth of the families living in Levittown moved.[41] This pattern took its toll. Despite his generally optimistic analysis of Levittown, New Jersey, the sociologist Herbert Gans found that those who moved to the new suburb from close-knit neighborhoods in Philadelphia suffered from homesickness and loneliness. Many missed their families, others the social life of their old communities. As one woman told him of life in Levittown, "It's too quiet here, nothing to do. In the city you can go downtown shopping, see all the people, or go visit mother. If there were more friendly people it would be better." Although their husbands commuted to Philadelphia for work, it seemed a world away to women who had no cars of their own. In the 1960s, when Gans was writing, the cost of long-distance telephone calls to distant family was often prohibitively expensive.[42]

What was a problem in Levittown was a problem in many a suburb. In an article on mental "crack-ups in the suburbs," Irwin Stein, a marriage counselor in White Plains, New York, summed up the difficulties women faced: "The suburban housewife is separated from the support she had when she lived in the city—the support of her own mother, who possibly lived in the same neighborhood, the support of many childhood women friends. An apartment house with sixty families offered her far more opportunity for meeting other women than does a block with perhaps six houses."[43] In a host of studies that came out in the 1950s and 1960s, the loneliness of female suburbanites was a recurring motif. Those who seemed most unhappy and homesick were often from working-class or close-knit ethnic families and neighborhoods; many of their new neighbors considered them too needy and overly aggressive in seeking out social contacts. In 1963, Robert Gutman concluded that the most unhappy women who had migrated to suburbs were those who were "expressive emotionally." He wrote, "It was as if the expressive women had not learned that the neighbor relationship is of a special sort, demanding more responsibility than acquaintanceship, yet allowing for less intensity and intimacy than friendship."[44] These women wanted to re-create the intimate bonds of the past, but could not. Their new social milieu demanded that they accept the fact that in modern life, transient, casual, and somewhat superficial connections were the dominant form of social relations. New residents should have few illusions about finding the same close bonds they had left behind.

Many believed that a sort of surface sociability flourished in American suburbs during the 1950s and 1960s.[45] Phyllis LaFarge noted that the young mothers who, like herself, were newly arrived in New Haven, worked hard to maintain a front of cheerfulness, which to her ears "did not ring true." To one woman she wanted to say, "'Look, I know how you feel; you're lonely, you're homesick. I feel the same way.' But something held me back. At last I realized that she was ashamed of what she felt, just as I was. . . . [These women] tried to deflect the eye of the beholder from what they felt. Why were they ashamed? Why was I ashamed?" She concluded, "Women are ashamed of loneliness because they feel they are failing to measure up to an ideal that is an important part of our tradition, one of the chief images of our uprootedness. . . . Most women felt that they should accept—and even enjoy—'moving on' as much as the cowpoke." Alas, this was harder than it seemed.[46] Failure to live up to the ideal of the happy relocator was a source of shame, so women kept up the façade of cheerfulness and hid their sadness behind brave, if hollow, pleasantries.

To find some social connection, they looked to organizations, joining in great numbers throughout the 1950s and 1960s.[47] Park Forest offered sixty-six adult groups that sought to address both community problems and the emotional needs of their members.[48] A suburban community in New England had eighty-nine clubs that social scientists of the era deemed "integrative devices. They tend to acquaint the newcomer with residents outside his particular neighborhood."[49] Another observer noted that sad and lonely women in the suburbs "cope[d] with these feelings by becoming a joiner. . . . 'If you move to suburbia and you aren't a joiner,' [said] . . . the wife of an arts book publisher, 'you are a dead duck. What is there to do? If you don't belong to clubs that have swimming or golf, or play bridge, or solicit for causes, or run Boy Scout troops, or attend a church, you're a very lonely person in suburbia.'"[50] Some claimed that women joined so many organizations that "hyperactivity" was becoming a "character trait" pervasive throughout suburbia.[51]

One group that appealed to the homesick and proliferated in America's suburbs was the Newcomers Club. A few had been founded in the decades before World War II, but the majority cropped up in the 1950s, 1960s, and 1970s. They continued to grow in the years thereafter, but at a slower rate. Unlike the Sons of New Hampshire, Sons of North Carolina, or Sons of Norway groups that had flourished in the nineteenth century, or even the Iowa picnics in the twentieth century, which focused on celebrating and memorializing places left behind, Newcomers Clubs paid attention to members' shared location in the present. They attempted to build a community based on members' common condition of being uprooted. Vance Packard wrote, "When members of a newcomer club move on—as they typically do—they usually immediately check in with the newcomer club at the next stop. Thus newcomer clubbing becomes a way of life and a world of its own, usually quite apart from the world of the people who consider the town their home town. There is little likelihood that by building their social life around other newcomers they will become a part of the town they live in, in any real sense. But that, perhaps, is the way many have come to prefer it."[52]

Most of the Newcomers Clubs were offshoots of the Welcome Wagon organization, a commercial institution founded in 1928 and present in thousands of towns across the country by the 1950s and 1960s. Businesses hired local women to visit area newcomers and tell them about the organizations, merchants, and culture of their new hometowns.[53] Such commercially sponsored visitors took on the welcoming role that neighbors had earlier played, as businesses realized that there was a thriving profit to be made in helping the uprooted settle in.

Other commercial enterprises joined them. In the 1950s, Donald McPherson opened Homerica, which boasted that "transplanting torn-up roots is our business." Homerica promised to help families who were moving to other parts of the country find new houses that matched their tastes. Other companies soon joined Homerica, and their reach expanded overseas. In the 1960s and 1970s, companies like Executive Homesearch promised to completely replicate in their new town the environment a family had left behind. A realtor boasted, "I can take a transferring family from Darien [Connecticut], and in any metropolitan area of the United States I can put these people in approximately the same environment as far as schools, types of neighbors, same income bracket, same family background, same education, anywhere across the country. They will not be changing their environment, they will be just changing their address."[54] These relocation experts were part of the totalizing structure of organizational life. If workers transferred their loyalties to corporations, the corporations would try to provide a substitute home for their transferred employees.

THE OLD NEIGHBORHOOD

While middle-class Americans were leaving cities for the suburbs, working-class, immigrant, and minority residents found new pressures to abandon older neighborhoods as well. Vito Cali recalled his feelings about the Chicago neighborhood his family left in search of higher status. Born in 1937 in Italy, he and his family came to Chicago in 1947. There they found a warm community in which to settle: "To this day, a week does not go by that I reflect back. . . . To go five blocks and know everyone by their first name in the area, and they know you . . . this is something that I probably will never see again. . . . And for this I'm sad. I'm very sad. . . . It gave me tremendous background feeling and tremendous pride of what I am." His neighborhood was "a community. A world within another world. . . . You never felt . . . that you left the old country sort of. You could go away to school, come back, and you're back home." Yet after a time, his father decided to move, partly to advance socially and partly to flee the poorer newcomers who were migrating into the area. Their new neighborhood, however, could not compare with the old. "[It was] cold. . . . Not knowing your neighbors. Strange in the sense of the . . . the warmth was gone. And this is the period that . . . every day, every chance we had, we'd go back to the old neighborhood. I would drive my mother to the old neighborhood to shop until there was no more stores in the old neighborhood. We still shop . . . the old Italian store . . . until the old Italian store just ceased to exist for lack of people. So there was a strong bond . . . that drew everyone back."[55]

Cali and his family left their old neighborhood willingly, if regretfully. Many working-class whites and blacks left similar neighborhoods but were given no choice in the matter. As municipalities across America pursued aggressive programs of urban renewal, thousands of city dwellers were forcibly relocated, their neighborhoods razed, and their communities dispersed. The purpose of urban renewal was to clear slums and rebuild fading downtowns, but in the process it also disturbed vital if poor neighborhoods.

About ten thousand people lived close together on a forty-eight-acre site in the West End neighborhood of Boston. Most of the residents were working-class immigrants, many of them Italian or Italian American. In 1957, after eight years of deliberations, the federal government approved the demolition of the neighborhood in order to build in its place expensive apartments, offices, and hospitals. [56] After they heard that the demolition of their neighborhood had been approved and was going to go forward, many residents were in despair. "I wish the world would end tonight. . . . I'm going to be lost without the West End. Where the hell can I go?" asked one. Herbert Gans, who studied the community and likened it to a tight-knit "urban village," reported that "the vast majority of West Enders had no desire to leave. . . . Those who had been born there cited the traditional belief that 'the place you're born is where you want to die.'" Indeed, many feared the social anonymity that awaited them outside of the West End. One resident told Gans, "I'm not afraid to die, but I don't want to. But if they tear the West End down and we are all scattered from all the people I know and that know me, and they wouldn't know where I was, I wouldn't want to die and people not know it."[57]

In his studies of West Enders, the psychologist Marc Fried concluded that many residents experienced profound grief when forced to move away from home. He recorded the comments of several: "I felt as though I had lost everything"; "I felt like my heart was taken out of me"; "I felt like taking the gaspipe"; "I lost all the friends I knew"; "I always felt I had to go home to the West End and even now I feel like crying when I pass by"; "I threw up a lot"; "I had a nervous breakdown." These emotions were widespread and long-lasting: "Among 250 women . . . 26 percent report that they still feel sad or depressed two years later, and another 20 percent report a long period (six months to two years) of sadness or depression. Altogether, therefore, at least 46 percent give evidence of a fairly severe grief reaction or worse. And among 316 men, the data show only a slightly smaller percentage (38 percent) with long-term grief reactions."[58]

Although the physical quality of their housing in their new locations was often an improvement, for many former residents of the West End these improvements did not make up for what they had lost. The Figellas, second-generation Italian Americans born in the West End, were happy with the physical attributes of their new house, "but all in all, they are dissatisfied with the move." Fried reported, "When asked what she dislikes about her present dwelling, Mrs. Figella replied simply and pathetically: 'It's in Arlington and I want to be in the West End.'" The Figellas were sociable people, yet they were isolated from their friends in their new house. Mr. Figella said, "I come home from work and that's it. I just plant myself in the house." Lots of their old neighbors felt similarly. The Borowski family had, at best, mixed feelings about the move. Mr. Borowski, who had not grown up in the West End, was fairly pleased with his new home. His wife, however, showed greater ambivalence: "If I knew the people were coming back to the West End, I would pick up this little house and put it back on my corner." She told Fried that she was not depressed about having to move, but when he asked "how she felt when the building she lived in was torn down, a strangely morbid association is aroused: 'It's just like a plant . . . when you tear up its roots, it dies! I didn't die but I felt kind of bad, It was home.'" But then she added cheerful words that were increasingly common in postwar America: "Don't look back, try to go ahead."[59]

Across the country, city dwellers pushed out of poor neighborhoods looked back wistfully at lost homes. In New Haven, twenty-five thousand people were forced to move between 1954 and 1968 to accommodate redevelopment efforts. When he was twelve, Harry DeBenedet and his family, residents of a multiethnic New Haven neighborhood called the Hill, had to leave their home and their community. According to DeBenedet, the redevelopment project "destroyed the entire neighborhood." The family left their house, in which DeBendet's mother had lived for forty or fifty years: "It was a difficult transition." They moved to nearby North Haven, but DeBenedet continued for many years to go back to the old neighborhood, or what was left of it. After school, he would take the bus or hitchhike, and once there, he would hang out with friends from the neighborhood who also had returned. He spoke of the "very, very strong magnetism" that the site of the old neighborhood held for its former residents. Another New

Haven resident, Theresa Argento, was forced to leave the close-knit Italian community of Wooster Square. Looking back on her life there, she recalled "the Italian songs" that floated out of windows, accompanied by the odor of sauces and meats cooking on stoves: "The aroma was unbelievable." When news came that the neighborhood would be redeveloped to accommodate a highway, her mother was devastated: "[She] was in tears." Eventually, Argento and her mother moved to another neighborhood in the city; the new neighborhood was attractive, but her mother "was so unhappy, so unhappy." It seemed so distant and removed from her old life: "She thought we took her to California."[60]

Of all the groups who suffered as a result of urban renewal programs, African Americans were particularly hard hit. An estimated 1,600 black neighborhoods were destroyed by urban renewal. Those who had to leave such areas felt what one psychiatrist termed "root shock," defined as "the traumatic sense of the loss of their life world."[61] Harlem alone lost over a third of its housing over a thirty-year period, and many residents felt a "lasting ache" for the homes they had been forced to vacate.[62] In Chicago, between 31st Street and 35th Street, African American residents were forced to leave homes they had occupied for years to make room for the Lake Meadows redevelopment project. One observer spoke of the pervasive feelings of "devastation" in the neighborhood: "Everybody who lived here was devastated." In the Roxbury neighborhood of Boston, black children returned to stand outside the family homes they had been forced to vacate and that had not yet been demolished. As one child noted of a forlorn playmate, "What's very sad about that building is that every time we go anywhere near that block with Willy, he makes us walk by so we can look at the house. . . . He'll point at the different windows and say . . . 'that was my brother's room.' . . . When he's saying this he always starts to cry. Always."[63]

At the time, mental health specialists and sociologists claimed that the working-class residents of neighborhoods undergoing urban renewal felt the loss of place more acutely than middle-class people did. They claimed the middle class took a sense of self from their professions and believed that their ambitions required movement. In contrast, working-class people received a sense of self from the social interactions they had with others who occupied the same streets, buildings, and shops. They had not crafted translocal selves; they were instead dependent on the here and now for their sense of who they were. Marc Fried claimed that the higher up the class ladder West Enders were, the less they mourned their old homes. Part of joining the middle class, he speculated, was developing a future-oriented perspective that was not tied to a definite locale.[64] One may also speculate that the middle class in the West End had learned the bourgeois emotional style that required them to suppress homesickness, while those below them in the social hierarchy had not yet learned this style. The middle class and working class may have felt similarly about leaving, but they followed different rules about acknowledging and expressing these feelings.

Among those forced to move, homesickness was joined by other emotions, especially anger. Residents repressed neither of these. Communities across the nation protested urban renewal plans and tried to defend their neighborhoods, with mixed success. Their protests were part of a larger culture of protest that redefined the American emotional style. Across the country during the late 1960s and 1970s, citizens, especially young people, showed a rising distrust of the organizational society and resistance to its demands for emotional repression. While Americans in the 1950s and early 1960s often had quietly chafed against the requirements of bureaucratic society, the generation that came of age in the late 1960s made their discontent known more clearly. They did not want to be moved around and did not want to be drafted or deployed for purposes, civilian or military, with which they did not agree.

THE DECLINE OF ORGANIZATIONAL SOCIETY

This mistrust of the organizational society was pervasive; its effects were particularly noticeable among troops in Vietnam. Soldiers, always prone to homesickness, acted on the emotion in ways that differed from the approaches of earlier generations of soldiers. As the war dragged on, they showed less deference and more outspokenness when they expressed their desire to go home.

For a time, there was optimism that the United States would be able to curb homesickness among its troops in Vietnam. Like other expanding institutions, the military claimed the right to relocate people, but then worked to provide them with the amenities of home. In 1965, the *New York Times* reported that there were more than 2 million Americans overseas: "Most of them are servicemen and their families, but some are in Europe and some are in Vietnam." The typical American abroad was "adaptable": "[He] likes to re-create home wherever he goes and the Government accommodates him when it can. It provides him with rock 'n' roll music over the armed services radio in Vietnam. It brings him the broadcasts of the pro football games." The paper suggested that as a result of these efforts there was "little complaining . . . in Vietnam."[65] Gen. William Westmoreland agreed with this assessment, noting that the army had made great progress in maintaining high morale among its men. He talked approvingly of the role the "PXs, clubs, and messes" played in keeping soldiers happy, and praised too the R and R program available to men after they had served six months of a

one-year tour of duty. He claimed, "[These efforts] helped during the period 1964–69 to generate the highest morale I have seen among U.S. soldiers in three wars."[66]

The Pentagon did supply more comforts than it had in earlier conflicts. It
attempted to turn military bases overseas into "Little America[s]." American foods, including hamburgers, steaks, Coca-Colas, and beer, were available at bases and base camps (although often the best foods were not
available to soldiers in more remote locations). On large bases like the one
at Long Binh, soldiers might find the PX, a grocery store, a pool hall, a
swimming pool, snack bars, and a library stocked with American magazines. Another base, Nha Be, offered a room equipped with a TV that carried the Armed Forces Network. Soldiers there could watch programs from
the three major networks, as well as football games. The USO also worked
to bring the comforts of home to soldiers, establishing seventeen clubs in
Vietnam. The clubs offered telephone services, showers, and American
food, as well as young women in miniskirts who served as hostesses.[67]

Soldiers in Vietnam were in somewhat better touch with their families
and homes than earlier generations. At least some of them could call home
using the Military Affiliate Radio System. By 1968, the army had set up
sixty sites across Vietnam, and despite the fact that conversations were brief
and often transmitted over static-filled connections, soldiers placed more
than 220,000 calls that year.[68] Soldiers sometimes also managed to see their
families during their year-long tours of duty, taking advantage of the two-
week R and R to meet their wives in Hawaii or other points midway between
the continental United States and Vietnam.[69]

Despite these new efforts and comforts, a significant portion of the 3
million soldiers who served in Vietnam between 1961 and 1973 felt too far
from home and increasingly alienated from the army. They did not believe
in the discipline or the hierarchy of the organization. The most dissatisfied
were the draftees, whose numbers increased as the war stretched on.
Reports from soldiers themselves make clear that morale was low and
homesickness high, despite government statements to the contrary. The
sense of alienation might appear even before soldiers left the country. Many
recruits and draftees found basic training particularly brutal. One soldier
recalled that sergeants would shout at men newly arrived at training camps,
"I want you to take your clothes off. . . . I want you to take off everything
that ever reminded you of being a civilian and put it in the box. . . . I want
everything." After they were naked, the young men would be taken to
shower, where another sergeant would instruct them, "Wash all that civilian scum off your bodies forever!"[70] But the showers could not wash
away the memories of home. Lynn Steele, who was drafted into the army
and served from 1968 to 1970, wrote his wife while still stateside that he

had "been pretty blue today. Had too much spare time." His wife had sent him pictures that he "mooned over . . . for ½ hr. or so." He liked them but they "made [him] mighty homesick." He tried to feel connected through letters, but confided, "Writing just doesn't cut it all the time. Have a horrible urge to call you, but it costs so much the way we talk."[71] Steele had not yet left his civilian self behind.

Part of the men's unhappiness may have stemmed from the makeup of the army itself. Whereas soldiers in World War II were on average twenty-six years old, soldiers in Vietnam were on average nineteen.[72] Many were leaving home for the first time and headed for a perilous destination. But even more significant were the other causes of distress and demoralization. By the late 1960s, as a result of the setback of the Tet Offensive, the increased visibility of the antiwar movement, the disillusionment of many soldiers because of inequitable draft laws, and the rise of a more rebellious spirit within the United States, soldiers became increasingly public in broadcasting their desire to return home.

By the late 1960s, some soldiers were wearing helmets on which they had written UUUU, which meant "the unwilling, led by the unqualified, doing the unnecessary for the ungrateful."[73] General Westmoreland observed the change as well: "It was only after the start of American withdrawal in 1969 that serious morale and disciplinary problems arose. That was to be expected. Men began to doubt the American purpose. Why die when the United States was pulling out? As the withdrawal continued, men were idle; idleness is the handmaiden of discontent."[74]

Such a change could be seen in the psychiatric casualty rates. In several essays on psychiatry in the army, Col. Franklin Jones reported a rise in what he called "nostalgic casualties" over the course of the Vietnam War. The use of the word *nostalgia* was no longer common among army medical officials, but it seemed to Jones to fit the situation of many soldiers in the conflict. Jones defined "nostalgic disorders" as relating to "separation from family and friends, boredom, social and sometimes physical deprivation." According to Jones, psychiatric casualties were low during the early years of the war, when U.S. soldiers served as military advisors, and stayed fairly low even as more men were deployed during the military buildup. These troops were in combat and too busy for complaints; it was only during the closing years of the war that nostalgic disorders increased. "Vietnam represented the epitome of a conflict in which nostalgic casualties occurred. During the early years of the war, the psychiatric casualty rate of about 12/1,000/year was lower even than that in non-combat overseas areas (Europe and Korea) at the same time." However, as a result of the long war, its growing unpopularity, racial tensions, and discontent, psychiatric evacuations rose. Jones believed that the rising rate of casualties also was connected to the policy of

Vietnamization, which began in 1969. Because this policy called for the Vietnamese to fight the conflict and took U.S. soldiers away from direct action, their boredom increased, as did their time to think about home. By 1972, the rate of psychiatric evacuations was 129 out of 1,000.

Soldiers' eagerness to return to the United States, their low morale, their skepticism of the military mission, and their familiarity with the drug culture flourishing back home made many turn to narcotics. While troops in earlier wars had used alcohol to escape from the present, soldiers in Vietnam, particularly those in "low-intensity combat situations," relied on other drugs as well. Jones commented, "Heroin reportedly displaced cannabis because it had no characteristic strong odor allowing detection, made time seem to go faster rather than slower as with marijuana and was compact and easily transportable."[75] The psychological relief that drugs brought made them quite popular (although precisely how popular has been the subject of recent debates).[76] A congressional investigation in 1971 found that drugs were "more plentiful than cigarettes or chewing gum" among soldiers in Vietnam. Two years later, in 1973, the Pentagon concluded that roughly a third of soldiers used heroin, and a fifth of the army was addicted to the substance.[77] Military doctors suggested that drug use, in addition to offering a temporary mental escape, was sometimes a means to a physical escape from war; they feared that soldiers might use drugs in order to be evacuated back to the United States. All it took was the discovery of heroin in a soldier's urine sample to send him home. By 1971, more soldiers were "being evacuated from Vietnam for drug use than for war wounds." Studies indicate that the majority discontinued their drug use upon their return home.[78]

This technique for escaping the war and returning home was effective only for a time, however. Eventually the army expanded its drug treatment programs and placed soldiers in detoxification programs close to the front, returning them to duty as soon as possible. The army also continued the policy of treating psychiatric problems by keeping soldiers close to their units and reiterating the fact that they would soon be returned to them.[79] This policy was part of an ongoing battle between the military and its troops over how far and how long from home soldiers should be deployed. The breakdown in organizational hierarchy and discipline meant that men were far less likely to silently put up with their homesickness, far less willing to be moved around for goals not their own.

The organizational culture that had taken shape in the interwar years, of which the draft was a potent symbol, was being challenged by a new spirit of rebelliousness. That spirit was visible across the nation, and particularly so on college campuses. When this generation of students entered the workforce, they showed their dissatisfaction with the systems and organizations they were supposed to join and manifested greater resistance to being moved to places to which they had no connection. Some suggest that this was a legacy of Vietnam that undermined not just faith in the government, but faith in the trustworthiness of most organizations.[80] While their fathers had been organization men, willing to move on, workers in the 1970s and after were more hesitant to break home ties and be moved at the will of the corporations for which they worked. Just as the armed services found it necessary to move to an all-volunteer force in 1973 because so many men were unwilling to submit to organizational and military demands, corporations likewise learned they now had to ask for volunteers willing to relocate.

Across the United States, workers began to show far less loyalty to their employers. They did not expect to spend their entire careers with the same corporation and were not willing to sacrifice all for their employers.[81] Vance Packard's study, *A Nation of Strangers*, published in 1972, suggested that Americans were beginning to protest the constant relocations that companies demanded of them. He cited a Harris Poll that asked respondents whether they would "like a job that involves being transferred to different places." Sixty-three percent said no. Other polls showed slightly lower percentages objecting to transfers, but the perception that employees were less willing to relocate spread.[82] A study of the offspring of the organization men Whyte had studied found, "Those who as children were moved around with their father's job, sometimes yearly, now find it astonishing that their parents not only put up with it, but embraced it eagerly. Reversing the organization man's credo, which placed the dictates of the organization ahead of almost everything else, many of the offspring have vowed that they would not let it happen to them."[83]

Companies worried about these trends, at least for a little while. In 1970, the *Wall Street Journal* reported that corporations faced pressure to "sweeten transfer allowances for reluctant workers." Companies were encountering "mounting employee reluctance to transfer," and CEOs were finding a less pliable workforce: "Once, they say, ambitious young men eager for a higher rung on the corporate ladder would leap at any transfer offer, with or without generous incidental benefits." That era, however, was passing. Given employees' resistance to being moved, even the most famous relocator of all, IBM, announced a new policy, claiming it had become "concerned with the effects of relocations upon employees and their families," and would therefore be more cautious in the future. The company also promised to inform workers that they need not move in order to advance their careers.[84] An expert on personnel issues noted in 1978, "The growing independence of today's employees and their concern about the quality of worklife as well as the growing number of women in the workforce and the influence of nonworking wives are making it increasingly difficult for corporations to persuade employees to accept transfers to a new location." The author concluded, "Corporations should no longer expect employees to jump when the company says 'Move!' It now takes special efforts and programs to get relocation to be accepted and to go smoothly."[85]

Much of this resistance was due to the social transformations of the 1960s and early 1970s. If male workers felt less loyalty to organizations than had their fathers' generation, their wives were even more outspoken on the subject. As a result of feminism, women were more willing to speak up about the trials of following their spouses or moving for their own careers. Wives of white-collar workers began to dismantle the myth of the happy spouse who would willingly and contentedly follow her husband anywhere his career took him. While many continued to move on, they did not try so hard to feign happiness at their situations. A wife of one corporate worker on the move confided, "I cried when we left Florida; I cried when we left Darien. It is an emotional upheaval no matter what. But this is the way my husband's work takes him. No doubt we will be transferred again within another two or three years.'" Another lamented:

> It is hard for me to say what I feel without sounding like a bitter woman. I know a move is much harder on a woman. Continually decorating *another* house, having *another* new group of people for dinner, lining up *another* new church, finding *another* new doctor and dentist can be a challenge the first few times, but it can also be very hectic and tiresome.... If you are ambitious, moving is a part of the package. Most of my friends seem to thrive as long as they are moving up. . . . I think sooner or later every family has to decide what is more important—money and position or roots. For me, family and friends—*old* friends— mean a great deal. . . . I think the security of having a real home with family and friends around that I don't have to say good-by to again means more to me than the security of a bigger pay check. . . . I've said more than I meant to . . . but I wanted you to know there is one soul out here who would like to resign from the rat race![86]

A study of relocated families in Roswell, Georgia, conducted in 1982, found that women who relocated as a result of their husbands' job transfer were more likely than their spouses to experience "boredom, loss, depression, and loneliness."[87] Martha Poage, who moved repeatedly for her husband's career, explained such feelings: "I have made friends only to lose most of them each time I moved, decorated houses only to sell them the following year. . . . When my children lost their friends and social standing in school, I lost my identity. I have been elated over some moves and cried over others. I have been lonely and isolated many times." According to Poage, many who moved suffered from "adjustment disorders." In fact, she maintained that "37% of job-related moves fail because the family does not form new relationships or set down permanent roots in the new location, or because of other family-related circumstances. In many of these cases, the employees quit their jobs, and many of these families return to their previous location."[88]

As a result of the women's liberation movement, women became more expressive of a range of previously proscribed emotions, including homesickness. Whereas wives in the nineteenth century had seen it as their lot to submit to the decisions of their husbands as they moved across the country, women in the late twentieth century were willing and able to discuss the costs of moving and often to protest moves. Although in the end they often acquiesced to relocation, they generally had greater input into family decisions and could speak more openly of their feelings about moving on. Adding complexity to the new dynamic was the fact that women themselves were beginning to feel pressure to move in order to forward their own careers, a scenario that became more common by the mid-1980s. Although by the end of the twentieth century, men still were more likely than women to be relocated by their employer, and were seemingly more willing to agree to corporate transfers, women's numbers were growing.[89] In a survey conducted in 2003, 30 percent of relocated workers were women.[90]

These changes in corporate life point in a number of directions. On the one hand, corporations still hope workers will move. A book published in 2009 reported that approximately a third of CEOs at Fortune 1,000 companies had worked in at least three different places before ascending to the top of the corporate ladder. Even those lower down the ladder are aware of the imperative to transfer. The vice president of human resources at UPS, John Saunders, told an interviewer, "We have a discussion [with employees]. 'Are you ready to relocate?' He says yes or no. If he says he can't, I'm not going to put him on our Ready to Promote list." The PR director of UPS explained why such transfers are necessary: "The company is committed to exposing you to a lot of different jobs." Many corporations share this outlook. According to the Census Bureau, companies move 4 million people (workers and their families) each year. Another study indicated that in 2007, 800,000 households moved because of work transfers.[91]

Businesses are also increasingly eager to send workers not just across the nation, but across the globe. Jack Welch, the former CEO of General Electric, said, "The Jack Welch of the future cannot be like me. I spent my entire career in the U.S. The next head of General Electric will be somebody who spent time in Bombay, in Hong Kong, in Buenos Aires. We have to send our best and brightest overseas and make sure they have the training that will allow them to be the global leaders who will make GE flourish in the future."[92] Management books at the end of the twentieth century called for "the development of globally capable leaders." "International assignments" were deemed the key to cultivating a global outlook on trade and commerce, and many large corporations have followed such advice. Philip Morris boasted 170,000 employees in 180 countries; General Electric hopes to have 25 percent of its managers deployed overseas for some period in order to increase their knowledge of global business practices and markets. Gillette and Colgate-Palmolive have similar initiatives, all designed to create a set of international managers.[93] There are, then, intense pressures on American workers to move both within and outside of the country for advancement.

Workers, however, have become more willing to talk about the costs of relocation. This is evident in the increasing rates of those turning down relocation offers from their companies. In 2003, the *New York Times* reported, "Fifty-four percent of the 316 human resources managers surveyed ... said they had employees who declined opportunities to relocate in 2002, up from 21 percent the previous year."[94]

A significant proportion of those transferred overseas also show misgivings. One study showed that an estimated 10 to 45 percent of all workers assigned overseas return early, for a variety of reasons.[95] Even the most ambitious and successful overseas workers find relocation emotionally taxing and show a new willingness to express their feelings about it. In 2008, a London newspaper featured the headline "Homesick Boss Quits Wolfson." The article reported on David Shrigley, who had moved to England from the United States in 2006, after being named chief executive of a microelectronics firm that designed chips for iPhones. He resigned that position two years later because, the *London Evening Standard* reported, he was "homesick for California" and "was missing friends and family back home."[96]

While Shrigley could give up his job because of homesickness, workers lower down on the totem pole faced greater risks. The long association between homesickness and a lack of ambition led one organizational psychologist to suggest that in the eyes of corporate leaders, those who will not move "have a big question mark" on their foreheads. Accordingly, he advised those who resist relocation to make clear to their employers that "it's purely a relocation issue, not a motivation issue."[97]

REFUGEES AND IMMIGRANTS

While native-born Americans struggled to find a way of expressing their emotions in an industrialized and bureaucratic society, the emotional rules and social structure seemed even more alien to newcomers entering the nation. Since the 1960s, there has been a rising tide of migrants flowing into the country. Some have been political refugees; others have been voluntary immigrants allowed into the country as a result of the Immigration Act of 1965, which eradicated the system of quotas established in the 1920s. In 2003, the Census Bureau estimated that 33.5 million U.S. residents, or 11.7 percent of the population, were foreign-born.[98]

The cold war era witnessed the first substantial influx of immigrants, many of whom were seeking temporary refuge. Cubans began arriving in 1959, Southeast Asians during the 1970s. Both groups were initially scattered about the United States rather than settled together as a group. This was a result of government policies designed to spread social service costs across states. The idea was that no single state or region should bear the brunt of supporting a surging refugee population. Yet these policies were remarkably inattentive to the social and psychological needs of those in exile from home. What they most wanted and needed was to be in communities of compatriots who spoke their language and knew their culture. Government policies, however, frustrated that desire.

Cuban refugees began to enter the United States in 1959, fleeing their country's revolution. By 1962, 248,070 had entered the country. Between 1962 and 1965, another 56,000 arrived; by 1977, the total number of Cuban refugees in the United States was over 650,000 and the Mariel boatlift increased that number by nearly 125,000 in 1980. In response to the initial wave of exiles, President Eisenhower established a Cuban Refugee Center to oversee resettlement. The following year, President Kennedy created the Cuban Refugee Program, designed to help refugees settle within the United States, but, officials hoped, outside of south Florida, where so many Cubans lived and where so many continued to come.

In 1964, the Johnson administration added an incentive for refugees to move. If they were unemployed and refused to leave south Florida, they would lose federal financial aid. The director of the Cuban Refugee Program explained that the purpose of this new rule was to "encourage the refugee who is caught in a vicious web of uncertainty, dependency, and propaganda to face the realities of life."[99] The realities, apparently, were that families and ethnic communities should scatter and that immigrants must cut ties and learn to be independent. At first, refugees followed the government's guidelines and relocated across the United States. However, during the 1970s, a sizable number began to return to the Miami area. A study conducted in 1978 found that 40 percent of Cubans in Dade County had lived elsewhere within the country. By 1980, more than half of all Cubans in the United States lived in the Miami metropolitan area. By 1990, the number had increased to half a million.[100] Many of them—most of them—believed or at least hoped they would be able to soon return to their own country. In the meantime, they took shelter in a thriving Cuban community that shared a climate and a culture with their homeland.

Cuban refugees moved to Miami to be close to extended family and countrymen and to help maintain a sense of their *Cubanidad,* their Cuban-ness. The most attractive place for refugees going to Miami was Little Havana, which had been home to a small Cuban population before the revolution. In Little Havana, newly arrived immigrants could find Cuban stores, Cuban radio stations, and Cuban foods. They joined organizations, called *municipios,* based on their township of origin in Cuba. There still are more than one hundred of these organizations within Miami, and they continue to serve as aid and social organizations for exiles. Some boast nearly a thousand members.[101] The continued vibrancy of life in Little Havana reflects migrants' strong desire to retain Cubanidad and remain both geographically and emotionally close to Cuba.

The Vietnam War produced a wave of refugees who arrived during the 1970s. Vietnamese, Cambodian, Hmong, and Laotian refugees came in the thousands. Just as refugee resettlement policies for Cubans had discouraged them from settling in areas where there were large populations of fellow migrants, policies for these Southeast Asians had the same goal. Refugees began to arrive in the spring of 1975; to deal with them the federal government ruled that no more than three thousand should settle in a single state. In 1981, the Bureau for Refugee Programs made a list of areas that had heavy concentrations of refugees. Newly arriving immigrants who did not have relatives in these areas were to be settled in other states and cities, with sparser immigrant populations.[102]

The unintended costs of such policies were high. Studies indicated that those who were scattered about rather than settled with their countrymen found it harder to adjust and were more likely to feel "homeless, displaced, and unwelcome than those who were resettled as groups."[103] A Vietnamese refugee living in New York told a reporter, "Supposing I stayed in Saigon. Maybe they would have killed me. But here, because of homesickness, I am half dead." In Mineola, Long Island, twenty-seven-year-old Han Nguyen said, "Much of the time I am very sad now . . . and I am weary and lonely. . . . I think a lot about not seeing my parents again." He had relatives in the country, but they were on the other side of the continent, in California.[104] Indeed, some found life in America so disorienting that despite the danger, they returned to Vietnam soon after arriving.[105] Vietnamese refugees probably would have been homesick and psychologically distressed even with more family members around them, for they had left much behind and experienced great trauma. Nevertheless, federal policies hindered their emotional adjustment.

On top of being scattered from friends and kin, many found the American style of life, centered as it was on the isolated, nuclear family, to be utterly foreign and unappealing. As one elderly Southeast Asian woman observed of her new life in the United States, "Over here, I don't like how we live in our house and keep a closed door where you can't visit each other. You have relatives living all around your neighborhood, but you can't visit each other, and it makes you very sad that you are dumb and you don't know their language." Many echoed this sentiment, lamenting that they had no one with whom to talk since they lived apart from other refugees.

Sixty-six-year-old Xee, a Hmong woman, observed, "You talk to yourself about loneliness and you think to yourself that if this life here is like this, then I want to return to Thailand." Xee was haunted by her homesickness, describing it this way: "When you go to sleep but can't fall asleep and you think about it [the past], and you keep rolling from side to side. And you think constantly about the past and missing your people because you have come to this country. You think very far to the tip of your toes. Then you think of different places. Doing this is like a rope that is being pulled back and forth. Then you think and think until you fall asleep."[106]

Many were unwilling to live with such deep feelings of melancholy, and in the late 1970s and 1980s, Southeast Asian refugees slowly circumvented the resettlement policies of the U.S. government that had dispersed them and created new communities. Like the Cubans who returned to Miami, Southeast Asian immigrants migrated within the United States to join such vibrant enclaves as Little Saigon in Orange County, California. From just a few businesses in the late 1970s, it grew to a community with more than two thousand shops, restaurants, and other ethnic businesses. It offers "pagoda-style mini malls, glittering jewelry booths, trendy fashion boutiques, fabric stores, hair salons, fancy restaurants, noodle shops and cafes, bakeries, supermarkets, laser-karaoke outlets, music stores, and night clubs—all reminiscent of the fallen capital of the former South Vietnam." On weekends, fifty thousand shoppers flood its streets, many of them arriving in chartered buses from as far away as San Jose. As one Vietnamese man explained, "I don't come to buy things. . . . I come to see people, strangers mostly, who come to do ordinary, everyday things, but in an environment where, because of the familiarity of faces and language, we never feel out of place."[107]

Yet many still do feel out of place in America. Joseph Westermeyer, a psychiatrist at the University of Minnesota, began hearing of the mental health problems of refugees in the late 1970s and convinced the university hospitals to open a psychiatric clinic for them, which saw a heavy traffic in melancholy individuals suffering from "adjustment reactions."[108] Similar clinics opened around the country. Sometimes refugees themselves became counselors at these facilities. Tong Nguyen, who left Vietnam in 1975, went to work for the local branch of Catholic Charities in order to help newly arrived refugees. Although he had lived in America for sixteen years, he still felt the tug of home: "Of course Minnesota is my home, but I never stop missing my real home." He tried to use his experience to help others making the same transition. Of his work with new refugees settling in Minnesota, he said, "We want to be friends with these people because we know why they have left their country. We know how much they have lost."[109] In San Diego, the Union of Pan Asian Communities opened its doors to homesick refugees and immigrants from across Asia and the Pacific. The organization's director, Beverly Yip, declared that problems were most profound for refugees from Southeast Asia, for whom "depression is probably the major health problem. . . . They've lost their home, they've lost their relatives, they've lost their jobs, they've lost their country." One refugee told a counselor that in America "even the moon looks different." The organization opened the East Wind Socialization Center, designed to meet the needs of chronically depressed immigrants.[110]

Joining these Asian and Cuban refugees have been a host of other immigrant populations, allowed entry as a result of the Immigration Act of 1965. Perhaps no group of newcomers has been more visible than Mexicans, who have been migrating to the United States since the nineteenth century, but who have come in ever increasing numbers during the twentieth, and who are currently the largest immigrant group in the country.[111]

A large number of Mexicans go north to support families back in Mexico, hoping to send money home and to return themselves sometime in the future with their pockets full of dollars. Their migrations are part of strategies for family improvement. Social scientists have concluded that the decision to migrate is not made by individuals, but by households and sometimes extended families, and that communal needs shape individual journeys. Rosa María Muñiz de Navarro, a housewife in Buena Vista, in the state of Jalisco, described her husband's reasons for migrating to the United States. They had been married for four years when he left: "He went to be able to build this house, make it larger, or rather to fix it—everything—a living room, rooms to sleep in for the children and for us, and a kitchen with running water. That was his dream and mine too."[112] Juan Carlos Estrella, a native of Tepic, worked in San Jose, California, for several years in the 1990s. Of his time there, he said, "Sometimes it is hard to be away from home, but the money is more [there]." Accordingly, he and his wife migrated north, worked, and then went home to Tepic with enough money to buy a house for themselves.[113]

Ties to one's spouse, to parents, and to siblings back in Mexico, are generally not lost in the process of migration and do not disappear in the face of the urban industrial order. In his study of migration from Oaxaca, the anthropologist Jeffrey H. Cohen concluded, "They migrate to support children, siblings, and parents. They risk their health and their lives for the good of their families and households. Usually they do not leave for long. Instead, they return to their hometowns after a year or two (sometimes three) to farm, to serve in local government, and to regain or perhaps renew their self-image as valuable, honest, and hardworking citizens of their communities." In a survey asking Oaxacans why they migrated, 79 percent of respondents listed as their first choice, and 96 percent as their second, the motivation "to better a family's living conditions."[114]

Mexican immigration patterns indicate that the extended family often motivates journeys, journeys that lead away from home but that are undergirded by a strong hope of return. The strength of extended family ties is evident in the remittances, or *remesas*, immigrants send to their families and hometowns. Mexican immigrants sent back as much as $2 billion in 1998. That amount has climbed steeply over the past decade, so steeply that when he was in office, President Vincente Fox celebrated Mexican immigrants who sent remesas as "national heroes." By 2006, Mexican immigrants were sending close to $24 billion back home each year.[115] Remittances reflect an ongoing concern for home and a desire to improve it, sometimes paying for subsistence needs, but also enabling larger investments in land, livestock, and farming supplies.[116] A reporter noted of life in the state of Guanajuato, "Remittances have created a peculiar economy in villages tucked among rolling corn and sorghum fields. There are few jobs, yet many houses have stereo systems, washing machines and three-piece living room sets."[117]

Remittances also fund community improvements. Across the United States, Mexican immigrants have formed state and hometown clubs. Migrants from Nayarit living in southern California can congregate at the state club, Casa Nayarit, in Wilmington. In Chicago, there is a Casa Jalisco as well as a Casa Michoacan.[118] These state clubs often organize smaller town and village associations. In 1998, Los Angeles was home to 170 hometown associations from eighteen different states in Mexico, and Chicago boasted over 120 different associations.[119] The Mexican government has worked to harness the immense energy of these groups and their devotion to home. It stipulates that if hometown groups send back money for town improvements, the city, state, and federal governments will each match those funds.[120] When their contributions are tallied together, the clubs end up sending significant amounts of money home. In 1995, hometown clubs from the state of Zacatecas sent $600,000 for fifty-six public improvement projects; Michoacan clubs in Illinois remitted $650,000 to their hometowns.[121]

The memory of home is strong and constant, evident not just in the money immigrants send there, but in return migration patterns. A study conducted in 1997 concluded that 50 percent of immigrants from western

Mexico returned after two years, and 70 percent returned within ten years.[122] Studies from the early twenty-first century show similar trends of large-scale return migration. For instance, in 2008–9, 636,000 Mexicans migrated to the United States and 433,000 left.[123] Even before they move back permanently to Mexico, many immigrants return for short visits throughout the year.

Mexico's government recognizes and endorses these back-and-forth migrations. In recent years, it has started a program called Paisano, designed to help immigrants coming home. At Christmas and Easter and during summer vacations, returning migrants, flooding into airports, bus stations, and town squares, are greeted by signs proclaiming, "Paisano: Bienvenidos a Casa" (Welcome home, countryman). The government distributes guides to these returnees that, among other things, tell them how to help their families and towns from afar, should they once again return to the United States.[124]

The remesas and the return migration bespeak an ongoing preoccupation with home. So too do immigrants themselves. Cuauhtémoc Menendez, a construction worker from Guadalajara who migrated to the United States in 1973 and eventually returned, observed, "When I was in the United States, the whole time, I think all the mojados feel the same way, they are in the United States but they are crying to go to Mexico. They are saving their money just to return. I think this is a sentiment that ties us all. Even though many earn some money and begin to have roots in the United States, nevertheless, they always think of returning."[125] A more recent immigrant, Ricardo Valencia, a native of Guadalajara, migrated to Nevada in January 2005 to pay off debts. His mind seemed always to be back in Mexico: "The day I got there, the next day I thought 'I want to leave!' because I've always been really close with my family. And I had never separated from the family. . . . But I had to stand it, we had to stand it. . . . Returning was always in mind." During his four years in the United States, he sent money to his family, and in 2009, he finally returned to them.[126]

While in the United States, immigrants gravitate to neighborhoods that re-create some of their hometown lives.[127] Vital ethnic enclaves have grown up in America's cities and, increasingly, in America's suburbs. In these neighborhoods are familiar foods, sounds, and faces. Basilio Prado, a native of Villa Hidalgo, said that while living in southern California and later in Las Vegas, he was able to settle in neighborhoods filled with people from his home state of Nayarit. "There were colonies" of people from his area: "In Long Beach there was one on Daisy Avenue; In Las Vegas on . . . the street called, the Mario. That's another colony and Mexican stores and all of, all of those apartments full of Mexicans." In San Bernadino, there was a colony on H. Street. In such places, Basilio found relief when he felt homesickness.[128] On the other hand, "nostalgia grabbed" Lizabeth Navarro when she lived in

North Carolina, for "there were hardly any Mexicans.... There was nothing, nothing." But elsewhere she found life more familiar: "I had family in Los Angeles, California, and it is easy to live in Los Angeles because it's almost like here in Mexico."[129]

These ethnic neighborhoods make the United States less alien, but they do not completely insulate newcomers from American social patterns and problems. There is a growing literature on depression and acculturative stress among Hispanic immigrants.[130] A source of anxiety and sadness among many Mexican immigrants is the vast difference between life north of the border and life south of it. Even though they find solace in their ethnic colonies, immigrants frequently discuss the isolating tendencies of American life. Carlos Ruiz, a native of the Federal District of Mexico living in Ogden, Utah, said that the United States lacks *calidez*, which he defined as "kindness, fraternity. The United States is cold. . . . What you miss is family, you miss the relationships with friends, get-togethers, parties, events. . . . There are lots of things."[131] When he first came to the United States, Genaro Rivera missed "family, friends, the rhythm of life," and dreamed "of being there [in Sonora] with . . . loved ones, the entertainment."[132] Ricardo Valencia compared life in Pahrump, Nevada, to San Blas, Mexico, where his wife and her family came from: "Over there [in Nevada] you get out of work and go home. That's it. Next day work, home, work, home or market, work, home, market. Its loops and loops. And here? Well, here in San Blas there's the beach, let's have a barbeque, be with your family. . . . It's more family involved. That is what is missed."[133] Immigrants from Mexico as well as refugees from Asia all said the same thing: life in the United States was lonelier and more isolated, families were smaller, and public life less lively.

The Mexican experience is quite typical. Immigrants from all countries miss extended families, public life, familiar tastes and sounds. They often perceive their time in the United States as but a temporary sojourn and contemplate return. An estimated 20 to 40 percent of all immigrants eventually do go back to their home countries.[134] Many nurse dreams of return for years before being able to realize them. Their dreams of returning home echo those of settlers at Jamestown, miners in California, and Italians in New York.

COMING HOME, STAYING HOME

Immigrants are not the only ones who question mobility and sometimes return to their roots. In recent years, Americans have become more place-bound. In his essay "Ever More Rooted Americans," Claude Fischer notes that mobility rates have declined in the United States, despite the continued cultural emphasis on restless mobility. Census figures support his contentions. In 1969–70, 18.4 percent of all Americans over the age of one moved. Numbers fluctuated throughout the 1970s, but peaked in 1984–85, when over 20 percent of all Americans moved. That number has declined ever since. In 2007–8, only 11.9 percent of Americans moved. Of course, changes in mobility rates can be attributed to many causes, and while economic conditions surely drive some to stay put, a longing for connection motivates others. As one researcher noted, in recent years, family "trumps money when people make decisions about where to live."[135] Richard Florida, who has studied why certain locations attract more residents than others, suggests, "Place provides an increasingly important dimension of our identity." His main interest is in the towns and cities that attract in-migrants because of their culture, lifestyle, and amenities; however, he recognizes that the idea of home exerts a powerful pull over Americans, leading many to stay put and others to eventually return to where they came from.[136] Karen N. fits into the latter category. She and her husband moved to Savannah, which they found beautiful; however, her time there was "compromised by a powerful undertow of omnipresent homesickness," and she and her husband ultimately decided to return to their roots and family in Connecticut. Of the move back, she writes, "At last I feel at peace."[137]

The past few decades have witnessed dramatic reverse migrations of Americans heading home. Particularly noteworthy have been the return of hundreds of thousands of African Americans to the South, often to the homes of their parents, grandparents, or kin, in search of "family connections." John Cromartie and Carol B. Stack, social scientists who have studied this remigration, argue that through return visits, the temporary stays of northern-born young children with kin in the South, and through memory, some northern blacks maintained a strong sense of southern identity. They point out that when blacks moved north, they "were attracted to urban enclaves where home folks had settled; likewise, people today are returning in the greatest numbers to the metropolitan and nonmetropolitan regions of the South that originally yielded the most northbound movers." By 1990, half a million blacks had returned to the South. Wille Foster, who left St. Louis for his native Mississippi, explained, "I liked St. Louis, but Mississippi is my home. I wanted to get back in the dirt I came out of."[138]

Other Americans who are returning home are retirees, who, after leaving home in search of opportunity, are now retracing their steps to their hometowns, particularly if relatives and children live there. These migrants are sometimes called "boomerang seniors."[139] In part as a result of such migration, there has been a resurgence of the multigenerational household. While in 1940, about 25 percent of the population lived in extended family arrangements, by 1980, only 12 percent did. Yet gradually, many became dissatisfied with the isolation of the nuclear family and began to seek out other arrangements. A survey conducted by the American Council of Life Insurance in the 1980s found that 93 percent of baby boomers believed there should be greater importance accorded to traditional family ties. And since 1980, the number of people in multi-generational homes has grown. In 2010 more than 49 million Americans, roughly 16 percent of the population, lived in such households.[140]

Some of the occupants of multigenerational households are "boomerang kids," who first came to national attention in the 1990s and were presumed to be returning home because of hard economic times. A Pew Research Center study indicates, however, that this pattern is not based wholly on economic necessity. As the director of the study noted, young people are also moving back because "they're becoming buddies with mom and dad, and they may not find it so unusual to still be living in their childhood bedroom."[141] Other factors behind the shift are the return of elderly adults to their offspring's houses and the increase of immigrants in the American population, for Latin Americans and Asians have imported traditions of extended family households.[142]

More than half a century ago, Talcott Parsons and other social scientists contended that in the modern industrial economy, extended families were a thing of the past. They suggested that the modern economy demanded fluidity, and indeed it did. The organizational society, widely celebrated in the 1950s and 1960s, required men and women to leave home if they hoped to embrace opportunities, to transfer their loyalties from family to organization, to master their homesickness, and to be cheerful as they did so. Since the 1970s, however, there has been greater resistance to these demands. While some have no choice but to accede to them in order to prosper in the modern economy, increasingly Americans have shown frustration with the constant uprooting so long required in capitalist society. Family life exerts a greater and greater pull on Americans, native and foreign-born alike. Families who live within the United States increasingly cluster together. Those separated from their kin by national boundaries maintain ties through constant communication, remittances, and back-and-forth migration, for they have migrated to enrich and sustain home and family life in distant locales and nurse dreams of return.

CONCLUSION

✧

Of Helicopter Parents, Facebook, and Walmart

Homesickness in Contemporary America

I f the sociological theories of the mid-twentieth century are being challenged by twenty-first-century demographic reversals, homeward migrations, the reemergence of the extended family, and a decline in mobility rates, one would not know it from the modern psychological advice and popular wisdom about homesickness. Americans still hear, and still believe, that they should learn to move on without pain and should avoid expressing their homesickness publicly. They learn such attitudes from books, magazines, and each other.

Immigrants and native-born alike know what the emotional rules are in American culture, and by observing them they make their homesickness almost invisible. Expert literature written for mental health practitioners, as well as popular culture, have ceaselessly promoted the idea that homesickness is a condition that, with proper training, can be eliminated in childhood. Consequently, those who feel it as adults are seen as maladjusted. That message has held steady since the early twentieth century, although there have been a few changes over the course of the century. First, the advice gradually has become gender neutral, offering the same models of emotional comportment for both boys and girls.[1] Second, over the course of the last quarter century, the idea that children and young adults should transfer their loyalties from family to an organization has disappeared, as faith in organizational culture has waned. Men and women are no longer expected to permanently ally themselves with a corporation or institution, but they are supposed to decisively cut the cord that binds them to parents and home and become free agents.

This promotion of mobile individualism is embedded in American mental health literature, which depicts homesickness as a condition that strikes the young and the premodern, but never the mature and well-adjusted. While the American Psychiatric Association's *Diagnostic and Statistical Manual of Mental Disorders*, published in 1952, made no mention of homesickness, it appeared in subsequent editions, chiefly as a childhood problem caused by the failure of youngsters to successfully separate from their families. The second edition, published in 1968, described children who were apprehensive in new surroundings as suffering from an "overanxious reaction of childhood." The third edition (1980) used the term "separation anxiety" to describe "excessive anxiety on separation from major attachment figures or from home." Children away from home might "experience anxiety to the point of panic." Their anxiety also had physical manifestations, which included "stomachaches, headaches, nausea, and vomiting." The fourth edition (1994) elaborated on the problem: "Some individuals become extremely homesick and uncomfortable to the point of misery. . . . They may yearn to return home and be preoccupied with reunion fantasies." Those who suffered from the problem were generally from "close-knit" families. According to psychologists, in the modern age, in which mobility and leave-taking have become commonplace, close familial bonds impede the proper socialization of children.[2]

More popular works brought these emotional models to the attention of the public. Dr. Benjamin Spock listed separation anxiety as a problem in *The Common Sense Book of Baby and Child Care* (1957) and counseled parents that if they were overly protective, their children would be overly dependent. Too much love and closeness were counterproductive. In a subsequent edition published in 1985, Spock maintained that if children were scared to go to school, parents must still send them, for "it's better for the child to outgrow dependence than to give in to it." The seventh edition, published in 1998, advised that the "basic aim" of parents and teachers "is to help the child separate from home and adjust to school and the outside world." Clearly, a chief goal of modern child rearing was to produce individuals accustomed to independence and mobility.[3] Modern scholars have elaborated on this advice, but the message is unvarying: children need to learn to leave home. In the words of the psychologist Christopher Thurber and the physician Edward Walton, children should be taught to "frame the separation as a positive developmental experience."[4]

From popular magazines such as *Parents,' PTA Magazine, Prevention*, and *Good Housekeeping*, parents have learned what to do if their children feel homesick at camp or on visits away from home. The advice has held steady for the past half century, suggesting that parents send care packages and letters, call (but not too often), and provide children with "ice-breakers" that will make them popular with their peers in their new surroundings.[5]

Books and magazines have offered a parallel stream of advice to children at risk of homesickness. Story books familiarize the very young with the idea of leaving home and offer advice on how to conquer homesickness. Unlike the tales written in the late nineteenth century, which celebrated children who ran back home when homesick, these stories strongly discourage such behavior. In *Arthur Goes to Camp*, Arthur begged his parents to bring him home and threatened to run away from camp if they did not. When he finally became involved with camp activities, though, he was happy in his new surroundings. Likewise, in *I Want to Go Home*, Big Bird left Sesame Street to visit his grandmother at the shore. While happy to see her, he nevertheless felt lonely and worried, and his grandmother diagnosed him as homesick. She kept him busy, and his homesickness began to abate, finally lifting when he made a new friend.[6]

Elmo's grandmother adopted similar tactics when her Muppet grandson came to visit. Although Elmo declared, "I miss Mommy and Daddy and Daisy . . . and my own room and Big Bird . . . and all my friends," his grandparents were so successful in distracting him with kittens, apple pies, pony rides, and marble games that he overcame his feelings and actually wanted to prolong his time away from home.[7] A pocket book, *Homesick Blues*, asked readers, "When you're away from home for a night or two, do you sometimes get the homesick blues?" The key to overcoming the feeling was to bring stuffed animals, a favorite pillow, or a good book and to call one's parents, make friends with other homesick children, and smile.[8] The message in all of these stories is that leaving home is natural and need not be painful. One can be happy anywhere. While Victorian tales told of loving young children who could not abide separation from mother and home, twentieth- and twenty-first-century stories portrayed such youngsters as crippled by their overly strong attachment to their parents.

At college, a host of resources—including counseling centers, freshmen orientation programs, books, and websites—offer advice about how to deal with homesickness. The advice has echoed what college students have heard their entire life: "Get involved"; "Call home"; "Talk about it"; "Seek out student resources."[9] A recent book for college students counsels those stricken with homesickness, "The knee-jerk reaction is to run back to the familiar. There's nothing wrong with visiting home once in a while, talking with a friend online or on the phone, visiting a friend at another campus, or bringing home cooking back to school with you. But do it in moderation. The cure to homesickness is not home—it's realizing how you made your old home so

Elmo waved and waved until the car was just a tiny
speck in the distance.
"Good-bye!" he called softly.
He had a shaky feeling in his tummy.

Elmo offers advice to young readers about how to conquer homesickness.
Source: Elmo Gets Homesick. "Sesame Workshop"®, "Sesame Street"®, and associated characters, trademarks, and design
elements are owned and licensed by Sesame Workshop. © 2011, Sesame Workshop. All Rights Reserved.

comfortable and doing the same things in your new home."[10] Some institutions believe parents too need help with this transition and offer advice to
facilitate their children's leave-takings. Pittsburg State University tells parents, "Time is the best cure," suggests they "put on a confident smile" when
their children leave for school, and warns them against calling too frequently
or making emergency visits to campus to rescue homesick students.[11]

Educators and mental health experts have studied children's and adoles-
cents' homesickness, but for the past fifty years these experts generally have
overlooked adult homesickness. In 1996, the psychologists M. A. L. van Tilburg, A. J. J. M Vingerhoets, and G. L. van Heck wrote, "After World War II the
interest in the phenomenon disappeared almost completely." As a result, scholarship on homesickness was "rather slim and scattered." Much of the scholarly
literature on adult homesickness has examined the emotion within immigrant

populations and has rarely attended to the pain caused by internal migration.[12] Little attention has been paid to the widespread evidence that native-born, seemingly well-adjusted, modern adults experience the feeling.

Part of the problem is that even the homesick themselves resist being labeled as such.[13] Homesickness is a sign of dependence and immaturity and therefore a sign of weakness. As Philip E. Slater explained in *The Pursuit of Loneliness*, "Independence training in American society begins almost at birth—babies are held and carried less than in most societies and spend more time in complete isolation—and continues, despite occasional parental ambivalence, throughout childhood and adolescence. When a child is admonished to be a 'big boy' or 'big girl' this usually means doing something alone or without help. . . . Signs of independence are usually rewarded."[14] In such a schema, homesickness has no place. Indeed, psychiatrists have noted how difficult it is for Americans to admit their need for emotional connections because they believe such a need is a sign of dependency and inadequacy. The psychiatrists Jacqueline Olds and Richard Schwartz described the resistance they encountered when trying to talk with their patients about an emotion much related to homesickness: loneliness. They treated a large number of patients who believed they were depressed but were in fact lonely. Yet few were willing to give their melancholy this appellation. The psychiatrists concluded, "Talking about loneliness in America is deeply stigmatized; we see ourselves as a self-reliant people who do not whine about neediness."[15]

Homesickness is a problem not just because it seems to be a sign of immaturity, but perhaps more crucially because it threatens individual and social progress, for it carries with it the temptation to return home. If acted upon it can disrupt market relations and render individuals less interchangeable, less fungible. It interferes with profits and contradicts the idea of fluidity that is at the base of the capitalist economy.

It is in this atmosphere, in a society that values independence, ambition, and optimism, that many adults feel compelled to repress their homesickness. Mobility is regarded as a time-honored American tradition, moving on a painless and natural activity. Those who feel grief at parting hide the emotion, believing it to be a sign of immaturity, maladjustment, and weakness. Instead of displaying homesickness, Americans express hopefulness and cheerfulness, two character attributes much valued in American society.[16] Trepidations about breaking home ties must be subordinated to sunny hopes for the future. Homesickness must be repressed.

In contrast, in the late twentieth century and early twenty-first, nostalgia, the longtime companion and sometime synonym of homesickness, has become a less troublesome emotion, signifying a diffuse, unthreatening, and painless longing for the past. By the 1970s, this new meaning of the word was firmly ensconced in popular parlance.[17] As an emotion, nostalgia has come to be widely celebrated, perhaps because it is now seen as harmless. Whereas the homesick may believe they can return home, the nostalgic know that moving backward in time is impossible. Nostalgia offers a way to establish connections with the past and with home that does not seriously undermine the present.

In this sense, nostalgia is not what it used to be. In the late nineteenth century and early twentieth, nostalgia as a longing for the past still caused pain, as people only gradually became accustomed to a tempo of change so rapid and inexorable that it made the past utterly different from the present. Today, however, most Americans take this fast pace of change for granted. The past is past, and by and large, contemporary Americans do not believe it is possible to return to it, nor do they mourn it, as earlier generations did. They may still yearn for lost times, for a sense of permanence in a world that is changing, but they also realize that the past is irrevocably lost. This is a hallmark of modern consciousness.

This mild nostalgia, which one scholar described as nostalgia "without melancholy," is in fact encouraged by popular culture and also by psychologists.[18] Recent psychological studies have described its benefits. A study published in 2008 found that nostalgia, in its modern sense, mitigated loneliness by bringing to mind past social relationships and situations. The researchers concluded, "Nostalgia magnifies perceptions of social support. . . . Nostalgia restores an individual's social connectedness." Having individuals engage in nostalgic thought could therefore "strengthen psychological resistance to the vicissitudes of life."[19] Americans' longings for lost times are now deemed mentally beneficial. Those who engage in a celebration of the past know that it is over, but they can return to bygone days in their minds. Such longings enrich mental and emotional life. In some sense, nostalgia has become an antidote to homesickness, for it can offer a sense of comfort and stability to those who are separated from home and kin. The modern advice about homesickness and nostalgia—to repress the former and express the latter—seems designed to mold individuals capable of living anywhere in the world.

Psychological advice and American folklore both enshrine and reinforce the ideology of individualism, promoting separation and ceaseless mobility as normal. Ordinary Americans have learned to follow the emotional pattern for rugged individualists: to separate, move on, and find consolation in sweet, nostalgic memories of lost times. The structure of daily life is built around this ideal. From children's books to the Welcome Wagon, American culture celebrates restlessness as a valuable national trait. It is also supported by the physical infrastructure of the nation, which encourages movement. Jet travel, introduced in the 1950s, has made journeys faster and easier, and made vast distances seem smaller. For those who cannot afford plane tickets, improved roadways have allowed them to become free-way flyers.

Despite the ease of travel, despite the cheerful countenance that Americans have learned to assume in public, despite the silence about homesickness and the emphasis on restless individualism, it is clear that we still live in the midst of a homesick culture. All across the country are signs of people dealing with the changes brought on by mobility, longing for someplace else, for family, for connections with what they have left behind. If we are blind to them it is because they are so very commonplace and the emotion is so rarely discussed. We have bought into and mouth the tenets of rugged individualism, but the facts of our daily life continually contradict that ideology.

STAYING CONNECTED

Those who leave home today are not unfettered individuals, cutting all ties with home. Instead, using their BlackBerrys, iPhones, Facebook accounts, and email, these migrants are better connected than past generations. Indeed, with their ever expanding range of devices, Americans seem positively obsessed with staying in touch. It is much harder to sustain the myth of the lonely individualist when individuals are hardly ever alone or on their own anymore. Even the training grounds for individualism and mobility—summer camps and colleges—have been fundamentally changed by technology. Parents and their children maintain nearly constant contact, so much so that a number of child-rearing experts complain that new obstacles have been thrown in the path to independence.

For instance, camp directors and college officials worry about "helicopter parents," who will not let their children venture out of reach. The stereotypical helicopter parents constantly call and email their children and remain intimately involved in the details of their lives, even from a distance. Although their numbers and behaviors may be exaggerated in popular accounts, it is indisputable that helicopter parents seem less intent on promoting separation and more intent on sustaining close bonds with their children than earlier generations. Summer camp directors complain that parents in fact suffer from "kidsickness" and "separation anxiety" when they leave their youngsters at camp, and some remain in continual communication with their offspring. [20] As one reporter noted, "Counter to the notion of a camp sojourn in which children go for weeks without speaking to their parents as they master a sense of independence, parents and offspring alike have come to expect a constant connection."[21] In response, many camps have adopted policies limiting campers' access to email and texting. It is harder, of course, to limit communications from parents, but some directors require parents to use one-way email services provided by companies such as CampMinder.com, Bunk1.com, or CampRegister.com, which control access, or in some cases, charge by the message, in order to discourage excessive communication.[22]

Educators and psychologists harbor similar fears about the college experience. Whereas in earlier decades, students left home for college and talked to their parents once a week, with new technologies students can and do communicate with their parents all the time. With "unlimited cell phone minutes, e-mail, text messages and Blackberries," the *New York Times* observes, college life today is far different from "the days of calling home once a week—collect—from the pay phone in the dormitory hallway." Mark Forrest, the associate director of counseling and psychological services at Rutgers, notes, "The good thing is that it eases their transition into a new environment because they can touch base with their loved ones and friends via e-mail and text messaging. But the drawback there is that it takes them a little longer to integrate into the new environment, because they're still keeping their old ties."[23] To help students become accustomed to their new environment, some suggest they reduce communication with family back home. Harlan Cohen, the author of an advice book for college students, writes, "It's easier than ever for students to be physically on campus and emotionally in a totally different place. Facebook, texting, and chatting can keep a student too dependent on a parent, friends, and significant others. I always suggest that students cut in half the time they communicate with people they know from home. Use that time to connect with new people on campus."[24] Drexel University's student newspaper offers similar advice: "It's nice to connect with family in a way that previously was not possible, but it's important for students to find themselves without advice from the family with whom they just spent the last two decades. . . . It's important to learn how to get through life without the help of your parents. . . . The phrase 'Tweeting my mom' just shouldn't ever be uttered."[25]

In discussing the rise of new styles of family life in which parents and children are in close and constant communication, Robert Epstein, an editor at *Psychology Today*, writes, "Parents' most important task is to help young people to become independent and autonomous. When we infantilize our young, we stifle their development." Many agree, noting that new technologies are hurting young people by keeping them from true independence.[26] The psychologist Peter Crabb points out that the spread of cell phones and other technologies ultimately "promotes immaturity and dependence." He suggests that the rising generation is not learning proper lessons of emotional control, observing that students call home to "seek succor" from their parents: "The call makes them feel better. But they are not learning to control their emotional states, which is part of becoming an adult."[27]

Young people and their parents seem largely unmoved by these concerns, however, and maintain close connections through the new technologies available to them. Ellen Kim, a student from California who left home to attend Rice University in Houston, willingly admitted, "Showing up at Rice was one of the most heart-wrenching moments of my life. . . . I missed my parents, my younger sister and my flea-bitten cat. . . . It was bad enough not being able to see them everyday. The truth was I didn't want to be the 'independent college student.'" Kim cried every day. "The most taxing part of coping with my homesickness was the suppression," for at first she did not want her parents or her peers to know of her feelings. "The last thing I wanted . . . was for everyone to think I was some immature cry baby. Seriously, I was 18 years old and unable to handle a few months on my own?" Yet despite her initial desire to hide her homesickness, she ultimately confessed to it: "I called home after that week and cried to my family." And her family cried as well. Kim's advice was that homesick students should follow her example. Rather than wean themselves completely from their families, they should use cell phones to stay in closer contact with them. She recommended to others who were homesick, "If you're feeling overwhelmed and can't find an outlet, call your family. . . . If you have one of those cell phone family plans, your five-hour call will be free! So why not?"[28]

While generations of psychologists might have responded to her question by saying that such frequent calls would impair her development as an independent individual, Kim can find a great deal of support among her peers. In fact, she seems quite typical. A survey conducted in 2004 found that 26 percent of freshmen living in dorms at UCLA "were in touch with their parents every day."[29] According to another study, college students were in contact with their parents, on average, more than ten times per week.[30] With the rise of social networking sites, there are even more ways for college students to stay in touch with those they have left behind. They can settle in their dorm rooms and still be in contact with their parents, siblings, and high school classmates. They have not left the old life completely behind; there is no clear line between past and present.

Fast transportation, cheap long-distance calling, and the rise of cell phones, texting, Skype, and social networking sites have all helped mobile American families stay in touch and maintain close bonds. In fact, one might speculate that Americans' contradictory desires—to move on and stay connected—have driven the spread of such technologies. Just as postal reform in the nineteenth century was inspired by the mobility of Americans and, in turn, allowed many to leave home with the reassurance that they could stay in touch, the technologies of the twentieth and twenty-first centuries have gained popularity because they fill such a deep social need. They make leaving home less intimidating, since one's mother or best friend is only a phone call or a mouse click away.[31]

Another institution in which homesickness has traditionally been a problem is the military. Here too, new technologies have left their mark, fundamentally reshaping the experience of deployment. Whereas in earlier wars, soldiers complained of the limited contact they had with home, they now enjoy unprecedented opportunities to call home, to email, and to acquire familiar goods. A survey in 2004 of one thousand soldiers deployed overseas found that 15 percent used the mail service, 50 percent emailed their friends and family, and 25 percent called them on the phone. The *Philadelphia Inquirer* noted in 2006 that in "tents, trailers and buildings throughout Iraq, the military has set up more that 1,250 phones and 3,500 computer terminals." These saw high traffic: on average, 160,000 soldiers were talking 11.6 million minutes per month on the phone. To help troops, a Brooklyn organization, Freedom Calls, set up teleconferencing centers in Iraq. As of 2006, roughly two thousand soldiers visit each day to call and see their families.[32] Charitable organizations have distributed free phone cards to soldiers.[33] These can be used at the sixty-odd calling centers that AT&T has established throughout Kuwait, Afghanistan, and Iraq.[34] Cell phones, too, present opportunities for unprecedented contact between the battlefield and the homefront.[35]

Lt. Col. Keith McVeigh, who began his career with the navy in 1983 but who now serves in the army, described communications with home when he first joined the military: "I could only contact my family by writing a letter or when we pulled into an overseas port, I could call them on a local country phone through an international operator and pay out of my own pocket." Contrasting that with his recent tour in Iraq, he explained that soldiers' "ability to call home is limited only to their access to a phone, funds and time limitations based on the number of phones in the calling center." Indeed, one sociologist found that among soldiers in Iraq "daily contact with family was prevalent." Given the new ease of staying in touch, McVeigh conjectured that homesickness might soon disappear.[36]

Not all his colleagues agree, however. Some believe that the increased contact with home makes their homesickness worse. One soldier explained that life back home was "a fantasy." For that reason, he did not want to know too much about what was going on there, fearing he would "miss it even more."[37] Yet despite the ambiguous effects of these new technologies, many of his fellow soldiers continue to eagerly avail themselves of them.

Immigrants to America do as well, using technology to sustain ties to their home countries. In the 1990s, when cheaper long-distance packages became available, newcomers to America began to call home more frequently than they had in the past. During these years, international calling grew more rapidly and proved more profitable than any other kind of long-distance phoning, representing a $6 billion enterprise in 1992. The rise of calling cards also aided immigrants. Basilio Prado, who had traveled from Villa Hidalgo, Mexico, to southern California, told interviewers he used cards to call home. He went through the minutes he'd purchased so quickly that he felt as though "they were made of smoke."[38] Ricardo Valencia said he went through "cards, cards, cards" talking to his family. When he first arrived he'd call home "almost every day. Every day. But then later about 3 times per week." Elizabeth Guardado, who lived in Texas and Colorado, called home to her family in Tepic quite regularly: "Every Saturday I would call my mom. . . . I would call to ask if she needed money or if there were any problems." She used telephone cards: "The one [with the picture] of Guadalupe was the one we would buy." William Hernandez, a native of the Canary Islands now living in Ogden, Utah, said he used phone cards to talk with his family in Spain two or three times each week: "I always talk with my parents because they are my parents. I have to call them. It's been two days since I've called them but I always call my family."[39] Others rely not on cards but on new long-distance calling plans, which allow families separated by vast distances to stay in touch affordably. Felicity Fouché, a South African living in Salt Lake City, calls her mother once or twice a week using a discounted long-distance service that costs her ten cents a minute.[40] Other immigrants text their families.[41]

Email, likewise, has changed the experience of immigration. During his time in Pahrump, Nevada, Ricardo Valencia signed up for a library card at the public library so he could use the computers to email home each week.[42] Sylvia Villarmia, a Filipina living in Houston, confided, "When I stay online every night to keep in touch with my children and grandchildren, I don't feel very homesick anymore. That is why I have all my gadgets like the webcam and the telephone."[43]

Immigrants also rely on modern technology to keep up with hometown news. Newspapers, long a salve to the homesick, are more accessible than ever. Christian Arias, a native of Villa Hidalgo, Mexico, said he got news of home from various web pages; Lizabeth Navarro recalled of her time in the United States, "Through the internet I would see the webpage of here, of Nayarit. I would get excited."[44] Felicity Fouché reads four South African newspapers and is sometimes better acquainted with her homeland's news than her family who remain there.[45] Likewise, Marjukka Ollilainen, a native of Finland who has lived in the United States for twenty years, stays current with Finnish news by reading papers online. In her weekly phone calls home to her father, a retired newspaperman, she often discovers that she knows the latest headlines before he does.[46] L. Marceline Santos-Taylor, the author of the "Manila Girl" column in the *Filipino Express*, a paper published in Jersey City, admitted, "[I'm] feeling just a wee bit homesick for the motherland. I haven't been back in two years." She kept up with her country's news by reading Philippine papers online. She also told her readers about "some websites [she visits] to quell these feelings of homesickness."[47]

Studies commissioned by the Carnegie Corporation suggest that all of these new modes of communication have affected immigrants' feelings about their lives in the United States and their connections to home. The organization sponsored two studies of immigrant life in America, one in 2002 and a second in 2009. The second study indicated that immigrants are better connected to their families and homelands than they were at the time of the first study. Whereas in 2002, only 28 percent of immigrants called home at least once a week, in 2009, 66 percent did, a reflection of the way that Skype, cell phones, and calling cards have changed communication patterns.[48]

While the homesick in America, native and foreign-born, may stay better connected than in years past, some suggest that this contact increases rather than decreases the longing for home. Maria Elena Rivera, a psychologist in Tepic, Mexico, believes that technology might in fact "magnificar la nostalgia," that is, magnify homesickness. Her sister, Carmen, had been living in San Diego for twenty-five years. With the rise of inexpensive long-distance calling, Carmen was able to phone home with greater frequency. Every Sunday she called the family home in Mexico, where her parents, siblings, and their offspring gathered for a large meal. Carmen always asked what the family was eating, who was there. Technology gave her new access to her family, but also made it clearer than ever that she was not with them. She could hear of the festivities but not participate in them.[49] Felicity Fouché noted that her homesickness came in waves, sometimes receding, sometimes advancing, and was often sparked by conversations with those back home: "You know, you'll get a call and everyone's getting together for some event."[50] The immediacy that phones and the Internet provide means that those away from home can know exactly what they are missing and when it is happening. The new technology gives the illusion that one can be in two places at once, but also highlights the impossibility of this. The Internet, social networking sites, and cell phones offer a sense of connection, yet using them is not the same as actually being home.

The new technologies are popular because they speak to enduring needs. The hope for lasting reunion has been long held but seldom realized, and throughout U.S. history, Americans have tried to bridge distance with the tools at hand. Antebellum Americans treasured daguerreotypes of loved ones and hoped to be reunited with them in heaven; Gilded Age Americans settled for short weekend reunions that relied on railroads and steamships; contemporary Americans send photos over their phones and make do with Facebook reunions, where everyone is together, but only virtually so.

COMMERCIAL CULTURE

If the new technologies have ambiguous effects on emotions—both assuaging and provoking homesickness, providing some solace but also increasing longing—the same is true for other cultural products of capitalism. It is, after all, capitalism that so often and relentlessly uproots Americans, luring them to new places, selling them new goods, destroying old landmarks and landscapes. Yet capitalism, with its technologies of reproducing, of mass producing, which can be so destructive, also offers familiarity through those very processes. Because corporate capitalism seeks the broadest possible market, it blankets states, regions, nations, and large parts of the earth with identical tastes, sounds, and images. And these mass-produced commodities, from food to entertainment, can be profoundly comforting to those who have been uprooted by market relations.

Take television. Many who moved during the second half of the twentieth century and the early years of the twenty-first found—and continue to find—comfort in television. A number of social scientists have demonstrated that viewers turn to television for a sense of friendship and sociability. Robert Kubey and Mihaly Csikszentmihalyi explained, "The medium clearly offers parasocial experiences. TV programs are well stocked with familiar faces and voices and viewing can help people maintain the illusion of being with others even when they are alone." They concluded, "People use television to help structure their experience and modulate moods."[51]

Of course, television watching, while a balm to the homesick, also has other effects on social life. Robert Putnam has drawn a strong link between the rise of television viewing, the privatization of leisure, and the decline of associational life.[52] Yet while television privatized leisure and removed individuals from their physical environs, it also offered a feeling of connection with others far away. Those on the move could watch the same shows they had enjoyed in their former homes. Johnny Carson had the same allure in North Dakota that he had in North Carolina and gave viewers a sense of predictable continuity, of familiarity, no matter where they moved. One scholar has suggested that by spreading a common entertainment across the country, television made regions more alike and created a shared, albeit commercial, national culture. In doing so, television made it easier for Americans to move comfortably from one place to another.[53]

For others, television spanned larger distances, bridging national boundaries. Eduardo Quezada, a Spanish-language newscaster for KMEX in Los Angeles, remembered how television eased his homesickness when he first came to the United States. Quezada, born in 1946, left his home in Hermosillo, Mexico, when he was seventeen to learn English. He was living in a one-room apartment in Long Beach and missed Hermosillo. He fiddled with the television in his room and was able to catch fleeting glimpses of a mariachi band and the Spanish commentary that accompanied it. The sounds comforted him, and the next weekend he stayed home to watch the same program. "It was not the news, or the entertainment," that he found compelling. "It was my language."[54] The millions in the Latin American diaspora who watch Univision and other Spanish-language programming know just what he means.

When satellite television began, it offered even greater access to scenes and sounds of home. A communications satellite was first put into space in 1965, a development that eventually allowed for far more varied television programming. Satellites reduced the cost of transmitting signals, and unlike older technologies, they carried multiple channels. Ruth Schwartz Cowan notes, "Satellites made special interest channels economically feasible, channels that would carry programs that appealed to only a segment [of] the nation's audience."[55] This became a boon for the homesick, who, before satellite television, could not find programming about their distant hometowns. With satellite, they could listen to the stations they had grown up with.

What many homesick migrants particularly want to see are sporting events. Sports teams are potent symbols of home pride and affiliation, and long after fans have moved from their hometowns, they continue to root for their favorites. During the 1980s, when satellite packages were too expensive for individual households, displaced Chicagoans routinely gathered at a bar in Los Angeles that had a satellite dish. These Cubs and Bears fans went to the Tin Horn Flats tavern for an opportunity to see their teams play and to connect with other Chicagoans who would line up early on Sunday morning during football season to catch pregame broadcasts.[56] In the 1970s, Cornhusker fans living in southern California cheered on their team by listening to low-wattage radio broadcasts of games. Now, with satellite television broadcasts, as many as two hundred Nebraskans living in Orange County still come together to watch Cornhusker games in Danny K's billiards pub. In all, an estimated 1,500 Nebraska fans can be found scattered at various drinking establishments across Huntington Beach, Palm Springs, and Santa Monica following their home team from afar.[57]

Since satellite television has become affordable for individual consumers, many households purchase packages that offer programming from their home countries. South Africans Felicity Fouché and her husband, both avid cricket and rugby fans, are able to watch live matches through their Direct TV account.[58] For homesick South Asians, Comcast offers the STAR India PLUS channel, which gives access to "top programs" from India, including "soap operas . . . as well as some of the nation's favorite reality and game shows." Another channel available to Comcast customers is TV Asia, which offers programs in a variety of languages. Its promotional blurb tells potential subscribers that it "is dedicated to bring the South-Asian American community together by delivering high quality entertainment. . . . TV Asia is sure to be your 'Home Away From Home.'"[59] In *The World Is Flat,* Thomas Friedman describes such trends as "the globalization of the local." He writes, "Even those individuals who have had to uproot themselves from developing countries to go West . . . have been able to take advantage of the flattening of the world to hold onto many aspects of their local culture, even if they are living in the midst of a different one thousands of miles away. Thanks to their ability to read their local newspapers online . . . thanks to Internet or satellite TV, the forces of particularization now seem to be as strong as the forces of homogenization."[60]

Migrants and immigrants find comfort in the "globalization of the local," but they also (perhaps counterintuitively) find comfort in the mass-produced commercial products of multinational corporations. Branded goods have become increasingly essential to social identity in America, and having access to them in new places helps maintain a stable sense of self. The endless repetition of chain stores and franchises that line America's boulevards and highways has created a society in which individuals can partake of the same foodstuffs, clothes, and experiences wherever they are. Chain stores homogenize American culture, but this may be one of their selling points to uprooted migrants eager for the familiar.[61] Perhaps home is where the Target is.

The U.S. military seems to have faith in that proposition. The *New York Times* reported in 2009 that on the Joint Base Balad in Iraq, "at the Subway [sandwich shop], workers from India and Bangladesh make sandwiches for American soldiers looking for a taste of home." The bases also provide massage parlors, swimming pools, and entertainment to keep soldiers content while serving their time.[62] One soldier recalled of his time in Iraq, "Access to items, be it food or other luxury items were never in short supply if located near a large base," because the PX or the Army and Air Force Exchange Service, as it is now generally called, is "the military version of Wal-Mart." In fact, in daily conversation, soldiers refer to the AAFES at Camp Victory in Iraq as Walmart and turn to it for their daily needs.[63] Precisely because it offers familiar goods, they will sometimes skip army rations and look for food there. One soldier explained, "[Soldiers] don't want any of the MRE [meals ready to eat]; they want, you know, some sandwiches, some chips, and that's all brand name, Lays, Ruffles . . . Pepsi Lime, Coke," so they go to the PX to buy it. "It's just like home. . . . I'm gonna drink a Diet Pepsi or a Coke and sit and watch a DVD."[64]

Iraqis, Greeks, Guatemalans, and Mexicans living in the United States find similar comfort in multinational chains that offer a familiar range of goods. For instance, some immigrants have been able to visit chain restaurants popular in their homelands that have spread to the United States. In July 2005, a Guatemalan chain, Pollo Campero, opened its doors in Chicago. On its first day of business, two hundred people lined up to buy fried chicken with a distinctive crust. Most of them were Guatemalans hungry for chicken, but many were also hungry for something else. A *Chicago Tribune* reporter explained:

> Patrons . . . waxed poetic about the juiciness and crispness of the chicken. But they also spoke of their childhoods in Guatemala, when a trip to Pollo Campero was seen as a gesture of love by their parents. They spoke of celebrating birthdays there, taking first dates for dinner. Regina Garcia, who moved to Chicago from Guatemala City, recalled how her entire family would go there after Sunday mass, a chance to linger for hours in conversation. She was in the first group that arrived shortly after dawn Friday. "This is something very special," she said. "It's part of all of our childhoods. It's a piece of our homeland."

According to the *Tribune*, Juan Jose Gutierrez, the CEO of Campero USA, "said the company benefits here from a built-in customer loyalty, tied to the sentimentality of immigrants far from home." Gutierrez made clear the connection between homesickness and his brand, remarking that "Campero appeals to nostalgia."[65]

Perhaps somewhat surprisingly, immigrants also admit to finding comfort in American chains that were present in their native countries. Because they first became acquainted with these chains in their homelands, they are reminders not of the United States but of Mexico or India or wherever they were first encountered. For instance, Ricardo Valencia recalled, "In Guadalajara I frequently visited Office Depot, Wal-Mart, Sam's, and the big stores." He found many of the same chains in Pahrump, Nevada, where he settled. "Sometimes they had the same things, things I had purchased for my children, my wife." When he got lonesome, Valencia was tempted to drink; to fight that impulse he went to Walmart instead of buying a beer. "I would buy things for them [his family]. . . . When I wanted not one but two beers, I would buy a little car, a Hot Wheels. Something small but for them." He noted, "Objects mentally transported me with my family. . . . On various occasions I would buy things and mail them through the post office."[66] The historian Donna Gabaccia points out that immigrants often first taste American foods in American chains in their home countries, and then find them familiar, and to some extent homelike, in their new land.[67] Branded goods sold by multinational corporations and large chain stores diminish diversity, but they also offer the familiar to immigrants who travel within the globalized economy.

Although they often standardize tastes, some corporations recognize the profits to be made by catering to the more distinctive preferences of ethnic enclaves. Immigrants therefore may find familiar grocery items on the shelves of larger chain supermarkets. Mexican beans and tortillas, Indian spices, and Chinese plum sauce are now widely marketed across the United States. A number of small ethnic food importing companies have been bought out by large multinationals with far-flung distribution centers and sophisticated marketing strategies. Hormel, for instance, purchased both Indian and Mexican food companies in order to reach new markets. These companies sell their goods largely through supermarkets, which, though they have not replaced ethnic grocers, have begun to carve a niche for themselves.[68]

There are some items that immigrants long for that cannot be found at Safeway or Stop and Shop, but that can be purchased in ethnic groceries, which stock their shelves with specialty goods more easily than in the past. In Jackson Heights, an Indian neighborhood in Queens, shoppers can buy chaat, kulfi, paan, and sarees, listen to Hindi music, and watch Hindi films. Kaushalya Devi, an immigrant, said, "I thought I would be in an alien land when I agreed to come and live with my son in America. But this is just like India!"[69] A Bengali woman, long settled in the United States, remarked on the increasing number of such businesses in her Indian community: "Twenty years ago, many things were not available; now almost everything, including fish from Bangladesh, is available in big cities."[70]

Given the global smorgasbord available to modern consumers and their enhanced ability to communicate with and travel to their homelands, some have predicted that homesickness will soon disappear. Certainly modern markets and technologies seem to bring the world closer together and reduce the sense of distance. However, the optimism that capitalism and technology can solve the problem and cure the pain of homesickness may be misplaced; certainly it is not new. Since at least the nineteenth century, commentators have predicted that homesickness would soon be eliminated, conquered once and for all by the forces of modernity.

In 1846, for instance, a French doctor wrote that acute homesickness, that is, nostalgia, "becomes more rare each day thanks to rapid communications which modern industry is beginning to establish among people who will soon be nothing more than one big family."[71] Throughout the nineteenth century, on both sides of the Atlantic, commentators continued to make such claims. In 1899, American observers predicted that although mild homesickness might continue to afflict individuals, "nostalgia has grown less common in these days of quick communication, of rapid transmission of news and of a widened knowledge of geography. The element of ignorance of one's surroundings and consequent sense of helplessness and despair of ever seeing home again which in times gone by so oppressed the sufferer from nostalgia, is now removed, except in the case of the very young or the densely ignorant."[72]

These happy predictions have continued into the twentieth and twenty-first centuries. In 1991, the writer Anton Shammas commented on the enhanced abilities of immigrants to bring to the United States an abundance of goods from their homelands: "Among other achievements, Amérka has made homesickness obsolete."[73] In 2009, an army officer reflecting on his time in Iraq likewise proclaimed that with all of the new communications technologies that help soldiers stay in touch, "homesickness should be a thing of the past, now."[74]

Such statements show a faith in the power of technology and capitalism to overcome distance. While nineteenth-century observers celebrated the railroad, steamboat, postal service, and telegraph as working wonders, contemporary Americans express the same optimism about computers, cell phones, airplanes, and cars. Some celebrate the abundance of products available everywhere, created by the machinery of corporate capitalism. As consumerism has become pervasive in American life, the ability to buy a sense of home has become easier. Chain stores and brand names have made the material world more homogeneous and in some ways more familiar. These innovations, from fast transport to global marketing to instantaneous communication, offer the seductive promise that leaving home and returning to it will be easy and painless. With the assurance that they can stay in touch with family and home, many have set off. Although the home one has left may be far away, the consumer economy provides the illusion that it is close at hand. Yet those who have suffered from homesickness know that even with such conveniences and technologies, the distances between an old home and a new one are great, and often unbridgeable. Despite the new inventions and economic connections, homesickness has not disappeared from the panoply of human emotions.

It has disappeared, however, from American discourse, and its meaning has fundamentally changed over the past several centuries. In the seventeenth and eighteenth centuries, the feeling could be found across colonial America before the words *nostalgia* and *homesickness* were even coined. Often there were few ways to assuage the emotion, given the constraints individuals encountered in hierarchical colonial society. There was little to do but tolerate it.

As more Americans gradually gained the liberty to come and go as they pleased, they had to sort out their often conflicting desires for home and for gain. Many came to believe that coping with homesickness was part of delaying gratification, that sacrifices in the present would lead to rewards in the future, and that leaving home might advance fortunes, prospects, and even home life. They were, however, more than willing to admit that striking off on one's own had costs. In the nineteenth century, many in the nation believed that it was acceptable to talk openly about these costs: miners cried when they received letters from home or heard familiar songs; soldiers wasted away from their yearnings. Homesickness was not yet shameful, for love and loyalty to home were the marks of a virtuous character.

By the twentieth century, as capitalism expanded and new theories of personality development took shape, Americans began to feel pressure to adapt to alien environments, to pull up stakes and move on, and show little distress in the process. In an age influenced by Darwinian notions of adaptation and psychological theories about emotional maturity, failure to separate from home came to be associated with failure more generally. Those who were homesick were considered premodern, unsophisticated, ill-equipped for the shifting and individualistic conditions of modern society. Fundamentally, homesickness was a mark of a childish nature. Consequently, by the end of the twentieth century, few native-born adults overtly discussed the emotion, although they displayed it in other ways.

Homesickness disappeared from adult discourse; it also disappeared from much of the historical record. As a result, restless individualism often came to be seen as an innate personality trait of Americans. Even those who criticized American restlessness nonetheless portrayed it as an inevitability.[75] But those who focused only on American individualism, and drew conclusions only from external behaviors and not internal desires, lost a sense of the fullness of the American experience.[76] In reality, Americans only slowly learned to leave home, only gradually began to regard moving on as a natural behavior. Even when they did leave, their mobility was not only or even primarily about individual self-aggrandizement; often people moved on with hopes of returning home to the family hearth enriched.

The history of America and American mobility is not just the history of moving forward and separating from family and kin. It also must include the "America house" in Odessa or Oaxaca, built with wages earned in the United States, the dream Stephen Crary had of going to the mines in California so that he might return to Connecticut to buy his wife a piano and his children ponies, the feelings of explorers who would have liked to beat it back across the Mississippi and the soldiers in the Mexican-American War who added western territory but longed for eastern ones. It is about suicidal slaves who did not want to come to the United States in the first place, and who could return to Africa only by supernatural means. It is about helicopter parents and boomerang kids, who have moved with greater ambivalence than widely acknowledged and who have been as much backward-looking as forward-facing. Americans in their migrations have consistently affirmed—in private writings, through purchases, through remittances sent home—a set of values that counter lonely individualism, that embrace community and connection. The culture in which we live is a homesick culture; the ideology of rugged individualism that holds sway, however, denies the relevance of the emotion, and so its many signs and artifacts frequently are not seen for what they are.

The wealth of communication technologies and their extraordinary popularity, the diversity of international goods on grocery store shelves, and the Bollywood programming available on satellite television are potent symbols of the emotional connections Americans try to sustain as they move on. Yet, in the end, those technologies, devices, applications, and products cannot make men and women forget about the miles that separate them from home. They are the next best thing to being there, but they are not the same as being there. They are not sufficient to make homesickness disappear, for in the end, easy travel, inexpensive communication, and name brands available worldwide, obscure but do not erase the fact of distance.

NOTES

INTRODUCTION

1. "Victim of Nostalgia: A Priest Dies Craving for a Sight of His Motherland," *Evening Bulletin* (San Francisco), August 12, 1887.
2. Katherine Lanpher, "A Manhattan Admonition," *New York Times*, August 31, 2004.
3. Ad Vingerhoets, "The Homesickness Concept: Questions and Doubts," in Tilburg and Vingerhoets, *Psychological Aspects of Geographical Moves*, 1.
4. Cressy, *Crossing Over*, 192.
5. "Homesick Russian Jews: Refugees Who Yearn for the Land of Persecution," *Dallas Morning News*, March 10, 1906.
6. P. N. Stearns, *American Cool*, 272.
7. Daniel Walker Howe makes the important point that part of the individualistic quest may lead to new communal affiliations (*Making the American Self,* 5).
8. Miranda A. L. van Tilburg, "The Psychological Context of Homesickness," in Tilburg and Vingerhoets, *Psychological Aspects of Geographical Moves*, 50; Vingerhoets, "The Homesickness Concept: Questions and Doubts," 1.
9. Tocqueville, *Democracy in America*, 536.
10. Turner, *The Frontier.*
11. Handlin, *The Uprooted*; Pierson, *The Moving American*; Jasper, *Restless Nation*; Packard, *A Nation of Strangers*; Minnen and Hilton, *Nation on the Move.*
12. Turner, *The Frontier*, 40.
13. Wilhelm, "New England in Southeastern Ohio," 23–25.
14. Kolodny, *The Land before Her*, 48, 37, 53; Henkin, *The Postal Age*, 60–61; Domoto, "A Japanese-American Nurseryman's Life."
15. Henkin, *The Postal Age*, 2, 29, 146–47.
16. Robert Hine made just this argument (*Community on the American Frontier,* 5).
17. Records of the Virginia Company of London, Court Book, November 21, 1621, in *The Records of the Virginia Colony* (Washington, DC: Government Printing Office, 1906), 1:566.
18. For discussions of the themes and mission of the history of emotions, see Plamper, "The History of Emotions," 238; P. N. Stearns and Stearns, "Emotionology," 813–36; Jan Lewis and Peter N. Stearns, introduction to P. N. Stearns and Lewis, *An Emotional History,* 1–14; Rosenwein, "Worrying about Emotions," 821; Reddy, "Historical Research," 302–15; Matt, "Current Emotion Research."
19. Rosenwein, "Worrying about Emotions," 821.
20. Starobinski, "The Idea of Nostalgia," 81.

CHAPTER 1

1. Johan Printz, "Report of Governor Johan Printz 1644[,] Relation to the Noble West India Company in Old Sweden sent out of New Sweden on June 11, Anno 1644," and "Report of Governor Printz, 1647[,] Report to the Right Honorable West India Company in Old Sweden, sent from New Sweden, February 20, 1647," in Myers, *Narratives*, 109, 128–29.

2. Bulkeley, *The Gospel-Covenant*, 14; Pettit, "God's Englishman," 58.

3. *Boston Gazette*, May 21–28, 1733; Piersen, "White Cannibals, Black Martyrs," 147–59.

4. Daniels, *Coming to America*, 30. Aaron Fogleman argues that perhaps as much as 75 percent of the colonial population was unfree ("From Slaves," 43).

5. Wokeck, *Trade in Strangers*, xxiv, 10, 22; Brite, *The Attitude*, 136, 138. On emigration restrictions, see Cressy, *Crossing Over*, 130–43; Marianne Wokeck, "Harnessing the Lure of the 'Best Poor Man's Country': The Dynamics of German-Speaking Immigration to British North America, 1683–1783," in Altman and Horn, *"To Make America"*; Altman, *Emigrants and Society*, 205. For examples of interrogation that migrants might face should they want to return to England, see "A Court at James Citty. The 9ᵗʰ Octob. 1626," in McIlwaine, *Minutes of the Council*, 116.

6. Kotchemidova, "From Good Cheer to 'Drive-by Smiling,'" 7–8.

7. Carol Z. Stearns, "'Lord Help Me Walk Humbly': Anger and Sadness in England and America, 1570–1750," in C. Z. Stearns and Stearns, *Emotions and Social Change*, 57. Nicole Eustace notes that there was a widespread perception that the lowliest in society, those with the least power, were inherently melancholic (*Passion*, 71–72).

8. McMahon, *Happiness*, 172–73.

9. Howe, *Making the American Self*, 38–39.

10. Nicholas Canny, "In Search of a Better Home? European Overseas Migration, 1500–1800," in *Europeans on the Move*, 280; Altman and Horn, introduction to *"To Make America,"* 15, 17.

11. Ida Altman, "A New World in the Old: Local Society and Spanish Emigration to the Indies," in Altman and Horn, *"To Make America,"* 30–58; Altman, *Emigrants and Society*, 247–74, 241–45; Altman, *Transatlantic Ties*, 37–39; Leslie Choquette, "Recruitment of French Emigrants to Canada, 1600–1760," in Altman and Horn, *"To Make America,"* 161.

12. Stirling, *An Encouragement*, 28–30; J. E. Cooke, *Virginia*, 6.

13. J. Smith, *The Generall Historie of Virginia*, 44.

14. A. Taylor, *American Colonies*, 38–39.

15. George Thorpe, A Letter to John Smith, Dec. 19, 1620, in Kingsbury, *The Records*, 3:417; John Smith, "A True Relation of such Occurrences and Accidents of Note as hath hap'ned in Virginia since the First Planting of that Colony which is now resident in the South Part thereof, till the Last Return," in Hale, *Jamestown Narratives*, 149; Kupperman, "Apathy," 28, 35, 36.

16. Kupperman, "Apathy," 25.

17. E. S. Morgan, "The First American Boom," 179–81; T. H. Breen, "Looking Out for Number One," 342–60.

18. Edward Hill to his Brother, Mʳ Jo. Hill, April 14, 1623, and Phoebus Caner to Mʳ Lawrence Ley, 1623, in "Notes Taken from Letters," in Kingsbury, *The Records*, 4: 234, 235.

19. "Records of the Virginia Company of London, The Court Book, November 3, 1619," in Kingsbury, *The Records*, 1: 256.

20. John Smith, "Generall Histories of Virginia by Captain John Smith, 1624; The Fourth Book," in L. G. Tyler, *Narratives*, 339.

21. J. E. Cooke, *Virginia*, 120–21.

22. William Rowlsley to his brother, April 3, 1623, in "Notes Taken From Letters," in Kingsbury, *The Records*, 4:235.

23. John Rolfe to Sir Thomas Dale, 1614, in L. G. Tyler, *Narratives*, 243.

24. "A Court at James Citty," 116; James Horn, "'To Parts beyond the Seas': Free Emigration to the Chesapeake in the Seventeenth Century," in Altman and Horn, *"To Make America,"* 115–16.

25. A. Taylor, *American Colonies,* 143.

26. Richard Frethorne to his parents, March 20, 1623; Richard Frethorne to his parents, April 2, 1623; Richard Frethorne to his parents, April 3, 1623, in Kingsbury *The Records,* 4: 58–62; A. E. Smith, *Colonists in Bondage,* 253; Emily Rose, "The Politics of Pathos: Richard Frethorne's Letters Home," in Applebaum and Sweet, *Envisioning an English Empire,* 92–108. Rose suggests that Frethorne wrote the letters knowing that they would be read by others and that they were used as part of a campaign to draw attention to the miserable conditions in Virginia.

27. Revel, *The Poor Unhappy.*

28. Horn, *Adapting,* 141, 425, 294–95, 302–4, 307, 309, 320; T. H. Breen, "Looking Out for Number One," 347–48.

29. D. H. Fischer, *Albion's Seed,* 264–74. Some historians contend that as early as the 1640s this backward-looking style, based on memories of English buildings, had become the norm in Virginia; others suggest it was not until the late seventeenth century that English styles became widespread. The later timeline is put forward by Horn, *Adapting,* 426–27.

30. D. H. Fischer, *Albion's Seed,* 239–40.

31. Bradford, *Bradford's History,* 33, 48, 79.

32. Bradford, *Bradford's History,* 156.

33. Winthrop, *Winthrop's Journal,* 1:58.

34. E. Johnson, *Wonder-Working Providence,* 45, 55.

35. "Memoirs of Captain Roger Clap," in Bercovitch, *Puritan Personal Writings,* 7–8.

36. Cressy, *Coming Over,* 191–93, 195.

37. D. H. Fischer, *Albion's Seed,* 28.

38. Cressy, *Coming Over,* 191–92, 200; Pettit, "God's Englishman," 60, 63, 58; Delbanco, "Looking Homeward," 362.

39. Winthrop, *Winthrop's Journal,* 2:11.

40. D. H. Fischer, *Albion's Seed,* 64–68.

41. D. H. Fischer, *Albion's Seed,* 55–56, 252–54, 468; Zuckerman, "The Fabrication of Identity," 200.

42. Cressy, *Coming Over,* 212; Poteet, "A Homecoming," 30–50.

43. Wokeck, *Trade in Strangers,* xxiii.

44. K. A. Miller et al., *Irish Immigrants,* 53; James Horn, "Tobacco Colonies: The Shaping of English Society in the Seventeenth-Century Chesapeake," in Canny, *The Oxford History,* 191.

45. K. A. Miller et al., *Irish Immigrants,* 53–54, 82–84, 137–38.

46. Risch, "Encouragement," 246–48, 273.

47. Brite, *The Attitude,* 138, 197–99.

48. Daniels, *Coming to America,* 30; Fogleman, "From Slaves," 43–44.

49. Mancke and Shammas, *The Creation,* 30.

50. Mannix, *Black Cargoes,* 119–21.

51. "A Journal of a Voyage made in the Hannibal of London, Ann. 1693–1694, from England to Cape Monseradoe, in Africa . . . by Thomas Phillips, commander of the said ship; from Churchill, Collections of Voyages and Travels (1732)," in Donnan, *Documents,* 402–3; Mannix, *Black Cargoes,* 119–21.

52. Quoted in Mannix, *Black Cargoes,* 114.

53. P. D. Morgan, *Slave Counterpoint,* 446.

54. *Virginia Gazette* (Purdie and Dixon), September 12, 1771.

55. *Virginia Gazette* (Purdie and Dixon), October 27, 1768, supplement.

56. *Virginia Gazette* (Purdie and Dixon), August 24, 1769, January 14, 1773; Windley, *Runaway Slave Advertisements*, 1:72–73, 128.
57. *Georgia Gazette*, July 2, 1766, in Windley, *Runaway Slave Advertisements*, 4:16.
58. *South Carolina Gazette*, July 8–July 15, 1756, in Windley, *Runaway Slave Advertisements*, 3:145–46.
59. *Virginia Gazette* (Dixon and Hunter), December 5, 1777.
60. Philip D. Morgan, "Colonial South Carolina Runaways: Their Significance for Slave Culture," in Heuman, *Out of the House of Bondage*, 71.
61. P. D. Morgan, *Slave Counterpoint*, 501.
62. *Virginia Gazette* (Dixon and Nicolson), April 24, 1779.
63. *Virginia Gazette* (Purdie and Dixon), July 14, 1774; Windley, *Runaway Slave Advertisements*, 1:151; *Virginia Gazette or American Advertiser*, February 22, 1786, in Windley, *Runaway Slave Advertisements*, 1:382.
64. P. D. Morgan, "Colonial South Carolina Runaways," 67.
65. P. D. Morgan, *Slave Counterpoint*, 642.
66. Grace Greenwood, "Sketches of Yankee Life and Character," *Independent*, January 6, 1870.
67. Earle, *Customs*, 92; Piersen, *Black Yankees*, 74–75.
68. R. W. Brown, *Memoir of Mrs. Chloe Spear*, 17; Piersen, *Black Yankees*, 74–76.
69. Sheldon, *A History*, 2:897; Piersen, *Black Yankees*, 74–76.
70. Greenwood, "Sketches of Yankee Life and Character," 1.
71. Elaine Forman Crane, "'I Have Suffer'd Much Today': The Defining Force of Pain in Early America," in Hoffman et al., *Through a Glass Darkly*, 398–99; See also McMahon, *Happiness*, 191.
72. Hofer, "Medical Dissertation," 380, 382; Starobinski, "The Idea of Nostalgia," 81–103.
73. Hofer, "Medical Dissertation," 381; Rosen, "Nostalgia," 32.
74. Rosen, "Nostalgia," 34–35; Starobinski, "The Idea of Nostalgia," 81–103.
75. Arnold, *Observations*, 1:206–9; Rosen, "Nostalgia," 39.
76. Rather, *Mind and Body*, 175–77; Zwingmann, "'Heimweh' or 'Nostalgic Reaction,'" 27; *The Oxford English Dictionary*, s.v. "homesickness."
77. Eustace, *Passion*, 476.
78. Howe, *Making the American Self*, 68.
79. Fea, *The Way of Improvement*, 6, 71; Wood, *The Radicalism*, 221.
80. *Gentleman's Magazine* 7 (1737): 242, quoted in Alan D. McKillop, "Local Attachment and Cosmopolitanism—The Eighteenth-Century Pattern," in Hilles and Bloom, *From Sensibility to Romanticism*, 199.
81. Arnold, *Observations*, 208.
82. McKillop, "Local Attachment and Cosmopolitanism," 191–218.
83. Bushman, *From Puritan to Yankee*, 267, 280.
84. Lynn Hunt, *Inventing Human Rights*, 29–30.
85. Wood, *The Radicalism*, 125–29, 145–46.
86. *Virginia Gazette* (Purdie and Dixon), April 16, 1767.
87. *Virginia Gazette* (Purdie), February 7, 1777.
88. Fithian, journal, November 21, 1773, 23–24.
89. Fithian, journal, January 16, 1774, 55.
90. Fithian, journal, June 5, 1774, 114–15.
91. Fithian, journal, July 4, 1774, 172–73; Fea, *The Way of Improvement*, 208–9.
92. Hugh Simm to Andrew Simm, December 2, 1768, Box 1, Item 6; Hugh Simm to Andrew Simm, November 14, 1772, Box 1, Item 10, Hugh Simm Collection, 1748–1810, Princeton University Library, Manuscripts Division.
93. Eustace, *Passion*; Knott, *Sensibility*; Burstein, *Sentimental Democracy*, 7.
94. Royster, *A Revolutionary People*, 35–37, 46.

95. Barber, *The History*, 11, 13–14.

96. Atkins, *The Diary*, 23.

97. Charles Lee to Benjamin Rush, December 12, 1775, in *The Lee Papers . . . 1754–1811* (New York, 1872–75), in Scheer and Rankin, *Rebels and Redcoats*, 103; McCullough, *1776*, 65.

98. General Schuyler to Governor Trumbull, December 19, 1776, in Force, *American Archives*, 1302.

99. Royster, *A Revolutionary People*, 60–61.

100. "To the President of Congress," September 24, 1776, in Washington, *The Writings*, 6:110.

101. Royster, *A Revolutionary People*, 71.

102. George Washington to his wife, June 18, 1775, in T. J. Fleming, *Affectionately Yours*, 54.

103. To Colonel William Malcolm, January 6, 1778, in Washington, *The Writings*, 10:269–70.

104. George Washington, "General Orders," July 18, 1775, in Washington, *The Writings*, 3:346; Bowman, *The Morale*, 63.

105. Royster, *A Revolutionary People*, 122.

106. S. Kennedy, "Letters, to his wife," June 7, 1776, June 10, 1776, 112, 113.

107. Waldo, "Valley Forge," 309, 318, 321.

108. Rosen, "Nostalgia," 38–40; Starobinski, "The Idea of Nostalgia," 96.

109. Starobinski, "The Idea of Nostalgia," 95–96; Bowman, *Morale*, 20–23; Cox, *A Proper Sense*, 38; Benjamin Rush, "Of the Mode of Education Proper in a Republic," in Rush, *The Selected Writings*, 90.

110. Benjamin Rush, "An Account of the Influence of the Military and Political Events of the American Revolution upon the Human Body," in Rush, *Medical Inquiries*, 1:279, 281, 285–86; *The Pennsylvania Packet and Daily Advertiser*, January 24, 1789.

111. Rush, "An Account of the Influence," 291–92.

112. Joseph Stansbury, "My Native Land," and "To Cordelia," in Sargent, *The Loyal Verses*, 95, 96–97; M. C. Tyler, *The Literary History*, 95–96.

113. Wallace Brown, *The Good Americans*, 159–62.

114. Ward, *Journal and Letters*, 43, 44, 385; Wrong, *Canada*, 407. For more examples, see Wrong, *Canada*, 373, 405. See also Richard Routh to Peter Frye, June 27, 1780, Richard Routh Correspondence, James Marshall and Marie-Louise Osborn Collection, Beinecke Library, Yale University, New Haven.

CHAPTER 2

1. Tocqueville, *Democracy in America*, 594. Tocqueville noted that such mobility seemed far easier for men than for their wives.

2. Domingo Sarmiento, "Travels in the United States in 1847," in *A Sarmiento Anthology*, 207; Pierson, *The Moving American*, 8. Modern historians have continued in this vein. See, for instance, Joyce Appleby, "New Cultural Heroes in the Early National Period," in Haskell and Teichgraeber, *The Culture of the Market*, 182.

3. Turner, *The Frontier*, 37.

4. P. K. Hall and Ruggles, "Restless," 834–35. The article considers only interstate movement by people born in the United States.

5. Sandage, *Born Losers*, 14, 27, 39, 81–82.

6. Potter, *People of Plenty*, 97.

7. Brandt, "A Short Natural History of Nostalgia," 58–59; McDannell and Lang, *Heaven*, 181–95, 198–203; Stannard, *The Puritan Way of Death*, 167–96; Douglas, *The Feminization of American Culture*, 200–226.

8. Faragher, *Sugar Creek*, 51.

9. "An Extraordinary Occurrence," *Federal Mirror* (Concord, New Hampshire), October 30, 1795; "Extract from a letter of a seaman on board the Jacob Jones, to his brother in

Boston, dated River Tigress, 20 miles below Canton," *Alexandria (Virginia) Gazette Commercial and Political*, April 13, 1815; *City Gazette and Commercial Daily Advertiser* (Charleston, SC), July 22, 1822; "Tea in Brazil," *Boston Weekly Messenger*, August 11, 1825; *Barre (Vermont) Patriot*, May 23, 1851.

10. "The Slave Trade," *Portsmouth (NH) Journal of Literature and Politics*, November 10, 1821; *Newburyport Herald*, August 3, 1821; *Lincoln Intelligencer* (Wiscasset, Maine), April 8, 1822.

11. "Melancholy Suicide," *Daily Evening Bulletin* (San Francisco), October 14, 1859; "Suicide of a Young Woman," *Daily Evening Bulletin*, February 16, 1860.

12. "Homesick Suicide," *New York Herald*, December 26, 1856.

13. "Another Homesick Suicide," *New York Herald*, January 12, 1857.

14. G. R. Taylor, *The Transportation Revolution*, 141–42.

15. G. R. Taylor, *The Transportation Revolution*, 74; Howe, *What Hath God Wrought*, 41, 564.

16. To go by sea to the Pacific Coast cost between $300 and $700 for a journey of four to eight months; to go overland cost between $180 and $200 per person. These were considerable sums in an age when an artisan's annual income was $375 and a clerk's $610. Howe, *What Hath God Wrought*, 816; Alter et al., "The Savings of Ordinary Americans," 750, 763.

17. P. N. Stearns, *American Cool*, 53, 20, 21, 38, 90, 42–50; Kotchemidova, "From Good Cheer to 'Drive-by Smiling,'" 10.

18. Wallace, *The Long, Bitter Trail*, 105–6.

19. Rozema, *Voices from the Trail of Tears*, 40.

20. Howe, *What Hath God Wrought*, 420.

21. Theda Perdue, "The Trail of Tears: Removal of the Southern Indians," in Weeks, *The American Indian Experience*, 109.

22. George Harkins quoted in Mintz, *Native American Voices*, 122.

23. "Plea from the Chickasaw," in Nabokov, *Native American Testimony*, 151; Perdue, "Trail of Tears," 110–11.

24. Ross to Senecas, April 14, 1834, in Moulton, *The Papers of John Ross*, 1:248–87, quoted in Mintz, *Native American Voices*, 123. See also Moulton, *John Ross*, 55.

25. John Howard Payne and Henry Rowley Bishop, "Home! Sweet Home!," in R. Jackson, *Popular Songs*, 80–82; H. R. Brown, *The Sentimental Novel*, 280; Hamm, *Yesterdays*, 167–69. Payne was still famous long after his death in 1852. He died in Tunis, where he had served as American consul. Americans thought it inappropriate for him to be buried away from home, so in 1883, his body was exhumed and brought back to the United States. So great was his celebrity that sixty years after his song first debuted and thirty-one years after his death, thousands of people filed past his coffin before he was interred in Oak Hill cemetery in Washington, DC. See "From a Foreign Grave, John Howard Payne's Body Brought Home," *New York Times*, March 23, 1883.

26. Payne, *John Howard Payne to His Countrymen*, 52.

27. H. G. Clauder to Theodore Schulz, March 17, 1837, Moravian Archives, Cherokee Mission, 290, quoted in Ehle, *Trail of Tears*, 363.

28. Andrew Jackson, "Second Annual Message," December 6, 1830, in Richardson, *A Compilation of the Messages and Papers of the Presidents*, 2:1084–85; see also Takaki, *A Different Mirror*, 87.

29. Howe, *What Hath God Wrought*, 128–31.

30. Sandage, *Born Losers*, 13–15, 72, 81.

31. Cashin, *A Family Venture*, 5, 17, 27, 32, 44, 65.

32. Cashin, *A Family Venture*, 70.

33. Owen, *John Owen's Journal*, 7–8.

34. Cashin, *A Family Venture*, 73.

35. Cashin, *A Family Venture*, 78–79.

36. J. E. Davis, "Changing Places," 658.

37. Jacobs, *Incidents*, 121; Gutman, *The Black Family*, 288–89. Even after the Civil War, some doctors dismissed the idea that slaves had felt homesickness when sold. See Hammond, *A Treatise on Insanity*, 413.

38. J. Ball, *Autobiography*, 19.

39. Keckley, *Behind the Scenes*, 29; H. Watson, *Narrative*, 32–33; Blassingame, *The Slave Community*, 161. Lawrence Levine discusses white perceptions of slaves as inscrutable and slaves' belief that it was necessary to hide their true emotions (*Black Culture*, 99–101).

40. Knight to Wm. M. Beall, June 30, 1844, May 22, 1845, Knight Papers, in *Records of Ante-Bellum Southern Plantations*, ed. Kenneth M. Stampp (Frederick, MD: University Publications of America), quoted in Kaye, *Joining Places*, 29.

41. John W. Cotton to William H. Wills, December 26, 1839, Wills Paper, Southern Historical Collection, University of North Carolina, quoted in Deyle, *Carry Me Back*, 218.

42. Henry Tucker to his father, February 17, 1804, in M. H. B. Coleman, *Virginia Silhouettes*, 9–15, quoted in Gutman, *The Black Family*, 288–89.

43. Steward, *Twenty-Two Years a Slave*, 42, 48, 47.

44. Mars, *Life*, 19.

45. C. Ball, *Fifty Years in Chains*, 115; Andrews, *To Tell a Free Story*, 82; *American National Biography*, s.v. "Ball, Charles."

46. Northup, *Twelve Years a Slave*, 47–48, 56–57, 186.

47. Kaye, *Joining Places*; Gutman, *The Black Family*, 263–67; Faust, "Culture, Conflict," 83–98; Jacobs, *Incidents*, 157.

48. Kaye, *Joining Places*, 129; interview with M. T. Judge, February 23, 1913, Nixon Papers, Alabama Department of Archives and History, Montgomery, Alabama, quoted in Deyle, *Carry Me Back*, 257, 260, 261. See also Franklin and Schweninger, *Runaway Slaves*, 49–74.

49. Interview with Susan Hamlin in George P. Rawick, ed., *The American Slave: A Composite Autobiography*, vol. 2, pt. 2 (Westport, CT: Greenwood Press, 1972), 235; Deyle, *Carry Me Back*, 246.

50. Abream Scriven to Dinah Jones, 1858, in *Blacks in Bondage: Letters from American Slaves*, ed. Robert S. Starobin (New York: New Viewpoints, 1974), quoted in Gutman, *The Black Family*, 36.

51. Albert J. Raboteau, *Canaan Land: A Religious History of African Americans* (New York: Oxford University Press, 2001), 49.

52. Deyle, *Carry Me Back*, 249–50.

53. McLachlan, *American Boarding Schools*, 227, 44–46, 124, 111–35.

54. Eliza Southgate Browne to her parents, May 12, 1797, in Browne, *A Girl's Life*, 4.

55. Mary Ann Bacon Wittlesey, "Diary of Mary Ann Bacon," in Buel, *Chronicles*, 66–67.

56. Buel, *Chronicles*, 230–32.

57. Howe, *Making the American Self*, 112, 128; Blauvelt, *The Work of the Heart*, 72.

58. Emily Dickinson to Austin Dickinson, February 17, 1848, in *The Letters*, 62–63.

59. Habegger, *My Wars*, 212.

60. Sidney Roby to Catherine Breese, December 18, 1844, correspondence, folder 2, box 9, Breese-Stevens-Roby Family Papers. For the chief work on the Roby letters, see Somerville, "Homesick," 178–96.

61. Sidney Roby to S. S. Breese, December 14, 1843, correspondence, folder 7, box 8; S. S. Breese to Sidney Roby, August 30, 1844, correspondence, box 9, folder 2, Breese-Stevens-Roby Family Papers.

62. Lucy Davis to Sabrina Bennet, September 25, 1846, in Kulick et al., *The New England Mill Village*, 399.

63. Robinson, *Loom and Spindle*, 38, 42.

64. Sally Rice to her parents, 1839, in Kulick et al., *The New England Mill Village*, 387–89.

65. Robinson, *Loom and Spindle*, 39.

66. Montrie, "'I Think Less of the Factory,'" 289–93. See also Zonderman, *Aspirations and Anxieties*, 71, 263, 265; Larcom, *A New England Girlhood*, 186–88.

67. Blewett, *Caught between Two Worlds*, 56.

68. Mary Ann Smith to Walter Smith, January 17, 1847, in Walter D. Smith Diary and Letters, 1842–1861, folder 112.01(c)02 (1847), Incoming Letters 1847, South Carolina Historical Society, Charleston.

69. Jemima W. Sanborn to Richard and Ruth Edwards Bennett, May 14, 1843, in Dublin, *Farm to Factory*, 90, 59–61.

70. Albee, *Confessions*, 150–52.

71. A. Putnam, "Diary"; Graff, *Conflicting Paths*, 43.

72. Francis Bennett Jr. Diary, January 10, 1852–December 31, 1854, Mss., American Antiquarian Society, quoted in Graff, *Conflicting Paths*, 83–84.

73. *Daily Sentinel and Gazette* (Milwaukee), January 1, 1848; *New York Herald*, January 4, 1857; *New York Herald*, January 7, 1858, 3.

74. *New York Times*, May 16, 1860.

75. Sons of New Hampshire, *Festival*, 5, 14, 29; Sons of New Hampshire, *Second Festival*, 73, 74,103; "Festival of the Sons of New Hampshire," *New York Times*, November 3, 1853; Kett, *Rites of Passage*, 101.

76. Kett, *Rites of Passage*, 101.

77. Faragher, *Sugar Creek*, 50; Throne, "Population Study," 316.

78. Winkle, *The Politics of Community*, 3.

79. *Hallowell (Maine) Gazette*, January 7, 1818, 2.

80. Wilkey, *Western Emigration*, 5.

81. Elias Lothrop to his wife, December 30, 1843, box 1, folder 1, Lothrop Family Papers.

82. Francis, "The Original manuscript Diary," January 4, 1846, 15.

83. *New Hampshire Sentinel*, February 16, 1837, 2. Tocqueville wrote that women on the frontier were "both sad and resolute" (*Democracy in America*, 593–94).

84. Fickes, Diary, April 17, 1856, April 28, 1856, June 8, 1856, June 19, 1856, July 20, 1856, January 1, 1857.

85. Larcom, *A New England Girlhood*, 259, 262–63, 270.

86. Owen and Sarah Ward to Amasa and Mary Angell, with postscript from Clarissa Ward to Amasa and Mary Angell, May 1, 1825, John Carpenter Angell Family Correspondence.

87. Erickson, *Leaving England*, 38–39.

88. Daniels, *Coming to America*, 146; H. B. Johnson, "The Location of German Immigrants," 1–41.

89. *The Emigrant's True Guide*, 2, 39, 43, 44, 46–52.

90. Flower, *The Errors of Emigrants*, 26, 28–29.

91. Newhall, *The British Emigrants' "Hand Book,"* 62; William Cobbett, *Emigrant's Guide in 10 Letters Addressed to the Taxpayers of England* (London, 1829), 34–35, quoted in Erickson, *Leaving England*, 241; Flower, *The Errors of Emigrants*, 26, 28–29.

92. Burlend and Burlend, *A True Picture of Emigration*, 7, 12, 13, 112, 113, 155, 156.

93. Jan George Zahn, to his siblings, August 26, 1856, in Brinks, *Dutch American Voices*, 389.

94. Jon N. Bjørndalen to his parents, January 5, 1844, in Blegen, *Land of Their Choice*, 183, 186.

95. Carl Blümner to his sister, March 18, 1841, in Kamphoefner et al., *News from the Land of Freedom*, 104–5.

96. Stott, *Workers in the Metropolis*, 84, 84n.

97. Moltmann, "American-German Return Migration," 378–92.

98. Henrietta Jessen to Eleanore and Doreas Williamsin, February 20, 1850, in Blegen, *Land of Their Choice*, 264.

99. Gro Svendsen journal, May 8, 1862, in Farseth and Blegen, *Frontier Mother*, 16.

100. Brite, *The Attitude*, 195–96; K. A. Miller, *Emigrants and Exiles*, 128–29, 243, 306–8.

101. Sjur J. Haaeim to Bishop Jacob Neumann, April 22, 1839, in Blegen, *Land of Their Choice*, 48–51; Blegen, *Norwegian Migration*, 81.

102. S. Stevall to Pastor Carlsson, in H. A. Barton, *Letters from the Promised Land*, 69–70.

103. "Journal of a Voyage," December 25, 1806, and "Diary of a Tour, Made Through the Interior Provinces of New Spain, in the Year 1807, by Captain Z. M. Pike, of the Army of the United States, When Under an Escort of Spanish Dragoons, July 1, 1807," in Hart and Hulber, *The Southwestern Journals of Zebulon Pike*, 157–58, 239.

104. Preuss, journal entries, June 12, 1842, August 11, 1842; *Exploring with Frémont*, 5, 38.

105. Stillson, *Spreading the Word*, 8.

106. Limerick, *The Legacy of Conquest*, 38.

107. Narcissa Prentiss Whitman diary, August 6, 1836; letter to Harriet, August 12, 1836; letter to "Brother Oren and Sister Nancy," October 24, 1836, 5, 15, 17.

108. Mary Richardson Walker diary, June 10, 1838; September 10, 1838.

109. Holland, "Diary," 18, quoted in Winders, *Mr. Polk's Army*, 129.

110. "From an Ohio Volunteer," *Tri-Weekly Ohio Statesman*, August 10, 1846.

111. "Hardships of the War," *Morning News* (New London, CT), September 10, 1846.

112. Scribner, *Camp Life*, 25, 35, 37; for further discussion of this episode, see Winders, *Mr. Polk's Army*, 130.

113. "Item from Baltimore," *New York Herald*, January 9, 1848.

114. Winders, *Mr. Polk's Army*, 121–23.

115. See, for instance, Larrey, *Surgical Essays*; Combe, *Observations*; Bucknill and Tuke, *A Manual*; Burrows, *Commentaries*.

116. G. Johnson, "The Medical Topography," 1.

117. "Nostalgia or Home Sickness," 1–2.

118. Rohrbough, *Days of Gold*, 35; Brian Roberts, *American Alchemy*, 69–74.

119. Mulford, *Prentice Mulford's Story*, 7; Starr, *Americans*, 63.

120. Stephen Crary to Rowena Crary, August 2, 1860, box 1, folder 6, Rowena and Stephen Crary Family Papers.

121. Elbridge Gerry Hall to his wife, May 20, 1849, typed transcript of letters from Elbridge Gerry Hall, BioFile.

122. Men living along the East Coast most frequently chose the sea route; those living inland, the overland route. Holliday, *The World Rushed In*, 50–51; Howe, *What Hath God Wrought*, 816.

123. Enos Christman to Ellen Apple, June 30, 1849, in diary, Enos Christman Journals and Correspondence.

124. Stillson, *Spreading the Word*, 88–89.

125. Unruh, *The Plains Across*, 125.

126. William Peacock to his wife, April 27, 1850, in *The Peacock Letters*, 10.

127. Tiffany, *Overland Journey*.

128. Webster, *The Gold Seekers*, 55.

129. Tiffany, *Overland Journey*, July 4, 1849, 74.

130. Backus, July 8, 1849, in *Overland Journey*.

131. William Peacock to his wife, August 24, 1850, in *The Peacock Letters*, 20.

132. Bianca Morse Federico and Myrtle Brown, eds., *Gold Rush: The Letters of Joel and Ann Brown, 1852, 1854–1855* (Washington, DC.: Federico, 1974), quoted in Jeffrey, *Frontier Women*, 118.

133. Alverson, *Sixty Years of California Song*, 28–29.

134. Alverson, *Sixty Years of California Song*, 28–32; Jeffrey, *Frontier Women*, 127.

135. William Taylor, *California Life Illustrated*, 78.

136. Christman, *One Man's Gold*, 204–5; S. L. Johnson, *Roaring Camp*, 139.

137. The feelings of women traveling to the trans-Mississippi West is one part of the history of homesickness that has garnered attention. See, for instance, Jeffrey, *Frontier Women*, 36–68; Faragher, *Women and Men on the Overland Trail*, 142–43, 173–78. For discussions of women who welcomed the liberation of life in the West, see Levy, *They Saw the Elephant*, 109.

138. Alverson, *Sixty Years of California Song*, 14.

139. Mary Ballou to her son Selden, October 30, 1852, in Ballou, *Voyage to California*, 6.

140. Rohrbough, *Days of Gold*, 135–66.

141. Ballou, *Voyage to California*, 1, 2–6, 8–9, 11; Ballou to her son Selden, October 30, 1852, 6.

142. Holliday, *The World Rushed In*, 53.

143. Henkin, *The Postal Age*.

144. Hafen, *The Overland Mail*, 45.

145. Enos Christman Journals and Correspondence, February 24, 1850.

146. William Taylor, *Seven Years' Street Preaching*, 284, 288; William Taylor, *California Life Illustrated*, 203.

147. "Letter from California," *Pittsfield (Massachusetts) Sun*, January 31, 1850.

148. Tocqueville, *Democracy in America*, 517–18. Benedict Anderson has likewise suggested that print culture, and in particular newspapers, helped create community among people who did not know each other (*Imagined Communities*).

149. Dana, *Two Years before the Mast*, 151; Henkin, *The Postal Age*, 43, 46.

150. Alonzo Delano quoted in Holliday, *The World Rushed In*, 318.

151. Lewis, "Photographing the California Gold Rush," 11–17; Henkin, *The Postal Age*, 57–60.

152. Abby Mansur to her sister Hannah, September 12, 1852; Abby Mansur to her sister Hannah and her brother, December 12 1852; Abby Mansur to her sister Hannah, 1854; Abby Mansur to her sister Hannah and her mother, December 9, 1854, in Abby T. Leighton Mansur Correspondence.

153. William Taylor, *California Life Illustrated*, 174.

154. William Taylor, *California Life Illustrated*, 213.

155. William Murray to his wife, November 14, 1852, in William Murray Letters.

156. William Murray to his wife, September 27, 1849, in William Murray Letters.

157. William Peacock to his wife, January 5, 1851, in *The Peacock Letters*, 23.

158. Daniel W. Coit, *Digging for Gold Without a Shovel*, ed. George P. Hammond (Denver: Old West, 1967), 98, quoted in Holliday, *The World Rushed In*, 414.

159. Holliday, *Rush for Riches*, 153.

160. William Peacock to his wife, January 5, 1851, in *The Peacock Letters*, 22–23.

161. William Taylor, *California Life Illustrated*, 282–84.

162. Elias Lothrop to his wife, September 14, 1850, box 1, folder 3; Elias Lothrop to his mother, September 21, 1851, box 1, folder 4, Lothrop Family Papers. For discussion of such decisions, see Rohrbough, *Days of Gold*, 262–63.

163. Enos Christman to Ellen Apple, April 10, 1852, in Enos Christman Journal and Correspondence.

164. Levi Kenaga to Benjamin Kenaga, March 28, 1866, box 2, series 1, folder 60, Kenaga Family Papers.

165. "Prevalence of Insanity in California—Causes," 241–42; Wilkins, "Insanity in California." 136–57; K. Thompson, "Early California," 45, 53–54.

166. Kotchemidova, "From Good Cheer to 'Drive-by Smiling.'"

CHAPTER 3

1. Alexander Hays to Mrs. Hays, June 15, 1862, in G. T. Fleming, *Life and Letters*, 232.

2. Benjamin Franklin Butler to Sarah Hildreth Butler, August 17, 1864; Benjamin Franklin Butler to Sarah Hildreth Butler, August 19, 1864; Benjamin Franklin Butler to Sarah Hildreth Butler, August 20, 1864, in Butler, *Private and Official Correspondence*, 5:65, 78, 85.

3. The historians Reid Mitchell, Aaron Sheehan-Dean, and Stephen W. Berry have explored how domestic ideals motivated Union and Confederate soldiers, leading them to see the war as a fight for home and for women. Similarly, Alice Fahs has demonstrated that Americans considered soldiers' domestic ties to their mothers as an admirable source of strength rather than a weakness. James McPherson, Frances Clarke, and David Anderson, however, have shown that this commitment to home could undermine men's fighting spirit. Mitchell, *The Vacant Chair;* Sheehan-Dean, *Why Confederates Fought,* 2, 4, 7, 10; S. W. Berry, *All That Makes a Man,* 171; Hess, *The Union Soldier,* 124, 126; Fahs, *The Imagined Civil War,* 105, 111–12; McPherson, *For Cause and Comrades,* 95, 134; Clarke, "So Lonesome I Could Die," 253–82; D. Anderson, "Dying of *Nostalgia*," 247–82; Megan J. McClintock, "The Impact of the Civil War on Nineteenth-Century Marriages," in Cimbala and Miller, *Union Soldiers,* 396.

4. McPherson, *Battle Cry of Freedom,* 306–7n; McPherson, *For Cause and Comrades,* 131; Sheehan-Davis, *Why Confederates Fought,* 59–60.

5. McPherson, *Battle Cry of Freedom,* 316–23.

6. Linderman, *Embattled Courage;* McPherson, *For Cause and Comrades,* 25. See also Fred Shannon, "The Life of the Common Soldier in the Union Army, 1861–1865," in M. Barton and Logue, *The Civil War Soldier,* 100; Hess, *The Union Soldier,* 96.

7. McPherson, *For Cause and Comrades,* 9, 174.

8. Clarke, "So Lonesome I Could Die," 254; Matt, "You Can't Go Home Again," 482–84.

9. U.S. Office of the Surgeon General, *The Medical and Surgical History of the War of the Rebellion,* part 1, vol. 1, *Medical History,* 639, 651–711. There is a statistical error in the final chart tallying African American cases; it says 334, but it should be 324. See also D. L. Anderson and Anderson, "Nostalgia and Malingering," 157.

10. Greene, *Letters,* preface.

11. Clara Downing to William Greene, January 2, 1861 [1862], in Greene, *Letters,* 16.

12. Linderman, *Embattled Courage,* 87–90. McPherson gives examples of women urging their husband to desert, indicating that while women's concerns about men's honor were common, they were not universal (*For Cause and Comrades,* 137).

13. Susan Greene to William Greene, January 7, 1862, in Greene, *Letters,* 26. Susan's desires vacillated. Sometimes she encouraged her son to use other means to get home, most of them involving a medical furlough.

14. Clara E. Downing to William Greene, January 19, 1862, in Greene, *Letters,* 48.

15. William Greene to Susan Greene, January 12, 1862, in Greene, *Letters,* 38.

16. William Greene to Susan Greene, February 1, 1862, in Greene, *Letters,* 64–65.

17. William Greene to Susan Greene, July, 1862, William Greene to Susan Greene, December 1, 1864, in Greene, *Letters,* 131, 271.

18. Fahs, *The Imagined Civil War,* 106.

19. Hess, *The Union Soldier,* 96.

20. Letter from Chauncey Herbert Cooke to his mother and father, October 20, 1862, in C. H. Cooke, "A Badger Boy in Blue," 84.

21. Charles Wright Wills, diary entry, September 17, 1861, in Wills, *Army Life,* 32.

22. Calvin Shedd to his wife and children, June 1, 1862, in Calvin Shedd Papers.

23. William G. Vardell to his wife, Jennie, June 8, 1863, box 1, William G. Vardell Letters. For further examples of Confederate soldiers' thoughts on home and duty, see Sheehan-Davis, *Why Confederates Fought,* 153.

24. William Gould to his sister, December 25, 1862; Richard Gould to his sister, February 3, 1863, in Harris and Niflot, *Dear Sister,* 28–29, 58–59.

25. Benjamin Kenaga to Fanny Reist Kenaga, August 19, 1864, series 1, box 2, folder 49, Kenaga Family Papers.

26. Benjamin Kenaga to Fanny Reist Kenaga, September 8, 1864, series 1, box 2, folder 49, Kenaga Family Papers.

27. "The Bull's Run Battle," *New York Herald,* July 27, 1861.

28. "Reporting on Bull Run," *New York Times,* July 23, 1861.

29. There is debate as to how the Emancipation Proclamation affected soldiers' will to fight. McPherson suggests it had a significant effect (*For Cause and Comrades,* 123); Chandra Manning says its effects were minimal (*What This Cruel War Was Over,* 86–95, 255n–256n).

30. McClellan to Ellen McClellan, September 25, October 5, 1862, McClellan Papers, Library of Congress, quoted in McPherson, *Battle Cry of Freedom,* 559.

31. James Fortiner to Emma, March 8, 1863, in Pantovic Collection.

32. John Vliet to Mr. Bodge, February 2, 1863, in Thomas W. Sweeny Papers, Henry E. Huntington Library, quoted in McPherson, *For Cause and Comrades,* 123.

33. Manning, *What This Cruel War Was Over,* 95.

34. Calvin Shedd to his wife and children, February 26, 1863, in Calvin Shedd Papers.

35. J. T. Calhoun, "Nostalgia," 130–32.

36. Atwell, *Civil War Diary,* March 27, 1862, 71.

37. Livermore, *My Story of the War,* 140.

38. Livermore, *My Story of the War,* 141.

39. Daniel Holt to his wife, March 7, 1863, in Greiner et al., *A Surgeon's Civil War,* 78–79. See also McPherson, *For Cause and Comrades,* 132.

40. George Dawson to his wife, October 19, 1861, in Bock, "One Year at War," 171–72.

41. Tally Simpson to his sister, December 2, 1862, in Everson and Simpson, "*Far, Far from Home,*" 160.

42. McPherson, *For Cause and Comrades,* 132.

43. John Collins, January 24, 1865, in Redkey, *A Grand Army of Black Men,* 70.

44. Marion Hill Fitzpatrick to Amanda, October 29, 1863, in Fitzpatrick, *Letters to Amanda,* 97.

45. Livermore, *My Story of the War,* 140–41.

46. Tally Simpson to his sister, November 10, 1861, in Everson and Simpson, "*Far, Far from Home,*" 90.

47. William Watson to his sister Ella, December 21, 1862, in Fatout, *Letters of a Civil War Surgeon,* 43.

48. "Maine Law for Soldiers," in Sears, *Mr. Dunn Browne's Experiences,* 227.

49. Attie, *Patriotic Toil,* 3.

50. Livermore, *My Story of the War,* 136–41.

51. James I. Robertson Jr., "Fun, Frolics, and Firewater," in M. Barton and Logue, *The Civil War Soldier,* 123.

52. Quoted in Wiley, *The Life of Billy Yank,* 153; McPherson, *For Cause and Comrades,* 92.

53. Abbott, *Personal Recollections,* August 30, 1864, 142.

54. Wiley, *The Life of Billy Yank,* 161; Wiley, *The Life of Johnny Reb,* 156.

55. Wiley, *The Life of Johnny Reb,* 317. For another description of sentimental music and its effects, see Robertson, "Fun, Frolics, and Firewater," 124–25.

56. George F. Root, "Just before the Battle, Mother"; Walter Kittredge, "Tenting on the Old Camp Ground," in Silber, *Soldier Songs,* 12–13, 50.

57. J. T. Calhoun, "Nostalgia," 130–32; S. M. Thompson, *Thirteenth Regiment,* 61; Numa Barned to A. Barned, March 27, 1863, quoted in Mitchell, *The Vacant Chair,* 26.

58. Elias Fogelsonger, January 22 1862, box 1, series 1, folder 29, Kenaga Family Papers.

59. William G. Vardell to his wife, June 8, 1863; William G. Vardell to his wife, June 30, 1863, William G. Vardell Letters, box 1.

60. For a discussion of soldiers' alienation from civilian life, see Linderman, *Embattled Courage,* 216–39.

61. Quoted in Ford, *The Story of the Fifteenth Regiment Massachusetts,* 62.

62. Porter, "The War Diary," 287.

63. "Dunn Browne's Thanksgiving in Camp," November 29, 1862, in Sears, *Mr. Dunn Browne's Experiences,* 47.

64. Thomas W. Smith to his brother, November 30, 1862, in T. W. Smith, *"We Have it Damn Hard Out Here,"* 69–70.

65. Charles Brackett to his wife, December 24, 1862, in Brackett, *Surgeon on Horseback,* 199–200.

66. John Samuel Apperson diary, December 24, 1862, in Apperson, *Repairing the "March of Mars,"* 332.

67. Letter from F. O. Danielson to his parents, June 22, 1862, in Check, "Civil War Letters," 7.

68. Richard Gould to his sister, January 13, 1864; Wesley Gould to his brother-in-law, October 25, 1862; Richard Gould to his sister, June 1, 1864, in Harris and Niflot, *Dear Sister,* 118, 35, 127.

69. Catton, "Hayfoot, Strawfoot!" 30–37; Shannnon, "The Life of the Common Soldier in the Union Army," 101.

70. Eric T. Dean Jr., "'Dangled over Hell': The Trauma of the Civil War," in M. Barton and Logue, *The Civil War Soldier,* 398–401. For a description of Confederate shortages, see Mitchell, *Civil War Soldiers,* 58–61, 160–67.

71. Lonn, *Desertion,* 30, 153.

72. Marrs, "Desertion and Loyalty," 59–63.

73. Lonn, *Desertion,* 16.

74. Benjamin Franklin Butler to Abraham Lincoln, May 1, 1864, in Butler, *Private and Official Correspondence,* 4:147–48.

75. William Fuller, "Thesis on Malingering," in Castel, "Malingering," 29–30.

76. Mitchell, *The Vacant Chair,* 142; Faust, *This Republic of Suffering,* 175.

77. Wesley to his sister, March 18, 1862; Richard Gould to Hannah, March 15, 1863; William Gould to his sister, September 25, 1863; James to Hannah, January 8, 1865, in Harris and Niflot, *Dear Sister,* 15, 67, 105, 150.

78. William R. Barry to his wife, Sarah, December 22, 1862, folder 256.01.01 © 01 Correspondence 1862, William R. Barry Correspondence.

79. Charles Brackett to his daughter, August 18, 1861; to his wife, September 23, 1861, in Brackett, *Surgeon on Horseback,* 9, 31–32. For more examples, see McPherson, *For Cause and Comrades,* 70.

80. J. R. Montgomery to his father, May 10, 1864, Museum of the Confederacy, Richmond, Virginia, quoted in Wiley, *The Common Soldier,* 133–35.

81. Castleman, *The Army of the Potomac,* 44.

82. Quoted in Wiley, *The Life of Billy Yank,* 292.

83. Richard Gould to Hannah, April 13, 1864, in Harris and Niflot, *Dear Sister,* 125.

84. Cyrus F. Boyd diary, February 16, 1863, in Boyd, *The Civil War Diary,* 125.

85. Benjamin Kenaga to Fanny Reist Kenaga, September 8, 1864, series 1, box 2, folder 49, Kenaga Family Papers.

86. Charles Mattocks to his mother, September 22, 1864, in Mattocks, *Unspoiled Heart,* 217.

87. McElroy, *Andersonville,* 60–62.

88. "The Prisoner of War in Texas," *Beadles Monthly, a Magazine of Today,* January 1866, 42–43.

89. U. S. Office of the Surgeon General, *The Medical and Surgical History of the War of the Rebellion,* part 1, vol. 1, *Medical History,* 148–49, 298–99, 638–39, 651–711.

90. Clarke, "So Lonesome I Could Die," 273n; Cunningham, *Doctors in Gray,* 184.

91. U. S. Office of the Surgeon General, *The Medical and Surgical History of the War of the Rebellion,* part 3, vol. 1, *Medical History,* 885–86; Peters, "Remarks," 75–76; J. T. Calhoun, "Nostalgia," 130–32.

92. Woodward, *Outlines of the Chief Camp Diseases*, 70; Bartholow, *A Manual*, 21–22; Ordronaux, *Manual of Instructions*.

93. Clarke, "So Lonesome I Could Die."

94. Peters, "Remarks," 75–76.

95. U. S. Office of the Surgeon General, *The Medical and Surgical History of the War of the Rebellion*, part 3, vol. 1, *Medical History*, 885–86.

96. J. T. Calhoun, "Nostalgia," 130–32.

97. John Taylor quoted in U. S. Office of the Surgeon General, *The Medical and Surgical History of the War of the Rebellion*, part 3, vol. 1, 885–86; see also D. L. Anderson and Anderson, "Nostalgia and Malingering," 160.

98. Bartholow, *A Manual*, 21–22.

99. John Taylor quoted in U. S. Office of the Surgeon General, *The Medical and Surgical History of the War of the Rebellion*, part 3, vol. 1, 885–86.

100. "Medical Society of the Second Division," 150.

101. "Testimony of Surgeon Stevenson," in "Contributions relating to the Causation and Prevention of Disease, And To Camp Diseases Together with A Report of the Diseases, Etc., Among the Prisoners at Andersonville, GA," in Flint, *Sanitary Memoirs*, 100.

102. "Sanitary Condition of Vermont Troops," 353.

103. Peters, "Remarks," 75–76.

104. Thomas Wentworth Higginson journal, February 11, 1864, in Looby, *The Complete Civil War Journal*, 192.

105. *New York Times*, November 28, 1863; Clarke, "So Lonesome I Could Die," 257; D. Anderson, "Dying of *Nostalgia*," 259–61.

106. Peters, "Remarks," 75. 75; U.S. Office of the Surgeon General, *The Medical and Surgical History of the War of the Rebellion*, part 3, vol. 1, *Medical History*, 885.

107. Clarke, "So Lonesome I Could Die," 267–68; Hess, *The Union Soldier*, 33, 36.

108. U.S. Office of the Surgeon General, *The Medical and Surgical History of the War of the Rebellion*, part 3, vol. 1, *Medical History*, 885–86.

109. J. T. Calhoun, "Nostalgia," 130–32, emphasis in original.

110. Thomas Wentworth Higginson journal, November 6, 1863, in Looby, *The Complete Civil War Journal*, 171–72; Ordronaux, *Manual of Instructions*, 63–64.

111. Clarke, "So Lonesome I Could Die," 268–69.

112. McPherson, *Battle Cry of Freedom*, 478–85.

113. Mitchell, *The Vacant Chair*, 76–77; Dammann and Bollet, *Images of Civil War Medicine*, 24.

114. Alcott, *Hospital Sketches*, 51–52.

115. Livermore, *My Story of the War*, 201–4.

116. Reid, *The Vacant Chair*, 71–87.

117. Walt Whitman, "Hospital Visits," in Bucke, *The Wound Dresser*, 42.

118. William G. Vardell to his wife, June 8, 1863, in William G. Vardell Letters.

119. Mitchell, *The Vacant Chair*, 135–37; Linderman, *Embattled Courage*, 216.

120. Linderman, *Embattled Courage*, 216–38; Mitchell, *Civil War Soldiers*, 56, 57, 88.

121. See, for instance, Sheehan-Dean, *Why Confederates Fought*, 6, 75, 88, 94.

122. Catton, *Reflections*; Linderman, *Embattled Courage*, 274–75.

123. For a discussion of this sense of loss, see Faust, *This Republic of Suffering*, 266–71; Linderman, *Embattled Courage*, 266–97.

CHAPTER 4

1. R. Edwards, *New Spirits*, 106.

2. This runs counter to George Rosen's analysis, which suggests that American discussions of the condition came later than European commentaries and essentially subsided after

the Civil War. In actuality, the Civil War invigorated discussions of the condition, and they expanded for the next four decades. See Rosen, "Nostalgia," 46.

3. Some historians, most notably Peter Fritzsche, suggest that this sense of the unrecoverability of times past developed earlier both in Europe and America as a result of the political upheavals of the eighteenth century. It seems clear that in the United States, however, the sense that return was impossible came more gradually, gaining wide acceptance only in the wake of the Civil War, massive immigration, urbanization, and industrialization. See Fritzsche, "Specters of History," 1587–618.

4. Mrs. S. H. Reed to William Randolph Barry, August 23, 1861, folder 256.01.01 © 01 (1861) in William R. Barry Correspondence.

5. W. T. Taylor, "Nostalgia," 122.

6. Chestnut and Pryor quoted in D. Anderson, "Down Memory Lane," 112–13, 117, 132.

7. Quoted in Blight, *Race and Reunion*, 42.

8. Blight, *Race and Reunion*; Litwack, *Been in the Storm So Long*, 301–2.

9. Quoted in Litwack, *Been in the Storm So Long*, 302.

10. "The Negroes of the Southwest," *New York Times*, November 28, 1863.

11. Quoted in Litwack, *Been in the Storm So Long*, 296–97.

12. Quoted in Litwack, *Been in the Storm So Long*, 306–7; Kaye, *Joining Places*, 212.

13. Vlach, *Back of the Big House*, ix, x.

14. Litwack, *Been in the Storm So Long*, 310.

15. Berlin, *The Making of African America*, 134; Foner, *Reconstruction*, 599; Clegg, *The Price of Liberty*, 256.

16. Williams, *The Liberian Exodus*, 2.

17. Clegg, *The Price of Liberty*, 259.

18. "Another Wail from Liberia," newspaper clipping, n.p., n.d, in Willis, Azor Scrapbook.

19. "The Azor Folks in Liberia. How they are getting on in the 'Land of Promise,'" newspaper clipping, n.p., May 13, 1879, in Willis, Azor Scrapbook.

20. Litwack, *Been in the Storm So Long*, 313; Robert G. Barrows, "Urbanizing America," in C. Calhoun, *The Gilded Age*, 106.

21. R. Edwards, *New Spirits*, 31.

22. "The Exodusters," *Christian Recorder*, February 17, 1881; Foner, *Reconstruction*, 600.

23. R. Edwards, *New Spirits*, 31.

24. Wells, *Crusade for Justice*, 79.

25. Julius L Mitchell to Mr. James Logan, August 31, 1904, in James Raymond Logan Scrapbook Collection, box 1, Correspondence 1904–1910.

26. Harleston, *The Toiler's Life*, 48–49, 61–62, 113–14.

27. Berlin, *The Making of African America*, 132, 134–35.

28. Clegg, *The Price of Liberty*, 260.

29. Sernett, *Bound for the Promised Land*, 21–22.

30. Quoted in Litwack, *Been in the Storm So Long*, 307.

31. "Negro Colonization," *Chicago Herald*, January 12, 1890, 4.

32. Quoted in Litwack, *Been in the Storm So Long*, 317.

33. Quoted in Sernett, *Bound for the Promised Land*, 20.

34. "Washington at Hampton," 325–26.

35. Edward J. Danzinger Jr., "Native American Resistance and Accommodation during the Late Nineteenth Century," in C. Calhoun, *The Gilded Age*, 182.

36. Danzinger, "Native American Resistance and Accommodation," 168.

37. Dodge, *Our Wild Indians*, 50, 311–14.

38. Quoted in Dee Brown, *Bury My Heart at Wounded Knee*, 31, 32, 34, 36.

39. Dee Brown, *Bury My Heart at Wounded Knee*, 100.

40. Dee Brown, *Bury my Heart at Wounded Knee*, 354; "The Poncas' Complaints: Col. Kemble's Story of How the Removal Was Effected," *New York Times*, February 15, 1880.

41. Dee Brown, *Bury my Heart at Wounded Knee*, 317–18, 328–30; Danzinger, "Native American Resistance and Accommodation," 170.

42. Adams, *Education for Extinction*, 22–23.

43. M. C. Coleman, *American Indian Children*, 41.

44. Adams, *Education for Extinction*, 28–51.

45. M. C. Coleman, *American Indian Children*, 60; Adams, *Education for Extinction*, 210–11; Ellis, *To Change Them Forever*, 98.

46. Stewart, *A Voice in Her Tribe*, 15, 16, 28–29; M. C. Coleman, *American Indian Children*, 80.

47. "Interview between Captain R. H. Pratt, Supt. Indian School, Carlisle, Pa, and Mr. Spears of the *New York Sun*," October 7, 1896, typed transcript, 1, 5, 8, 13, 14, box 19, folder 679, Richard Henry Pratt Papers.

48. *School News*, July 1880, 2, Beinecke.

49. "A Happy Little Caddo Boy who came last month, writes his first letter home," *School News*, September 1882, 4, Beinecke.

50. Adams, *Education for Extinction*, 225; Archuleta et al., *Away from Home*, 28; Ellis, *To Change Them Forever*, 107–9.

51. "Indian Girls Guilty of Arson," *New York Times*, February 8, 1898.

52. *School News*, July 1880, Beinecke.

53. "Roman Nose Goes to New York," *School News*, September, 1880, Beinecke.

54. *School News*, July 1882, 3, Beinecke.

55. Embe (Burgess?), *Stiya*, 1–7, 13, 15, 113, 115.

56. Alford, *Civilization*, 111; Stewart, *A Voice in Her Tribe*, 33; M. C. Coleman, *American Indian Children*, 178–79. Michael Coleman (178–89) and David Wallace Adams (*Education for Extinction*, 273–306) note that readjustment problems were common.

57. Zitkala-Ša, *American Indian Stories*, 108.

58. Hoganson, *Fighting for American Manhood*, 6, 27, 36, 37, quotes on 141, 152–53. See also Bederman, *Manliness and Civilization*, 170–71, 187–96.

59. "Nostalgia," *Congregationalist* 83 (August 11, 1898): 184.

60. "Died of Homesickness," *Kansas City Star*, July 29, 1898.

61. Hoganson, *Fighting for American Manhood*, 7.

62. *Aberdeen Daily News*, September 5, 1898. See also *St. Louis Republic*. June 3, 1900; *Biloxi Daily Herald*, March 15, 1902. For an example of the medical literature on the conflict and nostalgia, see Corson, "Nostalgia and Melancholia in the Tropics," 743.

63. Chudacoff, *The Age of the Bachelor*, 6.

64. "A Selfish Disease," *Alaska Dispatch*, September 4, 1900.

65. "Nostalgia," *Christian Advocate* 73 (September 22, 1898): 1552.

66. "Nostalgia, or Homesickness," *Appleton's Journal of Literature, Science and Art* 2 (October 9, 1869): 238.

67. "Nostalgia, or Homesickness," 660.

68. P. N. Stearns, *American Cool*, 54.

69. Kline, "The Migratory Impulse," 50–51, 57, 68, 78, 80.

70. P. N. Stearns, *American Cool*, 54.

71. Conwell, *Manhood's Morning*, 46, 47, 259.

72. Barrows, "Urbanizing America," in C. Calhoun, *The Gilded Age*, 102.

73. Chudacoff, *The Age of the Bachelor*, 48–55; Meyerowitz, *Women Adrift*, 2–20.

74. Darrow, *The Story of My Life*, 42.

75. Interview with Judge Wm. F. Harding (Sidney Saylor), *American Life Histories*.

76. Albert Wilbur to George Wilbur, September 3, 1876, box 12, folder 258, George W. Wilbur Family Papers.

77. Albert Wilbur to George Wilbur, October 12, 1876, box 12, folder 259, George W. Wilbur Family Papers.

78. Albert Wilbur to George Wilbur, January 3, 1877, box 12, folder 260, George W. Wilbur Family Papers.

79. George Wilbur to Sarah Ann Cook Wilbur, August 17, 1875, box 1, folder 9, George W. Wilbur Family Papers.

80. Albert Wilbur to Sarah Ann Cook Wilbur, January 7, 1879, box 20, folder 430, George W. Wilbur Family Papers.

81. Albert Wilbur to Sarah Ann Cook Wilbur, February 25, 1881, box 20, folder 435, George W. Wilbur Family Papers.

82. Quoted in Boyer, *Urban Masses*, 113–17; Chudacoff, *The Age of the Bachelor*, 164, 158.

83. Chudacoff, *The Age of the Bachelor*, 163–66.

84. P. N. Stearns, *American Cool*, 82.

85. "Heimweh-Homesickness," *Zion's Herald* 75 (May 19, 1897): 311. See also "His Father's Home," *Youth's Companion* 73 (March 23, 1889): 142; Robert Allyn, "Homesickness," *Christian Advocate* 47 (August 8, 1872): 254.

86. Victorians expected women to repress emotions more often than men; however, this was not true of homesickness. Some examples can be seen in discussions of women's anger and jealousy in P. N. Stearns, *American Cool*, 83.

87. Susan Coolidge, "How Alice and Lotty Went to the Farm," *Independent* 21 (September 9, 1862): 3.

88. Augusta Moore, "Homesickness in a Snow Storm," *New York Evangelist* 59 (March 22, 1888): 2.

89. Sangster, *The Art of Home-Making*, 226–28, 421–23.

90. "Country Girls in the City. Chapter II. Shall I Go to the City?," *Youth's Companion* 48 (December 2, 1875): 399.

91. Meyerowitz, *Women Adrift*, 48–49, 60–68.

92. Sangster, *The Art of Home-Making*, 228.

93. Meyerowitz, *Women Adrift*, 46–47, 82, 53–54, quote on 50.

94. For more on nostalgia, and why it became pervasive during the Gilded Age, see F. Davis, *Yearning for Yesterday*, 49; Lears, *No Place of Grace*, 12; Kammen, *Mystic Chords of Memory*, 255. For a different time frame, see Fritzsche, *Stranded in the Present*, 160–62; Fritzsche, "Specters of History," 1587–618.

95. Faragher, *Sugar Creek*, 219, 221–23.

96. Faust, *This Republic of Suffering*, 268.

97. Faust, *This Republic of Suffering*, 194–210.

98. Quoted in Berthoff, *An Unsettled People*, 396, 400.

99. Garland, *A Son of the Middle Border*, 440.

100. P. K. Hall and Ruggles, "'Restless,'" 836.

101. Peter Fritzsche has suggested that modern Americans experience a nostalgia free of melancholy, but that in earlier centuries individuals mourned the past with great sadness ("Specters of History," 1618).

102. Conwell, *Manhood's Morning*, 47.

103. Quoted in Burns, "The Country Boy," 60; L. M. Edwards, "Noble Domesticity," 27.

104. Burns, "The Country Boy," 62–63.

105. Conwell, *Manhood's Morning*, 47.

106. Alice Turner Curtis, "Homesickness," *New England Magazine* 21 (October 1899): 144.

107. Joseph C. Lincoln, "Coming Home," *Saturday Evening Post* 176 (November 21, 1903):14.

108. Page, *The Old South*, 143–48; D. Anderson, "Down Memory Lane," 110.

109. Blight, *Race and Reunion*, 286, 284, 313–15.

110. W. A. White, *The Autobiography*, 34–36.

111. K. Jackson, *Crabgrass Frontier*, 73–86.

112. Blair, *Bridging Two Eras*, 64–65.

113. Dona Brown, *Inventing New England*, 106–9, 135–68.

114. R. M. Taylor, "Summoning the Wandering Tribes," 23; R. M. Taylor, "The Olin Tribe."

115. "Notable Family Reunion," *New York Times*, May 8, 1887.

116. R. M. Taylor, "Summoning the Wandering Tribes," 21–23; More, *History of the More Family*, 22.

117. *Family Gathering on the French Homestead*, 3–5.

118. "New Hampshire's Old Home Week at Hand," *Boston Morning Journal*, August 16, 1902; "Old Home Week," *Boston Journal*, May 8, 1899. For rich imagery of Old Home Week, see Crooker, *Images of America*.

119. "Old Home Week," *Worcester (Massachusetts) Daily Spy*, August 1, 1902.

120. "'Old Home Week' the Rage," *Montgomery Advertiser*, April 23, 1903.

121. *Springfield (Massachusetts) Republican*, August 13, 1909.

122. Damon, "'Home Again.'"

123. *Springfield (Massachusetts) Daily Republican*, July 30, 1902; Dona Brown, *Inventing New England*, 128–29.

124. "'Old Home Week' the Rage."

125. Dona Brown, *Inventing New England*, 106; Craven, *The Legend of the Founding Fathers*, 91–92.

126. For family gatherings, relatives sometimes chartered trains for their return, as members of the Olin tribe did in 1887. Another way westerners returned to the East was by having a whole community charter a train, as a group of homesick Oklahomans did in 1913. See R. M. Taylor, "The Olin Tribe," 249, 250; R. M. Taylor, "Summoning the Wandering Tribes," 25–26; "Association for Homegoing Trip, Medford, Oklah," *Daily Oklahoman*, January 5, 1913.

127. Thomas F. Anderson, "'Old-Home Week' in New England," *New England Magazine* 34 (August 1906): 674–75.

128. "Nostalgia, or Homesickness," 238.

CHAPTER 5

1. Jacob Harms Dunnink to his family, December 15, 1851, in Brinks, *Dutch American Voices*, 33.

2. Byrne, *Irish Emigration*, 21.

3. Nugent, *Crossings*, 31–33, 45, 150; Peffer, *If They Don't Bring Their Women Here*, 1–2; Takaki, *Strangers from a Distant Shore*, 69, 71; "California: Opening of a New Steamship Line to China," *New York Times*, February 3, 1867.

4. G. R. Taylor and Neu, *The American Railroad Network*, 18; Trennert, "The Southern Pacific Railroad of Mexico," 266.

5. Dinnerstein and Reimers, *Ethnic Americans*, 11.

6. Wyman, *Round-Trip to America*, 4, 21; Bodnar, *The Transplanted*, 45, 52, 53, 71, 84.

7. Takaki, *Strangers from a Different Shore*, 244.

8. Park and Miller, *Old World Traits*, 150–51. For an example of the same phenomenon among Polish immigrants, see Thomas and Znaniecki, *The Polish Peasant*, 1493–94.

9. Hans Hansen to his father, May 4, 1890, in Zempel, *In Their Own Words*, 130–32.

10. Umberto Dini interviewed by Adrian Bernard, June 16, 1979, 3, box 1, *Italians in Chicago—Oral History*.

11. See, for instance, Johann Bauer to his mother, September 2, 1857, in Kamphoefner et al., *News from the Land of Freedom*, 157; Ann Whittaker to her brother James, January 1849, in Erickson, *Invisible Immigrants*, 183; John and Margaret Griffiths to Edward Roberts, March 4, 1850, in Erickson, *Invisible Immigrants*, 199.

12. Morwaska, *For Bread with Butter,* 125.
13. Quoted in Wyman, *Round-Trip to America,* 130–31.
14. Quoted in Caroli, *Italian Repatriation,* 77.
15. Quoted in Takaki, *Strangers from a Different Shore,* 62.
16. Gamio, *The Life Story,* 91.
17. Lasker, *Filipino Immigration,* 117; For another example, see "Field Notes by Theodosia M. Samano of Migratory Laborers Imperial Valley, California," 12–13, carton 15, folder 9, Paul Schuster Taylor Papers.
18. Wyman, *Round-Trip to America,* 63.
19. Virtanen, *Settlement or Return,* 175–76; Wyman, *Round-Trip to America,* 90.
20. Caren Lundgren and Carla Martinelli, in Coan, *Ellis Island Interviews,* 342–43, 63–64.
21. "Reminiscence of Phillipe Lemay," in Doty, *The First Franco-Americans,* 17–18.
22. Wyman, *Round-Trip to America,* 83.
23. Nugent, *Crossings,* 156–57.
24. Foerster, *The Italian Emigration,* 428.
25. Wyman, *Round-Trip to America,* 10–12; Takaki, *Strangers from a Different Shore,* 10; Sarna, "The Myth of No Return," 257–67.
26. Mrs. Rose Benjamin, box 1, folder 4, Essays by Jewish-American Immigrant Women.
27. Sarna, "The Myth of No Return," 257–67.
28. "Homesick Russian Jews: Refugees Who Yearn for the Land of Persecution," *Dallas Morning News,* March 10, 1906; Sarna, "The Myth of No Return," 257–58.
29. Quoted in Kobrin, "Rewriting the Diaspora," 1, 10, 9.
30. *Caravan Weekly Pictorial* (Brooklyn), November 6, 1958, box 1, folder "Syrian Ladies Aid Society (Brooklyn New York),"Near Eastern Miscellaneous Manuscripts.
31. Park and Miller, *Old World Traits,* 130; Moltmann, "American-German Return Migration," 389.
32. Wyman, *Round-Trip to America,* 97–98; "Russian Jews Homesick," *Chicago Herald,* July 10, 1891; Virtanen, *Settlement or Return,* 184; "How Our Immigrants Are Induced to Leave Us," *New York Times,* January 22, 1911.
33. Simonsen, "Returned Emigrants," 50.
34. Quoted in Saloutos, *They Remember America,* 33.
35. Gamio, *The Life Story,* 26; Anthony Jarzynkowski to his brother and family, December 9, 1890, in Kula et al., *Writing Home,* 265.
36. Khater, *Inventing Home,* 63. See also Wyman, *Round-Trip to America,* 150; Takaki, *Strangers from a Different Shore,* 244.
37. Wyman, *Round-Trip to America,* 128.
38. Gunda, "America in Hungarian Folklore," 160.
39. Quoted in Boroff, "A Little Milk," 12–21, 74–81.
40. Marianne and Anthony Betlijowski to Joseph Pipka, February 9, 1891, in Kula et al., *Writing Home,* 189–90.
41. John Chmielewiski to his mother, February 18, 1891, in Kula et al., *Writing Home,* 214.
42. Morwaska, *For Bread with Butter,* 1.
43. Emma Huhtasaari to her mother, May 1, 1905, April 5, 1909, in H. A. Barton, *Letters from the Promised Land,* 236–37.
44. Akhtar, *Immigration and Identity,* 16.
45. Orsi, *The Madonna of 115th Street,* 24.
46. Kraut, *The Huddled Masses,* 17; Sarna, "The Myth of No Return," 261–63.
47. Hans Øverland to his father, March 30, 1889, in Zempel, *In Their Own Words,* 88.
48. "Homesick Russian Jews," 8.
49. John Muszeński to his wife, February 27, 1891, in Kula et al., *Writing Home,* 360.

50. Barbara Di Nucci Hendrickson, "Memoirs of a Father's Daughter," 3, box 1, folder 1, Barbara Di Nucci Hendrickson Papers.

51. Filomena Mazzei, interviewed by Antoinette Lo Bosco, typed transcript, 7, box 1, *Italians in Chicago—Oral History.*

52. Mrs. N. Revel, "A Synopsis of My Life," box 1, folder 2, "Foreign Childhood and Education," Essays by Jewish-American Immigrant Women.

53. Pasqua Sparvieri, interviewed by Anthony Mansueto, February 28, 1980, typed transcript, 14–15, box 2, *Italians in Chicago—Oral History.*

54. Pasqua Sparvieri, 16.

55. Akhtar, *Immigration and Identity,* 26.

56. Emma Huhtasaari to her mother, May 1, 1905, in H. A. Barton, *Letters from the Promised Land,* 236.

57. Faustina Wisniewska (?) to her parents, n.d., in Kula et al., *Writing Home,* 446.

58. Sophie Kosciowlowski, interviewed by Leslie F. Orear, March 1971, typed transcript, 2, box 1, Polish Miscellaneous Manuscript Collections.

59. Orsi, *The Madonna of 115th Street,* 28.

60. Maria Valiani, interviewed by Anthony Mansueto, June 10, 1981, typed transcript, 14–15, box 5, *Italians in Chicago—Oral History Project.*

61. Pasqua Sparvieri, 14.

62. Maria Petra Mendiola Loisate, interviewed by Kate Moore, July 6, 1994, series KM, no. 061, *Ellis Island Oral History Project.*

63. There is a rich literature on ethnic neighborhoods and their offerings for homesick immigrants. See for instance, L. Cohen, *Making a New Deal,* 11–158; E. Ewen, *Immigrant Women,* 63; Diner, *Hungering for America,* 9, 65. Matt, "A Hunger for Home," 6–17. Andrew Heinze suggests that Jewish immigrants in such neighborhoods adopted a more American style of consumer behavior (*Adapting to Abundance,* 42).

64. Caroli, *Italian Repatriation,* 85.

65. Vecoli, "Chicago's Italians," 165, 178, 180.

66. David Vanderstel dissertation quoted in Robert P. Swierenga, "Local Patterns of Dutch Migration to the United States in the Mid-Nineteenth Century," in Vecoli and Sinke, *A Century of European Migrations,* 146.

67. Orsi, *The Madonna of 115th Street,* 34.

68. Foerster, *The Italian Emigration,* 431–32. Donna Gabaccia suggests that regional factors as well as these local connections often influenced immigrant destinations (*Militants and Migrants,* 81).

69. Salvatore Castagnola, "Land Where My Father Died," 85, box 6, Italian Miscellaneous Manuscript Collections.

70. Sartorio, *Social and Religious Life,* 19.

71. Elenora Rantanen, interview by Vienna Maki, March 30, 1981, typed transcript, 2, 4, box 6, folder R-4b, Finnish American Family History Project.

72. Ernesto Galarza, "The Galarza Family in the Mexican Revolution, 1910: From Mexico to Sacramento," in Dublin, *Immigrant Voices,* 231–33.

73. Sophie Nadrowska to her parents, December 2, 1890, in Kula et al., *Writing Home,* 363–64.

74. McIntosh, *American Food Habits,* 92.

75. Swanson, "Fritiof Colling," 76–87.

76. In contrast, the historian Hasia Diner maintains that immigrants often reveled in their abilities to buy luxury foods in the United States that had been out of reach in the Old World. As a result, they sought not the daily foods of home but the holiday dishes only rarely eaten in their homelands. See Diner, *Hungering for America.*

77. Ida Lindgren, to her mother, July 1870 in H. A. Barton, *Letters from the Promised Land,* 144.

78. Berta Serina Kingestad to her sister, July 17, 1886; Berta Serina Kingestad to her Parents, Brothers, and Sisters, February 27, 1889; Berta Serina Kingestad to her sister Anna, December 3, 1893, in Zempel, *In Their Own Words*, 29–30, 53.

79. T. Burgess, *Greeks in America*, 26.

80. Gabaccia, *We Are What We Eat*, 81.

81. Kraut, *The Huddled Masses*, 98–99; Diner, *Hungering for America*, 65.

82. Park and Miller, *Old World Traits*, 152.

83. Gabaccia, *We Are What We Eat*, 75, 67.

84. L. Cohen, *Making a New Deal*, 109–19.

85. H. A. Barton, *Letters from the Promised Land*, 287.

86. Balch, *Our Slavic Fellow Citizens*, 383.

87. B. Anderson, *Imagined Communities*.

88. T. L. Smith, "Religion and Ethnicity," 1174–78.

89. Simonsen, *Returned Emigrants*, 70.

90. Swierenga, "Local Patterns of Dutch Migration," 147.

91. M. Tierney to Scalabrini, November 7, 1904; M. Tierney to Scalabrini, March 7, 1905, in Scalabrini, *For the Love of Immigrants*, 332–33.

92. Orsi, *The Madonna of 115th Street*; L. Cohen, *Making a New Deal*, 87–90; *L'Italia*, August 19, 1894, reel 31, Italian Language Papers, *Chicago Foreign Language Press Survey*.

93. Renee Darmstadter, *The Jewish Community of New York City* (manuscript), quoted in Park and Miller, *Old World Traits*, 203–4.

94. Giovanni Battista Scalabrini, "On the Necessity of Protecting the Nationality of the Immigrants" (1891), in Scalabrini, *For the Love of Immigrants*, 64.

95. Metzker, *A Bintel Brief*, 101–2.

96. Castagnola, "Land Where My Father Died," 92.

97. Byrne, *Irish Emigration*, 27.

98. Bukowczyk, *And My Children Did Not Know Me*, 39.

99. Park and Miller, *Old World Traits*, 129; Foerster, *The Italian Emigration*, 393.

100. Leo Wolfson, *Jewish Communal Register of New York City (1917–1918)*, 859, quoted in Park and Miller, *Old World Traits*, 129; Holli and Jones, *Ethnic Chicago*, 82.

101. Weisser, *A Brotherhood of Memory*, 5, 17, 22, 26, 28, 31. For another view of landsmanshaftn, see Soyer, *Jewish Immigrant Associations*.

102. *L'Italia*, March 17, 1894, reel 30, Italian Language Papers, *Chicago Foreign Language Press Survey*.

103. Schrier, *Ireland*, 96–97; Saloutos, *They Remember America*, 30.

104. "The History of the Itoo Society," box 1, Joseph M. Couri Correspondence, Photographs, Documents folder, Near Eastern Miscellaneous Manuscripts.

105. "Covello Interview, 'Mutual Aid Societies,' interview with 'Italian—2nd Generation. Lawyer—42 yrs.,'" IA-BY-III, Covello Papers, quoted in Orsi, *The Madonna of 115th Street*, 51.

106. B. Fleischer, "A Jewish Order That Lives and Influences Jewish Life," *Sunday Jewish Courier*, September 14, 1919, reel 36, Jewish Papers, *Chicago Foreign Language Press Survey*.

107. *Abendpost*, June 22, 1929, reel 22, *Chicago Foreign Language Press Survey*.

108. Marietta Interlandi, interviewed by Therese Albini, October 17, 1979, *Italians in Chicago—Oral History*, box 1.

109. *Skandinaven* (daily edition), June 12, 1900, reel 46, *Chicago Foreign Language Press Survey*; *Lietuva*, January 27, 1905, Lithuanian papers, reel 42, *Chicago Foreign Language Press Survey*.

110. Horace Plunkett quoted in K. A. Miller, "Assimilation and Alienation," 103; Akhtar, *Immigration and Identity*, 25.

111. Hansen, *History of Sons of Norway*, 8–9.

112. Castagnola, "Land Where My Father Died," 96.
113. "Go Home for Christmas," *Sioux City Journal*, November 23, 1895.
114. K. A. Miller, *Emigrants and Exiles*, 544; Overland, *Immigrant Minds*, 23–34, 28; Bodnar, *The Transplanted*, 53, 128; Wyman, *Round-Trip to America*, 92–98; Choate, *Emigrant Nation*, 73, 102.
115. "Festival to Commemorate the Bringing of the Soil of Czechoslovakia to Chicago," *Denní Hlasatel*, November 16, 1922, reel 8, *Chicago Foreign Language Press Survey*; "Expedition of the Narodni Svaz Ceskych Katoliku," *Denní Hlasatel*, May 7, 1922, reel 8, *Chicago Foreign Language Press Survey*; Raphael Samuel, *Theatres of Memory*, Vol. 1: *Past and Present in Contemporary Culture* (London: Verso, 1994), 161, quoted in Fritzsche, *Stranded in the Present*, 50; see also 76–77, 132.
116. Park and Miller, *Old World Traits*, 137.
117. Balch, *Our Slavic Fellow Citizens*, 379.
118. K. A. Miller, *Emigrants and Exiles*, 3–8, 180, 341–42, 556; K. A. Miller, "Assimilation and Alienation," 107.
119. "Died by His Own Hand, Pangs of Nostalgia Drove Lonely Native to Meet Awful End," *Evening News* (San Jose), October 9, 1901.
120. "Self-Slain Irish Girl Was Homesick—Katie Clark Cuts Her Throat in Hour of Despondency," *Boston Sunday Journal*, August 23, 1903; "Homesick for Alps: Switzer a Suicide," *Boston Sunday Journal*, September 27, 1903.
121. "Two Homesick Greeks End Their Lives with Gas," *Tucson Citizen*, December 12, 1907.
122. *Anaconda Standard*, (Anaconda, Montana) April 15, 1907.
123. Metzker, *A Bintel Brief*, 115–16.
124. "Victim of Nostalgia; A Priest Dies Craving for a Sight of His Motherland," *Evening Bulletin* (San Francisco), August 12, 1887.
125. *Daily Charlotte Observer*, June 21, 1896.
126. The idea that homesickness caused psychosis among immigrants was not just an American idea. British doctors commented on the problem, most notably Isaac Frost, who studied homesick Austrian and German domestics in England, their suicidal tendencies, and religious and sexual abnormalities. See Frost, "Homesickness and Immigrant Psychoses," 801–47.
127. For a review of the debates and subsequent revisions, see Malzberg, "Mental Disease," 379–95.
128. "Twenty-Second Annual Report of the Committee on Lunacy," 23.
129. See, for instance, Malzberg, "Rates of Mental Disease," 545–48; Locke et al., "Immigration and Insanity," 301–6.
130. "Race and Insanity," *Science* 11 (June 8, 1888): 272.
131. Steiner, *On the Trail of the Immigrant*, 113.
132. "Homesick Russian Jews," 8.
133. McLaughlin, "Immigration and the Public Health," 391–95.
134. Dinnerstein and Reimers, *Ethnic Americans*, 64.
135. Choate, *Emigrant Nation*, 77, 81.
136. Warne, *The Immigrant Invasion*, 173; Wyman, *Round-Trip to America*, 101.
137. Wyman, *Round-Trip to America*, 102–3.
138. Higham, *Strangers in the Land*, 199.
139. Higham, *Strangers in the Land*, 11, 22, 33, 21–22.
140. Higham, *Strangers in the Land*, 138–43.
141. "Homesick Russian Jews," 8.
142. Sarna, "The Myth of No Return," 260.
143. Yiddish advice book, quoted in Kraut, *The Huddled Masses*, 112.
144. Metzker, *A Bintel Brief*, 117–18, 132–33.

145. K. A. Miller, "Assimilation and Alienation," 104.

146. Doty, *The First Franco-Americans*, 42.

147. Amadeo Yelmini, interviewed by Anthony Mansueto, May 4, 1980, typed transcript, 10, box 4, Italians *in Chicago—Oral History.*

148. *Caravan Weekly Pictorial* (Brooklyn), November 6, 1958, folder "Syrian Ladies Aid Society (Brooklyn New York)," box 1, Near Eastern Miscellaneous Manuscripts.

149. Hasia Diner suggests that the history of immigration is the history of emotions, in that the central questions about assimilation and ethnicity revolve around emotional adjustments and commitments. See Hasia R. Diner, "Ethnicity and Emotions in America: Dimensions of the Unexplored," in P. N. Stearns and Lewis, *An Emotional History,* 198.

150. K. A. Miller, *Emigrants and Exiles*, 121, 128, 489, 556; Wyman, *Round-Trip to America*, 90.

151. Akhtar, *Immigration and Identity*, 90, 94; Ritivoi, *Yesterday's Self*, 3.

152. Marcus Eli Ravage, "Our Sentimental Pilgrimage," *Saturday Evening Post* 195 (March 17, 1923): 4; Marcus Eli Ravage, "Our Sentimental Pilgrimage: The Return of the Native," *Saturday Evening Post* 195 (March 24, 1923): 138.

153. Ellen Raatikka, folder R-3, box 6, Finnish American Family History Project.

154. Lindberg, *The Background of Swedish Emigration*, 254.

155. Odorizzi, *Footsteps through Time*, 30.

156. Caroli, *Italian Repatriation*, 84.

157. Saloutos, *They Remember America*, 92, 65.

158. Sam Ori interviewed by Sandi Weisenberg, box 4, 34, *Italians in Chicago—Oral History.*

159. Handlin, "Immigrants Who Go Back," 72–73.

160. Saloutos, *They Remember America*, 65.

161. Wyman, *Round-Trip to America*, 139, 147–48.

162. Wyman, *Round-Trip to America*, 197–98.

163. Handlin, "Immigrants Who Go Back," 73.

164. Waldeman Ager, "Sjel til Salgs," Jul i Vesterheimen for 1935, n.p., quoted in Skardal, *The Divided Heart*, 272.

165. "Melody Made Him Homesick," *Anaconda Standard*, (Anaconda, Montana) April 26, 1901.

166. Martin Koster, interviewed by Janet Levine, July 18, 1993, series EI, no. 350, 21, *Ellis Island Oral History Project.*

167. Simonsen, "Returned Emigrants," 100.

CHAPTER 6

1. D. Ewen, *All the Years*, 231–32.

2. George Cohan, "Over There," in Silverman, *Of Thee I Sing*, 105–8.

3. D. M. Kennedy, *Over Here*, 153–54.

4. Keene, *Doughboys*, 2, 9.

5. Canfield, "Psychologists at War," 32, 104, 106, 241.

6. Bailey et al., *The Medical Department*, 57.

7. Arnold Rumbarger to his mother, June 17, 1918, reel 3, in Grinder, *World War I Survey.*

8. Keene, *Doughboys*, 36–37, 14.

9. Cpl. Paul Murphy, "An Account of my Personal Experience in World War I," April 1, 1963, 9, in Grinder, *World War I Survey*; "Memorandum for Captain Perkins from Capt. E. R. Padgett," August 30, 1918, Camp Meade file, box A10, quoted in Keene, *Doughboys*, 13.

10. Keene, *Doughboys*, 68–71.

11. Sherman Thomas, 4, reel 14, in Grinder, *World War I Survey.*

12. "Was Homesick, Henry County Boy Deserter Says," *Montgomery Advertiser*, June 6, 1918; "Homesick Soldier Boy," *Baltimore American*, November 9, 1917.

13. "Baker against Death Penalty," *Baltimore American*, February 28, 1918.

14. Keene, *Doughboys*, 14, 76, 24, 25.

15. "Camp Greenleaf Detention Camp Form Letter," reel 1, in Grinder, *World War I Survey*. Meghan Winchell makes this point about civilian women during World War II (*Good Girls*, 12–13).

16. Keene, *Doughboys*, 77–78; *Stars and Stripes*, May 30, 1919.

17. Pvt. Evan J. Miller to his mother from France December 23, 1917, reel 38, in Grinder, *World War I Survey*. Paul Fussell (*The Great War*, 42) notes that English department stores had a "Trench Requisites" department in which families could purchase goods for their sons at war, and Paul Moore (*Now Playing*, 211) describes the "gift packs" that Toronto department stores offered for Canadian soldiers serving overseas.

18. Pvt. Evan J. Miller to his father, March 12, 1918, reel 38, Grinder, *World War I Survey*.

19. J. J. Cooke, *Chewing Gum*, 14.

20. "Our Men in France Often Feel Homesick," *New York Times*, June 9, 1918.

21. *Mess Kit* 1 (September 1919): 6, reel 38, in Grinder, *World War I Survey*.

22. Allen, *Toward the Flame*, 181; David G. Bareuther to his family, October 15, 1917, in Evans, *American Voices of World War I*, 7; Perry A. Yost diary, March 25, 1918, in Evans, *American Voices of World War I*, 67; Shillinglaw, *An American in the Army*, 36; "Appreciation from the A.E.F.," *Mess Kit* 1 (September 1919): 19.

23. Yost diary, March 25, 1918, in Evans, *American Voices of World War I*, 67; Addison H. Smith to his mother, quoted in Evans, *American Voices of World War I*, 89.

24. J. J. Cooke, *Chewing Gum*, 14.

25. Allen, *Toward the Flame*, 59, 63, 64, 181.

26. Menninger and Nemiah, *American Psychiatry after WWII*, 4; Carrie H. Kennedy and Jeffrey A. McNeil, "A History of Military Psychology," in C. H. Kennedy and Zillmer, *Military Psychology*, 3.

27. U.S. Office of the Surgeon General, *Annual Report*, 479. Official records do not list Arnett's death.

28. "The Homesick Soldiers," *Tucson Citizen*, April 17, 1918.

29. "Homesickness Is Not Rheumatism So Don't Try to Make the Army Doctor Believe It Is," *Stars and Stripes*, December 27, 1918.

30. War Department, memo, Washington, February 7, 1918, in Bailey et al., *The Medical Department*, 64; "Strange Vagaries of Shell Shock," *Literary Digest*, June 8, 1918, 65–67.

31. Clarke, "So Lonesome I Could Die," 254.

32. Edgar Garland, 7, 11, reel 14, in Grinder, *World War I Survey*.

33. For discussions of the importance of emotional control in office culture, see P. N. Stearns, *American Cool*, 121–25.

34. Mandell, *The Corporation as Family*, 4.

35. P. N. Stearns, *American Cool*, 121–25.

36. Mandell, *The Corporation as Family*, 33, 38.

37. Norman Beasley, "A Business Founded on a Bet," *Business*, December 1920, 34–36.

38. U.S. Department of War, *Annual Report*, 70–71.

39. McWilliams, *Southern California Country*, 111,135, 162, 161; McWilliams, "What Are We Doing for the Interstate Migrant?," 3.

40. McWilliams, *Southern California Country*, 165–66, 167, 169, 170–71, 174; "Transplanting of East to West Shown by Our State Societies," *Los Angeles Times*, April 11, 1909.

41. "Southern California by Towns and Counties," *Los Angeles Times*, January 13, 1901; "Iowa Picnic Was a Success," *Los Angeles Times*, August 24, 1913; "Auld Lang Syne: Many Gather at Big Iowa Picnic," *Los Angeles Times*, August 13, 1917; "Iowa Picnic Brings Out 45,000 to Bixby Park," *Los Angeles Times*, August 15, 1926; "Thousands Crowd Park at Huge Iowa Picnic," *Los Angeles Times*, February 24, 1935; "100,000 at Iowa Picnic," *Los Angeles Times*, February 25, 1940; McWilliams, *Southern California Country*, 169.

42. "Society of the Sons of North Carolina," *Chicago Defender* (weekend edition), September 21, 1918; "Hundreds Attend Picnic," *Chicago Defender* (weekend edition), August 17, 1918.

43. Berlin, *The Making of African America*, 154, 155; Grossman, *Land of Hope*, 66.

44. Grossman, *Land of Hope*, 66, 96; "Letter from Mobile, Ala.," April 21, 1917, in "Letters of Negro Migrants of 1916–1918," 320.

45. Grossman, *Land of Hope*, 66–67; Berlin, *The Making of African America*, 172.

46. T. D. Black, *Bridges of Memory*, 526–27.

47. Grossman, *Land of Hope*, 6.

48. Wright, *12 Million Black Voices*, 92.

49. Wright, *American Hunger*, 1.

50. Quoted in Grossman, *Land of Hope*, 115.

51. "Letter from Pittsburg, Pa.," May 11, 1917, "Letter from Cleveland, Ohio, August 28, 1917," in "Additional Letters of Negro Migrants, 1916–1918," 459, 460.

52. Grossman, *Land of Hope*, 155; Ballard, *One More Day's Journey*, 24; Kiser, *Sea Island to City*, 211.

53. Grossman, *Land of Hope*, 156; Bontemps and Conroy, *Anyplace but Here*, 172; R. N. Brown, "Coming Home," 63.

54. Ballard, *One More Day's Journey*, 176; Sernett, *Bound for the Promised Land*, 187.

55. Ballard, *One More Day's Journey*, 15, 175, 177.

56. Grossman, *Land of Hope*, 94–95; Ballard, *One More Day's Journey*, 175.

57. Crew, *Field to Factory*, 28; Ballard, *One More Day's Journey*, 176.

58. Kiser, *Sea Island to City*, 84.

59. Bontemps and Conroy, *Anyplace but Here*, 172–73; Grossman, *Land of Hope*, 155.

60. Grossman, *Land of Hope*, 155.

61. Griffin, *'Who Set You Flowin'?"* 55; Lemke-Santangelo, *Abiding Courage*, 134.

62. R. N. Brown, "Coming Home," 24.

63. Lemke-Santangelo, *Abiding Courage*, 133–35.

64. "Bids South 'Good-Bye' Forever," *Chicago Defender* August 3, 1918.

65. Willie Mae Cotright, interviewed by Judith Dunning, 2002, typed transcript, 22, Rosie the Riveter World War II American Homefront Oral History Project.

66. Crew, *Field to Factory*, 73; Lemke-Santangelo, *Abiding Courage*, 52.

67. "Fish, Hominy and Cotton, or July Geddes, Negro of Etiwan," interview with George Brown, 9, 10, South Carolina Writers' Project Life History, *American Life Histories*.

68. J. N. Gregory, *The Southern Diaspora*, 17.

69. Grossman, *Land of Hope*, 43.

70. Sernett, *Bound for the Promised Land*, 201; Grossman, *Land of Hope*, 196–207.

71. Britomar Lathrop, *Britomar's Road Diaries* (Bloomington, Indiana: 1st Books Library, 2002), 3, 72, 201, 100, 178, 326.

72. H.E. Drobish, "Migration of Drought Refugees to California, April 17, 1935, Report written for the Emergency Relief Administration, State of California," in Folder 14, Carton 15, in Paul Schuster Taylor Papers; McWilliams, "What Are We Doing for the Interstate Migrant?," 3.

73. Johnson and Avina, Field Notes: Filipino Labor in California, 1935, Folder 3, Carton 15, Paul Schuster Taylor Papers.

74. Tom Vaser, Field Notes, 4, 5, folder 11, Carton 15, Paul Schuster Taylor Papers, Bancroft Library.

75. Vaser, Field Notes, 7, Paul Schuster Taylor Papers.

76. "200 Okie Ballads Recorded in Labor Camp," *New York Times*, October 2, 1940.

77. "Ballads of the Okies," *New York Times*, November 17, 1940.

78. Quoted in J. N. Gregory, *American Exodus*, 114.

79. *The Weed Patch Cultivator*—published weekly by the Arvin Migratory Camp 1, no. 18 (December 30, 1939): 1, microfilm of California Migrant Labor Camp Newsletters; Coded Administrative Camp Files, 1933–45; Records of the Office of the Director; Records of Region 9; Farm Security Administration; Records of the Farmers Home Administration (RG 96); National Archives-Pacific Sierra Region, San Bruno, CA, at Doe Library, University of California, Berkeley. See also J. N. Gregory, *American Exodus*.

80. U. S. Department of Agriculture, Bureau of Agricultural Economics and Farm Security Administration, "Population in Farm Security Administration Camps," Migratory Labor Camps, Current Report No. 1: An analysis of social and economic characteristics of families registering in FSA Migratory Labor Camps in California and Arizona from January to April, 1940 (Berkeley, August 1, 1940), 7, folder 42, carton 15, Paul Schuster Taylor Papers.

81. J. N. Gregory, *American Exodus*, 114, 116.

82. J. N. Gregory, *American Exodus*, 213, 222; J. N. Gregory, *Southern Diaspora*, 209.

83. "Statement of Miss Grace Abbott, Chief, Children's Bureau, Washington, D.C.," in U.S. Senate, *Relief for Unemployed Transients*, 23–24.

84. Uys, *Riding the Rails*, 11, 131–37, 82–89, 204, 201.

85. For positive assessments of the tramps' mobility, see "Statement of Miss Grace Abbott," 33; Uys, *Riding the Rails*, 11, 14, 15; "Statement of General Pelham D. Glassford," in U.S. Senate, *Relief for Unemployed Transients*, 126.

86. "Statement of Mrs. Margaret Ford, Executive Secretary, Travelers' Aid Society, Washington, D.C.," in U.S. Senate, *Relief for Unemployed Transients*, 60.

87. "Statement of General Pelham Glassford," 127.

88. Uys, *Riding the Rails*, 255, 260.

89. "257 Men Drop Out of Forest 'Army'; Some Homesick, Others Called Back by Parents," *New York Times*, April 11, 1933.

90. "The C.C.C.," *New York Times*, November 5, 1933.

91. "Whiskered Youths Back from Camps," *New York Times*, September 24, 1933; Frank and Ella Merryvale (Willard and Cornelia Mitchell), 14, *American Life Histories*.

92. "Never Had Nostalgia at Home," *New York Times*, July 13, 1935.

93. Groves, *The Drifting Home*, 38, 49; Hulbert, *Raising America*, 100–101.

94. J. B. Watson, *Psychological Care of Infant and Child*, 7, 11, 12, 43–44, 85, 77–78, 81–82. On Watson's influence and attitudes, see also Hulbert, *Raising America*, 11, 140–50.

95. Groves, *The American Family*, 201; Gruenberg, *We, the Parents*, 251–52, 262; Wylie, *Generation of Vipers*, 208; Hulbert, *Raising America*, 113.

96. Hulbert, *Raising America*, 35.

97. Conklin, *Principles of Adolescent Psychology*, 209–16.

98. McCann, "Nostalgia," 181.

99. Paris, *Children's Nature*, 18.

100. Paris, *Children's Nature*, 18, 30, quote on 138.

101. "Children and Parents," *New York Times*, July 16, 1939. See also Paris, *Children's Nature*, 140.

102. Levy, *Maternal Overprotection*, 30.

103. "Freshmen Are Aided," *New York Times*, September 15, 1935.

104. D. M. Kennedy, *Freedom from Fear*, 458–59, 495–96, 636–37, 710.

105. Pyle, *Last Chapter*, 5; Nichols, *Ernie's War*, 181; Linderman, *The World within War*, 302.

106. W. E. Gregory, "The Idealization of the Absent," 53–54.

107. "What Drives the American Soldier Forward," *New York Times*, September 12, 1943.

108. Nichols, *Ernie's War*, 178.

109. "Stimson Says Army Won't Linger Abroad," *New York Times*, December 10, 1944.

110. Pfau, "Miss Your Loving," 20–31; Grinker and Spiegel, *Men under Stress*, 182.

111. Brotz and Wilson, "Characteristics of Military Society," 374.

112. Hollingshead, "Adjustment to Military Life," 440–42.

113. Linderman, *The World within War*, 187. On this point, see also Rodgers, "Billy Yank and G.I. Joe," 93–121.

114. Napoli, "The Mobilization of American Psychologists," 32–36.

115. Wittson et al., "Cryptic Nostalgia," 57–59; Flicker and Weiss, "Nostalgia and Its Military Implications," 380–87.

116. Eisendorfer, "Clinical Significance," 146–49.

117. Rodgers, "Billy Yank and G.I. Joe," 117–18; Mitchell, *The Vacant Chair*, 31.

118. Frederick R. Hanson, "Organization of the Psychiatric Services in World War II," in *Combat Psychiatry*, 33, 39, 40.

119. "Red Cross Helps Yanks in Far East," *New York Times*, March 11, 1944.

120. "Businessmen to Aid U.S.O.," *Los Angeles Times*, April 7, 1942; "Endorse USO Program," *New York Times*, July 19, 1942.

121. Coffey, *Always Home*, 2, 5.

122. "Fraternity House for A Great Fraternity," *New York Times*, February 4, 1945; "The New York War Fund," *New York Times*, September 20, 1944.

123. Anita Christiansen and Mary Highfill, interviewed by Nadine Wilmot, 2005, 58–59, Rosie the Riveter, World War II American Homefront Oral History Project.

124. Earl Schneider, interviewed by Shaun Illingworth, November 18, 2002, Rutgers Oral History Archives, New Brunswick, History Department, http://oralhistory.rutgers.edu/Interviews/schneider_earl.html.

125. Brig. William J. Parkins, national program director, Salvation Army, "The USO Work of the Salvation Army," quoted in Winchell, "'To Make the Boys Feel at Home,'" 196.

126. Winchell, *Good Girls*, 34–36.

127. "The Civilian Side," *Los Angeles Times*, November 8, 1942; "Help the U.S.O. at Home," *Los Angeles Times*, June 28, 1942; "This Is a Woman's War Too," *New York Times*, February 7, 1943.

128. Winchell, "'To Make the Boys Feel at Home,'" 195–96.

129. "Need of U.S.O. to Fighting Men Told by Campaign Head," *Los Angeles Times*, July 19, 1942.

130. Meyer Berger, "Morale," *New York Times*, May 25, 1941.

131. Nichols, *Ernie's War*, 382–85.

132. "Anne McCaughey Diary," August 12, 1944, in Vining, *American Diaries of World War II*, 82, 95.

133. "William D. Askin Diary," January 18, 1945, in Vining, *American Diaries of World War II*, 255.

134. Quoted in Linderman, *The World within War*, 304.

135. Meyer Berger, "World's Biggest Retail Business: It Is the Army Exchange Service, with 8,000,000 Customers Who Buy Anything from Candy to Kayaks," *New York Times*, October 24, 1943; William Hurt to his parents, April 4, 1945, Hurt Letters and Papers, in J. J. Cooke, *Chewing Gum*, 123.

136. "World's Biggest Retail Business"; "Stores Near Front Aid Troop Morale," *New York Times*, May 28, 1943; Glenn Fowler, "Army's Post Exchange to Mark Sixtieth Anniversary Tomorrow," *New York Times*, July 24, 1955; "How the Home Front Thought and Behaved in World War II," *New York Times*, February 17, 1946.

137. Inada, *Only What We Could Carry*, xii.

138. Inada, *Only What We Could Carry*, xii.

139. K. A. Imamura to Walter Millsap, May 22, 1942, folder 1, box 1; American Council on Public Affairs, *The Displaced Japanese-Americans* (Washington, DC: American Council on Public Affairs, 1944?), 4, folder 34, box 2, Walter Millsap and Keikichi Akana Imamura Family Papers.

140. K. A. Imamura to Walter Millsap, July 22, 1942, written from the Assembly Center, Tulare, CA, box 1 folder 3; Toshiko Imamura to Walter Millsap, August 7, 1942, box 1, folder 3, Walter Millsap and Keikichi Akana Imamura Family Papers.
141. Keichi Imamura to Mr. Millsap, July 11, 1942, folder 2, box 1, Walter Millsap and Keikichi Akana Imamura Family Papers.
142. Uchida, *Desert Exile*, 103.
143. *Santa Anita Pacemaker* (Santa Anita Assembly Center), October 7, 1942, 12, box 2, folder 13, 94/8c, Holly H. Onomiya Papers.
144. Houston and Houston, *Farewell to Manzanar*, 35, 39.
145. "Pertinent Facts about Relocation Centers and Japanese Americans."
146. "A Year at Gila: Anniversary Booklet," July 20, 1943, folder 7, box 1, Gila River Relocation Center Records.
147. "Gila News-Courier Anniversary Supplement," September 12, 1943, 4, folder 8, box 1, Gila River Relocation Center Records.
148. Kikuchi, *The Kikuchi Diary*, 54, 67, 132–33.
149. Houston and Houston, *Farewell to Manzanar*, 100.
150. "A Year at Gila: Anniversary Booklet."
151. *Manzanar Free Press*, April 25, 1942, folder 46, box 2, Millsap and Imamura Family Papers.
152. "Second Year at Gila," Gila anniversary booklet, July 20, 1944, 3, folder 9, box 1, Gila River Relocation Center Records.
153. P. N. Stearns, *American Cool*, 189; Kotchemidova, "From Good Cheer to 'Drive-by Smiling.'"
154. Riesman et al., *The Lonely Crowd*, 25.

CHAPTER 7

1. Whyte, *The Organization Man*, 3.
2. Riesman et al., *The Lonely Crowd*.
3. Parsons, *The Social System*, 177–78.
4. Mintz and Kellogg, *Domestic Revolutions*, 182.
5. "The Return of the Multi-Generational Family Household."
6. William E. Henry, "Social Mobility as Social Learning: Some Elements of Change in Motive and in Social Context," in Kantor, *Mobility and Mental Health*, 46.
7. Warner, *The Corporation*, 60–61.
8. Berger et al., *The Homeless Mind*, 57, 64–67.
9. May, *Homeward Bound*.
10. "Problems of Homesick G.I.s," *Joplin (Missouri) Globe*, September 27, 1950.
11. "Sees No Need of Discipline for Protesting GIs," *Jefferson City (Missouri) Post Tribune*, January 9, 1946; "'Ike' Tells Homesick GIs He'll Rush Demobilization," *Charleston (West Virginia) Gazette*, January 19, 1946.
12. Rostker, *I Want YOU!*, 26.
13. Rostker, *I Want YOU!*, 27.
14. "Marine's Letter Bares Homesickness, Waiting, Bewilderment of War," *El Paso Herald Post*, January 18, 1951.
15. Melvin Horwitz to Dorothy Horwitz, November 11, 1952, in Horwitz and Horwitz, *We Will Not Be Strangers*, 143.
16. "'Operation Homefolk' to Start Tonight, Relatives, Sweethearts of Guardsmen Will Visit Camp," *Lubbock (Texas) Evening Journal*, November 10, 1950; "'Operation Homefolk' Unites GI's, Families," *Cumberland (Maryland) Times*, November 12, 1950.
17. Dorothea Dix, *Capital Times* (Madison, Wisconsin), December 24, 1951.
18. Ender and Segal, "V(E)-Mail," 88; Schumm et al., "Expectations," 649; Ender, "G.I. Phone Home," 437.

19. "Copters Deliver Turkeys in Korea," *New York Times*, November 22, 1951.
20. "Christmas Moves World to Prayer for Ending of War," *New York Times*, December 26, 1952.
21. Strecker, *Their Mothers' Sons,* 219, 205–7, 30, 34–35, 219.
22. Cuordileone, "'Politics in an Age of Anxiety,'" 522–26; Cuordileone, *Manhood,* 126–33; P. M. Edwards, *The Korean War,* 145; May, *Homeward Bound.*
23. "Problem of Homesick G.I.s."
24. "'Momism' Cited as Grave Danger," *Cedar Rapids Gazette*, December 25, 1950.
25. "Life Too Feminine, 'Momism' Blamed for Poor-Grade Soldiers," *Corpus Christi Times,* April 8, 1952; Standish, "Crisis in Courage," 24, 16, 21, 22.
26. Rodgers, "Billy Yank and G.I. Joe," 107, 113–14.
27. "New Soldiers for New Tasks," *New York Times,* July 23, 1950.
28. Marren, "Psychiatric Problems in Troops," 716–17; Carrie H. Kennedy and Jeffrey A. McNeil, "A History of Military Psychology," in C. H. Kennedy and Zillmer, *Military Psychology,* 8. For more on psychiatric care during the Korean War, see Menninger and Nemiah, *American Psychiatry after WWII,* 13–16; Norbury, "Psychiatric Admissions," 130–33; McGuire, *Psychology Aweigh!*
29. A. W. Johnson, "Combat Psychiatry," 307.
30. W. L. White, *Back Down the Ridge,* 50–51.
31. A. W. Johnson, "Combat Psychiatry," 305–8; Frederick R. Hanson, "Organization of the Psychiatric Services in World War II," in *Combat Psychiatry,* 33, 39, 40. Johnson estimates that only 60 percent of neuropsychiatric cases were returned; Hanson estimates 70 percent.
32. Whyte, *The Organization Man,* 3.
33. U.S. Census Bureau, "Annual Geographic Mobility Rates."
34. Whyte, *The Organization Man,* 275, 277. See also Gans, *The Levittowners,* 199.
35. Thoma and Lindemann, "Newcomers' Problems," 185–93.
36. Gordon and Gordon, "Psychiatric Problems," 546.
37. Phyllis LaFarge, "I Want to Go Home," *Redbook,* October 1967, 59, 153, 154.
38. K. T. Jackson, *Crabgrass Frontier,* 233.
39. K. T. Jackson, *Crabgrass Frontier,* 236–45.
40. Whyte, *The Organization Man,* 284–88.
41. Mintz and Kellogg, *Domestic Revolutions,* 185.
42. Gans, *The Levittowners,* 226, 242.
43. "Crackups in the Suburbs," *Cosmopolitan Magazine,* 149 (October 1960): 61.
44. Robert Gutman, "Population Mobility in the American Middle Class," in Duhl, *The Urban Condition,* 181–82. See also Riesman et al., *The Lonely Crowd,* 25; P. N. Stearns, *American Cool,* 193; Thoma and Lindemann, "Newcomers' Problems," 192.
45. Whyte, *The Organization Man,* 350.
46. LaFarge, "I Want to Go Home," 153–54.
47. R. D. Putnam, *Bowling Alone,* 16, 54.
48. Whyte, *The Organization Man,* 287–88.
49. Thoma and Lindemann, "Newcomers' Problems," 192.
50. "Crackups in the Suburbs," 61–63.
51. MacAllister et al., "The Adaptation of Women to Residential Mobility," 197–204.
52. Packard, *A Nation of Strangers,* 159.
53. "A Welcome Wagon," *New York Times,* July 7, 1929; "Earning It: Just Neighbors Being Friendly? Not Exactly," *New York Times,* May 19, 1996.
54. Packard, *A Nation of Strangers,* 160–68, 31.
55. Vito Cali, interviewed by Anthony Mansueto, April 22, 1980, typed transcript, 11, 14, 29, 30, *Italians in Chicago—Oral History,* box 4.

56. J. Douglas Porteous, "The Pathology of Forced Relocation," in Kaplan and Kaplan, *Humanscape*, 291–92.
57. Gans, *The Urban Villagers*, 289–90.
58. Marc Fried, "Grieving for a Lost Home," in Duhl, *The Urban Condition*, 151–52.
59. Fried, "Grieving for a Lost Home," 161–64.
60. Harry DeBenedet, interviewed by K. Smith, November 20, 2003; Theresa Argento, interviewed by Sarah Barca, March 9, 2004, in Oral Histories Documenting New Haven, Connecticut.
61. Fullilove, *Root Shock*, 20.
62. Fullilove, "Psychiatric Implications of Displacement," 1519.
63. Steven Morris, "Home Was Where the Bulldozer Is," *Chicago Tribune*, April 18, 1971; Thomas J. Cottle, "What It's Like to Grow Up Black in Boston," *Los Angeles Times*, October 10, 1974.
64. Fried, "Grieving for a Lost Home," 157.
65. "Washington: The Lonely Americans," *New York Times*, December 24, 1965.
66. Westmoreland, *A Soldier Reports*, 295; Appy, *Working-Class War*, 234–35.
67. Westheider, *The Vietnam War*, 81, 84, 85, 87–88, 90, 92.
68. Newborg and Bryan, "MARS Calling," 43–44; Moora, "Vietnam Calling," 13–15; The two articles differ on the number of MARS stations in Vietnam, with Newborg and Bryan estimating only 35.
69. Westheider, *The Vietnam War*, 92, 98.
70. Quoted in Appy, *Working-Class War*, 17, 87.
71. Correspondence from Lynn Steele to his wife, n.d., item no. 1371016024, Lynn Steele Collection.
72. Appy, *Working-Class War*, 27.
73. Appy, *Working-Class War*, 43.
74. Westmoreland, *A Soldier Reports*, 296.
75. Franklin Jones, "Military Psychiatry in Vietnam (1961–1975)," in Glass and Jones, *Psychiatry in the Army*, 1–28; Franklin D. Jones, "Military Psychiatry since World War II," in Menninger and Nemiah, *American Psychiatry after WWII*, 16, 23, 24; Longley, *Grunts*, 133–36.
76. Kuzmarov, *The Myth of the Addicted Army*.
77. Buzzanco, *Vietnam*, 114.
78. Jones, "Military Psychiatry since World War II," 5, 24.
79. Jones, "Military Psychiatry since World War II," 5.
80. Leiberger and Tucker, *The New Individualists*, 60.
81. G. E. Breen, *Middle Management Morale*, 43.
82. Packard, *A Nation of Strangers*, 278; Blomquist, "Study Shows Relocation Resistance Reversing," 55–56.
83. Leiberger and Tucker, *The New Individualists*, 38.
84. Danforth W. Austin, "Fattening a Friday," *Wall Street Journal*, August 26, 1970.
85. E. Miller, "Relocation," 43–45.
86. Packard, *A Nation of Strangers*, 30, 146.
87. Ammons et al., "Surviving Corporate Moves," 207–12.
88. Poage, *The Moving Survival Guide*, xiii, 1–2, 12–14.
89. Brett and Stroh, "Women in Management," 392–98; G. E. Breen, *Middle Management Morale*, 30.
90. Kilborn, *Next Stop, Reloville*, 165.
91. Kilborn, *Next Stop, Reloville*, 5–9, 62.
92. Welch quoted in J. S. Black et al., *Globalizing People*, 1.
93. Quoted in J. S. Black et al., *Globalizing People*, 3, 4, 5.

94. Melinda Ligoas, "Personal Business: Career Arc; Turning Down a Transfer Can Freeze a Career," *New York Times*, September 28, 2003.

95. "Homesickness," *Los Angeles Times*, May 19, 1986.

96. *Evening Standard* (London), September 8, 2008.

97. Ligoas, "Personal Business: Career Arc."

98. "The Foreign Born Population of the United States: 2003," accessed April 2010, www. census.gov/prod/2004pubs/p.20–551.pdf.

99. García, *Havana USA*, 13, 35, 22, 36–37, 45–47.

100. Boswell and Curtis, *The Cuban-American Experience*, 63–67; Grenier and Perez, "Miami Spice," 361–72.

101. García, *Havana USA*, 86–93; Thomas A. Tweed, "Diasporic Nationalism and Urban Landscape: Cuban Immigrants at a Catholic Shrine in Miami," in Orsi, *Gods of the City*, 133.

102. Hein, *From Vietnam*, 52–53.

103. M. Zhou and Bankston, *Growing Up American*, 35, 72.

104. "Vietnamese Refugees Here Find Plain Task Is Getting Job," *New York Times*, August 26, 1975; "A New Life in a Strange Land," *New York Times*, October 10, 1976.

105. "200 Refugees Fly from U.S. to Asia," *New York Times*, July 5, 1975.

106. Jane A. Bennett and Daniel F. Detzner, "Loneliness in Cultural Context: A Look at the Life-History Narratives of Older Southeast Asian Refugee Women," in Lieblich and Josselson, *The Narrative Study of Lives*, 114, 135, 137, 126–28.

107. M. Zhou and Bankston, *Growing Up American*, 75.

108. Joseph Westermeyer, "Mental Health of Southeast Asian Refugees: Observations over Two Decades from Laos and the United States," in Owan, *Southeast Asian Mental Health*, 69–77.

109. *Daily News* (Faribault, MN), January 11, 1992.

110. "Agency Softens Clash of Cultures—Asian-American Organization Fills a Social-Service Gap," *Los Angeles Times*, December 15, 1985.

111. Jeffrey S. Passel and D'Vera Cohn, "Mexican Immigrants: How Many Come? How Many Leave?" Pew Hispanic Center, 2009, i, accessed May 15, 2010, http://pewhispanic.org/files/reports/112.pdf.

112. Interview with Rosa María Muñiz de Navarro in M. P. Davis, *Mexican Voices/American Dreams*, 157–58; Conway and Cohen, "Consequences," 26–44.

113. Interview with Juan Carlos Estrella, conducted by Susan Matt and Luke Fernandez, translated by Luke Fernandez, Tepic, Mexico, December 13, 2009.

114. J. H. Cohen, *The Culture of Migration*, 8.

115. Conway and Cohen "Consequences," 29, 41–42; "Big Mexican Breadwinner: The Migrant Worker," *New York Times*, March 25, 2002; "Mexicans Miss Money from Relatives Up North," *New York Times*, October 26, 2007; Gobierno Federal, SEGOB, *Paisano: Bienvenidos a casa. Guia Invierno 2009* (Mexico City, 2009), 55.

116. Bryan R. Roberts et al., "Transnational Migrant Communities," 242.

117. "Mexicans Miss Money from Relatives Up North."

118. "Councilwoman Hahn Cuts Ribbon on Casa Nayarit," Janice Hahn, Council District 15, City of Los Angeles website, accessed April 20, 2011, http://cd15.lacity.org/Blog/LACITYP_006742; "Fedejal: A Road of Continuous Improvement," *MigrantENews*, accessed April 15, 2010, http://migrantenews.com/2010/03/fedejal-a-road-of-continuous-improvement/lang/en/; "Federation of National Michoacano Clubs in Illinois," National Alliance of Latin American and Caribbean Communities, accessed April 15, 2010, http://nalacc.org/index.php?id=214&tx_galileomembers_pi3%5Buid%5D=23&no_cache=1.

119. Alarcón, "The Development of Home Town Associations," 5.

120. *Paisano: Bienvenidos a casa*, 45.

121. Alarcón, "The Development of Home Town Associations," 3.

122. Reyes, *Dynamics of Immigration,* xi, ix, 69–70.

123. This is a typical pattern: In 2006–7, 1,026,000 Mexicans emigrated to the United States; that same year 479,000 returned to Mexico. In 2007–8, 814,000 emigrated to the United States, and 440,000 returned. See Passel and Cohn, "Mexican Immigrants," 1.

124. *Paisano: Bienvenidos a casa.*

125. Interview with Cuauhtémoc Menendez, in M. P. Davis, *Mexican Voices/American Dreams,* 188, 191.

126. Ricardo Valencia, San Blas, Mexico, interviewed by Luke Fernandez and Susan Matt, March 12, 2009, translated by Irasema Rivera, in author's possession.

127. Some might argue that these immigrant enclaves help migrants develop and maintain "transnational identities," which span national borders. For more on transnationalism, see Bryan R. Roberts et al., "Transnational Migrant Communities," 239; See also Nina Glick Schiller, Linda Basch, and Cristina Szanton Blanc, "From Immigrant to Transmigrant: Theorizing Transnational Migration," *Anthropological Quarterly* 68 (January 1995): 48–63.

128. Basilio Prado, Villa Hidalgo, Nayarit, Mexico, interviewed by Susan Matt, Luke Fernandez, and Irasema Rivera, March 11, 2009, translated by Irasema Rivera, in author's possession; "Way North of the Border," *New York Times,* September 30, 2005; Bryan R, Roberts et al., "Transnational Migrant Communities," 256.

129. Lizabeth O. Valderanna Navarro, Tepic, Mexico, March 9, 2009, interviewed by Susan Matt and Irasema Rivera, translated by Irasema Rivera, in author's possession.

130. See, for instance, González et al., "Acculturation"; Shattell et al., "Factors Contributing to Depression," 193–204; Hovey and Magañam, "Acculturative Stress," Mann and García, "Characteristics of Community Interventions," 87–93.

131. Carlos Ruiz, Ogden, UT, interviewed by Susan Matt and Irasema Rivera, July 20, 2009, translated by Irasema Rivera, in author's possession.

132. Genaro Rivera Lopez, interviewed by Susan Matt and Irasema Rivera, July 22, 2009, translated by Irasema Rivera, in author's possession.

133. Ricardo Valencia interview.

134. "No Hard Sign of Reverse Migration," *New York Times,* January 14, 2009.

135. C. S. Fischer, "Ever-More Rooted Americans," 177–98; U.S. Census Bureau, "Annual Geographic Mobility Rates," 1–4, quoted in Joel Kotkin, "There's No Place Like Home," *Newsweek,* October 19, 2009, 43.

136. Florida, *The Rise of the Creative Class,* 229–30; Florida, *Who's Your City,* 87–88. See also Deborah E. Popper and Frank J. Popper, "'The Organization Man' in the Twenty-first Century," in Platt, *The Humane Metropolis,* 210–11.

137. Karen N., "Her Savannah," unpublished manuscript, in author's possession.

138. Larry L. Hunt et al., "Who Is Headed South?" 112; Cromartie and Stack, "Reinterpretation of Black Return," 302, 310; Stack, *Call to Home,* xiv. R. N. Brown, "Coming Home," 220–21.

139. "Yes, Retirees, You Can Go Home Again," *Kiplinger's Retirement Report,* September 2008, accessed April 15, 2010, http://www.kiplinger.com//features//archives//2008/08/krr_yes_retirees_you_can_go_home_again.html; Haya El Nasser, "Older Seniors Return North," *USA Today,* February 22, 2007. Chad Berry documents the experience of southern white migrants to the Midwest, who upon retirement have returned in significant numbers to the South (*Southern Migrants,* 207–13).

140. Paul Taylor et al., "The Return of the Multi-Generational Family Household," Pew Research Center, March 18, 2010, 2, accessed April 12, 2010, http://pewsocialtrends.org/assets/pdf/752-multi-generational-families.pdf; Geoffrey Colvin, "What the Baby-Boomers Will Buy Next," *Fortune Magazine* 110 (October 15, 1984): 30.

141. Jennifer Ludden, "Boomerang Kids Drive Rise of Extended Family Living," March 18, 2010, accessed April 11, 2010, www.npr.org/templates/story/story.php?storyId= 124787436.

142. Taylor et al., "The Return of the Multi-Generational Family Household," 5.

CONCLUSION

1. P. N. Stearns, *American Cool*, 187.

2. American Psychiatric Association, *Diagnostic and Statistical Manual of Mental Disorders*, 2nd ed., 50; American Psychiatric Association, *Diagnostic and Statistical Manual of Mental Disorders*, 3rd ed., 50, 51; American Psychiatric Association, *Diagnostic and Statistical Manual of Mental Disorders*, 4th ed., 110–12.

3. Spock, *The Common Sense Book*, 348–51; Spock and Rothenberg, *Baby and Child Care*, 407; Spock and Parker, *Dr. Spock's Baby and Child Care*, 592.

4. Thurber and Walton, "Preventing and Treating Homesickness," 852.

5. "I Want to Come Home!," *Good Housekeeping* 222 (July 1996): 59; Susan Flagg Godbey and Therese Walsh, "Head Off Homesickness," *Prevention* 48 (August 1996): 44; Dorothy Dill Mason, "Not a Bit Homesick," *Parents' Magazine* 23 (September 1948): 136–37.

6. M. Brown, *Arthur Goes to Camp*; S. Roberts, *I Want to Go Home*.

7. Rabe, *Elmo Gets Homesick*.

8. *Homesick Blues? Here's What to Do*.

9. "Many College Freshmen Suffer from Temporary Homesickness," *Titusville Herald*, August 5, 1992.

10. H. Cohen, *The Naked Roommate*, 36.

11. "Homesickness: Students with the Blues," Student Prevention and Wellness, Pittsburg State University, accessed 5/12/10, www.pittstate.edu/office/activities/programs/ student-wellness/homesicknessparents.dot,.

12. Tilburg et al., "Homesickness," 899–12; Thurber and Walton, "Preventing and Treating Homesickness," 844.

13. Shirley Fisher, "The Psychological Effects of Leaving Home: Homesickness, Health, and Obsessional Thoughts," in Fisher and Cooper, *On the Move*, 154; Tilburg et al., "Homesickness," 899–12; Fisher, *Homesickness*, 25, 27, 118.

14. Slater, *The Pursuit of Loneliness*, 19.

15. Olds and Schwartz, *The Lonely American*, 8.

16. Fisher, "The Psychological Effects of Leaving Home," 154; Tilburg et al., "Homesickness," 899–12; Fisher, *Homesickness*, 25, 27, 118; Kotchemidova, "From Good Cheer to 'Drive-by Smiling,'" 5–37.

17. F. Davis, *Yearning for Yesterday*, 4.

18. Fritzsche, "Specters of History," 1618, 1591.

19. X. Zhou et al., "Counteracting Loneliness," 1028.

20. Christina Gillham, "When Your Child Is Away," *Newsweek*, July 28, 2008, 55.

21. Katie Hafner, "To: Mom and Dad Re: Homesickness," *New York Times*, July 31, 2003.

22. Hafner, "To: Mom and Dad Re: Homesickness"; "Fire Walls for the Homesick Virus," *New York Times*, August 14, 2008.

23. "When There's No Place Like Home," *New York Times*, July 29, 2007.

24. "Homesickness 101: 'Naked Roommate' Author's Tips on Surviving First Months at College," *Boston Globe*, October 10, 2009.

25. "Parental Advisory," *Triangle*, October 9, 2009, accessed October 2009, http://media. www.thetriangle.org/media/storage/paper689/news/2009/10/09/EdOp/Parental. Advisory-3799756.shtml.

26. Kathryn Tyler, "The Tethered Generation," *HR Magazine* 52, no. 5 (2007); "Colleges Ward Off Overinvolved Parents," *Wall Street Journal*, July 28, 2005.

27. Jane Gross, "A Long-Distance Tether to Home: New Technology Binds College Students and Parents," *New York Times*, November 5, 1999.

28. Ellen Kim, "Longing for Home Possible to Alleviate," *Rice Thresher*, September 18, 2009, accessed October 2009, www.ricethresher.org/home/index.cfm?event=displayArticlePr interFriendly&;uStory_id=384d778d-89e5–4818–9b5f-81a56b0e9162.

29. "Colleges Are Learning to Hold Parents' Hands," *Los Angeles Times*, November 28, 2004.

30. "In College, You Can Go Home Again and Again," *New York Times*, December 14, 2006.

31. Henkin, *The Postal Age*, 2, 29, 46–47.

32. "Front Lines a Click Away: Troops, Loved Ones Linked as Never Before," *Philadelphia Inquirer*, March 19, 2006.

33. "Teens' Effort for GIs Makes a Connection," *Boston Globe*, April 1, 2007.

34. "Camp AT&T: Your Communications Command Center," AT&T Military Headquarters, www.usa.att.com/military/camp/calling_centers.jsp, accessed November 17, 2009.

35. Email from LTC Keith McVeigh, November 9, 2009, in author's possession; "Staying in Touch with Home, for Better or Worse," *New York Times*, February 17, 2011.

36. Email from LTC Keith McVeigh; Ender, *American Soldiers in Iraq*, 23.

37. "Front Lines a Click Away."

38. Basilio Prado, Villa Hidalgo, Nayarit, Mexico, interviewed by Susan Matt, Luke Fernandez, and Irasema Rivera, March 11, 2009, translated by Irasema Rivera, in author's possession.

39. Ricardo Valencia, San Blas, Mexico, interviewed by Susan Matt and Luke Fernandez, March 12, 2009, translated by Irasema Rivera, in author's possession; Elizabeth Guardado, Tepic, Mexico, interviewed by Susan Matt and Irasema Rivera, March 10, 2009, translated by Irasema Rivera, in author's possession; William Hernandez, Ogden, UT, interviewed by Susan Matt and Irasema Rivera, July 2009, translated by Irasema Rivera, in author's possession.

40. Felicity Fouché, Salt Lake City, Utah, interviewed by Susan Matt, November 17, 2009, in author's possession.

41. Marjukka Ollilainen, Ogden, UT, interviewed by Susan Matt, April 20, 2010, in author's possession.

42. Ricardo Valencia interview.

43. Marivir Montebon, "Immigrants Tell How to Cope with Homesickness," April 1, 2009, Suite 101.com, accessed April 17, 2010, http://personaldevelopment.suite101.com/article.cfm.immigrants_tell_how_to_cope_with_homesickness.

44. Christian Arias, Villa Hidalgo, Nayarit, Mexico, interviewed by Susan Matt and Irasema Rivera, March 11, 2009, translated by Irasema Rivera; Lizabeth O. Valderana Navarro, Tepic, Mexico, interviewed by Susan Matt and Irasema Rivera, March 9, 2009, translated by Irasema Rivera, in author's possession.

45. Felicity Fouché interview.

46. Marjukka Ollilainen interview.

47. Manila Girl, "Feeling Homesick," *Filipino Express*, August 18, 2002.

48. Bittle et al., *A Place to Call Home*, 23, 3. For rates of phone calls home, see Farkas et al., *Now That I'm Here*, 60.

49. Maria Elena Rivera, Tepic, Mexico, December 12, 2009, interviewed by Susan Matt and Luke Fernandez, translated by Luke Fernandez.

50. Felicity Fouché interview.

51. Kubey and Cszikszentmihalyi, *Television*, 133, 173.

52. R. D. Putnam, *Bowling Alone*, 224, 228, 231, 235, 236, 238–42.

53. Cowan, *A Social History of American Technology*, 290; Cross and Szostak, *Technology and American Society*, 270; R. D. Putnam, *Bowling Alone*, 221, 63, 228; Meyrowitz, *No Sense of Place*, 119–20, 145–46.

54. "An Anchor at KMEX," *Los Angeles Times*, December 4, 2000.

55. Cowan, *A Social History of American Technology*, 291.

56. "Home Away from Home a Baseball Bar," *Los Angeles Times*, December 14, 1989.

57. "Orange Peeled a Look at Life inside the County: They Left Their Hearts in Nebraska," *Los Angeles Times*, March 7, 2005.

58. Felicity Fouché interview.

59. "South Asian Channels and Bundles," http://www.comcast.com/Corporate/Programming/IntlNetworks/southasian.html#STAR, accessed November 4, 2009.

60. Friedman, *The World Is Flat*, 507–8. Friedman gives credit for the phrase "the globalization of the local" to Indrajit Banerjee.

61. Ole O. Moen, "Mobility, Geographic and Social: The American Dream and American Realities," in Minnen and Hilton, *Nation on the Move*, 160.

62. "Big U.S. Bases Are Part of Iraq, but a World Apart," *New York Times*, September 8, 2009.

63. Email from LTC Keith McVeigh; Ender, *American Soldiers in Iraq*, 24.

64. LTC Keith McVeigh and SFC Scott Kibler, interviewed by Susan J. Matt, November 17, 2009, transcript in author's possession.

65. Oscar Avila, "Nostalgia Served Piping Hot," *Chicago Tribune*, July 30, 2005.

66. Ricardo Valencia interview.

67. Gabaccia, *We Are What We Eat*, 166.

68. "Hormel Venture with Patak Expands Ethnic Food," *Brandweek* 37 (February 5, 1996): 9; "Hormel Deal Brings Mexican Food Brands across Border," *Brandweek* 37 (July 15, 1996): 5. For more on this trend, see Gabaccia, *We Are What We Eat*.

69. "Jackson Heights: An Oasis for the Homesick," *News-India Times*, July 21, 1995.

70. Quoted in Ray, *The Migrant's Table*, 83.

71. Louis-Alexandre-Hippolyte Leroy-Dupré, "De la nostalgie" (Thèse de medicine, Paris, 1846), no. 134, 26, quoted in Roth, "Dying of the Past," 5–29.

72. "Are You Ever Homesick?" *Anaconda Standard*, (Anaconda, Montana) July 15, 1899.

73. Anton Shammas, "Amérka, Amérka: A Palestinian Abroad in the Land of the Free," in Wesley Brown and Ling, *Visions of America*, 291–300.

74. Email from LTC Keith McVeigh, November 9, 2009, in author's possession.

75. Jasper, *Restless Nation*, 11.

76. Hine, *Community on the American Frontier*, 5.

BIBLIOGRAPHY

ARCHIVAL MATERIALS

Angell, John Carpenter, Family Correspondence, 1825–59. Western Americana Collection, Beinecke Rare Book and Manuscript Library, Yale University, New Haven, CT.

Atwell, William B. *Civil War Diary of a Member of the 27ᵗʰOhio Infantry Regiment.* Western Americana Collection. Beinecke Rare Book and Manuscript Library, Yale University, New Haven, CT.

Backus, Gurdon. *Overland Journey from Burlington, Vermont.* Western Americana Collection. Beinecke Rare Book and Manuscript Library, Yale University, CT.

Ballou, Mary Bean. *Voyage to California.* Western Americana Collection. Beinecke Rare Book and Manuscript Library, Yale University, CT.

Barry, William R. Correspondence, 1855–64. South Carolina Historical Society, Charleston, SC.

Breese-Stevens–Roby Family Papers. Department of Rare Books and Special Collections, University of Rochester, NY.

[Brown, Rebecca Warren?]. *Memoir of Mrs. Chloe Spear, A Native of Africa, Who was Enslaved in Childhood, And Died in Boston, January 3, 1815, . . . Aged 65 Years.* By "A Lady of Boston." Boston, 1832. Photocopy of original, Howard University.

Christman, Enos. Journals and Correspondence. Western Americana Collection, Beinecke Rare Book and Manuscript Library, Yale University, New Haven, CT.

Crary, Rowena and Stephen. Family Papers. Western Americana Collection, Beinecke Rare Book and Manuscript Library, Yale University, New Haven, CT.

Damon, Fannie A. "'Home Again' sung to the air 'Home, Sweet Home.' Dedicated to the Old Folks' Picnic Ass'n, Westminster, Mass." Brown University Library, Providence, RI.

Domoto, Toichi. "A Japanese-American Nurseryman's Life in California: Floriculture and Family, 1883–1992." Oral history conducted in 1992 by Suzanne B. Riess. Regional Oral History Library, Bancroft Library, University of California, Berkeley.

Essays by Jewish-American Immigrant Women. Sponsored by the National Council of Jewish Women: 1925–1929. First Impressions of America, Princeton University Library Manuscripts Division, Princeton University, Princeton, NJ.

Fickes, Elizabeth Hukill. Diary, 1856–1857. Western Americana Collection, Beinecke Rare Book and Manuscript Library, Yale University, New Haven, CT.

Finnish American Family History Project. Immigration History Research Center, University of Minnesota, Minneapolis.

Francis, Samuel Dexter. "The Original manuscript Diary of Samuel Dexter Francis: Embracing Life in Vermont, 1841–1845; Travels in the Midwest & Life In Illinois, 1845–52; With the Day-By-Day Journal of His Trip Across the Plains and Life in Oregon, 1852–1862." Western Americana Collection, Beinecke Rare Books and Manuscript Library, Yale University, New Haven, CT.

Gila River Relocation Center Records, 1942–1945. Bancroft Library, University of California, Berkeley.

Hall, Elbridge Gerry. BioFile. The Society of California Pioneers, San Francisco.

Hendrickson, Barbara Di Nucci. Papers. Immigration History Research Center, University of Minnesota, Minneapolis.

"Italians in Chicago." Oral History Project. Immigration History Research Center, University of Minnesota, Minneapolis.

Italian Miscellaneous Manuscript Collections. Immigration History Research Center, University of Minnesota, Minneapolis.

Kenaga Family Papers. Western Americana Collection, Beinecke Rare Book and Manuscript Library, Yale University, New Haven, CT.

Logan, James Raymond. Scrapbook Collection. A very Institute Archives, College of Charleston, SC.

Lothrop Family Papers. Western Americana Collection, Beinecke Rare Book and Manuscript Library, Yale University, New Haven, CT.

Mansur, Abby T. Leighton. Correspondence, 1852–1874. Western Americana Collection, Beinecke Rare Book and Manuscript Library, Yale University, New Haven, CT.

Millsap, Walter, Keikichi Akana Imamura Family Papers. Western Americana Collection, Beinecke Rare Book and Manuscript Library, Yale University, New Haven, CT.

Murray, William. Letters. The Society of California Pioneers, San Francisco.

Near Eastern Miscellaneous Manuscripts Collection. Immigration History Research Center, University of Minnesota, Minneapolis.

Onomiya, Holly H. Papers, 1942–82. Bancroft Library, University of California, Berkeley.

Oral Histories Documenting New Haven, Connecticut (RU 1055). Manuscripts and Archives, Yale University Library, New Haven, CT.

Osborn, James Marshall and Marie-Louise Collection. Beinecke Rare Book and Manuscript Library, Yale University, New Haven, CT.

Pantovic Collection. A very Institute, College of Charleston, SC.

"Pertinent Facts about Relocation Centers and Japanese Americans." War Relocation Authority, Washington, DC. 1943? Beinecke Library Broadsides, Beinecke Rare Book and Manuscript Library, Yale University, New Haven, CT.

Polish Miscellaneous Manuscript Collections. Immigration History Research Center, University of Minnesota, Minneapolis.

Pratt, Richard Henry, Papers. Western Americana Collection, Beinecke Rare Book and Manuscript Library, Yale University, New Haven, CT.

Rosie the Riveter World War II American Homefront Oral History Project. Regional Oral History Office, Bancroft Library, University of California, Berkeley.

School News (Carlisle Barracks, PA.), Beinecke Rare Book and Manuscript Library, Yale University, New Haven, CT.

Shedd, Calvin. Calvin Shedd Papers. *The Civil War in Florida: Letters of a New Hampshire Soldier.* Special Collections, University of Miami Library, Coral Gables, FL.

Simm, Hugh. Collection, 1748–1810, Princeton University Library, Manuscripts Division, Princeton University, Princeton, NJ.

Smith, Walter D. Diary and Letters, 1842–61. South Carolina Historical Society, Charleston.

Steele, Lynn. Collection. Vietnam Virtual Archives, Texas Tech University. Accessed May 15, 2010. www.vietnam.ttu.edu/virtualarchive/.

Taylor, Paul Schuster. Papers, 1660–1997. Bancroft Library, University of California, Berkeley.

Tiffany, P. C. *Overland Journey from Mount Pleasant, Iowa to California.* Western Americana Collection, Beinecke Rare Book and Manuscript Library, Yale University, New Haven, CT.

Vardell, William G. Letters. South Carolina Historical Society, Charleston.

Walker, Mary Richardson. Diary. Walker Family Papers, Western Americana Collection, Beinecke Rare Book and Manuscript Library, Yale University, New Haven, CT.

Wilbur, George W. Family Papers. Western Americana Collection, Beinecke Rare Book and Manuscript Library, Yale University, New Haven, CT.

Willis, Edward. Azor Scrapbook. South Carolina Historical Society, Charleston.

PUBLISHED MATERIALS

Abbott, Lemuel Abijah. *Personal Recollections and Civil War Diary, 1864.* Burlington, VT: Free Press, 1908.

Adams, David Wallace. *Education for Extinction: American Indians and the Boarding School Experience, 1875–1928.* Lawrence: University Press of Kansas, 1995.

Akhtar, Salman. *Immigration and Identity: Turmoil, Treatment, and Transformation.* Northvale, NJ: Jason Aronson, 1999.

Alarcón, Rafael. "The Development of Home Town Associations in the United States and the Use of Social Remittances in Mexico." Washington, DC: Inter-American Dialogue, 2000. Accessed April 15, 2010. www.thedialogue.org/PublicationFiles/Alarcon.pdf.

Albee, John. *Confessions of Boyhood.* Boston: Richard G. Badger, Gorham Press, 1910.

Alcott, Louisa May. *Hospital Sketches.* 1863. Bedford, MA: Applewood Books, 1993.

Alford, Thomas Wildcat. *Civilization, and the Story of the Absentee Shawnees.* 1936. Norman: University of Oklahoma Press, 1979.

Allen, Hervey. *Toward the Flame: A War Diary.* 1926. Pittsburgh: University of Pittsburgh Press, 1968.

Alter, George, Claudia Goldin, and Elyce Rotella. "The Savings of Ordinary Americans: The Philadelphia Saving Fund Society in the Mid-Nineteenth Century." *Journal of Economic History* 54 (December 1994): 735–67.

Altman, Ida. *Emigrants and Society: Extremadura and America in the Sixteenth Century.* Berkeley: University of California Press, 1989.

———. *Transatlantic Ties in the Spanish Empire: Brihuega, Spain and Puebla, Mexico 1560–1620.* Palo Alto, CA: Stanford University Press, 2000.

Altman, Ida, and James Horn, eds. *"To Make America": European Emigration in the Early Modern Period.* Berkeley: University of California Press, 1991.

Alverson, Margaret Blake. *Sixty Years of California Song.* San Francisco: Sunset Publishing, 1913.

American Life Histories: Manuscripts from the Federal Writers Project, 1936–1940. Library of Congress. Accessed May 15, 2009. http://memory.loc.gov.

American Psychiatric Association. *Diagnostic and Statistical Manual of Mental Disorders.* 2nd ed. Washington, DC: American Psychiatric Association, 1968.

———. *Diagnostic and Statistical Manual of Mental Disorders.* 3rd ed. Washington, DC: American Psychiatric Association, 1980.

———. *Diagnostic and Statistical Manual of Mental Disorders.* 4th ed. Washington, DC: American Psychiatric Association, 1994.

Ammons, Paul, Josie Nelson, and John Wodarski. "Surviving Corporate Moves: Sources of Stress and Adaption among Corporate Executive Families." *Family Relations* 31 (April 1982): 207–12.

Anderson, Benedict. *Imagined Communities: Reflections on the Origin and Spread of Nationalism.* Rev. ed. London: Verso, 1991.

Anderson, David. "Down Memory Lane: Nostalgia for the Old South in Post–Civil War Plantation Reminiscences." *Journal of Southern History* 71 (February 2005): 105–36.

———. "Dying of *Nostalgia*: Homesickness in the Union Army during the Civil War." *Civil War History* 56, no. 3 (2010): 247–82.

Anderson, Donald Lee, and George Tryggve Anderson. "Nostalgia and Malingering in the Military during the Civil War." *Perspectives in Biology and Medicine* 28 (1984): 156–66.

Andrews, William L. *To Tell a Free Story: The First Century of Afro-American Autobiography, 1760–1865.* Urbana: University of Illinois Press, 1988.

Apperson, John Samuel. *Repairing the "March of Mars": The Civil War Diaries of John Samuel Apperson, Hospital Steward in the Stonewall Brigade, 1861–1865.* Edited by John Herbert Roper. Macon, GA: Mercer University Press, 2001.

Applebaum, Robert, and John Wood Sweet, eds. *Envisioning an English Empire: Jamestown and the Making of the North Atlantic World.* Philadelphia: University of Pennsylvania Press, 2005.

Appy, Christian G. *Working-Class War: American Combat Soldiers and Vietnam.* Chapel Hill: University of North Carolina Press, 1993.

Archuleta, Margaret, Brenda J. Child, and K. Tsianina Lomawaima, eds. *Away from Home: American Indian Boarding School Experiences, 1879–2000.* Phoenix: Heard Museum, 2000.

Arnold, Thomas. *Observations on the Nature, Kinds, Causes, and Prevention, of Insanity.* 2 vols. 2nd ed. London: Richard Philips, 1806.

Atkins, Josiah. *The Diary of Josiah Atkins.* New York: Arno Press, 1975.

Attie, Jeanie. *Patriotic Toil: Northern Women and the American Civil War.* Ithaca, NY: Cornell University Press, 1998.

Bailey, Pearce, Frankwood E. Williams, Paul O. Komora, Thomas W. Salmon, and Norman Fenton. *The Medical Department of the United States Army in the World War.* Vol. 10, *Neuropsychiatry in the United States.* Washington DC: U.S. Government Printing Office, 1929.

Balch, Emily Greene. *Our Slavic Fellow Citizens.* 1910. New York: Arno Press, 1969.

Ball, Charles. *Fifty Years in Chains, or, The Life of an American Slave.* 1859. Detroit: Negro History Press, 1971.

Ball, John. *Autobiography of John Ball, 1794–1884, compiled by his daughters: Kate Ball Powers, Flora Ball Hopkins, Lucy Ball.* In *Recollections of the Early Republic: Selected Autobiographies.* Edited by Joyce Appleby. Boston: Northeastern University Press, 1997.

Ballard, Allen B. *One More Day's Journey: The Story of a Family and a People.* New York: McGraw Hill, 1984.

Barber, Daniel. *The History of My Own Times.* 1827. Ann Arbor, MI: University Microfilms, 1963.

Bartholow, Roberts. *A Manual of Instructions for Enlisting and Discharging Soldiers With Special Reference to the Medical Examination of Recruits, and the Detection of Disqualifying and Feigned Diseases.* 1863. San Francisco: Norman Publishing, 1991.

Barton, H. Arnold, ed. *Letters from the Promised Land: Swedes in America, 1840–1914.* Minneapolis: University of Minnesota Press for the Swedish Pioneer Historical Society, 1975.

Barton, Michael, and Larry M. Logue, eds. *The Civil War Soldier: A Historical Reader.* New York: New York University Press, 2002.

Bederman, Gail. *Manliness and Civilization: A Cultural History of Gender and Race in the United States, 1880–1917.* Chicago: University of Chicago Press, 1995.

Bercovitch, Sacvan, ed. *Puritan Personal Writings: Autobiographies and Other Writings.* New York: AMS Press, 1982.

Berger, Peter, Brigitte Berger, and Hansfried Kellner. *The Homeless Mind: Modernization and Consciousness.* New York: Random House, 1973.

Berlin, Ira. *The Making of African America: The Four Great Migrations.* New York: Viking, 2010.

Berry, Chad. *Southern Migrants, Northern Exiles.* Urbana: University of Illinois Press, 2000.

Berry, Stephen W., II. *All That Makes a Man: Love and Ambition in the Civil War South.* New York: Oxford University Press, 2003.

Berthoff, Rowland. *An Unsettled People: Social Order and Disorder in American History.* New York: Harper & Row, 1971.

Bittle, Scott, Jonathan Rochkind, Amber Ott, and Paul Gasbarra. *A Place to Call Home: What Immigrants Say Now about Life in America.* New York: Public Agenda, Carnegie Corporation of New York, 2009.

Black, J. Stewart, Hal B. Gregersen, Mark E. Mendenhall, and Linda K. Stroh. *Globalizing People through International Assignments.* Reading, MA: Addison-Wesley, 1999.

Black, Timuel D., Jr. *Bridges of Memory: Chicago's First Wave of Black Migration.* Evanston, IL: Northwestern University Press, DuSable Museum of African American History, 2003.

Blair, Emily Newell. *Bridging Two Eras: The Autobiography of Emily Newell Blair, 1877–1951.* Edited by Virginia Jean Laas. Columbia: University of Missouri Press, 1990.

Blassingame, John. *The Slave Community: Plantation Life in the Antebellum South.* Rev. ed. New York: Oxford University Press, 1972.

Blauvelt, Martha Tomhave. *The Work of the Heart: Young Women and Emotion, 1780–1930.* Charlottesville: University Press of Virginia, 2007.

Blegen, Theodore C., ed. *Land of Their Choice: The Immigrants Write Home.* St. Paul: University of Minnesota Press, 1955.

———. *Norwegian Migration to America, 1825–1860.* New York: Arno Press, 1969.

Blewett, Mary H., ed. *Caught between Two Worlds: The Diary of a Lowell Mill Girl, Susan Brown, of Epson, New Hampshire.* Lowell, MA: Lowell Museum, 1984.

Blight, David. *Race and Reunion: The Civil War in American Memory.* Cambridge, MA: Belknap Press of Harvard University Press, 2001.

Blomquist, Ceil. "Study Shows Relocation Resistance Reversing." *Personnel Administrator* 27 (December 1982): 55–56.

Bock, H. Riley, ed. "One Year at War: Letters of Capt. Geo. W. Dawson, C.S.A." *Missouri Historical Review* 73 (January 1979): 165–97.

Bodnar, John. *The Transplanted: A History of Immigrants in Urban America.* Bloomington: Indiana University Press, 1985.

Bontemps, Arna, and Jack Conroy. *Anyplace but Here.* 1945. New York: Hill and Wang, 1966.

Boroff, David. "A Little Milk, a Little Honey." *American Heritage* 17 (October/November 1966): 12–21, 74–81.

Boswell, Thomas D., and James R. Curtis. *The Cuban-American Experience: Culture, Images, and Perspectives.* Totowa, NJ: Rowman & Allenheld, 1984.

Bowman, Allen. *The Morale of the American Revolutionary Army.* 1943. Port Washington, NY: Kennikat Press, 1964.

Boyd, Cyrus F. *The Civil War Diary of Cyrus F. Boyd, Fifteenth Iowa Infantry, 1861–1863.* Edited by Mildred Throne. Millwood, NY: Kraus, 1977.

Boyer, Paul. *Urban Masses and Moral Order in America, 1820–1920.* Cambridge, MA: Harvard University Press, 1978.

Brackett, Charles. *Surgeon on Horseback: The Missouri and Arkansas Journal and Letters of Dr. Charles Brackett of Rochester, Indiana, 1861–1863.* Compiled by James W. Wheaton. Carmel, IN: Guild Press, 1998.

Bradford, William. *Bradford's History of Plymouth Plantation 1606–1646.* Edited by William T. Davis. 1908. New York: Barnes and Noble, 1964.

Brandt, Anthony. "A Short Natural History of Nostalgia." *Atlantic Monthly* 242 (December 1978): 58–63.

Breen, George E. *Middle Management Morale in the '80s: An AMA Survey Report.* New York: American Management Association, 1983.

Breen, T. H. "Looking Out for Number One: Conflicting Cultural Values in Early Seventeenth-Century Virginia." *South Atlantic Quarterly* 78, no. 3 (1979): 342–60.

Brett, Jeanne M., and Linda K. Stroh. "Women in Management: How Far Have We Come and What Needs to Be Done As We Approach 2000?" *Journal of Management Inquiry* 8 (December 1999): 392–98.

Brinks, Herbert J., ed. *Dutch American Voices: Letters from the United States, 1850–1930.* Ithaca, NY: Cornell University Press, 1995.

Brite, John Duncan. *The Attitude of European States toward Emigration to the American Colonies and the United States, 1607–1820: A Part of a Dissertation Submitted to the Faculty of the Division of the Social Sciences in Candidacy for the Degree of Doctor of Philosophy.* 1937. Chicago: University of Chicago Libraries, 1939.

Brotz, Howard, and Everett Wilson. "Characteristics of Military Society." *American Journal of Sociology* 51 (March 1946): 371–75.

Brown, Dee. *Bury My Heart at Wounded Knee: An Indian History of the American West.* New York: Holt, Rinehart & Winston, 1970.

Brown, Dona. *Inventing New England: Regional Tourism in the Nineteenth Century.* Washington, DC: Smithsonian, 1995.

Brown, Herbert Ross. *The Sentimental Novel in America, 1789–1860.* New York: Pageant Books, 1959.

Brown, Marc. *Arthur Goes to Camp.* Boston: Little, Brown, 1982.

Brown, Robert Norman, II. "Coming Home: Black Return Migration to the Yazoo-Mississippi Delta." PhD diss., Louisiana State University, 2001.

Brown, Wallace. *The Good Americans: The Loyalists in the American Revolution.* New York: William Morrow, 1969.

Brown, Wesley, and Amy Ling, eds. *Visions of America: Personal Narratives from the Promised Land.* New York: Persea Books, 1993.

Browne, Eliza Southgate. *A Girl's Life Eighty Years Ago: Selections from the Letters of Eliza Southgate Browne.* New York: Charles Scribner's Sons, 1888.

Bucke, Richard M., ed. *The Wound Dresser: Letters Written to His Mother from the Hospitals in Washington during the Civil War.* New York: Bodley Press, 1949.

Bucknill, John Charles, and Daniel H. Tuke. *A Manual of Psychological Medicine Containing the History, Nosology, Description, Statistics, Diagnosis, Pathology, and Treatment of Insanity with an Appendix of Cases.* Philadelphia: Blanchard and Lea, 1858.

Buel, Elizabeth C. Barney, ed. *Chronicles of a Pioneer School from 1792–1833, Being the History of Miss Sarah Pierce and her Litchfield School.* Compiled by Emily Noyes Vanderpoel. Cambridge, MA: University Press, 1903.

Bukowczyk, John J. *And My Children Did Not Know Me: A History of the Polish Americans.* Bloomington: Indiana University Press, 1987.

Bulkeley, Peter. *The Gospel-Covenant; or The Covenant of Grace Opened. . . .* 2nd ed. London: Matthew Simmons, T. Kembe and A. Kembe, 1651.

[Burgess?], Embe. *Stiya: A Carlisle Indian Girl at Home Founded on the Author's Actual Observations.* Cambridge, MA: Riverside Press, 1891.

Burgess, Thomas. *Greeks in America.* 1913. New York: Arno Press, 1970.

Burlend, Rebecca, and Edward Burlend. *A True Picture of Emigration: Or Fourteen Years in the Interior of North America; Being a Full and Impartial Account of the Various Difficulties and Ultimate Success of an English Family who Migrated from Barwick-in-Elmet, Near Leeds, in the year 1831.* Edited by Milo Milton Quaife. New York: Citadel Press, 1968.

Burns, Sarah. "The Country Boy Goes to the City: Thomas Hovenden's *Breaking Home Ties* in American Popular Culture." *American Art Journal* 20, no. 4 (1988): 59–73.

Burrows, George Man. *Commentaries on the Causes, Forms, Symptoms, and Treatment, Moral and Medical, of Insanity.* London: Thomas and George Underwood, 1828.

Burstein, Andrew. *Sentimental Democracy: The Evolution of America's Romantic Self Image.* New York: Hill and Wang, 1999.

Bushman, Richard. *From Puritan to Yankee: Character and the Social Order in Connecticut, 1690–1765.* Cambridge, MA: Harvard University Press, 1967.

Butler, Benjamin F. *Private and Official Correspondence of Gen. Benjamin F. Butler, During the Period of the Civil War.* 5 vols. Norwood, MA: Plimpton Press, 1917.

Buzzanco, Robert. *Vietnam and the Transformation of American Life.* Malden, MA: Blackwell, 1999.

Byrne, Stephen. *Irish Emigration to the United States: What It Has Been, and What It Is. Facts and Reflections Addressed to Irish People Intending to Emigrate from their Native Land; and To Those Living in the Large Cities of Great Britain and of the United States.* 1873. New York: Arno Press, 1969.

Calhoun, Charles, ed. *The Gilded Age: Perspectives on the Origins of Modern America.* 2nd ed. Lanham, MD: Rowman & Littlefield, 2007.

Calhoun, J. Theodore. "Nostalgia, As a Disease of Field Service. A paper read before the Medical Society of the 2nd Division, 3rd Army Corps, Army of Potomac, February 10, 1864." *Medical and Surgical Reporter* 11 (1864): 130–32.

Canfield, Thomas Marley. "Psychologists at War: The History of American Psychology and the First World War." PhD diss., University of Texas at Austin, 1969.

Canny, Nicholas, ed. *Europeans on the Move: Studies on European Migration, 1500–1800.* Oxford: Clarendon Press, 1994.

———, ed. *The Oxford History of the British Empire.* Vol. 1, *The Origins of Empire.* Oxford: Oxford University Press, 1998.

Caroli, Betty Boyd. *Italian Repatriation from the United States, 1900–1914.* New York: Center for Migration Studies, 1973.

Cashin, Joan E. *A Family Venture: Men and Women on the Southern Frontier.* New York: Oxford University Press, 1991.

Castel, Albert, ed. "Malingering: Many . . . diseases are . . . feigned." *Civil War Times Illustrated* 16 (1977): 29–32.

Castleman, Alfred Lewis. *The Army of the Potomac: Behind the Scenes. A Diary of Unwritten History; From the Organization of the Army, by General George B. McClellan, to the Close of the Campaign in Virginia, about the First Day of January, 1863.* Milwaukee: Strickland, 1863.

Catton, Bruce. "Hayfoot, Strawfoot!" *American Heritage* 8, no. 3 (1957): 30–37.

———. *Reflections on the Civil War.* Garden City, NY: Doubleday, 1981.

Check, Earl. "Civil War Letters to New Sweden, Iowa." Translated by Emeroy Johnson. *Swedish-American Historical Quarterly* 36 (1985): 3–25.

Chicago Foreign Language Press Survey. Chicago: Chicago Public Library Omnibus Project of the Works Progress Administration of Illinois, 1942.

Choate, Mark I. *Emigrant Nation: The Making of Italy Abroad.* Cambridge, MA: Harvard University Press, 2008.

Christman, Enos. *One Man's Gold: The Letters and Journals of a Forty-Niner.* Edited by Florence Christman. London: Whittlesey House, 1931.

Chudacoff, Howard. *The Age of the Bachelor: Creating an American Subculture.* Princeton, NJ: Princeton University Press, 1999.

Cimbala, Paul, and Randall Miller. *Union Soldiers and the Northern Home Front: Wartime Experiences, Postwar Adjustments.* New York: Fordham University Press, 2002.

Clarke, Frances. "So Lonesome I Could Die: Nostalgia and Debates over Emotional Control in the Civil War North." *Journal of Social History* 42, no. 2 (2007): 253–82.

Clegg, Claude A., III. *The Price of Liberty: African Americans and the Making of Liberia.* Chapel Hill: University of North Carolina Press, 2004.

Coan, Peter Morton. *Ellis Island Interviews: In Their Own Words.* New York: Facts on File Press, 1997.

Coffey, Frank. *Always Home: Fifty Years of the USO.* Washington, DC: Brassey's, 1991.

Cohen, Harlan. *The Naked Roommate: And 107 Other Issues You Might Run Into in College.* Naperville, IL: Sourcebooks, 2005.

Cohen, Jeffrey H. *The Culture of Migration in Southern Mexico.* Austin: University of Texas Press, 2004.

Cohen, Lizabeth. *Making a New Deal: Industrial Workers in Chicago, 1919–1939.* New York: Cambridge University Press, 1991.

Coleman, Mary Haldane Begg, ed. *Virginia Silhouettes; Contemporary letters concerning Negro slavery in the state of Virginia, to which is appended, A dissertation on slavery with a proposal for the gradual abolition of it in the state of Virginia.* Richmond, VA: Dietz, 1934.

Coleman, Michael C. *American Indian Children at School, 1850–1930.* Jackson: University Press of Mississippi, 1993.

Combe, Andrew. *Observations on Mental Derangement: Being an Application of the Principles of Phrenology to the Elucidation of the Causes, Symptoms, Nature, and Treatment of Insanity.* Boston: Marsh, Capen & Lyon, 1834.

Conklin, Edmund S. *Principles of Adolescent Psychology.* New York: Henry Holt, 1935.

Conway, Dennis, and Jeffrey H. Cohen. "Consequences of Migration and Remittances for Mexican Transnational Communities." *Economic Geography* 74 (January 1998): 26–44.

Conwell, Joseph Alfred. *Manhood's Morning: A Book to Young Men between Fourteen and Twenty-Eight Years of Age.* Rev. ed. Philadelphia: Vir, 1903.

Cooke, Chauncey H. "A Badger Boy in Blue: The Letters of Chauncey H. Cooke." *Wisconsin Magazine of History* 4 (September 1920): 75–100.

Cooke, James J. *Chewing Gum, Candy Bars, and Beer: The Army PX in World War II.* Columbia: University of Missouri Press, 2009.

Cooke, John Esten. *Virginia: A History of the People.* Boston: Houghton, Mifflin, 1897.

Corson, E. S. "Nostalgia and Melancholia in the Tropics." *American Medicine,* November 7, 1903, 743–44.

Cowan, Ruth Schwartz. *A Social History of American Technology.* New York: Oxford University Press, 1997.

Cox, Caroline. *A Proper Sense of Honor: Service and Sacrifice in George Washington's Army.* Chapel Hill: University of North Carolina Press, 2004.

Craven, Wesley Frank. *The Legend of the Founding Fathers.* New York: New York University Press, 1956.

Cressy, David. *Crossing Over: Migration and Communication between England and New England in the Seventeenth Century.* Cambridge: Cambridge University Press, 1989.

Crew, Spencer R. *Field to Factory: Afro-American Migration, 1915–1940. An Exhibition at the National Museum of American History Smithsonian Institution.* Washington, DC: Smithsonian Institution, 1987.

Cromartie, John, and Carol B. Stack. "Reinterpretation of Black Return and Nonreturn Migration to the South, 1975–1980." *Geographical Review* 79 (July 1989): 297–310.

Crooker, Gary. *Images of America: New Hampshire Old Home Celebrations.* Charleston, SC: Acadia, 2009.

Cross, Gary, and Rick Szostak. *Technology and American Society: A History.* Upper Saddle River, NJ: Prentice Hall, 1995.

Cunningham, H. H. *Doctors in Gray: The Confederate Medical Service.* Baton Rouge: Louisiana State University Press, 1960.

Cuordileone, K. A. *Manhood and American Political Culture in the Cold War.* New York: Routledge, 2005.

———. "'Politics in an Age of Anxiety': Cold War Political Culture and the Crisis in American Masculinity, 1949–1960." *Journal of American History* 87 (September 2000): 515–45.

Dammann, Gordon, and Alfred Jay Bollet. *Images of Civil War Medicine: A Photographic History.* New York: Demos, 2008.

Dana, Richard Henry. *Two Years before the Mast.* 1840. New York: Buccaneer Books, 1984.

Daniels, Roger. *Coming to America: A History of Immigration and Ethnicity in American Life.* 2nd ed. New York: Harper Perennial, 2002.

Darrow, Clarence. *The Story of My Life.* New York: Charles Scribner's Sons, 1932.

Davis, Fred. *Yearning for Yesterday: A Sociology of Nostalgia.* New York: Free Press, 1979.

Davis, Jack E. "Changing Places: Slave Movement in the South." *Historian* 55 (1993): 657–76.

Davis, Marilyn P. *Mexican Voices/American Dreams: An Oral History of Mexican Immigration to the United States.* New York: Henry Holt, 1990.

Delbanco, Andrew. "Looking Homeward, Going Home: The Lure of England for the Founders of New England." *New England Quarterly* 59, no. 3 (1986): 358–86.

Deyle, Steven. *Carry Me Back: The Domestic Slave Trade in American Life.* New York: Oxford University Press, 2005.

Dickinson, Emily. *The Letters of Emily Dickinson.* Edited by Thomas H. Johnson. Vol. 1. Cambridge, MA: Belknap Press of Harvard University Press, 1958.

Diner, Hasia R. *Hungering for America: Italian, Irish and Jewish Foodways in the Age of Migration.* Cambridge, MA: Harvard University Press, 2001.

Dinnerstein, Leonard, and David M. Reimers. *Ethnic Americans: A History of Immigration and Assimilation.* New York: Harper & Row, 1975.

Dodge, Richard Irving. *Our Wild Indians: Thirty Three Years Personal Experience among the Red Men of the Great West.* Hartford, CT: A. D. Worthington, 1883.

Donnan, Elizabeth, ed. *Documents Illustrative of the History of the Slave Trade to America.* Vol. 1, *1441–1700.* Washington, DC: Carnegie Institution, 1930.

Doty, C. Stewart. *The First Franco-Americans: New England Life Histories from the Federal Writers' Project 1938–1939.* Orono: University of Maine at Orono Press, 1985.

Douglas, Ann. *The Feminization of American Culture.* New York: Knopf, 1978.

Dublin, Thomas, ed. *Farm to Factory: Women's Letters, 1830–1860.* New York: Columbia University Press, 1993.

———. *Immigrant Voices: New Lives in America, 1773–1986.* Urbana: University of Illinois Press, 1993.

Duhl, Leonard J., ed. *The Urban Condition: People and Policy in the Metropolis.* New York: Basic Books, 1963.

Earle, Alice Morse. *Customs and Fashions in Old New England.* New York: Scribner's Sons, 1893.

Edwards, Lee M. "Noble Domesticity: The Paintings of Thomas Hovenden." *American Art Journal* 19, no. 1 (1987): 4–38.

Edwards, Paul M. *The Korean War.* Westport, CT: Greenwood Press, 2006.

Edwards, Rebecca. *New Spirits: Americans in the Gilded Age, 1865–1905.* New York: Oxford University Press, 2006.

Ehle, John. *Trail of Tears: The Rise and Fall of the Cherokee Nation.* New York: Anchor Books, 1997.

Eisendorfer, A. "Clinical Significance of Extramural Psychiatry in the Army." *War Medicine* 5 (1944): 146–49.

Ellis, Clyde. *To Change Them Forever: Indian Education at the Rainy Mountain Boarding School, 1893–1920.* Norman: University of Oklahoma Press, 1996.

Ellis Island Oral History Project. Alexandra, VA: Alexander Street Press, 2003.

The Emigrant's True Guide: Comprising Advice and Instruction In every Stage of the Voyage to America; such as Choice of a Ship, Provisions and Clothing for the Voyage; Hints during the Voyage; Custom-

House Laws; What to Do on Landing; Interesting Anecdotes, Etc., Also, Information Which the Emigrant Needs on Arrival; Such as, Choice of Lodgings; Ways of Sharpers; How to get Employment; Where to Look for Land; Steamboat, Canal, and Railroad Routes; Rates of Travel in All Directions; How to Preserve Health, Etc. Etc. New York: J. Winchester, New World Press, 1844.

Ender, Morton G. *American Soldiers in Iraq: McSoldiers or Innovative Professionals?* New York: Routledge, 2009.

———. "G.I. Phone Home: The Use of Telecommunications by the Soldiers of Operation Just Cause." *Armed Forces and Society* 21 (Spring 1995): 435–53.

Ender, Morton G., and David R. Segal. "V(E)-Mail to the Foxhole: Soldier Isolation, (Tele) Communication, and Force Projection Operations." *Journal of Political and Military Sociology* 24 (Summer 1995): 83–104.

Erickson, Charlotte. *Invisible Immigrants: The Adaptation of English and Scottish Immigrants in Nineteenth-Century America.* Coral Gables, FL: University of Miami Press, 1972.

———. *Leaving England: Essays on British Emigration in the Nineteenth Century.* Ithaca, NY: Cornell University Press, 1994.

Eustace, Nicole. *Passion Is the Gale: Emotion, Power, and the Coming of the American Revolution.* Chapel Hill: University of North Carolina Press for the Omohundro Institute of Early American History and Culture, Williamsburg, VA, 2008.

Evans, Martin Marix, ed. *American Voices of World War I: Primary Source Documents 1917–1920.* Chicago: Fitzroy Dearborn, 2001.

Everson, Guy R., and Edward H. Simpson Jr., eds. *"Far, Far from Home": The Wartime Letters of Dick and Tally Simpson, Third South Carolina Volunteers.* New York: Oxford University Press, 1994.

Ewen, David. *All the Years of American Popular Music.* Englewood Cliffs, NJ: Prentice-Hall, 1977.

Ewen, Elizabeth. *Immigrant Women in the Land of Dollars: Life and Culture on the Lower East Side, 1890–1925.* New York: Monthly Review Press, 1985.

Fahs, Alice. *The Imagined Civil War: Popular Literature of the North and South, 1861–1865.* Chapel Hill: University of North Carolina Press, 2001.

Family Gathering on the French Homestead in Dunstable, Mass. October 8, 1879. n.p., 1879.

Faragher, John Mack. *Sugar Creek: Life on the Illinois Prairie.* New Haven, CT: Yale University Press, 1986.

———. *Women and Men on the Overland Trail.* New Haven, CT: Yale University Press, 1979.

Farkas, Steve, Ann Duffett, and Jean Johnson. *Now That I'm Here: What America's Immigrants Have to Say about Life in the U.S. Today.* With Leslie Moye and Jackie Vine. New York: Public Agenda, Carnegie Corporation, 2002.

Farseth, Pauline, and Theodore C. Blegen, eds. and trans. *Frontier Mother: The Letters of Gro Svendsen.* Northfield, MN: Norwegian American Historical Association, 1950.

Fatout, Paul, ed. *Letters of a Civil War Surgeon.* West Lafayette, IN: Purdue University, Studies in the Humanities Series, 1961.

Faust, Drew Gilpin. "Culture, Conflict, and Community: The Meaning of Power on an Ante-Bellum Plantation." *Journal of Social History* 14 (Fall 1980): 83–97.

———. *This Republic of Suffering: Death and the American Civil War.* New York: Knopf, 2008.

Fea, John. *The Way of Improvement Leads Home: Philip Vickers Fithian and the Rural Enlightenment in Early America.* Philadelphia: University of Pennsylvania Press, 2008.

Fischer, Claude S. "Ever-More Rooted Americans." *City & Community* 1 (June 2002): 177–98.

Fischer, David Hackett. *Albion's Seed: Four British Folkways in America.* New York: Oxford University Press, 1989.

Fisher, Shirley. *Homesickness, Cognition, and Health.* London: Psychology Press, 1989.

Fisher, Shirley, and Cary L. Cooper, eds. *On the Move: The Psychology of Change and Transition.* New York: John Wiley, 1990.

Fithian, Philip Vickers. *The Journal and Letters of Philip Vickers Fithian, A Plantation Tutor of the Old Dominion, 1773–1774*. Edited by Hunter Dickinson Farish. Williamsburg, VA: Colonial Williamsburg, 1957.

Fitzpatrick, Marion Hill. *Letters to Amanda: The Civil War Letters of Marion Hill Fitzpatrick, Army of Northern Virginia*. Edited by Jeffrey C. Lowe and Samuel Hodges. Macon, GA: Mercer University Press, 1998.

Fleming, George Thornton, ed. *Life and Letters of Alexander Hays, Brevet Colonel United States Army, Brigadier General and Brevet Major General, United States Volunteers. Compiled by Gilbert Adams Hays*. Pittsburgh: Gilbert Adams Hays, 1919.

Fleming, Thomas J., ed. *Affectionately Yours, George Washington: A Self-Portrait in Letters of Friendship*. New York: Norton, 1967.

Flicker, David, and Paul Weiss. "Nostalgia and Its Military Implications." *War Medicine* 4 (1943): 380–87.

Flint, Austin, ed. *Sanitary Memoirs of the War of the Rebellion*. Vol. 1. New York: Hurd and Houghton, 1867.

Florida, Richard. *The Rise of the Creative Class and How It's Transforming Work, Leisure, Community, and Everyday Life*. New York: Basic Books, 2003.

———. *Who's Your City? How the Creative Economy Is Making Where to Live the Most Important Decision of Your Life*. New York: Basic Books, 2008.

Flower, George. *The Errors of Emigrants: Pointing Out Many popular Errors Hitherto Unnoticed; With a Sketch of the Extent and Resources of the New States of the North American Union, And a Description of the Progress and Present Aspect of the English Settlement in Illinois founded by Morris Birkbeck and George Flower, in the year 1817*. London: Cleave, 1841.

Foerster, Robert F. *The Italian Emigration of Our Times*. 1924. New York: Arno Press, 1969.

Fogleman, Aaron S. "From Slaves, Convicts, and Servants to Free Passengers: The Transformation of Immigration in the Era of the American Revolution." *Journal of American History* 85 (1998): 43–76.

Foner, Eric. *Reconstruction: America's Unfinished Revolution, 1863–1877*. New York: Harper & Row, 1988.

Force, Peter. *American Archives: Fifth Series. Containing A Documentary History of the Untied States of America from the Declaration of Independence, July 4, 1776 to the Definitive Treaty of Peace with Great Britain, September 3, 1783*. Volume 3. Washington, DC: M. St. Clair and Peter Force, 1853.

Ford, Andrew E. *The Story of the Fifteenth Regiment Massachusetts Volunteer Infantry in the Civil War, 1861–1864*. Clinton, MA: W. J. Coulter, 1898.

Franklin, John Hope, and Loren Schweninger. *Runaway Slaves*. New York: Oxford University Press, 1999.

Friedman, Thomas L. *The World Is Flat: A Brief History of the Twenty-First Century*. Updated and expanded ed. New York: Farrar, Straus and Giroux, 2006.

Fritzsche, Peter. "Specters of History: On Nostalgia, Exile, and Modernity." *American Historical Review* 106 (December 2001): 1587–618.

———. *Stranded in the Present: Modern Time and the Melancholy of History*. Cambridge, MA: Harvard University Press, 2004.

Frost, Isaac. "Homesickness and Immigrant Psychoses: Austrian and German Domestic Servants the Basis of Study." *Journal of Mental Science* 84 (1938): 801–47.

Fullilove, Mindy Thompson. "Psychiatric Implications of Displacement: Contributions from the Psychology of Place." *American Journal of Psychiatry* 153, no. 12 (1996): 1516–523.

———. *Root Shock: How Tearing Up City Neighborhoods Hurts America and What We Can Do about It*. New York: One World Books, 2004.

Fussell, Paul. *The Great War and Modern Memory*. 25th anniversary ed. New York: Oxford University Press, 2000.

Gabaccia, Donna. *Militants and Migrants: Rural Sicilians Become American Workers*. New Brunswick, NJ: Rutgers University Press, 1988.

———. *We Are What We Eat: Ethnic Food and the Making of Americans*. Cambridge, MA: Harvard University Press, 1998.

Gamio, Manuel, comp. *The Life Story of the Mexican Immigrant: Autobiographic Documents*. New York: Dover, 1971.

Gans, Herbert J. *The Levittowners: Ways of Life and Politics in a New Suburban Community*. New York: Pantheon, 1967.

———. *The Urban Villagers: Group and Class in the Life of Italian-Americans*. New York: Free Press, 1962.

García, María Cristina. *Havana USA: Cuban Exiles and Cuban Americans in South Florida, 1959–1994*. Berkeley: University of California Press, 1996.

Garland, Hamlin. *A Son of the Middle Border*. New York: Macmillan, 1923.

Glass, Albert Julius, and Franklin D. Jones. *Psychiatry in the Army: Lessons for Community Psychiatry*. Edited by Franklin Jones, Linette R. Sparacino, and Joseph M. Rothberg. Defense Technical Information Center. Accessed December 2008. http://handle.dticmil/100.2/ADA434941.

González, Hector M., Mary N. Haan, and Ladson Hinton. "Acculturation and the Prevalence of Depression in Older Mexican Americas: Baseline Results of the Sacramento Area Latino Study on Aging." *Journal of the American Geriatrics Society* 49 (July 2001): 948–53.

Gordon, Richard E., and Katherine K. Gordon. "Psychiatric Problems of a Rapidly Growing Suburb." *AMA Archives of Neurology and Psychiatry* 79 (May 1958): 543–48.

Graff, Harvey J. *Conflicting Paths: Growing Up in America*. Cambridge, MA: Harvard University Press, 1995.

Greene, William B. *Letters from a Sharpshooter: The Civil War Letters of William B. Greene, Co. G, 2nd United States Sharpshooters (Berdan's) Army of the Potomac, 1861–1865*. Transcribed by William H. Hastings. Paoli, WI: Historic Publications, 1993.

Gregory, James N. *American Exodus: The Dust Bowl Migration and Okie Culture in California*. New York: Oxford University Press, 1989.

———. *The Southern Diaspora: How the Great Migrations of Black and White Southerners Transformed America*. Chapel Hill: University of North Carolina Press, 2005.

Gregory, W. Edgar. "The Idealization of the Absent." *American Journal of Sociology* 50 (July 1944): 53–54.

Greiner, James M., Janey L. Coryell, and James R. Smither, eds. *A Surgeon's Civil War: The Letters and Diary of Daniel M. Holt, M.D.* Kent, OH: Kent State University Press, 1994.

Grenier, Guillermo J., and Lisandro Perez. "Miami Spice: The Ethnic Cauldron Simmers." In *Origins and Destinies: Immigration, Race, and Ethnicity in America*, edited by Silvia Pedraz and Ruben Rumbaut, 361–72. Belmont, CA: Wadsworth, 1996.

Griffin, Farah Jasmine. *"Who Set You Flowin'?" The African-American Migration Narrative*. New York: Oxford University Press, 1995.

Grinder, Dale R., ed. *World War I Survey: Papers*. Compiled by U.S. Military History Institute. Frederick, MD: University Publications of America, 1985.

Grinker, Roy R., and John P. Spiegel. *Men under Stress*. Philadelphia: Blakiston, 1945.

Grossman, James R. *Land of Hope: Chicago, Black Southerners, and the Great Migration*. Chicago: University of Chicago Press, 1989.

Groves, Ernest R. *The American Family*. Chicago: J. B. Lippincott, 1934.

———. *The Drifting Home*. Boston: Houghton Mifflin, 1926.

Gruenberg, Sidonie Matsner. *We, the Parents: Our Relationship to Our Children and to the World Today*. New York: Harper & Brothers, 1939.

Gunda, Bela. "America in Hungarian Folklore." *New Hungarian Quarterly* 15 (1974): 156–62.

Gutman, Herbert G. *The Black Family in Slavery and Freedom, 1750–1925.* New York: Vintage Books, 1977.

Habegger, Alfred. *My Wars Are Laid Away in Books: The Life of Emily Dickinson.* New York: Random House, 2001.

Hafen, LeRoy. *The Overland Mail, 1849–1869: Promoter of Settlement, Precursor of Railroads.* 1926. New York: AMS Press, 1969.

Hale, Edward Wright, ed. *Jamestown Narratives: Eyewitness Accounts of the Virginia Colony, the First Decade, 1607–1617.* Champlain, VA: Round House Press, 1998.

Hall, Patricia Kelly, and Steven Ruggles. "'Restless in the Midst of Their Prosperity': New Evidence on the Internal Migration of Americans, 1850–2000." *Journal of American History* 91 (December 2004): 829–46.

Hamm, Charles. *Yesterdays: Popular Song in America.* New York: Norton, 1979.

Hammond, William A. *A Treatise on Insanity in Its Medical Relations.* 1883. New York: Arno, 1973.

Handlin, Oscar. "Immigrants Who Go Back." *Atlantic Monthly* 198 (July 1956): 70–74.

———. *The Uprooted: The Epic Story of the Great Migrations That Made the American People.* Boston: Little, Brown, 1951.

Hansen, Carl G. O. *History of Sons of Norway: An American Fraternal Organization of Men and Women of Norwegian Birth or Extraction.* Minneapolis: Sons of Norway Supreme Lodge, 1944.

Hanson, Frederick R. *Combat Psychiatry: Experiences in the North African and Mediterranean Theaters of Operation, American Ground Forces, World War II.* Washington, DC: Government Printing Office, 1949.

Harleston, Edward Nathaniel. *The Toiler's Life: Poems.* Philadelphia: Jenson Press, 1907.

Harris, Robert F., and John Niflot, comps. *Dear Sister: The Civil War Letters of the Brothers Gould.* Westport, CT: Praeger, 1998.

Harrower, John. *The Journal of John Harrower: An Indentured Servant in the Colony of Virginia, 1773–1776.* Edited by Edward Miles Riley. Williamsburg, VA: Colonial Williamsburg, 1963.

Hart, Stephen Harding, and Archer Butler Hulber, eds. *The Southwestern Journals of Zebulon Pike, 1806–1807.* Albuquerque: University of New Mexico Press, 2006.

Haskell, Thomas L., and Richard F. Teichgraeber III, eds. *The Culture of the Market: Historical Essays.* New York: Cambridge University Press, 1993.

Hein, Jeremy. *From Vietnam, Laos, and Cambodia: A Refugee Experience in the United States.* New York: Twayne, 1995.

Heinze, Andrew R. *Adapting to Abundance: Jewish Immigrants, Mass Consumption, and the Search for American Identity.* New York: Columbia University Press, 1990.

Henkin, David M. *The Postal Age: The Emergence of Modern Communications in Nineteenth-Century America.* Chicago: University of Chicago Press, 2006.

Hess, Earl J. *The Union Soldier in Battle: Enduring the Ordeal of Combat.* Lawrence: University Press of Kansas, 1997.

Heuman, Gad, ed. *Out of the House of Bondage: Runaways, Resistance and Marronage in Africa and the New World.* London: Frank Cass, 1986.

Higham, John. *Strangers in the Land: Patterns of American Nativism, 1860–1925.* New York: Atheneum, 1966.

Hilles, Frederick W., and Harold Bloom, eds. *From Sensibility to Romanticism: Essays Presented to Frederick A. Pottle.* New York: Oxford University Press, 1965.

Hine, Robert V. *Community on the American Frontier: Separate but Not Alone.* Norman: University of Oklahoma Press, 1980.

Hofer, Johannes. "Medical Dissertation on Nostalgia." Translated by Carolyn Kiser Anspach. *Bulletin of the Institute of the History of Medicine* 2 (1934): 376–91.

Hoffman, Ronald, Mechel Sobel, and Fredrika J. Teuta, eds. *Through A Glass Darkly: Reflections on Personal Identity in Early America*. Chapel Hill: University of North Carolina Press for the Omohundro Institute of Early American History and Culture, 1997.

Hoganson, Kristin L. *Fighting for American Manhood: How Gender Politics Provoked the Spanish-American and Philippine-American Wars*. New Haven, CT: Yale University Press, 1998.

Holland, James K. "Diary of a Texan Volunteer in the Mexican War." *Southwestern Historical Quarterly* 30 (July 1926): 1–33.

Holli, Melvin G., and Peter d'A. Jones. *Ethnic Chicago: Revised and Expanded*. Grand Rapids, MI: William B. Eerdmans, 1984.

Holliday, J. S. *Rush for Riches: Gold Fever and the Making of California*. Oakland: Oakland Museum of California; Berkeley: University of California Press, 1999.

———. *The World Rushed In: The California Gold Rush Experience*. New York: Simon and Schuster, 1981.

Hollingshead, August B. "Adjustment to Military Life." *American Journal of Sociology* 51 (March 1946): 439–47.

Homesick Blues? Here's What to Do! Middleton, WI: Pleasant Company Publications, 1999.

Horn, James. *Adapting to a New World: English Society in the Seventeenth-Century Chesapeake*. Chapel Hill: University of North Carolina Press for the Institute of Early American History and Culture, 1994.

Horwitz, Dorothy G., and Melvin Horwitz. *We Will Not Be Strangers: Korean War Letters between a M.A.S.H. Surgeon and His Wife*. Urbana: University of Illinois Press, 1997.

Houston, Jeanne Wakatsuki, and James D. Houston. *Farewell to Manzanar*. New York: Bantam Books, 1973.

Hovey, Joseph D., and Cristina Magañam. "Acculturative Stress, Anxiety, and Depression among Mexican Immigrant Farmworkers in the Midwest United States." *Journal of Immigrant Health* 2 (2000): 119–31.

Howe, Daniel Walker. *Making the American Self: Jonathan Edwards to Abraham Lincoln*. New York: Oxford University Press, 1997.

———. *What Hath God Wrought: The Transformation of America, 1815–1848*. New York: Oxford University Press, 2007.

Hulbert, Ann. *Raising America: Experts, Parents, and a Century of Advice about Children*. New York: Knopf, 2003.

Hunt, Larry L., Matthew O. Hunt, and William W. Falk. "Who Is Headed South? U.S. Migration Trends in Black and White, 1970–2000." *Social Forces* 87, no. 1 (2008): 95–119.

Hunt, Lynn. *Inventing Human Rights: A History*. New York: Norton, 2007.

Inada, Lawson Fusao, ed. *Only What We Could Carry: The Japanese American Internment Experience*. Berkeley: Heyday Books, California Historical Society, 2000.

Jackson, Kenneth T. *Crabgrass Frontier: The Suburbanization of the United States*. New York: Oxford University Press, 1985.

Jackson, Richard, ed. *Popular Songs of Nineteenth-Century America: Complete Original Sheet Music for 64 Songs*. New York: Dover, 1976.

Jacobs, Harriet. *Incidents in the Life of a Slave Girl*. 1861. Mineola, NY: Dover, 2001.

Jasper, James M. *Restless Nation: Starting Over in America*. Chicago: University of Chicago Press, 2000.

Jeffrey, Julie Roy. *Frontier Women: The Trans-Mississippi West, 1840–1880*. New York: Hill and Wang, 1979.

Johnson, A. W. "Combat Psychiatry, Historical View." *Medical Bulletin of the U.S. Army, Europe* 26 (1969): 305–8.

Johnson, Edward. *Wonder-Working Providence of Sion's Saviour in New England*. Edited by J. Franklin Jameson. New York: Scribner's, 1910.

Johnson, George. "The Medical Topography of Texas and the Diseases of the Army of Invasion." *Boston Medical and Surgical Reporter* 36 (May 19, 1847): 1.

Johnson, Hildegard Binder. "The Location of German Immigrants in the Middle West." *Annals of the Association of American Geographers* 41 (March 1951): 1–41.

Johnson, Susan Lee. *Roaring Camp: The Social World of the California Gold Rush*. New York: Norton, 2001.

Kammen, Michael. *Mystic Chords of Memory: The Transformation of Tradition in America*. New York: Vintage, 1993.

Kamphoefner, Walter D., Wolfgang Helbich, and Ulrike Sommer, eds. *News from the Land of Freedom: German Immigrants Write Home*. Translated by Susan Carter Vogel. Ithaca, NY: Cornell University Press, 1991.

Kantor, Mildred B., ed. *Mobility and Mental Health: Proceedings of the Fifth Annual Conference on Community Mental Health Research, Social Science Institute, Washington University, 1963*. Springfield, IL: Charles C. Thomas, 1965.

Kaplan, Stephen, and Rachel Kaplan, eds. *Humanscape: Environments for People*. North Scituate, MA: Duxbury Press, 1978.

Kaye, Anthony E. *Joining Places: Slave Neighborhoods in the Old South*. Chapel Hill: University of North Carolina Press, 2007.

Keckley, Elizabeth. *Behind the Scenes; or, Thirty Years A Slave and Four Years in the White House*. New York: G. W. Carleton, 1868.

Keene, Jennifer D. *Doughboys, the Great War, and the Remaking of America*. Baltimore: Johns Hopkins University Press, 2001.

Kennedy, Carrie H., and Eric A. Zillmer, eds. *Military Psychology: Clinical and Operational Applications*. New York: Guilford Press, 2006.

Kennedy, David M. *Freedom from Fear: The American People in Depression and War, 1929–1945*. New York: Oxford University Press, 1999.

———. *Over Here: The First World War and American Society*. New York: Oxford University Press, 2004.

Kennedy, Samuel. "Letters, to his wife—in 1776." *Pennsylvania Magazine of History and Biography* 8 (1884): 111–16.

Kett, Joseph F. *Rites of Passage: Adolescence in America, 1790 to the Present*. New York: Basic Books, 1977.

Khater, Akram Fouad. *Inventing Home: Emigration, Gender, and the Middle Class in Lebanon, 1870–1920*. Berkeley: University of California Press, 2001.

Kikuchi, Charles. *The Kikuchi Diary: Chronicle from an American Concentration Camp. The Tanforan Journals*. Edited by John Modell. Urbana: University of Illinois Press, 1973.

Kilborn, Peter T. *Next Stop, Reloville: Life inside America's New Rootless Professional Class*. New York: Times Books, Henry Holt, 2009.

Kingsbury, Susan Myra. *The Records of the Virginia Company of London*. 4 vols. Washington, DC: Government Printing Office, 1906–35.

Kiser, Clyde Vernon. *Sea Island to City: A Study of St. Helena Islanders in Harlem and Other Urban Centers*. 1932. New York: Atheneum, 1969.

Kline, Linus W. "The Migratory Impulse vs. Love of Home." *American Journal of Psychology* 10 (October 1898): 1–81.

Knott, Sarah. *Sensibility and the American Revolution*. Chapel Hill: University of North Carolina Press, 2008.

Kobrin, Rebecca. "Rewriting the Diaspora: Images of Eastern Europe in the Bialystok Landsmanshaft Press, 1921–1945." *Jewish Social Studies* 12 (Spring 2006): 1–38.

Kolodny, Annette. *The Land before Her: Fantasy and Experience of the American Frontiers, 1630–1860*. Chapel Hill: University of North Carolina Press, 1984.

Kotchemidova, Christina. "From Good Cheer to 'Drive-by Smiling': A Social History of Cheer-fulness." *Journal of Social History* 39 (Fall 2005): 5–37.

Kraut, Alan. *The Huddled Masses: The Immigrant in American Society, 1880–1921.* Arlington Heights, IL: Harlan Davidson, 1982.

Kubey, Robert, and Mihaly Cszikszentmihalyi. *Television and the Quality of Life: How Viewing Shapes Everyday Experience.* Hillsdale, NJ: Lawrence Erlbaum, 1990.

Kula, Witold, Nina Assorodobraj-Kula, and Marcin Kula. *Writing Home: Immigrants in Brazil and the United States 1890–1891.* Edited and translated by Josephine Wtulich. Boulder, CO: East European Monographs, 1986.

Kulick, Gary, Roger Parks, and Theodore Z. Penn, eds. *The New England Mill Village.* Cambridge, MA: MIT Press, 1982.

Kupperman, Karen Ordahl. "Apathy and Death in Early Jamestown." *Journal of American History* 66 (June 1979): 24–40.

Kuzmarov, Jeremy. *The Myth of the Addicted Army: Vietnam and the Modern War on Drugs.* Amherst: University of Massachusetts Press, 2009.

Larcom, Lucy. *A New England Girlhood Outlined from Memory.* Boston: Houghton Mifflin, 1898.

Larrey, Baron D. J. *Surgical Essays.* Translated by John Rever. Baltimore: N. G. Maxwell, 1823.

Lasker, Bruce. *Filipino Immigration to the Continental United States and to Hawaii.* 1931. New York: Arno Press, 1969.

Lathrop, Britomar. *Britomar's Road Diaries.* Bloomington, IN: 1st Books Library, 2002.

Lears, T. J. Jackson. *No Place of Grace: Antimodernism and the Transformation of American Culture, 1880–1920.* New York: Pantheon, 1981.

Leiberger, Paul, and Bruce Tucker. *The New Individualists: The Generation after the Organization Man.* New York: HarperCollins, 1991.

Lemke-Santangelo, Gretchen. *Abiding Courage: African-American Migrant Women and the East-Bay Community.* Chapel Hill: University of North Carolina Press, 1996.

Levine, Lawrence W. *Black Culture and Black Consciousness: Afro-American Folk Thought from Slavery to Freedom.* New York: Oxford University Press, 1977.

Levy, David M. *Maternal Overprotection.* New York: Columbia University Press, 1943.

Levy, Jo Ann. *They Saw the Elephant: Women in the California Gold Rush.* Norman: University of Oklahoma Press, 1992.

Lewis, Robert. "Photographing the California Gold Rush." *History Today* 52, no. 3 (2002): 11–17.

Lieblich, Amia, and Ruthellen Josselson, eds. *The Narrative Study of Lives.* Vol. 5. Newbury Park, CA: Sage, 1997.

Limerick, Patricia Nelson. *The Legacy of Conquest: The Unbroken Past of the American West.* New York: Norton, 1987.

Lindberg, John S. *The Background of Swedish Emigration to the United States: An Economic and Sociological Study in the Dynamics of Migration.* Minneapolis: University of Minnesota Press, 1930.

Linderman, Gerald F. *Embattled Courage: The Experience of Combat in the American Civil War.* New York: Free Press, 1997.

———. *The World within War: America's Combat Experience in World War II.* New York: Free Press, 1997.

Litwack, Leon. *Been in the Storm So Long: The Aftermath of Slavery.* New York: Knopf, 1979.

Livermore, Mary Ashton Rice. *My Story of the War: A Woman's Narrative of Four Years Personal Experience as Nurse in the Union Army, and in Relief Work at Home, in Hospitals, Camps, and at the Front, during the War of Rebellion With Anecdotes, Pathetic Incidents, and Chilling*

Reminiscences Portraying the Light and Shadows of Hospital Life and The Sanitary Service of the War. Hartford, CT: A. D. Worthington, 1890.

Locke, Ben Z., Morton Kramer, and Benjamin Pasamanick. "Immigration and Insanity." *Public Health Reports* 75 (April 1960): 301–6.

Longley, Kyle. *Grunts: The American Combat Solider in Vietnam.* Armonk, NY: M. E. Sharpe, 2008.

Lonn, Ella. *Desertion during the Civil War.* 1928. Lincoln: University of Nebraska Press, 1998.

Looby, Christopher, ed. *The Complete Civil War Journal and Selected Letters of Thomas Wentworth Higginson.* Chicago: University of Chicago Press, 2000.

MacAllister, Ronald J., Edgar W. Butler, and Edward J. Kaiser. "The Adaptation of Women to Residential Mobility." *Journal of Marriage and the Family* 35 (May 1973): 197–204.

Malzberg, Benjamin. "Mental Disease and 'The Melting Pot.'" *Journal of Nervous and Mental Disease* 72 (1930): 379–95.

———. "Rates of Mental Disease among Certain Population Groups in New York State." *Journal of the American Statistical Association* 31 (September 1936): 545–48.

Mancke, Elizabeth, and Carole Shammas. *The Creation of the British Atlantic World.* Baltimore: Johns Hopkins University Press, 2005.

Mandell, Nikki. *The Corporation as Family: The Gendering of Corporate Welfare, 1890–1930.* Chapel Hill: University of North Carolina Press, 2002.

Mann, Alison S., and Alexandra A. García. "Characteristics of Community Interventions to Decrease Depression in Mexican-American Women." *Hispanic Health Care International* 3 (2005): 87–93.

Manning, Chandra. *What This Cruel War Was Over: Soldiers, Slavery, and the Civil War.* New York: Knopf, 2007.

Mannix, Daniel P. *Black Cargoes: A History of the Atlantic Slave Trade, 1518–1865.* In collaboration with Malcolm Cowley. New York: Viking Press, 1962.

Marren, J. J. "Psychiatric Problems in Troops in Korea During and Following Combat." *United States Armed Forces Medical Journal* 7 (1956): 715–26.

Mars, James. *Life of James Mars, A Slave Born and Sold in Connecticut. Written by Himself.* 3rd ed. Hartford, CT: Case Lockwood, 1866.

Marrs, Aaron W. "Desertion and Loyalty in the South Carolina Infantry, 1861–1865." *Civil War History* 50 (2004): 47–65.

Matt, Susan J. "Current Emotion Research in History: Or, Doing History from the Inside Out." *Emotion Review* 3, no. 1 (2011): 1–8.

———. "A Hunger for Home: Homesickness and Food in a Global Consumer Society." *Journal of American Culture* 30 (Spring 2007): 6–17.

———. "You Can't Go Home Again: Homesickness and Nostalgia in U.S. History." *Journal of American History* 94, no. 2 (2007): 469–97.

Mattocks, Charles. *Unspoiled Heart: The Journal of Charles Mattocks of the 17th Maine.* Edited by Philip Racine. Knoxville: University of Tennessee Press, 1994.

May, Elaine Tyler. *Homeward Bound: American Families in the Cold War Era.* New York: Basic Books, 1988.

McCann, Willis H. "Nostalgia: A Review of the Literature." *Psychological Bulletin* 38 (1941): 165–82.

McCullough, David. *1776.* New York: Simon & Schuster, 2005.

McDannell, Colleen, and J. Bernhard Lang. *Heaven: A History.* New Haven, CT: Yale University Press, 1998.

McElroy, John. *Andersonville: A Story of Rebel Military Prisons.* 1879. Greenwich, CT: Fawcett, 1962.

McGuire, Frederick L. *Psychology Aweigh! A History of Clinical Psychology in the United States Navy, 1900–1988.* Washington, DC: American Psychological Association, 1990.

McIlwaine, H. R., ed. *Minutes of the Council and General Court of Colonial Virginia.* 2nd ed. Richmond: Virginia State Library, 1979.

McIntosh, Elaine N. *American Food Habits in Historical Perspective.* Westport, CT: Praeger, 1995.

McLachlan, James. *American Boarding Schools: A Historical Study.* New York: Charles Scribner's Sons, 1970.

McLaughlin, Allan. "Immigration and the Public Health." *Public Opinion* 39 (September 23, 1905): 391–95.

McMahon, Darrin M. *Happiness: A History.* New York: Atlantic Monthly Press, 2006.

McPherson, James M. *Battle Cry of Freedom: The Civil War Era.* New York: Oxford University Press, 1988.

———. *For Cause and Comrades: Why Men Fought in the Civil War.* New York: Oxford University Press, 1997.

McWilliams, Carey. "What Are We Doing for the Interstate Migrant?" Los Angeles: Division of Immigration and Housing, 1939.

———. *Southern California Country: An Island on the Land.* 1946. Freeport, NY: Books for Libraries Press, 1970.

"Medical Society of the Second Division, Third Corps, Army of the Potomac, Discussion on Nostalgia." *Medical and Surgical Reporter* 11, no. 10 (1864): 150–52.

Menninger, Roy W., and John C. Nemiah, eds. *American Psychiatry after WWII, 1944–1994.* Washington, DC: American Psychiatric Press, 2000.

Metzker, Isaac, ed. and comp. *A Bintel Brief: Sixty Years of Letters from the Lower East Side to the Jewish Daily Forward.* Garden City, NY: Doubleday, 1971.

Meyerowitz, Joanne J. *Women Adrift: Independent Wage Earners in Chicago, 1880–1930.* Chicago: University of Chicago Press, 1988.

Meyrowitz, Joshua. *No Sense of Place: The Impact of Electronic Media on Social Behavior.* New York: Oxford University Press, 1985.

Miller, Ernest. "Relocation: When Employees Say No." *Personnel* 55 (1978): 43–45.

Miller, Kerby A. "Assimilation and Alienation: Irish Emigrants' Responses to Industrial America, 1871–1921." *Irish Studies* 4 (1985): 87–112.

———. *Emigrants and Exiles: Ireland and the Irish Exodus to North America.* New York: Oxford University Press, 1985.

Miller, Kerby A., Arnold Schrier, Bruce D. Boling, and David N. Doyle. *Irish Immigrants in the Land of Canaan: Letters and Memoirs from Colonial and Revolutionary America, 1675–1815.* New York: Oxford University Press, 2003.

Minnen, Cornelis A. van, and Sylvia L. Hilton. *Nation on the Move: Mobility in U.S. History.* Amsterdam: vu University Press, 2002.

Mintz, Steven, ed. *Native American Voices: A History and Anthology.* 2nd ed. St. James, NY: Brandywine Press, 2000.

Mintz, Steven, and Susan Kellogg. *Domestic Revolutions: A Social History of American Family Life.* New York: Free Press, 1988.

Mitchell, Reid. *Civil War Soldiers: Their Expectations and Their Experiences.* New York: Viking, 1998.

———. *The Vacant Chair: The Northern Soldier Leaves Home.* New York: Oxford University Press, 1993.

Moltmann, Günter. "American-German Return Migration in the Nineteenth and Early Twentieth Centuries." *Central European History* 13 (December 1980): 378–92.

Montrie, Chad. "'I Think Less of the Factory than of My Native Dell': Labor, Nature, and the Lowell 'Mill Girls.'" *Environmental History* 9 (April 2004): 275–95.

Moora, Robert F. "Vietnam Calling—Via MARS." *Army Digest,* May 1968, 13–15.

Moore, Paul S. *Now Playing: Early Moviegoing and the Regulation of Fun.* Albany: State University of New York Press, 2008.

More, David Fellows. *History of the More Family and an Account of their Reunion in 1890.* Binghamton, NY: Samuel P. More, 1893.

Morgan, Edmund S. "The First American Boom: Virginia, 1618 to 1630." *William and Mary Quarterly,* 3rd ser., 28, no. 2 (1971): 170–98.

Morgan, Philip D. *Slave Counterpoint: Black Culture in the Eighteenth-Century Chesapeake and Lowcountry.* Chapel Hill: University of North Carolina Press for the Omohundro Institute of Early American History and Culture, 1998.

Morwaska, Ewa. *For Bread with Butter: The Life-Worlds of East Central Europeans in Johnstown, Pennsylvania, 1890–1940.* New York: Cambridge University Press, 1985.

Moulton, Gary E., ed. *The Papers of John Ross.* Norman: University of Oklahoma Press, 1985.

Mulford, Prentice. *Prentice Mulford's Story, Life by Land and Sea.* New York: F. J. Needham, 1889.

Myers, Albert Cook, ed. *Narratives of Early Pennsylvania, West New Jersey and Delaware, 1630–1707.* New York: Barnes & Noble, 1959.

Nabokov, Peter, ed. *Native American Testimony: A Chronicle of Indian-White Relations from Prophecy to the Present, 1492–2000.* New York: Penguin, 1999.

Napoli, Donald S. "The Mobilization of American Psychologists, 1938–1941." *Military Affairs* 42 (February 1978): 32–36.

Newborg, William F., and Robert O. Bryan. "MARS Calling." *Army,* March 1969, 43–44.

Newhall, J. B. *The British Emigrants' "Hand Book," And Guide to the New States of America.* London: Wiley and Putnam, 1844.

Nichols, David, ed. *Ernie's War: The Best of Ernie Pyle's World War II Dispatches.* New York: Random House, 1986.

Norbury, F. B. "Psychiatric Admissions into a Combat Division in 1952." *Medical Bulletin of the U.S. Army Far East,* July 1953, 130–33.

Northup, Solomon. *Twelve Years a Slave: Narrative of Solomon Northup, a Citizen of New York, Kidnapped in Washington City, in 1841 and Rescued in 1853, From a Cotton Plantation Near the Red River, in Louisiana.* 1854. New York: Dover, 1970.

"Nostalgia or Home Sickness." *Boston Medical and Surgical Journal* 39 (August 2, 1848): 1.

Nugent, Walter. *Crossings: The Great Transatlantic Migrations, 1870–1914.* Bloomington: Indiana University Press, 1992.

Odorizzi, Irene M. *Planinsek. Footsteps through Time.* Arlington, VA: Washington Landmark Tours, 1978.

Olds, Jacqueline, and Richard S. Schwartz. *The Lonely American: Drifting Apart in the Twenty-first Century.* Boston: Beacon Press, 2009.

Ordronaux, John. *Hints on the Preservation of Health in Armies For the Use of Volunteer Officers and Soldiers bound with Manual of Instructions for Military Surgeons on the Examination of Recruits and Discharge of Soldiers.* 1863. San Francisco: Norman, 1990.

Orsi, Robert A., ed. *Gods of the City: Religion and the American Urban Landscape.* Bloomington: University of Indiana Press, 1999.

———. *The Madonna of 115th Street: Street Faith and Community in Italian Harlem.* New Haven, CT: Yale University Press, 1985.

Overland, Orm. *Immigrant Minds, American Identities: Making the United States Home, 1870–1930.* Urbana: University of Illinois Press, 2000.

Owan, T. C., ed. *Southeast Asian Mental Health: Treatment, Prevention, Services, Training, and Research.* Rockville, MD: National Institute of Mental Health, 1985.

Owen, John. *John Owen's Journal of his Removal from Virginia to Alabama in 1818.* Edited by Thomas MacDory Owen. Publications of the Southern History Association. Baltimore: Friedenwald, 1897.

Packard, Vance. *A Nation of Strangers*. New York: David McKay, 1972.

Page, Thomas Nelson. *The Old South: Essays Social and Political*. 1892. Chautauqua, NY: Chautauqua Press, 1919.

Park, Robert E., and Herbert A. Miller. *Old World Traits Transplanted*. 1921. New York: Arno Press and New York Times, 1969.

Paris, Leslie. *Children's Nature: The Rise of the American Summer Camp*. New York: New York University Press, 2008.

Parsons, Talcott. *The Social System*. Glencoe, IL: Free Press, 1951.

Payne, John Howard. *John Howard Payne to His Countrymen*. Edited by Clemens de Baillou. Athens: University of Georgia Press, 1961.

Peacock, William. *The Peacock Letters*. Stockton, CA: San Joaquin Pioneer & Historical Society, 1950.

Peffer, George Anthony. *If They Don't Bring Their Women Here: Chinese Female Immigration before Exclusion*. Urbana: University of Illinois Press, 1999.

Peters, Dewitt C. "Remarks on the Evils of Youthful Enlistments and Nostalgia." *American Medical Times, being a weekly series of the New York Journal of Medicine* 6 (1863): 75–76.

Pettit, Norman. "God's Englishman in New England: His Enduring Ties to the Motherland." *Proceedings of the Massachusetts Historical Society* 101 (1989): 56–70.

Pfau, Ann Elizabeth. "Miss Your Loving: Women in the Culture of American World War II Soldiers." PhD diss., Rutgers University, 2001.

Piersen, William D. *Black Yankees: The Development of an Afro-American Subculture in Eighteenth-Century New England*. Amherst: University of Massachusetts Press, 1988.

———. "White Cannibals, Black Martyrs: Fear, Depression, and Religious Faith as Causes of Suicide among New Slaves." *Journal of Negro History* 62 (1977): 147–59.

Pierson, George. *The Moving American*. New York: Knopf, 1973.

Plamper, Jan. "The History of Emotions: An Interview with William Reddy, Barbara Rosenwein, and Peter Stearns." *History and Theory* 49 (May 2010): 237–65.

Platt, Rutherford H., ed. *The Humane Metropolis: People and Nature in the 21st Century City*. Boston: University of Massachusetts Press, Lincoln Institute of Land Policy, 2006.

Poage, Martha. *The Moving Survival Guide: All You Need to Know to Make Your Move Go Smoothly*. Guilford, CT: Globe Pequot Press, 2005.

Porter, W. C. "The War Diary of W. C. Porter." Edited by J. V. Frederick. *Arkansas Historical Quarterly* 11 (1952): 286–314.

Poteet, James M. "A Homecoming: The Bulkeley Family in New England." *New England Quarterly* 47 (March 1974): 30–50.

Potter, David M. *People of Plenty: Economic Abundance and the American Character*. Chicago: University of Chicago Press, 1954.

Preuss, Charles. *Exploring With Frémont: The Private Diaries of Charles Preuss, Cartographer for John C. Frémont on His First, Second, and Fourth Expeditions to the Far West*. Edited and translated by Erwin G. Gudde and Elisabeth K. Gudde. Norman: University of Oklahoma Press, 1958.

"Prevalence of Insanity in California—Causes." In *Transactions of the Medical Society of the State of California, During the Years 1870 and 1871*. Sacramento: Russell & Winterburn, 1872, 241–42.

Putnam, Archelaus. "Diary of Archelaus Putnam of New Mills." *Danvers Historical Society Collections* 4 (1916): 51–72; 5 (1917): 49–69; 6 (1918): 11–29.

Putnam, Robert D. *Bowling Alone: The Collapse and Revival of American Community*. New York: Simon and Schuster, 2000.

Pyle, Ernie. *Last Chapter*. New York: Henry Holt, 1946.

Rabe, Tish Sommers. *Elmo Gets Homesick*. Racine, WI: Western Publishing, Children's Television Workshop, 1990.

"Race and Insanity." *Science* 11 (June 8, 1888): 272.

Rather, L. J. *Mind and Body in Eighteenth Century Medicine: A Study Based on Jerome Gaub's De regimine mentis.* Berkeley: University of California Press, 1965.

Ray, Krishendu. *The Migrant's Table: Meals and Memories in Bengali-American Households.* Philadelphia: Temple University Press, 2004.

Reddy, William. "Historical Research on the Self and Emotions." *Emotion Review* 1, no. 4 (2009): 302–15.

Redkey, Edwin S., ed. *A Grand Army of Black Men: Letters from African-American Soldiers in the Union Army, 1861–1865.* New York: Cambridge University Press, 1992.

"The Return of the Multi-Generational Family Household." Pew Research Center, March 18, 2010. Accessed April 12, 2010. http://pewsocialtrends.org/assets/pdf/752-multi-generational-families.pdf.

Revel, James. *The Poor Unhappy Transported Felon's Sorrowful Account of his Fourteen Years Transportation, at Virginia, in America. In Six Parts.* York: C. Croshaw, ca. 1800.

Reyes, Belinda I. *Dynamics of Immigration: Return Migration to Western Mexico.* San Francisco: Public Policy Institute of California, 1997.

Richardson, James D. *A Compilation of the Messages and Papers of the Presidents.* Vol. 2. New York: Bureau of National Literature, 1911.

Riesman, David, with Nathan Glazer and Reuel Denny. *The Lonely Crowd.* 1961. New Haven, CT: Yale University Press, 2000.

Risch, Erna. "Encouragement and Aid to Immigrants, 1607–1830." PhD diss., University of Chicago, 1931.

Ritivoi, Andreea Deciu. *Yesterday's Self: Nostalgia and the Immigrant Identity.* Lanham, MD: Rowman & Littlefield, 2002.

Roberts, Brian. *American Alchemy: The California Gold Rush and Middle-Class Culture.* Chapel Hill: University of North Carolina Press, 2000.

Roberts, Bryan R., Reanne Frank, and Fernando Lozano-Ascensio. "Transnational Migrant Communities and Mexican Migration to the U.S." *Ethnic and Racial Studies* 22 (March 1999): 238–66.

Roberts, Sarah. *I Want to Go Home.* New York: Random House, Children's Television Network, 1985.

Robinson, Harriet H. *Loom and Spindle, or Life Among the Early Mill Girls With a Sketch of "The Lowell Offering" And Some of Its Contributors.* 1898. Kailua, HI: Press Pacifica, 1976.

Rodgers, Thomas E. "Billy Yank and G.I. Joe: An Exploratory Essay on the Sociopolitical Dimensions of Soldier Motivation." *Journal of Military History* 69 (January 2005): 93–121.

Rohrbough, Malcolm J. *Days of Gold: The California Gold Rush and the American Nation.* Berkeley: University of California Press, 1997.

Rosen, George. "Nostalgia: A 'Forgotten' Psychological Disorder." *Clio Medica* 10 (1975): 28–51.

Rosenwein, Barbara H. "Worrying about Emotions in History." *American Historical Review* 107 (June 2002): 821–45.

Rostker, Bernard. *I Want YOU! The Evolution of the All-Volunteer Force.* Santa Monica, CA: RAND, 2006.

Roth, Michael S. "Dying of the Past: Medical Studies of Nostalgia in Nineteenth-Century France." *History and Memory* 3 (1991): 5–29.

Royster, Charles. *A Revolutionary People at War: The Continental Army and American Character, 1775–1783.* Chapel Hill: University of North Carolina Press, 1979.

Rozema, Vicki, ed. *Voices from the Trail of Tears.* Winston-Salem, NC: John F. Blair, 2003.

Rush, Benjamin. *Medical Inquiries and Observations.* 4 vols. 2nd ed. Philadelphia: J. Conrad, 1805.

———. *The Selected Writings of Benjamin Rush.* Edited by Dagobert D. Runes. New York: Philosophical Library, 1947.

Saloutos, Theodore. *They Remember America: The Story of the Repatriated Greek-Americans*. Berkeley: University of California Press, 1956.

Samuel, Raphael. *Theatres of Memory*. Vol. 1, *Past and Present in Contemporary Culture*. London: Verso, 1994.

Sandage, Scott A. *Born Losers: A History of Failure in America*. Cambridge, MA: Harvard University Press, 2005.

Sangster, Margaret E. *The Art of Home-Making in City and Country, in Mansion and Cottage*. New York: Christian Herald Bible House, 1898.

"Sanitary Condition of Vermont Troops." *Medical and Surgical Reporter* 7 (January 4, 11, 1862): 353.

Sargent, Winthrop, ed. *The Loyal Verses of Joseph Stansbury and Doctor Jonathan Odell: Relating to the American Revolution*. Albany, NY: J. Munsell, 1860.

Sarmiento, Domingo. *A Sarmiento Anthology*. Edited by Allison Williams Bunkley. Translated by Stuart Edgar Grummon. Princeton, NJ: Princeton University Press, 1948.

Sarna, Jonathan D. "The Myth of No Return: Jewish Return Migration to Eastern Europe, 1881–1914." *American Jewish History* 71 (1981): 256–68.

Sartorio, Enrico C. *Social and Religious Life of Italians in America*. Boston: Christopher, 1918.

Scalabrini, John Baptist. *For the Love of Immigrants: Migration Writings and Letters of Bishop John Baptist Scalabrini (1839–1905)*. Edited by Silvano M. Tomasi. New York: Center for Migration Studies, 2000.

Scheer, George F., and Hugh F. Rankin. *Rebels and Redcoats*. Cleveland, OH: World, 1957.

Schrier, Arnold. *Ireland and the American Emigration, 1850–1900*. Minneapolis: University of Minnesota Press, 1958.

Schumm, Walter R., D. Bruce Bell, Morten G. Ender, and Rose E. Rice. "Expectations, Use and Evaluation of Communication Media among Deployed Peacekeepers." *Armed Forces and Society* 30 (Summer 2004): 649–62.

Scott, Emmett, J. "Additional Letters of Negro Migrants, 1916–1918." *Journal of Negro History* 4 (October 1919): 412–65.

———. "Letters of Negro Migrants of 1916-1918." *Journal of Negro History* 4 (July 1919): 290-340.

Scribner, Benjamin Franklin. *Camp Life of a Volunteer: A Campaign in Mexico; Or, A Glimpse at Life in Camp by "One Who Has Seen the Elephant."* 1847. Austin, TX: Jenkins, 1975.

Sears, Stephen W., ed. *Mr. Dunn Browne's Experiences in the Army: The Civil War Letters of Samuel W. Fiske*. New York: Fordham University Press, 1998.

Sernett, Milton C. *Bound for the Promised Land: African American Religion and the Great Migration*. Durham, NC: Duke University Press, 1997.

Shattell, Mona M., Katherine M. Smith, Ann Quinlan-Colwell, and José A. Villalba. "Factors Contributing to Depression in Latinas of Mexican Origin Residing in the United States: Implications for Nurses." *Journal of American Psychiatric Nurses Association* 14 (2008): 193–204.

Sheehan-Dean, Aaron. *Why Confederates Fought: Family and Nation in Civil War Virginia*. Chapel Hill: University of North Carolina Press, 2007.

Sheldon, George. *A History of Deerfield, Massachusetts*. 2 vols. Deerfield, MA: E. A. Hall, 1896.

Shillinglaw, David Lee. *An American in the Army and YMCA, 1917–1920: The Diary of David Lee Shillinglaw*. Edited by Glen E. Holt. Chicago: University of Chicago Press, 1971.

Silber, Irwin, ed. and comp. *Soldier Songs and Home-Front Ballads of the Civil War*. New York: Oak, 1964.

Silverman, Jerry, ed. *Of Thee I Sing: Lyrics and Music for America's Most Patriotic Songs*. New York: Citadel Press, 2002.

Simonsen, Reidar Grunde. *Returned Emigrants: A Study of Repatriated Norwegians*. Thesis, University of Oslo, 1982.

Skardal, Dorothy Burton. *The Divided Heart: Scandinavian Immigrant Experience Through Literary Sources.* Lincoln: University of Nebraska Press, 1974.

Slater, Philip E. *The Pursuit of Loneliness: American Culture at the Breaking Point.* Boston: Beacon Press, 1970.

Smith, Abbot Emerson. *Colonists in Bondage: White Servitude and Convict Labor in America, 1607–1776.* Chapel Hill: University of North Carolina Press for the Institute of Early American History and Culture, 1947.

Smith, John. *The Generall Historie of Virginia, New-England, and the Summer Isles: with the names of the Adventurers, Planters, and Governours from their first beginning AN:1584 to this present 1624.* 1624. London: World, 1966.

Smith, Thomas W. *"We Have it Damn Hard Out Here": The Civil War Letters of Sergeant Thomas W. Smith, 6th Pennsylvania Cavalry.* Edited by Eric J. Wittenberg. Kent, OH: Kent State University Press, 1999.

Smith, Timothy L. "Religion and Ethnicity in America." *American Historical Review* 83 (1978): 1155–185.

Somerville, James. "Homesick in Upstate New York: The Saga of Sidney Roby, 1843–1847." *New York History* 72 (April 1991): 178–96.

Sons of New Hampshire. *Festival of the Sons of New Hampshire: with the speeches of Messrs. Webster, Woodbury, Wilder, Bigelow, Parker, Dearborn, Hubbard, Goodrich, Hale, Plummer, Wilson, Chamberlain, and others, together with the names of those present, and letters from Distinguished Individuals, Celebrated in Boston, November 7, 1849.* Boston: James French, 1850.

———. *Second Festival of the Sons of New Hampshire, Celebrated in Boston, November 2, 1853, Including also an account of the proceedings in Boston on the day of the funeral at Marshfield, and the subsequent obsequies commemorative of the death of Daniel Webster, their Late President.* Boston: James French, 1854.

Soyer, Daniel. *Jewish Immigrant Associations and American Identity in New York, 1880–1939.* Cambridge, MA: Harvard University Press, 1997.

Spock, Benjamin. *The Common Sense Book of Baby and Child Care.* New York: Duell, Sloan, and Pearce, 1957.

Spock, Benjamin, and Steven Parker. *Dr. Spock's Baby and Child Care, Revised and Updated.* 7th ed. New York: Pocket Books, 1998.

Spock, Benjamin, and Michael B. Rothenberg. *Baby and Child Care.* New York: E. P. Dutton, 1985.

Stack, Carol B. *Call to Home: African-Americans Reclaim the Rural South.* New York: Basic Books, 1996.

Standish, Anthony. "Crisis in Courage, Part One: Fighters and Non-Fighters." *United States Army Combat Forces Journal,* April 1952, 13–24.

Stannard, David E. *The Puritan Way of Death: A Study in Religion, Culture, and Social Change.* New York: Oxford University Press, 1977.

Starobinski, Jean. "The Idea of Nostalgia." *Diogenes* 54 (Summer 1966): 81–103.

Starr, Kevin. *Americans and the Californian Dream, 1850–1915.* New York: Oxford University Press, 1973.

Stearns, Carol Z., and Peter N. Stearns, eds. *Emotions and Social Change: Toward a New Psychohistory.* New York: Holmes & Meier, 1988.

Stearns, Peter N. *American Cool: Constructing a Twentieth-Century Emotional Style.* New York: New York University Press, 1994.

Stearns, Peter N., and Jan Lewis, eds. *An Emotional History of the United States.* New York: New York University Press, 1998.

Stearns, Peter N., and Carol Z. Stearns. "Emotionology: Clarifying the History of Emotions and Emotional Standards." *American Historical Review* 90 (October 1985): 813–36.

Steiner, Edward. *On the Trail of the Immigrant*. 1906. New York: Arno Press, 1969.

Steward, Austin. *Twenty-Two Years a Slave, And Forty Years A Freeman, Embracing A Correspondence of Several years, While President of Wilberforce Colony, London, Canada West*. 1856. New York: Negroes University Press, 1968.

Stewart, Irene. *A Voice in Her Tribe: A Navajo Woman's Own Story*. Edited by Doris Ostrander Dawdy. Soccoro, NM: Ballena Press, 1980.

Stillson, Richard T. *Spreading the Word: A History of Information in the California Gold Rush*. Lincoln: University of Nebraska Press, 2006.

Stirling, William Alexander. *An Encouragement to Colonies*. 1624. New York: Da Capo Press, 1968.

Stott, Richard B. *Workers in the Metropolis: Class, Ethnicity, and Youth in Antebellum New York City*. Ithaca, NY: Cornell University Press, 1990.

Strecker, Edward A. *Their Mothers' Sons: The Psychiatrist Examines an American Problem*. Philadelphia: J. B. Lippincott, 1951.

Swanson, Mary Towley. "Fritiof Colling: Artist for Homesick Swedes." *Minnesota History* 55 (1996): 76–87.

Takaki, Ronald. *A Different Mirror: A History of Multicultural America*. Boston: Little, Brown, 1993.

———. *Strangers from a Distant Shore: A History of Asian Americans*. New York: Penguin Books, 1990.

Taylor, Alan. *American Colonies: The Settlers of North America*. New York: Penguin, 2002.

Taylor, George Rogers. *The Transportation Revolution, 1815–1860*. Vol. 4, *The Economic History of the United States*. New York: Rinehart, 1951.

Taylor, George Rogers, and Irene D. Neu. *The American Railroad Network, 1861–1890*. Cambridge, MA: Harvard University Press, 1956.

Taylor, Robert M., Jr. "The Olin Tribe: Migration, Mutual Aid, and Solidarity of a Nineteenth-Century Rural American Kin Group." PhD diss., Kent State University, 1979.

———. "Summoning the Wandering Tribes: Genealogy and Family Reunions in American History." *Journal of Social History* 16, no. 2 (1982): 21–37.

Taylor, W. T. "Nostalgia, or Home Sickness." *American Medical Bi-Weekly* 10 (March 15, 1879): 121–23.

Taylor, William. *California Life Illustrated*. New York: Carlton & Porter, 1861.

———. *Seven Years' Street Preaching in San Francisco, California: Embracing Incidents, Triumphant Death Scenes, Etc.* Edited by W. P. Strickland. New York: Carlton & Porter, 1856.

Thoma, Lucy, and Erich Lindemann. "Newcomers' Problems in a Suburban Community." *Journal of the American Institute of Planners* 27 (August 1961): 185–98.

Thomas, William I., and Florian Znaniecki. *The Polish Peasant in Europe and America*. Vol. 2, 1918–1920. 2nd ed. New York: Dover, 1958.

Thompson, Kenneth. "Early California and the Causes of Insanity." *Southern California Quarterly* 58 (1976): 45–62.

Thompson, S. Millett. *Thirteenth Regiment of New Hampshire Volunteer Infantry in the War of the Rebellion, 1861–1865: A diary covering three years and a day*. Boston: Houghton, Mifflin, 1888.

Throne, Mildred. "Population Study of an Iowa County in 1850." *Iowa Journal of History* 57 (October 1959): 305–30.

Thurber, Christopher, and Edward Walton. "Preventing and Treating Homesickness." *Child and Adolescent Psychiatric Clinics of North America* 16 (2007): 843–58.

Tilburg, Miranda A. L. van, and Ad J. J. M. Vingerhoets, eds. *Psychological Aspects of Geographical Moves: Homesickness and Acculturation Stress*. Tilburg, Netherlands: Tilburg University Press, 1997.

Tilburg, Miranda A. L. van, Ad J. J. M. Vingerhoets, and G. L. van Heck. "Homesickness: A Review of the Literature." *Psychological Medicine* 26 (September 1996): 899–912.

Tocqueville, Alexis de. *Democracy in America.* Edited by J. P. Mayer. Translated by George Lawrence. New York: Harper & Row, 1966.

Trennert, Robert A., Jr. "The Southern Pacific Railroad of Mexico." *Pacific Historical Review* 35 (August 1966): 265–84.

Turner, Frederick Jackson. *The Frontier in American History.* New York: Henry Holt, 1921.

"Twenty-Second Annual Report of the Committee on Lunacy of the Board of Public Charities of the Commonwealth of Pennsylvania for the Year Ending September 30, 1904." In *The Thirty-Fifth Annual Report of the Board of Commissioners of Public Charities of the Commonwealth of Pennsylvania for 1904, also the Report of the General Agent and Secretary, Statistics, and the Report of the Committee on Lunacy.* Harrisburg, PA: State Printer, 1906.

Tyler, Lyon Gardiner, ed. *Narratives of Early Virginia, 1606–1626.* New York: Barnes and Noble, 1946.

Tyler, Moses Coit. *The Literary History of the American Revolution, 1763–1783.* Vol. 2. New York: G. P. Putnam's Sons, 1897.

Uchida, Yoshiko. *Desert Exile: The Uprooting of a Japanese-American Family.* Seattle: University of Washington Press, 2002.

U.S. Census Bureau. "Annual Geographic Mobility Rates, by Type of Movement, 1947–2008." *Current Population Survey,* April 2009. Accessed April 2010. www.census.gov/population/www/socdemo/migrate.html.

U.S. Department of War. *Annual Report of the Secretary of War for the Fiscal Year Ended June 30, 1920.* Washington, DC: Government Printing Office, 1920.

U.S. Office of the Surgeon General. *Annual Report of the Surgeon General, U.S. Navy, Chief of the Bureau of Medicine and Surgery to the Secretary of the Navy for the Fiscal Year 1919.* Washington, DC: Government Printing Office, 1919.

———. *The Medical and Surgical History of the War of the Rebellion (1861–65).* Washington, DC: Government Printing Office, 1870–88.

U.S. Senate. *Relief for Unemployed Transients. Hearings before a Subcommittee of the Committee on Manufactures.* Seventy-Second Congress, Second Session on S. 5121, January 13–25, 1933. Washington, DC: Government Printing Office, 1933.

Unruh, John D., Jr. *The Plains Across: The Overland Emigrants and the Trans-Mississippi West, 1840–1860.* Urbana: University of Illinois Press, 1979.

Uys, Errol Lincoln. *Riding the Rails: Teenagers on the Move during the Great Depression.* New York: TVBooks, 1999.

Vecoli, Rudolph J. "Chicago's Italians Prior to World War I: A Study of Their Social and Economic Adjustment." PhD diss., University of Wisconsin, 1963.

Vecoli, Rudolph J., and Suzanne M. Sinke, eds. *A Century of European Migrations, 1830–1930.* Urbana: University of Illinois Press, 1991.

Vining, Donald, ed. *American Diaries of World War II.* New York: Pepys Press, 1982.

Virtanen, Keijo. *Settlement or Return: Finnish Emigrants (1860–1930) in the International Overseas Return Migration Movement.* Helsinki: Finnish Historical Society, 1979.

Vlach, John Michael. *Back of the Big House: The Architecture of Plantation Slavery.* Chapel Hill: University of North Carolina Press, 1993.

Waldo, Albigence. "Valley Forge, 1777–1778. Diary of Surgeon Albigence Waldo, of the Connecticut Line." *Pennsylvania Magazine of History and Biography* 21 (1897): 299–323.

Wallace, Anthony F. C. *The Long, Bitter Trail: Andrew Jackson and the Indians.* New York: Hill and Wang, 1993.

Ward, George Atkinson. *Journal and Letters of the late Samuel Curwen, Judge of Admiralty, Etc., An American Refugee in England, from 1775–1784, Comprising Remarks on the Prominent Men* and Measures of that Period. To which are Added, Biographical Notices of Many American Loyalists and other Eminent Persons. 1842. New York: AMS Press, 1973.

Warne, Frank Julian. The Immigrant Invasion. New York: Dodd, Mead, 1913.

Warner, W. Lloyd. The Corporation in the Emergent American Society. New York: Harper and Brothers, 1962.

"Washington at Hampton." Southern Workman, 42 (June 1913): 325–26.

Washington, George. The Writings of George Washington from the Original Manuscript Sources, 1745–1799. Edited by John C. Fitzpatrick. 37 vols. Washington, DC: Government Printing Office, 1931–44.

Watson, Henry. Narrative of Henry Watson, a Fugitive Slave. 3rd ed. Boston: Bela Marsh, 1850.

Watson, John B. Psychological Care of Infant and Child. 1928. New York: Arno Press, New York Times, 1972.

Webster, Kimball. The Gold Seekers of '49: A Personal Narrative of the Overland Trail and Adventures in California and Oregon from 1849 to 1854. Manchester, NH: Standard Book Company, 1917.

Weeks, Philip, ed. The American Indian Experience: A Profile, 1524 to the Present. Wheeling, IL: Forum Press, 1988.

Weisser, Michael R. A Brotherhood of Memory: Jewish Landsmanshaftn in the New World. New York: Basic Books, 1985.

Wells, Ida B. Crusade for Justice: The Autobiography of Ida B. Wells. Edited by Alfreda M. Duster. Chicago: University of Chicago Press, 1970.

Westheider, James E. The Vietnam War. Westport, CT: Greenwood Press, 2007.

Westmoreland, William C. A Soldier Reports. Garden City, NY: Doubleday, 1976.

White, W. L. Back Down the Ridge. New York: Harcourt, Brace, 1953.

White, William Allen. The Autobiography of William Allen White. New York: Macmillan, 1946.

Whitman, Narcissa Prentiss. Diary. Typewritten transcription. 1931.

Wilkins, E. T. "Insanity in California." Transactions of the Medical Society of the State of California, during the Years 1870 and 1871, 1872–73, 136–57.

Whyte, William H., Jr. The Organization Man. New York: Simon and Schuster, 1956.

Wiley, Bell Irvin. The Common Soldier of the Civil War. New York: Charles Scribner's Sons, 1975.

———. The Life of Billy Yank: The Common Soldier of the Union. Indianapolis: Bobbs-Merrill, 1952.

———. The Life of Johnny Reb: The Common Solider of the Confederacy. Baton Rouge: Louisiana State University Press, 1943.

Wilhelm, Hubert G. H. "New England in Southeastern Ohio." Pioneer American Society Transactions 2 (1979): 13–30.

Wilkey, Walter. Western Emigration. Narrative of a Tour to, And one Year's Residence in "Edensburgh," (Illinois,) By Major Walter Wilkey, An honest yeoman of Mooseboro' State of Maine. New York: Sackett & Sargent, 1839.

Williams, Alfred Brockenbrough. The Liberian Exodus: An account of Voyage of the First emigrants in the Bark "Azor," and their Reception at Monrovia, with a description of Liberia—Its Customs and Civilization, Romances and Prospects. Charleston, SC: News and Courier Book Presses, 1878.

Wills, Charles W. Army Life of an Illinois Solider: Including a Day by Day Record of Sherman's March to the Sea, Letters and Diary of the Late Charles W. Wills, Private and Sergeant 8th Illinois Infantry; Lieutenant and Battalion Adjutant 7th Illinois Cavalry; Captain, Major and Lieutenant Colonel 103rd Illinois Infantry. Compiled by Mary E. Kellogg. Washington, DC: Globe, 1906.

Winchell, Meghan K. Good Girls, Good Food, Good Fun: The Story of USO Hostesses during World War II. Chapel Hill: University of North Carolina Press, 2008.

———. "'To Make the Boys Feel at Home': USO Senior Hostesses and Gendered Citizenship." *Frontiers* 25 (2004): 190–211.

Winders, Richard Bruce. *Mr. Polk's Army: The American Military Experience in the Mexican War.* College Station: Texas A&M Press, 1997.

Windley, Lathan A., comp. *Runaway Slave Advertisements: A Documentary History from the 1730s to 1790.* 4 vols. Westport CT: Greenwood Press, 1983.

Winkle, Kenneth J. *The Politics of Community: Migration and Politics in Antebellum Ohio.* Cambridge: Cambridge University Press, 1988.

Winthrop, John. *Winthrop's Journal: "History of New England" 1630–1649.* Edited by James Kendall Hosmer. 2 vols. New York: Charles Scribner's Sons, 1908.

Wittson, C. L., H. I. Harris, and W. A. Hunt. "Cryptic Nostalgia." *War Medicine* 3 (1943): 57–59.

Wokeck, Marianne S. *Trade in Strangers: The Beginnings of Mass Migration to North America.* University Park: Pennsylvania State University Press, 1999.

Wood, Gordon. *The Radicalism of the American Revolution.* New York: Knopf, 1992.

Woodward, Joseph Janvier. *Outlines of the Chief Camp Diseases of the United States Armies.* 1863. New York: Hafner, 1964.

Wright, Richard. *American Hunger.* 1944. New York: Harper & Row, 1977.

———. *12 Million Black Voices.* 1941. New York: Thunder Mouth's Press, 1988.

Wrong, George M. *Canada and the American Revolution: The Disruption of the First British Empire.* New York: Cooper Square, 1966.

Wylie, Philip. *Generation of Vipers.* 1942. New York: Rinehart, 1955.

Wyman, Mark. *Round-Trip to America: The Immigrants Return to Europe, 1880–1930.* Ithaca, NY: Cornell University Press, 1993.

Zempel, Solveig, ed. and trans. *In Their Own Words: Letters from Norwegian Immigrants.* Minneapolis: University of Minnesota Press, 1991.

Zhou, Min, and Carl L. Bankston III. *Growing Up American: How Vietnamese Children Adapt to Life in the United Sates.* New York: Russell Sage Foundation, 1998.

Zhou, Xinye, Constantine Sedikides, Tim Wildschut, and Ding-Guo Gao. "Counteracting Loneliness: On the Restorative Function of Nostalgia." *Psychological Science* 19 (2008): 1023–29.

Zitkala-Ša. *American Indian Stories, Legends, and Other Writings.* Edited by Cathy N. Davidson and Ada Norris. New York: Penguin Books, 2003.

Zonderman, David A. *Aspirations and Anxieties: New England Workers and the Mechanized Factory System, 1815–1849.* New York: Oxford University Press, 1992.

Zuckerman, Michael. "The Fabrication of Identity in Early America." *William and Mary Quarterly,* 3rd ser., 34 (April 1977): 183–214.

Zwingmann, Charles A. A. "'Heimweh' or 'Nostalgic Reaction': A Conceptual Analysis and Interpretation of a Medico-Psychological Phenomenon." PhD diss., Stanford University, 1959.

INDEX